COMPETITION LAW IN SOUTH ASIA

Since 2000, South Asian countries have increasingly engaged in competition law reform. Yet, apart from India and Pakistan, the countries in this region have had little success enforcing these laws. *Competition Law in South Asia* analyses the mechanisms and institutions through which Bangladesh, Bhutan, India, Pakistan, Maldives, Nepal, Sri Lanka, and Afghanistan have adopted modern competition legislation or policy. The book argues that the success (or failure) of competition law reform in these countries is strongly impacted by the unique interplay of mechanisms and legal and political institutions engaged by these countries in adopting their competition legislation or policy. The book provides an in-depth comparative analysis of the adoption and implementation continuum in India and Pakistan, the compatibility and legitimacy generated by the adoption process, and its impact on implementation of the adopted competition legislation. Taking a far-reaching, comparative approach, the book draws lessons not only for countries in South Asia but also for emerging economies across the globe. This title is also available as open access on Cambridge Core.

AMBER DARR is a lecturer in competition law at the University of Manchester and a senior research fellow with the UCL Centre for Law, Economics and Society. She is an appointed Advocate of the Supreme Court of Pakistan.

Global Competition Law And Economics Policy

This series publishes monographs highlighting the interdisciplinary and multijurisdictional nature of competition law, economics, and policy. Global in coverage, the series should appeal to competition and antitrust specialists working as scholars, practitioners, and judges.

Competition Law in South Asia

POLICY DIFFUSION AND TRANSFER

AMBER DARR
University of Manchester

CAMBRIDGE
UNIVERSITY PRESS

CAMBRIDGE
UNIVERSITY PRESS

Shaftesbury Road, Cambridge CB2 8EA, United Kingdom

One Liberty Plaza, 20th Floor, New York, NY 10006, USA

477 Williamstown Road, Port Melbourne, VIC 3207, Australia

314–321, 3rd Floor, Plot 3, Splendor Forum, Jasola District Centre, New Delhi – 110025, India

103 Penang Road, #05–06/07, Visioncrest Commercial, Singapore 238467

Cambridge University Press is part of Cambridge University Press & Assessment, a department of the University of Cambridge.

We share the University's mission to contribute to society through the pursuit of education, learning and research at the highest international levels of excellence.

www.cambridge.org
Information on this title: www.cambridge.org/9781009247177

DOI: 10.1017/9781009247184

When citing this work, please include a reference to the DOI 10.1017/9781009247184

First published 2023

A catalogue record for this publication is available from the British Library.

Library of Congress Cataloging-in-Publication Data
NAMES: Darr, Amber, author.
TITLE: Competition law in South Asia : policy diffusion and transfer / Amber Darr, Coventry University.
DESCRIPTION: Cambridge, United Kingdom ; New York, NY : Cambridge University Press, 2022. | Series: Global competition law and economics policy | Includes bibliographical references and index.
IDENTIFIERS: LCCN 2022033903 (print) | LCCN 2022033904 (ebook) | ISBN 9781009247177 (hardback) | ISBN 9781009247139 (paperback) | ISBN 9781009247184 (epub)
SUBJECTS: LCSH: Antitrust law–South Asia.
CLASSIFICATION: LCC KNC750 .D37 2022 (print) | LCC KNC750 (ebook) | DDC 343.5407/21–dc23/eng/20220924
LC record available at https://lccn.loc.gov/2022033903
LC ebook record available at https://lccn.loc.gov/2022033904

ISBN 978-1-009-24717-7 Hardback
ISBN 978-1-009-24713-9 Paperback

For my parents, Mansoor and Humaira Darr

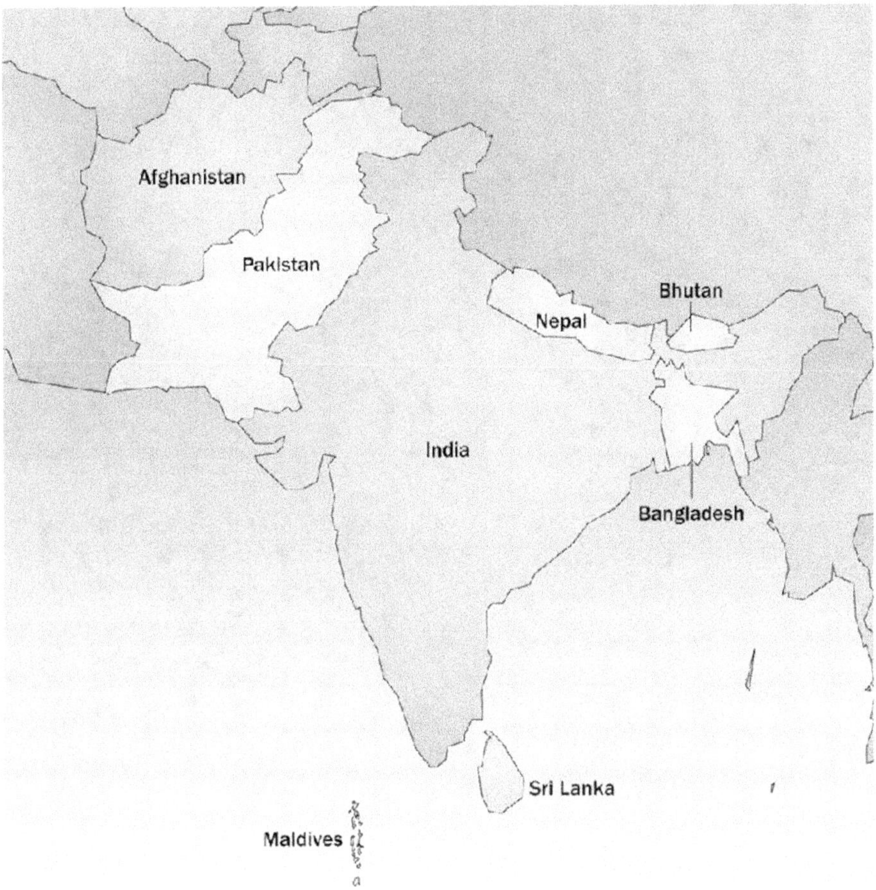

Map of South Asia

Contents

Maps, Figures, and Boxes

MAPS

FIGURES

BOXES

Tables

Preface

In late August 2010, when I was still practising law in Pakistan, I received an unexpected and rather anxious call from the chairman of a multi-national cement company that I had been advising, asking to meet me urgently. It appeared that the chairman had just been delivered an order of the Competition Commission of Pakistan (CCP)[1] penalising his company in the sum of Pak Rupees 405 million[2] for participating in a cartel, and he urgently needed advice on strategising an appropriate course of action. He insisted that his company had not engaged in any illegal activity and was upset that the CCP had not provided his counsel a reasonable opportunity of being heard. Most importantly, he was vehement that CCP be prevented from recovering the penalty because paying it would effectively shut down the company's operations in Pakistan.

Reading the order in his office a short while later, I realised that the CCP had fined my client in exercise of its powers under the Competition Ordinance 2007[3] for being a member of the All Pakistan Cement Manufacturers Association (APCMA), which in its view operated as a cartel.[4] The order noted that the CCP had been alerted to the existence of a possible cartel by a news item regarding the APCMA's decision to raise the price of cement. Upon entering and searching the offices of the APCMA as well as of some of its member cement companies the CCP had discovered a 2003 agreement that had confirmed its suspicions.[5] In October 2008, the CCP had taken *suo motu* notice of cartelisation in the cement sector, and after

1 F. No. 4/2/Sec.4/CCP/200UU8 *In the Matter of Show Cause Notices Issued to all Pakistan Cement Manufacturers Association and Its Member Undertakings* order dated 27.08.2009 ('the APCMA Order').

2 This was equivalent to approximately United States Dollars 5.3 million as per the exchange rate of the day.

3 Ordinance No. LII of 2007 dated 02.10.2007 ('the 2007 Ordinance').

4 APCMA order (n.1) para 40.

5 ibid para 10.

several hearings held over a period of ten months, it had found the APCMA and its member companies guilty of facilitating and participating in a cartel, and had fined each of them in a sum equalling 7.5 per cent of their respective annual turnovers.[6]

I found the CCP's order interesting in several respects: in more than two-thirds of its seventy-five-page order the CCP only reproduced the constitutional objections raised by the APCMA and its member companies without actually any of resolving any of the issues relating to the constitutionality of the 2007 Ordinance or of the CCP. Further, in interpreting the provisions of the 2007 Ordinance to decide the issue of cartelisation, the CCP relied extensively on foreign materials: citing economists such as Adam Smith and Joseph Stiglitz, not ordinarily known to Pakistani lawyers, and quoting on EU jurisprudence, which did not have binding force in the Pakistani legal system. The only references to Pakistani precedents in the order were in respect of issues of due process, evidence, and procedure. With regard to my client's argument that it could not be held liable for a cartel agreement that had been organised three years before it had joined the APCMA and which in any event had not been brought to its notice even after joining the APCMA, the order invoked the 1980 judgment of the European Court of Justice in *Van Landewyck SARL and others* v. *the Commission*.[7] The order also failed to provide any justification for fixing the penalty at 7.5 per cent of the average turnover of all alleged participants of the cartel, regardless of their role or extent of participation.

I realised that although there were several grounds on which my client could appeal the order, actually doing so was fraught with difficulty. In terms of section 42 of the 2007 Ordinance, an order passed by two or more members of the CCP, (as this order was), could only be appealed before the Supreme Court of Pakistan. However, despite being named as the final and only competition appellate authority in the 2007 Ordinance, the Supreme Court had no specialist competition knowledge and, therefore, was unlikely to rule on the merits of the CCP's argument. It was also not clear whether in hearing a matter in its competition jurisdiction, the Supreme Court would exercise its general powers to decide the constitutional objections that the CCP order had failed to resolve. This meant that if the Supreme Court confirmed the CCP's order and called upon my client to pay the penalty in full, my client would not only be deprived of a meaningful resolution of its competition and constitutional arguments and objections but would also exhaust its only appellate remedy. My colleagues and I therefore advised my client to adopt a two-pronged strategy: first, to avail of its statutory right of appeal and file the appeal before the Supreme Court within the limitation period, and second, to utilise the constitutional remedy available to it of challenging the order before the high court in its inherent jurisdiction.

6 ibid para 56.

7 ibid para 31(l), pp 55–56, *Van Landewyck SARL and others v the Commission* [1980] ECR 3125.

It turned out my client along with the APCMA and other member companies had already filed petitions before the Islamabad High Court soon after the CCP had issued the show cause notice in October 2008. Although the Islamabad High Court had at first restrained the CCP from deciding the matter while the petitions remained pending, in January 2009 it had dismissed the petitions for being premature and had allowed the CCP to proceed with the hearings. In August 2009, just as the CCP was getting ready to pass its final order, the APCMA and the cement companies had once again challenged the matter, this time before the Lahore High Court. The Lahore High Court too had initially restrained the CCP from passing a final order, however, later it had allowed the CCP to pass the order while restraining it from taking any adverse action against the parties. Simply put, this meant that while the CCP could conclude its hearings and pass an order, it could neither restrain the operatioins of the APCMA or its member companies nor recover penalties from any of them.[8]

The next hearing before the Lahore High Court was fixed for two days later. Although my client had previously shared a counsel with some of the other member companies, it now appointed me to represent it before the court in a bid to distance itself from cement companies that had been members of the APCMA in 2003 when the alleged cartelisation had been agreed. Arriving in court two days later I found myself among some of the most prominent lawyers in the country making erudite and impassioned arguments on behalf of the APCMA and its member companies. Even as I waited my turn, I not only knew that I had little to add to these arguments, but also that it was not permissible for me to press factual grounds (that distinguished my client from the other parties) in the constitutional jurisdiction in which the high court was hearing the matter: the appropriate forum for such arguments would have been a specialist appellate forum, however, the 2007 Ordinance did not provide for any such authority. I nevertheless made my case as best as possible and sought comfort in at the thought that the order Lahore High Court's interim restraining the CCP from taking adverse action against the parties would remain in place until such time as the high court finally decided these petitions.

As things turned out, however, there was not to be a final order in these proceedings. While the date fixed for the announcement of the order was still a few days away, the judge who had been hearing the petitions was elevated to the Supreme Court and left the matter to be decided by his successor. This of course meant that the petitions would have to be argued afresh. It also meant that the case files would be relegated to the bottom of an ever-growing pile of undecided cases and the matter would not be easily or quickly re-listed for hearing. My annoyance at this outcome notwithstanding, I knew that the APCMA and its member companies, including my client, were pleased because the restraining order issued in earlier

8 ibid paras 11–13 and 58; also p 75.

hearings would continue and the CCP would not be able to recover any penalties from them.

***

It was in the APCMA case that I witnessed for the first time the panic that competition enforcement could provoke in business entities. It was also the first time that I saw the courts quite as reluctant to engage with or comment upon the constitutionality or operations of a regulatory body. In the months following the APCMA proceedings, orders restraining the CCP from recovering penalties and postponing rather than resolving the constitutional objections raised by the aggrieved parties started pouring in from high courts across the country. This meant that even though the CCP continued to hear and decide competition matters it recovered penalties only on the rare occasions when the parties paid these voluntarily. In time, the interactions between the courts and the CCP came to follow a predictable pattern: the courts restrained the CCP from recovering penalties and allowed the restraining order to continue indefinitely, while the CCP increasingly issued orders that were unlikely to be challenged before the courts.

In time I came to the view that at its core, this 'failure' of competition enforcement in Pakistan was linked to the fact that no one – not the CCP tasked to enforce it, the businesses challenging it, the lawyers filing petitions and appeals against it or the courts hearing these – really understood what competition legislation was intended to achieve. For the businesses, the 2007 Ordinance was merely an updated version of the anti-monopoly law it had replaced,[9] and, therefore, essentially anti-business and anti-development, a view that seemed to be reinforced by the CCP's somewhat aggressive enforcement strategy in that period. The lawyers engaged for these cases were largely unfamiliar with competition concepts or jurisprudence and, therefore, preferred to focus on constitutional objections, while the courts remained indecisive, perhaps waiting for more clarity on the status of the 2007 Ordinance which had still not been ratified by the parliament. It seemed to me that this inability to fully understand the rationale and objectives of the competition legislation was aggravated by the fact that the 2007 Ordinance had been introduced by an executive order of a military-led government without meaningful institutional engagement with other state institutions or the public.

In October 2012 when I started my PhD at University College London (UCL) I was keen to explore the link between the process through which Pakistan had adopted its competition legislation and the subsequent implementation of the law in the country. To do so, I decided to compare the adoption and implementation of competition laws in India and Pakistan. While I was initially drawn to India due to

9 Pakistan had promulgated a Monopolies and Restrictive Trade Practices (Control and Prevention) Ordinance in 1970. However, for various political reasons the ordinance was never meaningfully enforced.

its proximity and ancient historical ties with Pakistan as well as its seemingly steadier record of competition enforcement, I was ultimately convinced of the utility of a comparative analysis due to this passage in an article by Rodolfo Sacco that I had come across early in my research:

> As long as we confine ourselves to the study of a single legal system, we will . . . try to capture its features in a synchronic systematic view. We will try to see statute, scholarly formula, proposals for change, the tradition of the schools, the arguments of judges, and the holdings of cases as compatible with one another. The study of domestic law does not allow us to reject completely the great optical illusion founded on the synchronic view. We do not reject it until we find in different legal systems that identical statutes or scholarly formulas give rise to different applications, that identical applications are produced by different statutes or different scholarly formulas, and so forth.[10]

I was also aware that India and Pakistan shared an interesting mix of commonalities and distinctions that were of particular interest for my proposed study. Both countries had adopted their competition legislation within a few years of each other and in both countries the legislation was based on foreign models, expressed similar goals, and provided for similar competition enforcement systems. Further, the legal and political instituitons in India and Pakistan were of an identical age due to the countries having been simultaneously carved out in 1947 from the former British Indian Empire and having largely retained the legal culture and system introduced by the British. These similarities notwithstanding, the political histories and economic priorities of the countries had diverged considerably after their creation, which in turn, had impacted their law-making processes. India had remained a parliamentary democracy throughout and until 1991 had resisted liberal economic legislation. When it finally adopted laws to facilitate the goals of liberalisation it did so through the parliament and in consultation with a range of stakeholders. Pakistan, on the other hand, had struggled with democracy, but had remained committed to a capitalist and feudal ideology. While this made Pakistan more amenable to liberal economic legislation it also meant that in the majority of cases such legislation was introduced in the country through an executive ordinance rather than through the parliament.[11]

In my PhD I focused on the mechanisms through which India and Pakistan adopted their competition legislations and the unique interplay of their respective, political and legal institutions in the course of adoption. I discovered that the adoption processes in both countries had not only determined the substance of the competition legislations, but also their compatibility with and legitimacy in the countries, and had thereby set the stage for their subsequent implementation. India

10 Rodolfo Sacco, 'Legal Formants: A Dynamic Approach to Comparative Law (Installment II of II)' (1991) 39, American Journal of Comparative Law, 343, 385.

11 I discuss these issues more fully in Chapter 2.

had adopted its competition legislation after debates with a range of democratic institutions that lasted over two years and in doing so had enhanced (though not perfected) the compatibility and legitimacy of the Indian competition legislation and had facilitated its implementation. The adoption of the Pakistani competition legislation, on the other hand, had been largely outsourced to a World Bank-led team, which had only superficially addressed the issues of compatibility and legitimacy of the legislation. Consequently after an aggressive start, competition enforcement in the country had all but petered out.

The fact that competition enforcement in the two countries had been shaped, at least in part, by the mechanisms and institutions through which the laws had been initially been adopted, also provided hope that the countries may rechart their competition enforcement by engaging different mechanisms and legal and political institutions in the interpreting and implementing the legislation. Most importantly, however, I realised that for either country to achieve meaningful competition outcomes and to realise the economic benefits of a competitive society, it would have to strike an appropriate balance between the international and domestic legitimacy of its competition legislation: while international legitimacy was necessary for the country to attract international investment, domestic legitimacy was imperative for the legislation to be accepted, understood, and utilised in the country itself. Failure to strike this balance on the part of either country would not only lead to the legislation being rendered irrelevant but would also thwart the economic aims for which the countries had adopted the legislation in the first place.

***

This book has grown out of my PhD research. Having examined the links between the adoption and implementation of competition legislation in India and Pakistan I was curious to understand the competition experience of the remaining South Asian countries,[12] whose distinct modern-day political boundaries and complicated relationships belie a strong geographic, historic, and economic connection, comparable struggles with democracy, broadly similar stages of economic development, and analogous relationships with multi-lateral agencies and developed economies.

Most importantly for my purpose, each of the six remaining South Asian countries had engaged with modern competition laws almost concurrently with India and Pakistan, albeit in different ways: Sri Lanka had adopted a modern competition law in 1987 (the Fair Trading Commission Act), and a consumer protection law in 2003 (Consumer Affairs Authority Act) which also provided for a 'competition promotion division', but was still to issue even a single order regarding anti-competitive

[12] I define South Asia as per the Charter of the South Asian Association for Regional Cooperation (SAARC) established in 1985, in terms of which the region comprises of eight countries namely (in alphabetical order), Afghanistan, Bangladesh, Bhutan, India, Maldives, Nepal, Pakistan, and Sri Lanka.

practices; Nepal had adopted the Competition Promotion and Market Protection Act, 2063 in 2007, however, its national competition authority, the Competition Promotion and Market Protection Board, appeared to be largely inactive; Bangladesh had adopted a competition law in 2012 and had established a national competition authority but was still to operationalise it; Maldives had adopted a Competition and Fair Business Practices Act in 2020 after extensive deliberations that lasted nearly four years, and Bhutan, claiming it did not need a sophisticated competition legislation due to its small economy, had adopted a National Competition Policy in 2015, which it had updated in 2020. Even Afghanistan, beset as it was with political crises, had adopted an Intellectual Property law which included a provision dealing with 'unfair commercial practices', and in 2011 had circulated a draft competition law, which is yet to be enacted.

The proposition I aim to explore for the remaining six South Asian countries is the same as the one I had explored for India and Pakistan in the course of my PhD: I argue that a country that is able to generate compatibility and legitimacy for the legislation at the adoption stage is likely to have greater success in implementing it. To understand the extent of compatibility and legitimacy generated in each of these countries, I evaluate the mechanisms and institutions through which these countries have engaged with the competition legislation and the progress each country has made along the deliberation-enactment-implementation continuum. As in the case of India and Pakistan, I turn to the literatures on diffusion and policy transfer, comparative law, and new development economics, to understand each country's motivation for adopting modern competition legislation, to predict the extent of compatibility and legitimacy likely to be generated in the adoption processes of these countries, and the degree of success each country is likely to enjoy in implementing its competition legislation.

However, unlike in the case of India and Pakistan, where I had compared the entire deliberation-enactment-implementation continuum for both Indian and Pakistani competition legislation, for the remaining South Asian countries I disassemble the continuum and adapt its constituent parts for each country as appropriate: in case of Afghanistan and Bhutan, for instance, I focus only on the deliberation phase as the countries are still to enact a competition legislation; in case of Bangladesh, Maldives and Nepal, that have already adopted some version of a competition legislation but have not commenced implementation, I examine the deliberation as well as the enactment phase; and finally, in the case of Sri Lanka which has tentatively ventured into implementation, I examine the entire continuum, albeit given the absence of competition orders it is not possible to do so in as much depth as in the case of India and Pakistan.

My primary aim in undertaking this exercise, beyond satisfying my personal curiosity about the state of competition reform in the countries that comprise the South Asian region, is to plug an important gap in competition law and South Asian scholarship. I contribute to competition scholarship in two ways: first, I move away from viewing competition legislation as a self-contained economic solution and see it instead as legal organism that co-exists with, and is shaped by other institutions pre-existing in the adopting countries; and second, I evaluate the 'success' of competition legislation from the perspective of the host countries rather than from that of the multi-lateral agencies that bring legislation to these countries. I contribute to South Asian scholarship by producing the a first-ever study of competition laws in South Asia. Although South Asian countries are important players in the global marketplace whether as sellers of raw materials and increasingly of services, as buyers of processed goods or as destinations for foreign investment, these are often viewed only as passive recipients of Western competition (and other legislative) models rather than as independent political and economic actors that play a critical role in shaping not only the content of the legislation that they adopt but also the manner in which the legislation is subsequently implemented. In examining the South Asian experience in the very legal and political context in which it takes place, this book deepens the understanding of competition enforcement in South Asia and thereby creates opportunities for more meaningful competition enforcement across the region.

***

Notwithstanding its focus on South Asia and competition, the book aims to speak to all developing countries that adopt laws based on Western or foreign models and to the authorities entrusted with implementing these laws. A growing number of developing countries adopt not just competition legislation but also other a range of regulatory laws and establish authorities to implement them in the hope that doing so will facilitate their economic transformation. Unfortunately, however, these countries often struggle with bridging the gap between law on the books and law in action in their contexts.

The book essentially offers a two-fold message to all these countries: first that any mechanism or strategy that a country employs for adopting legislation based on foreign models has trade-offs, and second, that regardless of which mechanism and strategy that a country ultimately settles upon for the intial adoption, it remains open for it to adjust and re-chart its strategy and thereby the implementation trajectory of its adopted legislation to suit its evolving priorities. Understanding the trade-offs is important because the strategy and mechanisms that a country employs for the adoption of legislation or legal principles is largely dictated by the relationship between the institutions pre-existing in the country and the country's political priorities, rather than an objective assessment of an objectively best mode of adoption. For instance, for some countries, such as India, generating domestic legitimacy through initial consensus-building may be more important, while for others such as Pakistan, acquiring a legislative model which has international legitimacy may be a greater priority. It is important to appreciate, however, that a country that disproportionately prioritizes domestic legitimacy may drift away from internationally accepted concepts and outcomes, while a country that disproportionately values international legitimacy, may remain unable to implement the law in its domestic context.

The possibility of course correction is relevant not only for the adopting countries but also for the authorities established for implementing the adopted laws and stems from the fact that countries continue to adopt legal principles in interpreting the adopted laws at the implementation stage. This in turn means that regardless of the strategy employed by a country for initial adoption, it remains open for the government bodies or independent authorities designated to interpret and implement the legislation to adopt a different strategy and thereby not only to fine tune the meaning but also the extent of compatibility and legitimacy of the legislation in the domestic contexts and, in doing so, to re-chart its implementation trajectory.

Beyond the governments and competition authorities of South Asian and other developing countries, this book is also likely be of interest to scholars specialising in EU and US competition law, comparative law, and economics who are interested in how principles from developed, legally sophisticated jurisdictions, travel to and are adopted and implemented in emerging and developing economies. Scholars interested in comparative law will particularly benefit from the theoretical framework utilised in this book, which although constructed to examine the links between adoption and implementation of borrowed competition laws, is equally relevant for all regulatory laws adopted from western models and provides robust tools for analysing the spread of legal principles across developing countries and understanding the factors in the host countries that are likely to affect implementation of these laws. The book also offers scholars interested in development and new institutional economics, greater insight into the role of pre-existing legal and political institutions in the implementation and success of borrowed economic institutions.

This book also speaks to multi-lateral agencies that play an important, if not a critical role in defining the direction of law reform in developing economies. In the South Asian story, for instance, the World Trade Organisation (WTO) features prominently among factors that prompted these countries to adopt competition laws, the World Bank, the International Monetary Fund (IMF), and the Asian Development Bank (ADB) have played an important role in the specific competition legislations adopted, and the United Nations Conference on Trade and Development (UNCTAD) has made, and continues to contribute to capacity building for the implementation of competition legislation in these countries. In most instances, the multi-lateral agencies engaging with particular countries do not engage with, and appear not to fully appreciate, the impact of the legal and political institutions pre-existing in these countries, on the enforcement of these laws and, therefore, factor these only cursorily, if at all, in prescribing competition or other regulatory solutions for these countries or in designing capacity building programmes for them. I believe that in embedding the adoption and implementation of competition legislations in the contexts of the adopting countries and in underscoring the significance of their pre-existing institutions, this book will help multilateral agencies understand the limitations of their solutions and advice in bringing about meaningful economic reform in developing countries and, may therefore, encourage them to propose more context-specific adoption and implementation strategies for competition as well as other regulatory laws designed for these countries.

***

This book explores the story of competition law in South Asia in nine chapters. Chapter 1 establishes the theoretical framework for assessing the impact of the process through which legislation is adopted, on its subsequent implementation. Integrating strands from diffusion and transfer, new institutional economics, and comparative law literatures, this chapter argues that for a borrowed law 'to continue to grow in and become a part of'[13] the adopting country, it must be compatible with the context of the country and enjoy a degree of legitimacy in it. To this end, the chapter explores the meaning of and connection between the concepts of 'compatibility' and 'legitimacy': in case of 'compatibility' it also explores features of the adopted law and the context must be compatible with each other, while in case of 'legitimacy' it elaborates its internal and external dimensions and argues that both dimensions are relevant and necessary for the successful implementation of adopted legislation. The chapter also explores how compatibility and legitimacy influence and shape the subsequent implementation of adopted laws.

Chapters 2 and 3 describe different aspects of the South Asian experience of adoption of competition laws. Chapter 2 compares the adoption of modern competition laws in India and Pakistan, while Chapter 3 examines the pre-conditions of transfer and the adoption experience in the remaining siz South Asian countries before evaluating the South Asian experience as a whole. These chapters note where each country is located on the deliberation-enactment-implementation continuum in relation to competition legislation and examine the legal and political institutions pre-existing in each country and engaging in the deliberation, enactment, or implementation of competition legislation. The chapters also identity the factors that have motivated South Asian countries to consider adopting competition legislation, and the transfer mechanisms and institutions these countries have employed in this regard. The chapters predict the extent of compatibility and legitimacy that the adopted competition enjoys or is likely to enjoy, in the specific context of each adopting country.

[13] Alan Watson, *Legal Transplants: An Approach to Comparative Law* (2nd edn, University of Georgia Press 1993).

Chapters 4–7 focus on the Indian and Pakistani competition experience. Chapter 4 establishes the manner in which the adoption processes employed by the two countries have shaped their competition enforcement authorities. It compares the structures, mandates, and compositions of these authorities as well as their decision-making strategies and provides an overview of implementation of competition laws in the two countries by comparing a range of features ('indicators') of the orders of competition authorities. Chapter 5 evaluates the Indian and Pakistani competition authorities' interpretaion of the statutory provisions relating to anti-competitive agreements and in doing so provides a basis for understanding the interpretative strategies of these authorities in relation to other competition principles provided in the legislation. Chapter 6 examines the penal strategies of the Indian and Pakistani competition authorities, focusing particularly on the sanctions and penalties that the authorities have imposed in the first decade of their operations. It also examines how the penal strategies have been shaped by the strategies and institutions through which competition legislation was adopted in either country. Chapter 7 examines the interaction of the Indian and Pakistani competition authorities and the pre-existing dispute resolution authorities in the two countries and explores the manner in which this interaction shapes the implementation trajectory of competition legislation in the countries. The adoption processes through which the countries had acquired the legislation, and the extent of compatibility and legitimacy these processes had generated, form the backdrop for the discussions in all four chapters.

Chapter 8 examines the state of competition enforcement in the remaining six South Asian countries and explores how the adoption processes through which each of these countries have adopted their competition legislation has impacted their enforcement efforts. In the case of countries that are still to adopt competition laws, the chapter predicts their implementation prospects. The chapter also explores how countries that are in the hiatus stage and are still to embark upon implementation may learn from the Indian and Pakistani experience, and ends with discussing the patterns of diffusion and transfer and implementation of competition legislation throughout the region. Having established the gap in competition enforcement in Chapter 8, Chapter 9 explores how governments and competition authorities in all South Asian countries may be motivated to engage more meaningfully with competition enforcement and argues that governments are more likely to support competition enforcement in their contexts if they are convinced of competition's potential to help deliver their broader economic and social goals. The chapter also proposes some implementation strategies for these countries.

***

The idea of this book has been with me ever since I started my PhD in 2012 and it is both exciting and daunting to send the final product out into the world. As I do so,

I am very sensible of the tremendous debt of gratitude I owe to my supervisors Professor Iaonnis Lianos and Professor Riz Mokal for their supervision, guidance, and support throughout my time at UCL and beyond. A very special thank you also to my PhD examiners Professor Frederic Jenny and Professor Josef Drexl for their engagement with my work, their faith in its value and their encouragement in transforming the PhD into a manuscript. I am also very grateful to several lawyers, economists, and competition experts throughout South Asia for very generously sharing with me their time, experience, and insights. In particular I would like to thank in India (in alphabetical order): Professor Aditya Bhattacharjea (Delhi School of Economics, Delhi University); Mr Percival Billimoria (now with Chambers of P.S. Billimoria, Delhi); Dr Geeta Gauri and Mr M.S. Sahoo (former members, Competition Commission of India); Dr Seema Gaur (former advisor, Competition Commission of India); Mr John Handoll (National Practice Head, Shardul Amarchand Mangaldas, Delhi); Mr Dhanendra Kumar (former chairperson Competition Commission of India); Mr K.K. Sharma (former Director General Investigations Competition Commission of India) and Mr Udai Mehta (CUTS India). In Pakistan (in alphabetical order): Mr Ijaz Ahmed (partner, Ijaz Ahmed and Associates, Karachi); Mr Uzair Karamat Bhandari (partner Bhandari, Naqvi and Riaz, Lahore); Mr Bilal Hamid and Major General (retd.); Rehmat Khan (CFO and chairman, Pakistan Cement Company Limited Islamabad); Ms Rahat Kaunain Hassan, Ms Vadiyya Khalil, and Dr Joseph Wilson (present and former chairpersons of the Competition Commission of Pakistan); Mr Ejaz Ishaq Khan (partner, Aqlaal Islamabad); Mr Ikram-ul-Haque Qureshi (former director Legal Competition Commission of Pakistan); Mr Salman Akram Raja (partner, Raja Muhammad Akram and Company) and Mr Asif Saad (former CEO, Lotte Pakistan Limited). In Bangladesh I would like to acknowledge Mr M.A. Razzaque (chairman, RAPID Dacca); in Nepal Mr Apurba Khatiwada (lawyer and associate SAWTEE Kathmandu), and in Sri Lanka Mr Gamunu Chandrasekera (attorney, Chambers of Nihal Jayawardene PC Colombo) and Dr Dushni Weerakoon (executive director of the Institute of Policy Studies Sri Lanka) without whose guidance many of the questions in my mind would have remained unclarfified.

I would also like to extend a very special thank you to my colleagues at University of Manchester for their encouragement and enthusiasm for this work, to my former colleagues at Coventry Law School for their support with different aspects of the writing process and to the ASPiRE Fellowship at the Centre for Financial and Corporate Integrity at Coventry University which allowed me the time to focus on my research.; to the Centre for Law, Innovation, and Development, KIMEP University Kazakhstan, the CLS Staff Forum, the BRICS Competition Law and Policy Forum, the UCL Work in Progress Forum; the University of Glasgow, the University of Reading, the Institute of Business Administration Karachi; School of Law Lahore University of Management Sciences, and the Research Society of International Law, Islamabad for providing me a platform to share my research at various stages and and the opportunity to engage with an informed and interested audience which helped further refine my thinking.

Finally, I extend profound and most heartfelt thanks to my family – especially to my sister Aisha for being the wisest sounding-board in my moments of self-doubt – and to my wonderful friends for their love, friendship, and understanding throughout this long journey: I have been lucky to have some of the very best in my corner.

Abbreviations

2007 Ordinance	Competition Ordinance 2007
2007 Amendment Act	Competition (Amendment) Act 2007
2009 Ordinance	Competition Ordinance 2009
2010 Ordinance	Competition Ordinance 2010
AAEC	appreciable adverse effect on competition
Afghani Act	Draft Competition Act 2011
Bangladeshi Act	Competition Act 2012
Bhutanese Policy	Competition Policy 2020
CCI	Competition Commission of India
CCP	Competition Commission of Pakistan
DG	Director General Investigations
General Enforcement Regulations	Competition Commission (General Enforcement) Regulations 2007
Indian Act	Competition Act 2002
Indian Tribunal	Competition Appellate Tribunal, India includes the NCLAT in any post-2017 references
Manes Report	Eric David Manes, 'A Framework for a New Competition Policy and Law: Pakistan' (The International Bank for Reconstruction and Development 2007)
NCLAT	National Company Law Appellate Tribunal
Nepalese Act	Competition Promotion and Market Protection Act 2063, 2007
Pakistani Act	Competition Act 2010
Pakistani Tribunal	Competition Appellate Tribunal, Pakistan
Raghavan Report	Report of the High Level Committee on Competition Policy & Law 2000
SAARC	South Asian Association for Regional Cooperation
SAFTA	South Asian Free Trade Area
South Asian Six	Afghanistan, Bangladesh, Bhutan, Maldives, Nepal, and Sri Lanka
Sri Lankan Act	Consumer Affairs Authority Act 2003

Authorities

COMPETITION APPELLATE TRIBUNAL INDIA

Alkem Laboratories Limited v CCI and other
Appeals 9/2016, 14/2016, and 15/2016 decided 10.05.2016
All India Organization of Chemists & Druggists (AIOCD) and others v CCI and others
Appeals 21/2013, 6/2014, and 7/2014 decided 09.12.2016
Bengal Chemist & Druggists Association and others v CCI and another
Appeal 37/2014 decided 10.05.2016
Coal India Limited and another v CCI and others
Appeal 80/2014 decided 09.12.2016
Director, Karak Pharmaceuticals Pvt. Ltd v CCI and others
Appeal 42/2014 decided 07.12.2015
Appeal 15/2012 decided 29.08.2012
Dr. L.H. Hiranandani Hospital v CCI and another
Appeal 19/2014 decided 18.12.2015
ECP Industries Ltd v CCI
Appeal 47/2015 decided 01.03.2016
Excel Crop Care Limited v CCI & others
Appeals 79/2012, 80/2012, and 81/2012 decided 29.10.2013
Film Distribution Association, Kerala v Eros International Media Ltd. & others
Appeal 68/2012 decided 03.01.2013
Film Distributors Association, Kerala v CCI and others
Appeal 61/2015 decided 03.07.2015
Gulf Oil Corporation Ltd v Competition Commission of India & others
Appeals 82/2012, 83/2012, 84/2012, 85/2012, 86/2012, 87/2012, 88/2012, 89/2012, and 90/2012 decided 18.04.2013

IATA Agents Association of India v Uniglobe Mod Travels (P) Ltd. & others
Appeal 8/2012 decided 10.07.2013
Indian Jute Mills Association v CCI and others
Appeals 73/2014, 77/2014, 78/2014, 83/2014, 84/2014, 85/2014, 86/2014, 87/2014, 88/2014 and 8/2015, 9/2015, 10/2015, 11/2015, 12/2015, 13/2015, 14/2015, and 15/2015 decided 01.07.2016
International Cylinder (Pvt.) Ltd v CCI
Appeals 21/2012 to 65/2012 decided 20.12.2013
Jose C. Mundadan v CCI and others
Appeal 55/2015 decided 17.08.2015
Jose C. Mundadan v CCI and others
Appeal 56/2015 decided 27.04.2016
Kansan News Pvt. Ltd v Fastway Transmissions Pvt. Ltd. & others
Appeal 137/2012 decided 10.01.2013
Kerala Film Exhibitors Association and another v CCI and others
Appeal 100/2015 decided 04.02.2016
Kingfisher Airlines Limited v CCI and others
Appeal 15/2012 decided 29.08.2012
MDD Medical Systems India Private Limited v CCI and others
Appeals 93/2012, 94/2012 and 95/2012 decided 25.02.2013
Nandu Ahuja, Sunil Arjan Lulla, Jyoti Deshpande v CCI & another
Appeals 1/2012, 2/2012, 3/2012 decided 05.08.2013
Nandu Ahuja, Sunil Arjan Lulla, Jyoti Deshpande v CCI & another
Appeals 11/2013, 12/2013, 13/2013 decided 17.01.2014
National Insurance Company Ltd v CCI
Appeals 94/2015, 95/2015, 96/2015 and 97/2015 decided 09.12.2016
President All Kerala Chemists and Druggists and another v CCI and others
Appeals 5/2016 decided 10.05.2016
Shib Sankar Nag Sarkar and another v *CCI and others*
Appeal 34/2014 decided 10.05.2016
Steel Authority of India Limited v Jindal Steel & Power Limited
Appeal 1/2009 decided 15.02.2010
Tamil Nadu Film Exhibitors Association v CCI and another
Appeal 14/2014 decided 28.04.2015
Telugu Film Chamber of Commerce v Cinergy Independent Film Service Pvt. Ltd & others
Appeal 15/2013, decided 14.10.2015
Toyota Kirloskar Motor Private Limited v CCI and others
Appeals 60/2014, 61/2014 and 62/2014 decided 09.12.2016
Travel Agents Association of India v Uniglobe Mod Travels (P) Ltd. & others
Appeal 24/2011 decided 10.07.2013

COMPETITION COMMISSION OF INDIA

A Foundation for Common Cause & People Awareness v PES Installations (Pvt.) Limited
Case 43/2010 decided 16.4.2012
All India Online Vendors Association and Flipkart India Private Limited
Case 20/2018 decided 06.11.2018
Ashish Ahuja v Snapdeal.com & Another
Case 17/2014 decided 19.05.2014
Automobile Dealers Association v Global Automobiles & others
Case 33/2011 decided 03.07.2012
Bio Med Private Limited v Union of India & others
Case 26/2013 decided 04.06.2015
Builders Association of India v Cement Manufacturers Association & others
Case 29/2010 decided 20.06.2012
Builders Association of India v Cement Manufacturers Association and others
Case 29/2010 decided 31.08.2016
Cartelization in Public Sector Insurance Companies
Suo Motu Case 2/2014 decided 10.07.2015
Crown Theatre v Kerala Film Exhibitions Federation
Case 16/2014 decided 08.09.2015
Deepak Verma v Clues Network
Case 34/2016 decided 26.07.2016
Delhi Vyapar Mahasangh v Flipkart and Amazon
Case 40/2019 decided 13.01.2020.
ESYS Information Technologies Pvt. Ltd. v Intel Corporation (Intel Inc.) & others
Case 48/2011 decided 16.01.2014
Express Industry Council of India v Jet Airways (India) Limited & others
Case 30/2013 decided 17.11.2015
Fast Track Call Cab (Pvt.) Ltd and Meru Travel Solutions (Pvt.) Ltd v ANI Technologies (Pvt.) Ltd.
Case 6/2015 and 74/2015 decided 19.07.2017.
FICCI v United Producers/Distributors Forum & others
Case 1/2009 decided 25.5.2011
Financial Software and Systems Pvt. Limited v ACI Worldwide Solutions Private Limited and others
Case 52/2013 decided 13.01.2015
Fx Enterprise Solutions India Pvt. Ltd. v Hyundai Motor India Limited
Case 36/2014 & 82/2014 decided 14/06/2017

In re Alleged cartelisation by steel producers
RTPE 9/2008 decided 09/01/2014
In re: Cartelisation in respect of zinc carbon dry cell batteries market in India
Suo Motu Case 02/2016 decided 19.04.2018
In re: Cartelisation in the supply of Electric Power Steering Systems
Suo Motu Case No. 07 (01)/2014 decided 09.08.2019
In re: Jasper Infotech Private Limited (Snapdeal) v KAFF Appliances (India) Pvt. Ltd. (Kaff)
Case 61/2014 decided 15.01.2019
Indian Foundation of Transport Research & Training v Sh. Bal Malkait Singh & others
Case 61/2012 decided 16.02.2015
Indian Sugar Mills Association & Others v Indian Jute Mills Association & others
Case 38/2011 decided 03.04.2014
Jasper Infotech Private Limited (Snapdeal) v Kaff Appliances (India) Pvt. Ltd. (Kaff)
Case 61/2014 decided 29.12.2014
K. C. Marketing, Maharashtra v OPPO Mobiles MU Private Limited
Case 34/2018 decided 08.11.2018
Kannada Gratiakara Koota Shri Ganesh Chetan v Karnataka Film Chamber of Commerce & others
Case 58/2012 decided 27.07.2015
Kerala Cine Exhibitors Association v Kerala Film Exhibitors Federation & others
Case 45/2012 decided 23.06.2015
Magnus Graphics v Nilpeter India Pvt. Ltd. & others
Case 65/2013 decided 02.12.2014
Maruti & Company v Karnataka Chemists & Druggists Association & others
Case 71/2013 decided 28.07.2016
Matrimony.com Limited v Google
Cases 07 and 30/2012 decided 08.02.2018
Mega Cabs (Pvt.) Ltd v ANI Technologies (Pvt.) Ltd
Case 82/2015 decided 09.02.2016
Meru Travel Solutions (Pvt.) Ltd. v Uber India Systems (Pvt.) Ltd.
Case 96/2015 decided 10.02.2016
Meru Travel Solutions Private Limited (MTSPL) v Uber India Systems (Pvt). Ltd.
Case 81/2015 decided 22.12.2015
MP Merhotra v Kingfisher Airlines Limited & others
Case 4/2009 decided 09.01.2012
Mr Mohit Manglani v Flipkart India Private Limited and others
Case 80/2014 decided 23.04.2015

Mr Ramakant Kini v Dr L.H. Hiranandani Hospital, Powai, Mumbai
Case 39/2012 decided 05.02.2014
Mr Umar Javeed and others. v Google LLC and others
Case 39/2018 decided 16.04.2019.
Neeraj Malhotra v Deustche Post Bank Home Finance Ltd. & others
Case 5/2009 decided 02.12.2010.
P.K Krishnan v Paul Madavana Alkem Laboratories & others
Case 28/2014 decided 01.12.2015
Re Alleged Cartelization by Cement Manufacturers
RTPE 52/2006 decided 30.07.2012
Re Alleged Cartelization by Cement Manufacturers v Shree Cement Limited and others
RTPE 52/2006 decided 31.08.2016
Re Aluminum Phosphide Tablets Manufacturers
Suo motu Case 2/2011 decided 23.04.2012
Reliance Big Entertainment Limited v Tamil Nadu Film Exhibitors Association & others
Case 25/2010 decided 16.02.2012
Rohit Medical Store v Macleods Pharmaceutical Limited & others
Case 78/2012 decided 29.01.2015
Rubtub Solutions Pvt. Ltd. v MakeMyTrip India Pvt. Ltd. (MMT) and others
Case 01/2020 decided 24.02.2020
Sheth & Co. & others
Suo Motu Case 4/2013 decided 10.06.2015
Shivam Enterprises v Kiratpur Sahib Truck Operators Transport Society Limited & others
Case 43/2013 decided 04.02.2015
Shri B.P Khare v Orissa Concrete and Allied Industries & Others
Ref Case 5/2011 decided 21.02.2013
Shri Dhanraj Pillay & others v Hockey India
Case 73/2011 decided 31.05.2013.
Shri Ghanshyam Das Vij v Bajaj Corporation Limited & others
Case 68/2013 decided 12.01.2015
Shri Jyoti Swaroop Arora v Tulip Infratech Limited & others decided
Case 59/2011 03.02.2015
Shri Shamsher Kataria v Honda Siel Cars India Limited & others
Case 3/2011 decided 25.08.2014.
Shri Sonam Sharma v Apple Inc. USA & others
Case 24/2011 decided 19.03.2013.
Shri Sunil Bansal & others v Jaiprakash Associates Ltd and others
Cases 72/2011, 16/2012, 34/2012, 53/2012, 45/2013 decided 26.10.2015

Shri T. G. Vinayakumar v Association of Malayalam Movie Artists and others
Case No. 98/2014 decided 24.03.2017
Swastik Stevedores Private Limited v Dumper Owner's Association & others
Case 42/2012 decided 21.01.2015
Uniglobe Mod Travels Pvt. Limited v Travel Agents Federation of India & others
Case 3/2009 decided 04.10.2011
Varca Druggist & Chemist and others v Chemists & Druggists Association Goa and others
MRTP Case No. C-127/2009/DGIR (4/28) decided 11.06.2012
Vijay Gupta v Paper Merchants Association Delhi & others
Case 7/2010 decided 24.03.2011
XYZ v Alphabet Inc
Case 07/2020 decided 09.11.2020

COMPETITION APPELLATE TRIBUNAL PAKISTAN

1-Link Guarantee Ltd and others v CCP and others
Appeal 1-26/2012 decided 20.03.2013
Al-Rahim Foods (Pvt.) Limited v CCP and others
Appeal 3/2016 decided 25.01.2017
Bahria Town (Pvt.) Limited v CCP
Appeal 3/2017 decided 10.05.2017
Colgate Palmolive (Pakistan) Limited v Competition Commission of Pakistan and another
2019 C L D 254
Engro Foods (Pvt.) Ltd. and 2 others v Competition Commission of Pakistan
2019 C L D 981
Ghulam Fareed and 8 others v Competition Commission of Pakistan and another
2019 C L D 279
HASCOL Petroleum Ltd v CCP and others
Appeal 7/2016 decided 21.12.2016
Institute of Business Management v CCP
Appeal 5/2016 decided 07.06.2017
Institute of Chartered Accountants of Pakistan v Competition Commission of Pakistan
CA 274/2009 decided 19.03.2009.
Nauman Anwar Butt v DHL
Appeal 2/2016 decided 21.12.2016

Pakistan Poultry Association v CCP
Appeal 9/2016 decided 28.09.2016
Pakistan Poultry Association v Competition Commission of Pakistan
2018 C L D 759
Pakistan State Oil Limited v Competition Commission of Pakistan
2019 C L D 538
PTCL v CCP
Appeal 4/2017 decided 10.05.2017
Raja Asir Munir and another v DHL Pakistan (Pvt.) Limited and 2 others
2018 C L D 725
Reckitt Benckiser Pakistan Ltd v CCP
26.11.2015
Saleem Habib Godial v CCP
Appeal 1/2016 decided 29.03.2017
Synthetic Fibre Development v CCP
Appeal 12/2016 decided 07.06.2017
Tara Crop Sciences (Pvt.) Limited v CCP and other
Appeal 2/2015 decided 30.11.2016
Toyota Sahara Motors v CCP
Appeal 1/2016 decided 29.03.2017
University of Faisalabad v CCP
Appeal 4/2016 decided 07.06.2017
University of South Asia v CCP
Appeal 10/2016 decided 28.09.2016.
WAH Engineering College v CCP
Appeal 6/2016 decided 07.06.2017

COMPETITION COMMISSION OF PAKISTAN

1-Link Guarantee Limited & Member Banks case
File 1/24/ATM Charges/C&TA/CCP/2011 decided 28.06.2012
All Pakistan Cement Manufacturers Association case
File 4/2/Sec 4/CCP/2008 decided 27.08.2009
All Pakistan Newspaper Society case
File 06/Sec 3/CCP/08 decided 23.04.2009
Dredging Companies case
File 3(17)/L.O/CCP/2009 decided 23.07.2010
In the Matter Phase II Review of Acquisition of Careem Inc. By Uber Technologies, Inc. through Augusta Acquisition B.V,
File No: 1032/Merger-CCP/19 order dated 31.012020
GCC Approved Medical Centres case
File 2(2)/JD(L)/POEPA/CCP/2011 decided 29.06.2012

Institute of Chartered Accountants of Pakistan case
File 3/Sec-4/CCP/08 decided 04.12.2008
Jamshoro Joint Venture Limited and LPG Association of Pakistan case
File 3/LPG/DIR(INV)/M&TA/CCP/2009 decided 14.12.2009
Karachi Stock Exchange case
File 1/Dir(Inv.) KSE/CCP/08) decided 18.03.2009
LDI Operators case
File 5(114)/Reg/ADG-SCP/LHC/CCP/13 decided 30.04.2013
NFC Employees Co-operative Housing Society
File no. 80/NFCEHS/C&TA/CCP/2016 decided 27.11.2018
Pakistan Automobile Manufacturers Authorized Dealers Association & Member Undertakings
File 1/101/PAMADA/C & TA/CCP/2013 decided 10.04.2015
Pakistan Banking Association case
File 2/sec-4/CCP/07 decided 10.04.2008.
Pakistan Engineering Council
File 2(32)/Comp Cell/CCP/2015 decided 20.04.2016
Pakistan Flour Mills Association
F.No:89/PFMA/C &TA/CCP/2016 decided13.12.2019.
Pakistan Jute Mills Association and its member mills
File CCP/Cartels/03/2010 decided 03.02.2011
Pakistan Poultry Association
File 42/PPA/C & TA/CCP/2015 decided 29.02.2016
Pakistan Poultry Association
File CCP/Cartels/04/2010 decided 16.08.2010
Pakistan Ship's Agents' Association
File 08/APPMA/CMTA/CCP/10/1709 decided 22.06.2011
Pakistan Vanaspati Manufacturers Association case
File 1(15)/PVMA-ISB decided 30.06.2011
PESCO Tender Order/Amin Brothers Engineering et al. case
File 13/PESCO/CMTA/CCP/2010 decided 13.05.2011
Port Qasim Authority and Engro Vopak Terminal Limited case
Files 6/LP/CMTA/CCP/2010 & 2/(192)/AGR/Exm./Reg/CCP/2010 decided 29.06.2011
Reliance Paints
File no. 31/RP/C&TA/CCP/2015 decided 30.03.2018
Takaful Pakistan Ltd. And Travel Agents' Association of Pakistan
File 9/M(A&R)/CAA-TAAP/CCP/2007 decided 29.01.2010
Urea Manufacturers
F. NO: 01/UREA/C&TA/CCP/2010 decided 29.03.2013
Wateen Telecom (Pvt.) Limited and Defence Housing Authority case
File 09/Reg/Comp/CAP/CCP/2010 decided 22.03.2011

INDIAN HIGH COURTS

Amir Khan Productions (Pvt.) Limited v Union of India
WP 358/2010 decided 18.08.2010
Arun Kumar Bajoria v CCI & another
WP (C) 2471/2016 decided 21.03.2016
DLF Home Developers Limited v CCI & another
WP 6361 and 4362/2014 decided 10.10.2014
Google Inc. & others v CCI & another
WP 7084/2014 decided 27.04.2015
Gujarat Guardian Limited v CCI and others
WP 7766/2010 decided 23.11.2010
Hyundai Motor India Limited v CCI and others
WA 340/2015 decided 23.07.2018
Hyundai Motors India Limited & BMW India Pvt. Limited v CCI and another
WP 31808 and 31809/2012 decided 04.02.2015
Interglobe Aviation Limited v Secretary CCI
WP 6805/2010 decided 06.10.2010
Telefonaktiebolaget LM Ericsson v CCI & others
WP 1006/2014 decided 16.04.2016

INDIAN SUPREME COURT

Brahm Dutt v Union of India
(2005) 2 Supreme Court Cases 431
Commissioner of Income Tax v Chhabil Dass Agrawal
(2014) 1 SCC 603
Competition Commission of India v Steel Authority of India Limited
(2010) 10 SCC 744
Excel Crop Care Limited v CCI
2017 8 SCC 47
His Holiness Kesavananda Bharati Sripadagalvaru and others v State and Kerala and another
AIR 1973 SC 1461

PAKISTANI HIGH COURTS

Islamabad Feeds (Pvt) Limited & others v Federation of Pakistan etc.
WP 4942/2020 decided 16.09.2021
LPG Association of Pakistan v Federation of Pakistan and others
2021 C L D 214

Pakistan Banking Association v Federation of Pakistan and others
CP 938/2008 decided 07.11.2008

PAKISTANI SUPREME COURT

Anjuman e Ahmedya v Deputy Commissioner
PLD 1966 Supreme Court 639
Chief Justice of Pakistan, Mr Justice Iftikhar Muhammad Chaudhry v The President of Pakistan through the Secretary and others
PLD 2010 SC 61
Rana Aftab Ahmed Khan v Muhammad Ajmal and another
PLD 2010 SC 1066
Sindh High Court Bar Association v The Federation of Pakistan
PLD 2009 SC 879
Syed Zafar Ali Shah v General Parvez Musharraf, Chief Executive and others
PLD 2000 SC 869

OTHERS

Ceylon Oxygen Ltd. v Fair Trading Commission
SLR-Year-1997-Vol.2p 372
Jyoti Baniya v The Federation of Nepali National Transport Entrepreneurs and Others
Nepal Law Report 2068 (2011/12), Volume 4, Decision No. 8598, Decision Date 10-19-2067 (12-5-2010 AD)
Van Landewyck SARL and others v the Commission
[1980] ECR 3125

Statutes and Statutory Instruments

AFGHANISTAN

Draft Competition Act 2011

BANGLADESH

Bangladesh Laws (Revision and Declaration) Act 1973
Competition Act 2012
Constitution of Bangladesh 1972

BHUTAN

Competition Policy 2015
Competition Policy 2020
Consumer Protection Act 2012
Information, Communications and Media Act 2018

BRITISH

Government of India Act 1935
Indian Independence Act 1947

INDIA

Competition (Amendment) Act 2007
Competition Act 2002
Competition Bill 2020

Competition Commission of India (Selection of Chairperson and other Members of the Commission) Rules 2003
Constitution of India 1950
Consumer Protection (E-commerce) Rules 2020.
Finance Act 2017
Monopolies and Restrictive Trade Practices Act 1969
S.O. 1198(E) dated 14.10.2003
S.O. 1240(E) dated 15.05.2009
S.O. 1241(E) dated 15.05.2009
S.O. 1242(E) dated 15.05.2009
S.O. 340(E) dated 31.03.2003
S.O. 715(E) dated 19.06.2003
The Competition Commission of India (Lesser Penalty) Regulations 2009

NEPAL

Competition Promotion and Market Protection Act 2063 (2007)
Consumer Protection Act 2054 (1998)
Electronics Trading Act (2063) 2008
Interim Constitution of Nepal 2063 (2007)
Privacy Act (2075) 2018
The Consumer Protection Act (2075) 2018

PAKISTAN

Competition Appellate Tribunal Rules 2015
Competition Commission (General Enforcement) Regulations 2007
Competition Commission (Salary, Terms and Conditions of Chairman and Members) Rules 2009
Competition Ordinance 2007
Competition Ordinance 2009
Competition Ordinance 2010
Constitution (Amendment) Order 2007
Constitution of the Islamic Republic of Pakistan 1973
Laws (Continuance in Force) Order 1958
Monopolies and Restrictive Trade Practices (Control and Prevention) Ordinance, 1970
Notification No. F.15(1)/2010-A.V dated 27.07.2011
Notification No. F.21(1)/2011-Admn-III dated 29.05.2012
Ordinance No. CI of 2002
Ordinance No. LVI of 1980
Ordinance No. XIV of 1982

Ordinance No. XXVI of 1980
Personal Data Protection Bill 2020
Proclamation of Emergency and Provisional Constitutional Order No. 1 of 2007
Provisional Constitution Order 1969

SRI LANKA

Consumer Affairs Authority Act 2003
Draft Personal Data Protection Act 2019
Electronic Transactions (Amendment) Act 2017
Electronic Transactions Act 2006
Fair Trading Commission Act 1987
Information and Communication Technology (Amendment) Act 2008
Information and Communication Technology Act 2003

OTHER

Notice on agreements of minor importance which do not appreciably restrict competition under Article 101(1) of the Treaty on the Functioning of the European Union (2014/C 291/01)
Treaty for the Functioning of Europe (TFEU)
EU Guidelines on Application of Article 81
Clayton Act, ch. 323, 38 Stat. 730 (1914)
The Sherman Act 1890 15 U.S.C. §§ 1-38
Commission Regulation (EU) No. 330/2010 of 20.04.2010
Commission Regulation (EU) No. 461/2010 of 27.05. 2010
Commission Regulation (EU) No. 1217/2010 of 14.12.2010
Commission Regulation (EU) No. 1218/2010 of 14.12.2010

1

The Theoretical Framework

1.1 INTRODUCTION

The Law and Development movement, launched in the 1960s by the US Agency for International Development, the Ford Foundation, and other private American donors, placed law at the centre of the development process. Although this movement soon faltered, largely due to its emphasis on encouraging countries to transplant laws without requiring them to adapt these to their contexts, its failure underscored the importance of *compatibility* of the borrowed laws.[1] A review of the literature relating to the movement reveals that laws that were not compatible with the context of the adopting country sometimes did not 'take at all': in many cases these laws though 'promoted by the reformers, remained on the books but were ignored in action' while in other cases these laws 'were captured by local elites and put to uses different from those the reformers intended'.[2] The evidence for the importance of compatibility that emerged in relation to this movement was so overwhelming that by the time the movement had ended there was 'explicit recognition', even at the World Bank, 'of the failures of transplants and of top-down methods, which [...] led to a rejection of one-size-fits-all approach and [...] placed a renewed stress on the need for context specific project development based on consultation of all "stakeholders"'.[3]

Notwithstanding the recognition that compatibility was, and is, important for law reform to deliver the results for which it is undertaken, there has been little clarity, particularly in comparative law literature, as to how this compatibility may be generated or how it impacts the subsequent success of the borrowed law. This chapter argues that compatibility between the adopted law and the context is generated in the course of

[1] David M Trubek, 'The "Rule of Law" in Development Assistance: Past, Present, and Future" in David Trubek and Alvaro Santos (eds), *The New Law and Economic Development: A Critical Appraisal* (CUP 2006), 79.

[2] ibid.

[3] ibid 91.

adoption of the borrowed law and affects not only the extent to which the law is understood, utilised, and applied in the adopting country but also the pace at which it integrates into the adopting country's pre-existing legal system. To study the connection between the adoption and implementation of borrowed laws, particularly economic laws, this chapter proposes an analytical framework that integrates elements from comparative law literature, the political science literatures of policy diffusion and transfer, and new institutional economics (NIE) literature. Policy diffusion and transfer literatures indicate that countries have diverse motivations for adopting laws which also impact the mechanisms through which they adopt these laws; comparative law literature suggests that the context of the adopting country, through the actors that engage in the adoption process, plays a critical role in shaping the content of the adopted law and thereby lays the foundations of its subsequent performance in the adopting country; and new institutional economics literature elaborates the connection between the institutions through which laws are adopted on their subsequent implementation.[4]

This chapter is, therefore, organised as follows: Section 1.2 discusses comparative law, diffusion and transfer, and new institutional economics literatures as the three pillars of this analysis and highlights their respective contribution to the proposed framework; Section 1.3 outlines the attributes of successful transplants as derived from the different literatures and explores whether compatibility alone is sufficient to generate these attributes; Section 1.4 presents the integrated analytical framework and explains how it may be configured for analysing the competition experience of individual South Asian countries; Section 1.5 outlines the framework in action.

1.2 THE THEORETICAL PILLARS

Comparative law literature, the literature on policy diffusion and transfer, and new institutional economics offer insights into different aspects of the adoption of laws. This section examines each of these literatures to glean factors that may be used in designing a framework for analysing the links between the adoption and implementation of borrowed laws.

1.2.1 *Legal Transplant Literature: The Clue is in the Context*

Legal transplant literature as a branch of comparative law literature recognises that legal rules or systems of law move from one country or people to

[4] Drawing upon the work of Douglass North, the term 'institutions' as used throughout this work includes formal institutions (such as laws), informal ones (such as conventions and codes of behaviour), created ones (such as statutes), or evolving ones (such as common law). However, the term does not include political, economic, or legal 'organisations' or 'authorities' that come into existence and operate through an institutional framework. Douglass C. North, *Institutions, Institutional Change, and Economic Performance* (CUP 1990), 4–5.

another,[5] but warns against the borrowing of laws that are not compatible with the context of the adopting countries or spirit of the peoples for whom they are intended. The emphasis on context notwithstanding, there is little consensus amongst scholars as to what is included in context, why it matters, or how compatibility with context may be generated.

Montesquieu and Kahn-Freund, speaking nearly two centuries apart, view context as the institutions, political law, and social and political context of a country,[6] whilst Mattei suggests that context also includes the pre-existing legal system of the adopting country.[7] Amongst scholars, writing specifically about competition law transplants, Shahein is of the view that context comprises the 'specific political, economic and social environment' of countries,[8] Trebilcock and Iacobucci suggest that 'particularities of history, initial conditions, institutional traditions, and political economy considerations' of countries are also relevant,[9] and Gal argues that the context encompasses 'almost all issues which relate to the relationship between law and society'.[10]

Watson includes actors within the meaning of context arguing that 'legislators, jurists, or judges' allow 'social economic, and political factors to impinge on legal development' and suggests that 'this culture has to be understood and injected into the equation before one can begin to erect a theory of law and society'.[11] Sacco expands upon the role of actors arguing that the meaning of the transplant in the adopting country, not only in implementing but also in deliberating and enacting it, is likely to be influenced by all factors that may be capable of influencing the views of an interpreter, including the implicit patterns along which the adopting society is organised.[12] Legrand and Chen-Wishart endorse the role of actors as interpreters; however, they appear to focus on the interpretation that takes place at the implementation rather than the adoption stage.[13]

5 Alan Watson, *Legal Transplants: An Approach to Comparative Law* (2nd edn, University of Georgia Press 1993), 21.

6 Charles de Secondat Montesquieu and others, *The Spirit of the Laws* (CUP 1989), 8, 610; Otto Kahn-Freund, 'On Uses and Misuses of Comparative Law*' (1974) 37 The Modern Law Review 1, 12, 13.

7 Ugo Mattei, 'Efficiency in Legal Transplants: An Essay in Comparative Law and Economics' (1994) 14 IRL International Review of Law & Economics 3, 17.

8 Heba Shahein, 'Designing Competition Laws in New Jurisdictions: Three Models to Follow' in Richard Whish and Christopher Townley (eds), *New Competition Jurisdictions: Shaping Policies and Building Institutions* (Edward Elgar 2012), 51, 55.

9 Michael J. Trebilcock and Edward M. Iacobucci, 'Designing Competition Law Institutions' (2002) 25 World Competition 361, 471.

10 Michal Gal, 'The "Cut and Paste" of Article 82 of the EC Treaty in Israel: Conditions for a Successful Transplant' (2007) 9 European Journal of Law Reform 467, 473.

11 Alan Watson, *The Evolution of Law* (Johns Hopkins University Press 1985) 118.

12 Rodolfo Sacco, 'Legal Formants: A Dynamic Approach to Comparative Law (Installment II of II)' (1991) 39 The American Journal of Comparative Law 343, 384–85.

13 Pierre Legrand, 'The Impossibility of Legal Transplants' (1997) 4 Maastricht Journal of European and Comparative Law 111, 114; Mindy Chen-Wishart, 'Legal Transplant and

For Montesquieu, context is significant because in his view laws, whether they form the government or support it, are related to the nature and principle of the government of the country in which they are made.[14] Similarly for Kahn-Freund, legal rules 'which organize constitutional, legislative, administrative or judicial institutions and procedures ... are ... "organic"' and 'any attempt to use a pattern of law outside the environment of its origin continues to entail the risk of rejection'.[15] Legrand considers context significant because it informs the meaning of the law. He argues that whilst it may be possible to transplant the *words* of a law, it is not possible to transfer its *original meaning* because the 'epistemological assumptions [of interpreters of the law]' in the adopting country 'are ... historically and culturally conditioned' to the adopting country rather than to the originating country, and, therefore, it is likely that as they interpret the words of the adopted legislation they will not provide them with the meanings ascribed to them in the originating country.[16] Teubner, whilst agreeing with Legrand to the extent that the meaning of laws is rooted in their originating contexts, argues that this means that transplants may be 'legal irritants' in the host country and force the law to develop in unexpected directions.[17]

Watson is an outlier in this discussion to the extent that he argues that 'a foreign rule can be successfully integrated into a very different system ... which is constructed on very different principles from that of the donor'[18] because 'usually legal rules are not peculiarly devised for the particular society in which they now operate'.[19] However, a closer reading of his work suggests that he recognises that the law of one country may diverge from that of another due to the impact of 'the Spirit of a People' in that country.[20] Ewald explains this apparent dichotomy in Watson's writings by distinguishing between 'Strong Watson', who takes the rigid position that there is no 'interesting relationship to be discovered between law and society', and 'Weak Watson', who argues that compatibility between the legal transplant and the context of the borrowing country must be examined with 'cautious awareness of [its]... complexity'.[21] Grossfeld also attempts to square Watson's thesis with that of Montesquieu and Kahn-Freund by arguing that whilst

Undue Influence: Lost in Translation or a Working Misunderstanding?' (2013) 62 The International and Comparative Law Quarterly 1.

14 Montesquieu (n.6).

15 Kahn-Freund (n.5), 12–13, 27. Kahn-Freund's discussion leaves open the possibility that laws that are not organically related to the context, such as economic laws are believed to be, may be more easily transplanted.

16 Legrand (n.13).

17 Gunther Teubner, 'Legal Irritants: Good Faith in British Law or How Unifying Law Ends up in New Divergences' (1998) 61(1) The Modern Law Review 11, 12.

18 Watson (n.5), 55, 56.

19 ibid 95, 96.

20 Watson (n.11), 42.

21 William Ewald, 'Comparative Jurisprudence (II): The Logic of Legal Transplants' (1995) 43 The American Journal of Comparative Law 489, 491, 509.

the 'recurrence of legal forms' endorses 'Watson's observation that the native element in the law of any country is relatively slight', it is necessary to draw a distinction between legal rules, which may be transplanted relatively easily, and institutions that are more attuned to the context of their country of origin and therefore cautions that importing institutions 'without such evaluation [of compatibility with the context of the adopting country] is "*un grand hazard*"'.[22]

Context is important for competition scholars for its role in operationalising competition transplants. Trebilcock and Iacobucci emphasise that context is important for designing appropriate competition authorities because 'no single institutional model of a competition agency will be optimal for all countries ... given particularities of history, initial conditions, institutional traditions, and political economy considerations'.[23] Discussing the Israeli competition law experience, Gal argues that 'the receiving state's knowledge, commonality with the state of origin' are essential pre-conditions for it to be receptive to the legal transplant,[24] and Shahein, speaking of competition transplants generally, argues that competition laws, like most other laws, are embedded in a specific political, economic, and social environment and must be appropriately 'contextualised' to operate in the adopting country.[25]

Interestingly, however, although legal transplant scholars accept the importance of compatibility with context, they do not fully examine how this necessary compatibility may be generated. Legrand, for instance, recognises that historical and cultural factors affect how a borrowed law is interpreted in the host country. However, he focuses on the divergence in the meanings given to the law in the originating and host country rather than on strategies for generating compatibility at the adoption stage, and thereby bridging this gap.[26] Teubner too emphasises the importance of a positive relationship between the transplant and the legal system of the host country but does not offer any suggestions for creating conditions for harmonising this interaction.[27] Similarly, Chen-Wishart stops short of considering whether the subsequent development of a borrowed law may be correlated with the extent of compatibility created in the course of adoption, even though she makes the important point that more interesting than the issue of whether or not legal transplants are possible is the question of 'how the transplant develops in the recipient legal system'.[28]

Amongst comparative law scholars, Sacco, Mattei, and Berkowitz et al. are unusual in their attention to the adoption stage. Sacco, for instance, recognises

[22] Bernhard Grossfeld, *The Strength and Weakness of Comparative Law* (Clarendon; OUP 1990), 43, 46. Interestingly, however, Grossfeld does not define institutions.

[23] Trebilcock and Iacobucci (n.9), 471.

[24] Gal (n.10), 473.

[25] Shahein (n.8), 55.

[26] Legrand (n.13).

[27] Teubner (n.17).

[28] Chen-Wishart (n.13), 3.

the possibility of actors at the adoption stage considering and generating compatibility in selecting and interpreting a transplant.[29] Mattei adds to the understanding of the adoption stage by highlighting the 'efficiency' of a legal doctrine as a possible reason for a country adopting it; however, he does not explore the relationship, if any, between efficiency and compatibility with the machinery of justice, which he claims is necesary for the transplant to succeed.[30] Berkowitz et al. emphasise the process through which laws are introduced, arguing that transplants imposed either directly or through colonisation are less likely to be compatible with the host country; however, they do not recommend an alternate processes of adoption.[31]

Legal transplant literature also provides some insight into what may be considered a successful legal transplant. Whilst Kahn-Freund alludes to success in negative terms as the adopted law 'not being rejected',[32] Watson refers to it more directly as the legal transplant continuing to grow in and becoming a part of the borrowing country, and clarifies that simply ascribing a different meaning to the transplant should not be confused with its rejection in the adopting country.[33] Mattei sees success as the compatibility of the transplant with the 'machinery of justice' in the adopting country, without which he believes the 'impact' of the transplant may be lost.[34] Teubner is of the view that the success of a legal transplant lies in its ability to interact productively with other elements in the legal organism in which it is transplanted,[35] whilst Berkowitz et al. argue that the performance of a transplant may be judged by the extent to which actors in the adopting country are able to understand, apply, and utilise it.[36]

Competition law scholars add to this discussion by approaching the success of transplanted competition laws as a process rather than an end goal which, once achieved, may be forgotten. So, for instance, Trebilcock and Iacobucci consider performance of competition authorities to be an indicator of the success of the transplanted law under which these authorities are established, and suggest that the quality of performance is directly linked with the compatibility and suitability of the transplant for the adopting country;[37] for Shahein, the success of a legal transplant depends on the extent to which the adopting country is able to appropriately

[29] Sacco (n.12).
[30] Mattei (n.7).
[31] D Berkowitz, K Pistor and JF Richard, 'Economic Development, Legality, and the Transplant Effect' (2003) 47(1) European Economic Review, 165, 174.
[32] Kahn-Freund (n.5).
[33] Watson (n.5).
[34] Mattei (n.7).
[35] Teubner (n.17).
[36] Berkowitz et al (n.31).
[37] Trebilcock and Iacobucci (n.23), 466.

'contextualise' the transplant for its purposes;[38] whilst Gal, in her analysis of the Israeli competition legislation, recognises that the benchmarks of success may vary from the adoption to the implementation stages due to the country's different goals at each stage. She observes that while in the course of transplantation, actors engaging with the Israeli competition law were motivated by the desire to meet the country's international political objectives, in implementing the law their focus had shifted to having their decisions understood and accepted within the country.[39]

1.2.2 *Policy Diffusion and Transfer: Bringing a Method to the Spread*

Comparative law and diffusion and transfer scholars have long called for synergies between the two.[40] Policy diffusion and transfer are defined as processes through which knowledge about policies, administrative arrangements, institutions, and ideas in one political system are used in the development of policies, administrative arrangements, institutions, and ideas in another political system. Diffusion and transfer are deemed to be 'a consequence of interdependence',[41] and are increasingly recognised for providing an important explanation for the spread of a policy or a practice.[42] However, diffusion and transfer must not be considered synonymous with convergence. Although diffusion and transfer sometimes results

[38] Shahein (n.25).

[39] Gal (n.24), 482.

[40] For instance, among political science scholars, Giraldi (n.40) 279 is of the view that diffusion (and, by extension, transfer) 'can lead to the spread of all kinds of things' ranging from specific instruments, standards, and institutions (both public and private), to broad policy models, ideational framework, and institutional settings, and Weyland (n.42) 18 adds templates (principles or general guidelines for designing programmes or institutions) and concrete policies (models or specific options from the menu offered by a policy model) in this list. Among lawyers, see Esin Örücü, 'Law as Transposition' (2002) International and Comparative Law Quarterly 51(2), 205; William Twining, 'Social Science and Diffusion of Law' (2005) Journal of Law and Society, 32, 203, 205; Ioannis Lianos, 'Global Governance of Antitrust and the Need for a BRICS Joint Research Platform in Competition Law and Policy' in Tembinkosi Bonakele, Eleanor Fox, Liberty Mncube (eds) Competition Policy for the New Era (Oxford University Press 2017).

[41] Fabrizio Giraldi 'Transnational Diffusion: Norms, Ideas and Policies' in Walter Carlsnaes, Thomas Risse-Kappen, and Beth A Simmons (eds) *Handbook of International Relations* (SAGE 2012), 454, 459; Charles R Shipan and Craig Volden, 'Policy Diffusion: Seven Lessons for Scholars and Practitioners' (Nov/Dec 2012) 72(6) Public Administration Review 788–96, 788.

[42] Dietmar Braun, Fabrizio Gilardi, Katharina Füglister, and Stéphane Luyet, 'Ex Pluribus Unum: Integrating the Different Strands of Policy Diffusion Theory' (2007) Politische Vierteljahresschrift S38, 40, 41. For similar views in respect of policy transfer, see David P Dolowitz and David Marsh, 'Learning from Abroad: The Role of Policy Transfer in Contemporary Policy-Making' (2000) 13 GOVE Governance 5, 6.

in convergence, it is not necessary that it should, and even when convergence does occur, it is relative rather than absolute.[43]

The commonalities between diffusion and transfer notwithstanding, there are important differences between them. Diffusion, also referred to as 'pattern finding',[44] refers to the often wave-like spread of ideas and policies across geographically clustered countries that are distinguished by variegated socio-economic, political, and cultural characteristics.[45] On the other hand, transfer, also described as 'process tracing'[46] refers to the intentional import of policies or programs by a country for implementation in its own context.[47] Therefore, while diffusion is a disembodied process which takes place independently of actors or agents,[48] the element of intentionality in transfer integrates the motivations, epistemological leanings, and institutional constraints[49] of agents at work in the transfer process.[50] Finally, while diffusion is studied through quantitative, statistical methods of analysis, transfer may be analysed qualitatively, taking into account the 'preconditions for transfer in the recipient state', the 'kind of actors pushing … the transfer process' and so on.

Diffusion and transfer literatures bolster the idea of context so important to legal transplant literature by suggesting that the outcome of diffusion and transfer may vary according to the *setting* in which it takes place, which includes the initial conditions of the diffusion or transfer as well as intervening factors that may affect its operation and force.[51] More particularly, policy transfer literature argues that all institutional constraints of rules, norms, expectations, and traditions that limit free play of individual will and calculation, also structure the actions and values of agents transferring policies through these institutions, and thereby not only impact the outcomes of transfer, but are also themselves transformed in the process.[52] The literature also indicates that as a policy develops and moves through the cycle of transfer, new actors and institutions become involved, that may shape the outcome

43 David Marsh and JC Sharman, 'Policy Diffusion and Policy Transfer' (2009) 30 Policy Studies 269, 271, 278–79; Giraldi in Carlsnaes, Risse-Kappen, and Simmons (n.40), 456, 484; Kurt Gerhard Weyland *Bounded Rationality and Policy Diffusion: Social Sector Reform in Latin America* (Princeton University Press 2006), chapter 1.

44 Marsh and Sharman, ibid 276.

45 Weyland (n.42), 19.

46 Marsh and Sharman (n.42), 276.

47 Adam J Newmark, 'An Integrated Approach to Policy Transfer and Diffusion' (2002) 19 Policy Studies Review 151, 170, 17.

48 Martino Maggetti and Fabrizio Gilardi, 'Problems (and Solutions) in the Measurement of Policy Diffusion Mechanisms (2016) 36 Journal of Public Policy 87, 4.

49 David Dolowitz and David Marsh, 'Who Learns What from Whom: A Review of the Policy Transfer Literature' (1996) 44 Political Studies 343, 354.

50 Mark Evans, 'Policy Transfer in Critical Perspective' (2009) 30 Policy Studies 243, 244.

51 Marsh and Sharman (n.42) 279.

52 Dolowitz and Marsh, 'Who Learns What from Whom' (n.48), 354–56; Marsh and Sharman (n.42) 275.

according to their unique knowledge, interests, and preferences regarding transfer strategies.[53] Integrating elements from diffusion and transfer literatures to a study of transplanted laws enables an examination of the motivations for the spread of legal rules from one country to another and of the institutions that shape this spread, and thereby offers a deeper insight into the structure and development of legal systems.[54]

Mechanisms for the diffusion and transfer of policies are categorised as 'voluntary or coercive' or 'horizontal or vertical'. A country may either voluntarily adopt policies due to dissatisfaction with an existing policy, policy failure, elections, the need to reduce uncertainty, or to legitimize previous decisions[55] or it may be coerced into adopting a policy due to express or implied pressure from foreign governments or multi-lateral agencies.[56] Coercive transfer is more likely to take place in developing countries reliant on multi-lateral agencies for financial and other assistance.[57] Voluntary and coercive diffusion and transfer overlap with the categories of horizontal and vertical diffusion and transfer: diffusion or transfer is considered horizontal when states learn about different policies from other states, compete with each other, or adopt a policy that neighbouring states may have adopted, while diffusion and transfer is considered vertical when states receive incentives for adopting the policy innovation from politically or economically more powerful bodies.[58]

The literature describes several different mechanisms through which diffusion and transfer takes place, however, the terminology used to identify these mechanisms is often inconsistent. For instance, there is considerable overlap between *coercion* and *contractualisation*. *Coercion* refers to diffusion or transfer of policies through international organizations or countries; it is deemed to be direct when a policy is transferred from one government to another or through supra-national institutions[59] and indirect when it is brought about by externalities such as

[53] David P Dolowitz, and David Marsh, 'The Future of Policy Transfer Research' (2012) 10 Political Studies Review, 339, 341. Gal (n.10) 482 also argues that the priorities of actors engaged in transplanting laws may vary from the adoption to the implementation stage.

[54] Mathias Reimann, 'The Progress and Failure of Comparative Law in the Second Half of the Twentieth Century' (2002) 504 American Journal of Comparative Law 671, 685.

[55] Dolowitz and Marsh, 'Who Learns What from Whom' (n.48) 346–47.

[56] ibid; also Newmark (n.46). Certain scholars argue that diffusion can only be voluntary while transfer may be both voluntary or coercive. See Torben Heinze, 'Mechanism-Based Thinking on Policy Diffusion: A Review of Current Approaches in Political Science' (Freie Univ Berlin, FB Politik- und Sozialwiss, Kolleg Forschergruppe 'The Transformative Power of Europe' 2011) 3, 19–20; Maggetti and Gilardi (n.47), 4.

[57] Marsh and Sharman (n.42) 272.

[58] Dorothy Daley, James Garand, 'Horizontal Diffusion, Vertical Diffusion, and Internal Pressure in State Environmental Policymaking, 1989–1998' (2005) 33 American Politics Research 615, 620.

[59] Direct coercion includes regulatory policies advanced by IFIs, or rules introduced by states exerting military or economic power. It includes IFI's 'recommending' the adoption of a policy as a conditionality of financial assistance, and 'convincing' governments by 'knowledge provision, advice and insinuation' that the suggested changes are desirable for the country. See

advancements in technology and economic pressures.[60] *Contractualisation* on the other hand refers to the diffusion and transfer of policies in response to a bargain between states in relation to a legal rule; when their negotiations include trade-offs linking two or more issue areas; and when the results are formalised by an international treaty (or any other form of bilateral agreement).[61]

Similarly, the term *emulation* whether absolute or partial, is used interchangeably with *learning*,[62] *mimicry*, *socialization*, *copying*,[63] *lesson-drawing*, *cost-saving*, and *problem-solving*,[64] while also being independently defined as the mechanism 'whereby knowledge of policy innovations is borrowed from other entities'[65] for its normative and social characteristics rather than its objective content or consequences.[66] *Emulation* is therefore distinct from *socialisation* and *learning* which refer to the range of mechanisms whereby adopting countries learn from the laws and experience of others in order to develop laws suitable for their domestic contexts. *Learning* for this purpose, includes 'rational or comprehensive' learning in which policymakers aggregate statistical information about the experience of the original country,[67] and 'bounded' learning where policymakers rely on cognitive shortcuts in arriving at their conclusions regarding the attractiveness or appropriateness of a policy even if doing so may introduce errors in the process.[68] To complicate matters further, *learning* is sometimes referred to as *lesson drawing* as well as *copying*, *emulation*,[69] *hybridization*, and *synthesis*[70] all of which represent different degrees

Newmark (n.46) 155; Marsh and Sharman (n.42) 272; Jean-Frédéric Morin and Richard E Gold, 'An Integrated Model of Legal Transplantation: The Diffusion of Intellectual Property Law in Developing Countries' [2015] International Studies Quarterly 782; Giraldi in Carlsnaes, Risse-Kappen, and Simmons (n.40) 464, 465; Weyland (n.42) 39.

60 Dolowitz and Marsh, 'Who Learns What from Whom' (n.48) 348, 349.

61 Morin and Gold (n.60) 782.

62 Richard Rose, 'What Is Lesson-Drawing?' (1991) II Journal of Public Policy 3.

63 Marsh and Sharman (n.42) 272.

64 Morin and Gold (n.60) 782; Colin J Bennett, 'What Is Policy Convergence and What Causes It?' (1991) 1991 British Journal of Political Science 215, 220–21.

65 Newmark (n.46).

66 Giraldi in Carlsnaes, Risse-Kappen, and Simmons (n.40) 475–78.

67 According to Weyland (n.42) in Chapter 1, rational or comprehensive learning may also be characterised as 'Bayesian updating' which suggests that policymakers have prior beliefs which shift in the light of information from and experience of other countries. Also see Giraldi in Carlsnaes, Risse-Kappen, and Simmons (n.40) 471.

68 In 'bounded learning', the policymakers are unable to systematically compute extensive information and end up (a) placing excessive importance on information, that for logically accidental reasons, has special immediacy and grabs their attention ('availability'); (b) attaching undue weight to the short-term success or failure of a policy which they mistake for proof of the inherent quality of the underlying programme or model ('representativeness'), and (c) relying more on an initial value which strongly affects their subsequent judgements ('anchoring'). Weyland (n.42) ch 1.

69 Marsh and Sharman (n.42) 271, 272.

70 These are explained as processes through which elements of programmes in two or more countries are combined to develop a policy best suited to the adopting country. Dolowitz and Marsh, 'Who Learns What from Whom' (n.48) 351.

of *learning*.[71] *Learning* is described as *socialisation* in situations where a state 'clearly frames the cognitive dimension of the appropriate rule ... as well as the internalization of international norms and policies and their domestic counterparts'[72] to understand the appropriateness of a foreign rule and to ensure that the rule in question resonates with established social norms and fits with the collective identity of the adopting country.[73]

In adapting the typology of diffusion and transfer mechanisms for the spread of laws, it is important that only such departures are made from the existing terminology as are absolutely necessary for rationalising and clarifying terminology.[74] To this end these mechanisms may be consolidated in four broad categories: (a) *coercion*, which has the same meaning as given to it in diffusion and transfer literatures but includes *contractualisation* on the basis that contracting parties (especially if one of these is a developing country) do not have equal bargaining power and their contractual agreements do not always result in balanced outcomes;[75] (b) *emulation*, which is redefined to refer only to mechanisms through which a country adopts a law for its normative and legitimation value without an attempt to understand or apply the principles contained in the legislation; (c) *regulatory competition*, also referred to as 'international economic competition' or simply 'competition' refers to a situation in which a country adopts a law or policy because it is engaged in a 'race to the bottom' (ie when law-makers adopt the lowest regulatory standards of competing countries to avoid capital flight) or 'race to the top' (ie when law-makers focus on reputational rather than economic competition) to attract or retain economic resources, with another country;[76] and (d) *socialisation* which includes all mechanisms that a country employs to persuade itself of the appropriateness of the law for its domestic context and to the internalising of the principles, beliefs, and norms of a foreign community (Table 1.1).

A closer reading of the diffusion and transfer mechanisms indicates that countries are often motivated to adopt foreign policies or ideas in their search for legitimacy. Weyland, for instance, hints at the need to 'look good before global public opinion'

71 ibid.

72 Heinze (n.57).

73 Morin and Gold (n.60) 783.

74 My sensitivity in this regard is borne out of Evans (n.49) critiquing Rose (n.63) for failing to relate lesson-drawing with 'the broader literature of policy transfer'. Evans is of the view that 'it is important for Rose to clarify his term within this context to lend clarity to the debate for students and scholars alike'. I also note that Lianos 'Global Governance of Antitrust' (n.51) 9–10 includes the mechanisms of *coercion, competition*, and *contractualisation* under the head of '*externalities*'. However, I do not subscribe to this categorisation in order to remain in alignment with the terminology originally provided in the diffusion and transfer literatures.

75 Morin and Gold (n.60) 782.

76 Giraldi in Carlsnaes, Risse-Kappen, and Simmons (n.40) 468–70. Also Marsh and Sharman (n.42) 271, 272; Morin and Gold (n.60) 782, 783.

TABLE 1.1. *Rationalising the typology of mechanisms of policy diffusion and transfer for laws*

New Categories	Mechanisms included
Coercion	Coercion; Contractualisation*
Emulation	Copying; Mimicry
Regulatory Competition	Competition; International Economic Competition
Socialization	Learning; Lesson-drawing (excluding emulation); Hybridization, Synthesis

*This categorisation may not be appropriate if the contracting countries are of equal bargaining power.

and concern for 'international legitimacy' as important factors in this regard,[77] while Marsh and Sharman suggest that 'emulation may be a deliberate ploy by governments to acquire legitimacy', particularly in the case of developing countries that often seek to 'legitimize themselves by mimicking developed states'.[78]

Giraldi further clarifies that a country's desire for international legitimacy stems from its need to secure domestic legitimacy because states 'are sensitive to the reaction of the international community as it can affect their domestic legitimation and power'.[79] Linos, like Giraldi, affirms the significance of domestic legitimacy. She argues that polices and ideas diffused or transferred through 'democratic institutions' have the potential of conferring 'critical domestic legitimacy' on the diffused policy or idea.[80] More specifically she is of the view that when laws spread through democracy, elected leaders have an interest in maintaining their popularity to win re-election and, therefore, are likely to pay greater attention to the preferences of ordinary citizens and domestic interest groups rather than blindly following the dictates of their foreign colleagues or international organizations.[81] Democratic institutions are therefore more likely to generate legitimacy than if the laws had been adopted through non-democratic institutions. In her view, therefore, domestic legitimacy while partly attributable to international legitimacy is equally shaped by the domestic institutions engaging in the process of diffusion or transfer.

The discussion of legitimacy in the context of policies and ideas may be easily extended to the spread of laws. It may be argued that countries adopt foreign laws, as they adopt foreign policies or ideas, not only due to a need to gain or enhance their international legitimacy but also to bolster their domestic legitimacy. It may further

77 According to Weyland (n.42) 39–42. the need to 'look good before global public opinion' and to gain 'international legitimacy' is relevant even in diffusion or transfer through learning (or socialisation), albeit it is not the sole or even the primary motivation in these cases.

78 Marsh and Sharman (n.42) 272.

79 Giraldi in Carlsnaes, Risse-Kappen, and Simmons (n.40), 23.

80 Katerina Linos, *The Democratic Foundations of Policy Diffusion: How Health, Family and Employment Laws Spread across Countries* (OUP 2013) ch 1, 2; ch 2.

81 ibid.

be argued that as in the case of diffused or transferred policies or ideas, domestic legitimacy while linked to and, at least partly derived from international legitimacy, may also be *created* by the engagement of appropriate institutions in the adopting country. Legitimacy, so defined, is both a motivation for and an outcome of the domestically executed process of adoption; however, the literature does not explore these aspects of legitimacy in any depth.

1.2.3 *New Institutional Economics: Bridging the Gap between Process and Outcome*

Both legal transplant and diffusion and transfer literatures leave certain critical questions unanswered: legal transplant literature does not fully explain the processes and institutions through which compatibility with context may be generated or enhanced, while diffusion and transfer literatures do not link the mechanisms of the spread of laws with the outcomes beyond the primary outcome of the law being introduced in a new context. New institutional economics, with its focus on institutions and outcomes not only offers insight into these questions but also affords a fuller understanding of the notion of the 'success' of adopted economic laws and policies.

Although the term institutions feature extensively in the discussion of context in legal transplant literature and of the process of diffusion and transfer in diffusion and transfer literature neither literature defines institutions nor explains the precise role they play in the spread or adoption of laws. In placing institutions at the heart of economic development and defining 'institutions' broadly to include both formal and informal rules that organize social, legal, and political aspects of a society as well as 'any form of constraint that human beings devise to shape human interaction' whether formal or informal, created, or evolved over time new institutional economics offers important insight into the role of institutions in generating successful economic law reform.[82]

In particular this literature argues that the compatibility of new institutions with the context of the country in which they operate is critical to their ability to yield high economic growth. According to North, institutions may be compatible with context, if they evolve organically from the context of the country through an evolutionary process rather than being introduced by 'a discontinuous change' brought about by revolution or conquest or adopted due to any other external pressure.[83] Rodrik endorses the importance of compatibility for high-performing economic institutions, however, he recognises the possibility of institutions being introduced in a country other than through organic processes and argues that such institutions may be made compatible by being adapted for the context of the adopting country through bottom-up, participatory

[82] Douglass North, *Institutions, Institutional Change and Economic Performance* (CUP 1990), ch 1 p 4. However, this definition does not include organisations which come into existence and operate through an institutional framework.

[83] ibid 101.

institutions.[84] He argues that economic institutions are a form of 'technology' which may either be 'general purpose . . . codified and . . . readily available on world markets', or 'highly specific to local conditions' and containing 'a high degree of tacitness' due to the fact that 'much of the knowledge that is required [about the technology] is in fact not written down . . .'.[85] He further argues that when the desired 'technology' is general purpose, a country may simply import a blueprint by following a 'largely top-down' approach which relies 'on expertise on the part of technocrats and foreign advisors', while if the 'technology' is highly specific to context, a country must resort to 'bottom-up' mechanisms for eliciting and aggregating local information in devising the technology most appropriate for the country.[86] Most importantly for present purposes, Rodrik clarifies that the categories of general purpose and specific technology are 'only caricatures', and that in actual fact, even 'an imported blueprint requires domestic expertise for successful implementation' and 'when local conditions differ greatly, it would be unwise to deny the possible relevance of institutional examples from elsewhere'.[87]

Acemoglu and Robinson strike a somewhat different note by arguing that economic institutions need to be 'inclusive' to yield economic growth. They distinguish between inclusive economic institutions that 'encourage participation by the great mass of people in economic activities', and extractive institutions that are 'designed to extract income and wealth from one subset of society to benefit a different subset'.[88] In an argument reminiscent of Rodrik, they state that an economic institution is inclusive or extractive depending on the political institutions through which it is created: extractive political institutions allow the concentration of power in the hands of a narrow elite and place few constraints on the exercise of this power, and thereby allow the all-powerful economic elite to structure economic institutions to extract resources from the rest of society. In contrast, inclusive political institutions distribute power more broadly in society and make it harder for any one group to usurp power. This in turn generates inclusive economic institutions that distribute resources more equitably.[89] Reading Acemoglu and Robinson in conjunction with Rodrik, it may be argued that bottom-up-participatory institutions are also inclusive, and are, therefore, critical for creating compatible and inclusive economic institutions that may yield economic growth in the adopting country.

[84] Dani Rodrik, *One Economics, Many Recipes: Globalization, Institutions and Economic Growth* (Princeton University Press 2007), ch 5.

[85] ibid.

[86] ibid. Rodrik also notes that although the institutions through which a country may elicit and aggregate local information may be 'as diverse as the institutions that they help create . . . the most reliable forms of such mechanisms are participatory political institutions', because while nothing prevents authoritarian regimes from utilising local knowledge nothing compels them to do so either.

[87] ibid.

[88] Daron Acemoglu and James A Robinson, *Why Nations Fail: The Origins of Power, Prosperity, and Poverty* (Crown Publishers 2012) ch 15, 429–30.

[89] ibid.

In elaborating the role of political institutions in generating high yielding economic institutions, new institutional economics plugs the important gap between the *process* through which countries acquire economic institutions and the *outcomes* these economic institutions may deliver in the adopting country. More importantly, North's rather broad definition of institutions, and by extension, of economic institutions, may be deemed to include legislation while Rodrik's discussion on economic institutions as a form of 'technology' which developing countries may acquire from their more developed counterparts and adapt for their contexts, suggests that economic institutions, like legal transplants, are transferrable and indeed are often codified in the form of statutes. Given these overlaps it may be argued that the attributes of successful legal transplants are also relevant for successful economic institutions and the benchmarks for assessing the success of legal transplants may be equally utilised for measuring the success of economic institutions included in these legal transplants.

1.3 CONSTRUCTING THE INTEGRATED FRAMEWORK

This section integrates elements from the theoretical pillars discussed in the preceding section and maps them on to the life cycle of an adopted legislation to construct a framework for evaluating the impact of the adoption process on the subsequent implementation of the adopted legislation.

1.3.1 *The Life Cycle of a Statute*

The life of a statute, bounded on one side by the moment in which a country first conceives the idea of adopting a new legislation and on the other when the adopted legislation is repealed, goes through at least three distinct phases: in the first phase, the adopting country considers and deliberates the parameters of the proposed statute, in the second phase, the country formally introduces the statute in its national legal corpus, and in the third phase, the country proceeds with the interpretation and enforcement of the adopted statute. The first two phases comprise the adoption stage while the third phase belongs to the implementation stage. It is important to emphasise here that this delineation of phases and stages is heuristic only and does not detract from the complexity of continuing diffusion, transfer, and adoption of legal principles in interpreting the adopted legislation in the implementation stage (Figure 1.1).

In each of the phases comprising the adoption and the implementation stages, different institutions and actors acting through the constraints of these institutions interact with and shape the legislation proposed to be adopted. The institutions that a country engages in the adoption process depend, at least in part, on the country's motivation for adopting a law and the mechanism it engages in this regard. In turn, the nature of these adopting institutions that is whether they are bottom-up, participatory, and inclusive or top-down and exclusive, determines the extent to which the

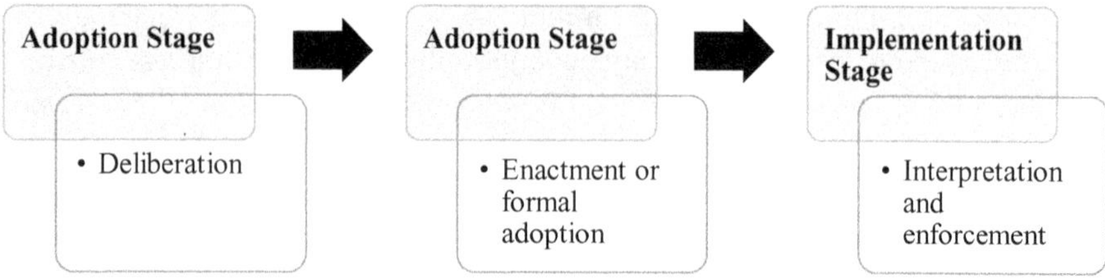

FIGURE 1.1. Adoption and implementation stages of adopted statutes

proposed legislation is adapted to the context of the adopting country and later, accepted as valid and authoritative in that country. The adoption process also shapes the content of the adopted legislation including the provisions for the structure, mandate, and composition of the enforcement authorities that it proposes to establish. In doing so, the institutions engaging in the adoption process lay the groundwork for the operation of these authorities at the implementation stage.

1.3.2 *Adoption and Implementation: A Stepwise Enquiry of the Literature*

The literatures explored in Section 1.2 provide the building blocks for a sequential, stepwise analysis of the adoption stage (comprising the deliberation and enactment phases) and the implementation stage. Each step of this analysis includes institutions relevant to that stage. In doing so it automatically includes actors operating through the agency conferred upon by institutions and subject to their constraints.

1.3.2.1 Step 1: Setting the Stage

The first step of the analysis relates to the adoption stage which includes the deliberation and the enactment phases. It combines the concept of context from legal transplant literature and pre-conditions of transfer particularly from policy transfer literature to establish the institutional backdrop against which the transfer or adoption of law takes place. This step, therefore, involves an examination of key legal and political institutions pre-existing in the context of the adopting country and engaged by it in the process of adoption. To understand whether these institutions are participatory, bottom-up and inclusive or top-down and exclusive, this analysis evalutes their operation, experiential depth, and authority in the context in which they operate with reference to their structure and historical evolution.

1.3.2.2 Step 2: Tracing the Process

The next step which also relates to the adoption stage utilises the idea of policy transfer as process-tracing to track the stages of adoption as these unfold in the context of the adopting country, starting from an evaluation of the country's motivations for considering the idea of adoption of a particular legislation through to when the legislation is formally introduced in the pre-exisitng legal system of the country. This step also entails identifying the country's preferred diffusion and transfer mechanisms as well as an assessment of the range, nature, and depth of the institutions engaged in each of the deliberation and enactment phases of the adoption stage.[90] The aim of this step is to gauge the adopted legislation's compatibility with the context of the adopting country (as emphasised in the legal transplant and new institutional economic literatures) as well as its legitimacy in that context (as highlighted in the diffusion and transfer literature) and thereby to estimate the potential for its successful implementation (discussed more fully in Step 3).

1.3.2.3 Step 3: Evaluating the Outcome

The third and final step proceeds from the underlying premise highlighted in the Law and Development movement that an adopted law may be considered successful if if is transformed into a 'law in action' rather than remaining merely a 'law in the books' and if local elites do not capture it for for their own ends.[91] The benchmarks of success identified in the literatures discussed in Section 1.2 suggest that to assess the success of an adopted legislation its independent performance as well as its interaction with the country's pre-existing legal system must be examined.[92] To evaluate the performance of the adopted legislation and, therefore of the enforcement authorities that it establishes, this step draws upon legal transplant literature to assess the extent to which the adopted law continues to grow in, and is understood, utilised, and applied in the adopting country;[93] whilst to understand the interaction between the adopted legislation with elements pre-existing in the legal organism of the adopting country, this step examines the extent to which the interaction facilitates or obstructs the performance of the adopted legislation.

To this end, this step requires an analysis of the decisions of the enforcement authorities which interpret and apply the provisions of the adopted legislation, as well as the decisions of general authorities pre-existing in the country's legal system which render their opinion on the constitutive, substantive, or procedural aspects of the adopted legislation (Table 1.2).

[90] There is a likelihood that these institutions may be distinct from the institutions already highlighted in Step 1.
[91] See Trubek (n.1 and 3).
[92] See in particular, Trebilcock and Iacobucci and Teubner in Section 1.2.1.
[93] See generally Section 1.2.1.

TABLE 1.2. *Theoretical sources of the analytical framework*

	Source		
Stage	Legal Transplant	Diffusion and Transfer	New Institutional Economics
ADOPTION	• There must be compatibility between the adopted legislation and the context of the adopting country. • Context includes social, political, and legal institutions. • Actors play an important role in shaping the adopted law.	• Policies are diffused and transferred through: (a) coercion; (b) emulation; (c) regulatory competition; and (d) socialisation. • The mechanism that a country employs depends on its motivation for acquiring the legislation and its pre-existing institutional landscape. • Diffusion is a disembodied process while transfer takes place through actors who act within institutional constraints.	• Institutions must be compatible with the context to yield economic growth. • The design of institutions engaged in the adoption process (whether they are bottom-up, participatory, and inclusive or top-down and exclusive) determines whether the adopted legislation may yield economic growth. • The historic depth of the institutions engaged in the adoption process is also relevant.
IMPLEMENTATION	• The adopted legislation must continue to grow in and become a part of the context of the adopting country. • It should be compatible with the machinery of justice in the country. • It should interact productively with other elements in the adopting country's legal organism. • It must be understood, utilised, and applied in the adopting country.	• Outcomes are not critical to the study of diffusion and transfer. • Convergence, though a possible outcome, is only likely to be a matter of degree. • The legitimacy of the law in the adopting country depends on the mechanism and institutions engaged by the country in the adoption process. • The range of institutions engaged in the transfer of a legislation affects its legitimacy.	• The law should not remain 'law in the books' and must become 'law in action'. • The law should not be captured by local elites for their own ends.

1.3.3 *The Framework of Analysis*

The adoption and implementation stages as described above when integrated into a framework reveal factors generated in the adoption process that impact its subsequent implementation. (Figure 1.2).

In the adoption stage the deliberation and enactment phases may also be independently examined to yield distinct insights. Evaluation of the deliberation phase helps identify the country's preferred diffusion or transfer strategy as it unfolds in the pre-existing institutional landscape of the adopting country, its motivation for adopting the legislation, and the range and nature of institutions engaged in the phase. In the enactment phase the adopting country engages new institutions, which may lead to a shift in its diffusion and transfer strategy. An analysis of this phase, therefore, entails a fresh evaluation of the diffusion and transfer strategy employed by the country and the nature and range of institutions directly engaged in the enactment and helps understand the extent and qualtiy of compatibility and legitimacy generated at the adoption stage. In considering institutions in both these phases it is important to consider the branches of state to which these institutions

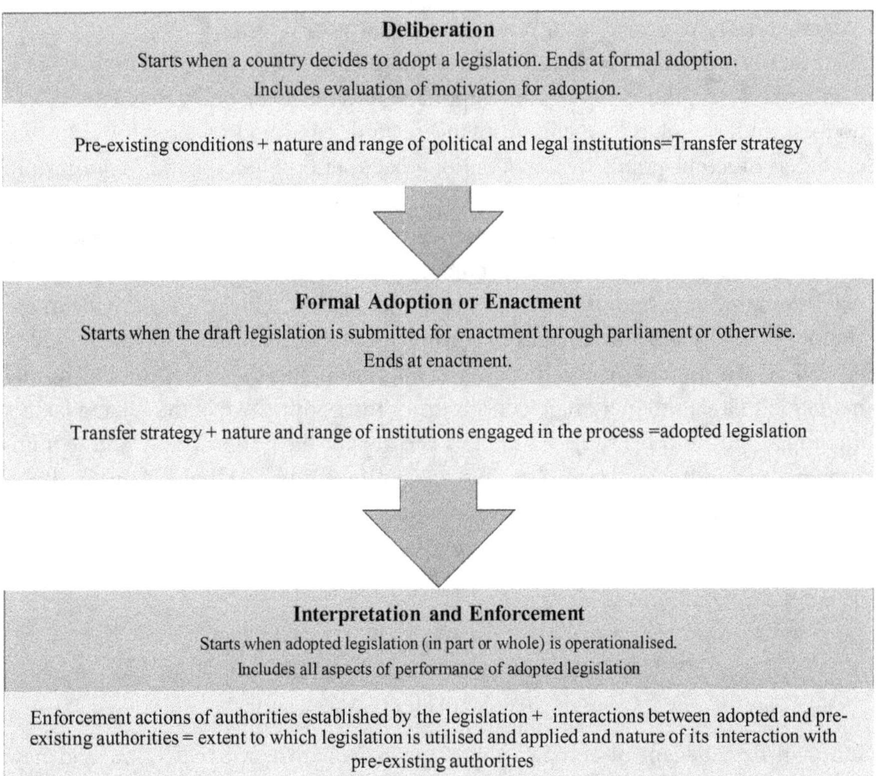

FIGURE 1.2. The integrated analytical framework

relate; the quality and extent of their interaction with each other, and their ability (or lack thereof) to aggregate local knowledge and adapt the adopted legislation in light of this knowledge. Cumulatively, this phase-wise analysis of the adoption stage is expected to yield a more nuanced understanding of the institutions and strategies that have shaped the provisions of the adopted legislation particularly those relating to the structure, mandate, and composition of the competition authorities the legislation purports to establish.

The implementation stage comprises the interpretation and enforcement phases and is, therefore, analytically distinct from, though connected to the two phases of the adoption stage. The analysis of the implementation stage entails an evaluation of the independent performance of the adopted legislation by an assessment of the decisions of the enforcement authorities and of the interaction of the adopted legislation with the country's pre-existing legal system, as reflected in the decisions of the general courts pre-existing in the country in respect of the challenges to the orders of these authorities. This analysls offers insight into the extent to which the adopted legislation is 'understood, utilised and applied' in the adopting country and has thereby become a law in action rather than simply remaining a law in the books. It also helps understand the extent to and pace at which the adopted legislation has integrated into the context of the adopting country.

While some overlap in successive stages and phases of this analytical framework is inevitable, it has the distinct and important advantage of being segmented and modular and, therefore, capable of being re-configured and adapted for countries located at different points in the adoption-enactment-implementation continuum. In practice this means that regardless of whether the country is only deliberating upon the legislation it proposes to adopt, has formally adopted the legislation, or has commenced the interpretation and enforcement of its provisions, this framework may be employed to understand the extent of its compatibility and legitimacy in the adopting country and to predict the implementation trajectory of the adopted legislation. An important insight derived from arranging the adoption and implementation of a statute in a single continuum is the significance of the related factors of compatibility and legitimacy: arguably the greater the compatibility and legitimacy generated in the adoption stage, the greater the likelihood that not only will the adopted legislation will be understood, applied, and utilised in the implementation stage but also that it will enjoy a productive interaction with its pre-existing legal system.

1.4 COMPATIBILITY, LEGITIMACY, AND THE INTERPLAY OF INSTITUTIONS

Although the concept of compatibility appears in both comparative law and new institutional economics literatures and legitimacy is explicitly mentioned in the diffusion and transfer literatures, these literatures appear to assume that these concepts are widely understood and therefore, do not explore these in any depth. This section examines these concepts and their interrelations and offers suggestions as to how these may be measured.

1.4.1 *The Nature of Compatibility*

In emphasising but not defining compatibility comparative law and new institutional economics literatures appear to suggest that the word may be understood in its ordinary English meaning. Authoritative English dictionaries state that any two objects (or ideas) may be considered compatible if they are able 'to exist or occur together without problems or conflict'.[94] It follows that 'compatibility' is 'the fact of being able to exist, live, or work successfully with something or someone else'.[95]

This common core notwithstanding, compatibility as discussed in comparative law literature is somewhat static and binary while that referred to in new institutional economics literature has a dynamic and evolutionary quality. Comparative law seems to hold that compatibility with context either exists or does not at the time of adopting a legislation. Also, it focuses more on describing elements within the context that the adopted legislation must be compatible with, rather than on processes through which compatibility may be generated or enhanced.[96] In terms of this literature an adopted legislation is compatible with the context of the adopting country if it is compatible with the social and political institutions pre-existing in the country, particularly its machinery of justice, its particularities of history, initial conditions, institutional traditions, political economy, and all other factors that may impinge upon the relationship between law and society.[97] This literature further suggests that the adopted legislation and the context interact with each other through actors that engage with the adoption process most often from within the institutions pre-existing in the adopting country, however, it does not explore the nature of this interaction or its impact in particular depth.

On the other hand, new institutional economics recognises that compatibility may not only be created but also enhanced in the course of adoption of legislation and possibly beyond.[98] North for instance, argues that compatibility is generated when an economic institution organically evolves from the context of the country, while Rodrik is of the view that an economic institution may be *made* compatible with the context of the country if it is adapted for context in

94 Oxford English Dictionaries <www.lexico.com/en/definition/compatible> accessed 9 September 2021.

95 Cambridge English Dictionary <https://dictionary.cambridge.org/dictionary/english/compatibility> accessed 22 November 2019.

96 Section 1.2.1.

97 Section 1.2.1.

98 Section 1.2.3.

accordance with the local knowledge and information aggregated through bottom-up, participatory, and inclusive institutions.[99]

1.4.2 *The Dimensions of Legitimacy*

Legitimacy, as discussed in the diffusion and transfer literature, is both a motivation for and an outcome of the diffusion and transfer process. Scholars argue that countries often adopt foreign ideas, policies, and, by extension laws, in the quest for international and domestic legitimacy. This section explores the concept of legitimacy to understand its significance as well as the processes through which it may be created or enhanced.

1.4.2.1 Understanding Legitimacy

The concept of legitimacy has its roots in political philosophy[100] and political science and sociology,[101] where it is defined as a subjective '*belief* that a rule, institution or leader has the right to govern'.[102] Legitimacy, so defined, is difficult to measure and is, therefore, often understood in terms of its sources (that is as being derived from legality,[103] authority,[104] and justice[105]) or its attributes (such as its ability to create efficiency, expertise and accountability, and fairness or justice).[106] It may, therefore, be argued that a rule, institution, or government is legitimate if it has been made according to the law (ie it has legality) and if it is recognised as having the force of law in the country (ie it has necessary authority). Equally, it may be argued that a rule, institution, or government has legitimacy if it is procedurally effective (ie if it is efficient and has the necessary expertise for carrying out its purposes), and if it creates or adopts mechanisms for accountability.

99 ibid.

100 Peter Fabienne, 'Political Legitimacy' The Stanford Encyclopedia of Philosophy (Summer 2017 edn), Edward N Zalta (ed) <https://plato.stanford.edu/archives/sum2017/entries/legitimacy/> accessed 14 August 2017.

101 Ian Hurd, 'Legitimacy' <http://pesd.princeton.edu/?q=node/255> accessed 14 August 2017; Routledge, 'Authority v. Legitimacy' <http://cw.routledge.com/textbooks/alevelphilosophy/data/AS/WhyShouldIBeGoverned/Authorityandlegitimacy.pdf> accessed 14 August 2017.

102 Ian Hurd (n.102).

103 ibid. It is argued that not all legal acts are necessarily legitimate and not all legitimate acts are necessarily legal because there is always the possibility that rulers might legally impose laws which the citizens believe to be lacking in legitimacy.

104 Routledge (n.102). Authority too may exist independently of legitimacy. For example, a state has authority if it maintains public order and makes laws that are generally obeyed by its citizens. However, it is only when the citizens *perceive* these laws to be right, justified, and supported by good reasons that the authority of the state (or indeed of a law made by the state) may be deemed to be legitimate.

105 Ian Hurd (n.102). Justice denotes adherence to an external moral standard.

106 Rizwaan Jameel Mokal, 'On Fairness and Efficiency' (2003) 66 Modern Law Review 452, 453.

Among the various aspects of legitimacy, justice is particularly interesting because it features among the sources as well as the attributes of legitimacy. This suggests that legitimacy is not only the *outcome* of processes that are recognised as fair and just but must also *generate* fairness and justice. It is further interesting to note that unlike other sources and attributes of legitimacy, justice whether as a source or as an attribute of legtimacy relates to the *substance* of the rule or instrument,[107] rather than its *formal* (ie its legality and authority) or *functional* (ie its efficiency, expertise, and accountability) aspects. It may be argued that while it is entirely possible for a rule, institution, or government to display all three aspects of legitimacy (ie substantive, formal, and functional), it is equally likely that the presence of only one or more of these aspects may be sufficient to generate the belief that the rule, institution, or government is legitimate.[108] It is most appropriate, therefore, to view legitimacy on a scale with *formal* legitimacy at one end, *formal* plus *functional* legitimacy towards the middle, and *formal* plus *functional* plus *substantive* legitimacy, (which may collectively be referred to as *perfect legitimacy*), at the other.

This discussion further suggests that a country's desire for international legitimacy which derives from the country *aligning* itself with policies or laws for their reputational value rather than substantive appropriateness, is a desire for *formal*, and perhaps *functional* rather than *substantive* legitimacy. It may therefore also be argued that international legitimacy gains somewhat of a *substantive* character when a country leverages it for domestic legitimacy, because the domestic audience is unlikely to be persuaded to endorse a policy or law unless it has the potential to generate justice and fairness in addition to its claims of efficiency, expertise, and accountability. However, the extent or quality of this *substantive* legitimacy or indeed how it compares with the *formal* and *functional* legitimacy of an institution or rule is likely to vary from case to case depending on the legislative maturity of the country in question.

1.4.2.2 Significance of Legitimacy

The clue to understanding the significance of legitimacy lies in Linos' reference to 'critical domestic legitimacy'.[109] It may be argued that legitimacy of a rule is critical for

107 Despite 'justice' being included in most conceptions of legitimacy and despite sharing a common basis with legitimacy in fundamental political values (such as equality), certain scholars are of the view the two do not place the same demands on society and, are, therefore, not interchangeable. Rawls, in particular, is of the view that legitimacy is a weaker idea than justice and that laws or decisions made by particular political institutions may be legitimate without being just. In his view, therefore, legitimacy is part of justice, but justice is not an attribute of legitimacy. Fabienne (n.101).

108 For instance, Tom Tyler argues that 'the antecedents of legitimacy lie in people's judgment about the procedures through which legal authorities make rules … people defer to rules primarily because of their judgments about how those rules are made, not their evaluation of their content'. Tom R Tyler and others, 'Procedural Fairness and Compliance with the Law' (1997) 133(II) Swiss Journal of Economics and Statistics (SJES), 219, 225.

109 Linos (n.81).

its enforcement because for people to obey a rule, they must view it as legitimate at least to a certain degree. This means that people will obey a rule that is created through a process which is seen as fair, legal, or correct even if these policies or laws do not actually benefit them.[110] People are also likely to obey a rule if they have trust in the rule-making body, quality of interpersonal treatment, evidence of the body's neutrality, and the extent of participation that the body allows in the formulation of the rule regardless of whether the rule is substantively just and fair.[111] It follows, therefore, that while legitimacy of a rule, institution, or government is a necessary pre-condition for its effective enforcement, even partial (ie only formal and functional legitimacy) legitimacy may suffice for this purpose.

In addition to enforcement, legitimacy of a rule, institution, or government is desirable for its reputational effect. For instance, when a country adopts a policy or law for international legitimacy, it sends out a signal that it is a progressive member of the international community and, therefore, fit for future interaction and collaboration. When the same country leverages its international legitimacy for domestic legitimacy it signals to its citizens that it is engaged in internationally recognised reform and is, therefore, an appropriate candidate not only for exercising power and authority but also for delivering progress in the domestic context. Conversely, when a country aims for domestic legitimacy by introducing effective, just, and fair reform, it not only catalyses the reorganisation of its legal, economic, or social context but creates the opportunity for leveraging the soundness of its domestic law reform for recognition and legitimacy abroad.

It is likely that countries adopting laws or polices to gain international legitimacy, also seek effective, fair, and just reform domestically. Such countries may, therefore, simultaneously seek formal international legitimacy that derives from the reputational capital and authority of international precedents and substantive domestic legitimacy that stems from the proposed legislation's capacity for generating justice and fairness in the country. For instance, a government may recognise that a country needs reorganisation in a particular economic or social sphere and be committed to bringing about appropriate meaningful reform for this purpose. In carrying out this reform, the country may consult international precedents, perhaps to understand the area and perhaps also to garner support for its proposed reform. Such a law, when introduced, would not only enjoy formal, functional, and substantive legitimacy in the domestic context, but will also send a positive signal abroad, and thereby play a positive role in bringing about material change in the country.

1.4.2.3 Generating Legitimacy

The discussion about the sources of legitimacy provides insight into how legitimacy is generated. Weber, for instance, suggests that legitimacy stems from *tradition* (ie

[110] Ian Hurd (n.102).

[111] Tom R Tyler and others (n.109).

people have faith in a particular political or social order because it has been there for a long time); *charisma* (because they have faith in the rulers), and *legality* (because they trust its lawfulness).[112] *Tradition* and *charisma*, so defined, may be understood to be facets of authority,[113] which together with legality serve as mechanisms for generating legitimacy, albeit of the formal rather than functional or substantive variety.

Locke adds a further dimension to this discussion by highlighting public 'consent' as a pre-condition of legitimacy.[114] He argues that consent is necessary not only for the original institutionalisation of political authority but also for the ongoing evaluation of the performance of a political regime,[115] albeit while the original institutionalization requires *express* consent, *tacit* consent may suffice for subsequent evaluation. Simmons introduces the idea of *actual* consent. He is of the view that there is no 'content-independent' duty to the obey the state, and actual consent may only be given if the rules, institutions, or other commands of the state confer a benefit of the people[116] that is, if they are fair and just in addition to being procedurally effective. Actual consent, therefore, generates substantive legitimacy rather than the purely formal or functional legitimacy created by authority or legality. Despite its desirability, actual consent is not practicable in most modern democracies which operate on the basis of *constructive* consent – that is, these democracies assume that the public has consented to a rule if their elected representatives give their consent and if the public trusts in the legality and authority of the process through which a rule is made even when it does not delve into the substantive fairness of the rule. Arguably, even constructive consent is better than no consent, and a country in which the adopted law enjoys legitimacy based derived from constructive of consent, not only sends out positive signals abroad but also by enhancing the possibility of the law being obeyed, creates the potential for bringing about material change at home. Given that bottom-up, participatory, and inclusive institutions[117] are more capable of garnering actual or constructive consent it may be argued that laws adopted through domestic democratic institutions are likely to enjoy a more perfect legitimacy than those adopted through institutions, that while recognised as legal or having authority do not have the capacity to elicit or aggregate consent from the public.[118]

112 Fabienne. (n.101).

113 See Section 1.4.2.1.

114 Although Locke speaks of legitimacy of political authority, his ideas may be extended to laws, which are evidence of the exercise of such authority.

115 Fabienne. (n.101) Section 1.3.

116 ibid. This may be distinguished from Plato's views in the *Republic*, that legitimate authority is not founded on consent or even on giving people what they want. Routledge. (n.102).

117 See Section 1.2.3.

118 This discussion resonates with Linos' comments about creating critical domestic legitimacy by transferring policies and laws through 'democratic institutions' rather than through elite networks. Although Linos does not define or describe democratic institutions, she may be deemed to be referring to any bottom-up, participatory, institutions that have the capacity to garner public consent whether directly or through elected representatives. See n.81 and text thereto.

1.4.3 *Compatibility and Legitimacy: Two Sides of the Same Coin?*

Juxtaposing the concepts of compatibility and legitimacy reveals commonalities between the two. Compatibility relates to the ability of the adopted law to co-operate and co-exist with institutions pre-existing in the context of the adopting country, while legitimacy relates to the extent to which the law is obeyed and enforced in the country, its ability to send positive signals internationally as well as domestically, and its potential for bringing about meaningful social or economic reform in the country.

Both compatibility and legitimacy are also dynamic rather than static which means that whilst both may be generated as the proposed legislation is considered for adoption in the deliberation phase or even as it is formally enacted they may be enhanced as the adopted legislation is interpreted in the implementation stage. New institutional economics scholars such as Rodrik for instance, argue that compatibility may be generated if the blueprint (of an economic institution) is adapted for the context of the adopting country in light of the tacit local knowledge aggregated by bottom-up and participatory institutions, while diffusion and transfer scholars, such as Linos, argue that adopted policies may be legitimised by public consent garnered through democratic institutions. Arguably, continued engagement with bottom-up and participatory democratic institutions post-adoption is likely to continue to mould the adopted legislation in light of local knowledge and to renew the intial consent given to it, thereby enhancing both its compatibility and legitimacy as it proceeds through the implementation stage.

This discussion suggests that bottom-up and participatory democratic institutions may generate compatibility, as per new institutional economics literature, due to their capacity to aggregate local knowledge, and legitimacy as per diffusion and transfer literature, due to their power to garner public consent whether actual or constructive. Interestingly, Acemoglu and Robinson, in arguing that inclusive economic institutions are created through inclusive political institutions, draw these two seemingly distinct strands together. In defining inclusive political institutions as institutions that distribute power more broadly in society, they give a nod not only to new institutional economics' reference to bottom-up and participatory institutions but also to diffusion and transfer literature's reference to democratic institutions and to the idea of justice and fairness as a source of legitimacy. Similarly in defining inclusive economic institutions as institutions that distribute resources more equitably in society, their discussion resonates with the idea of justice and fairness as an attribute of substantive legitimacy. This suggests that adoption through bottom-up, participatory, and inclusive institutions is not only likely to generate greater compatibility but also to enhance the quality and extent of legitimacy that the legislation enjoys in the country.

1.5 THE FRAMEWORK IN ACTION

The integrated analytical framework developed and presented in this chapter hinges on the core concepts of compatibility and legitimacy: the analysis of the pre-conditions of transfer, the institutional context, and the interplay of institutions at the adoption stage aims to establish the extent and nature of compatibility and legitimacy generated at that stage, while that of the independent performance and interaction of the enforcing authorities at the implementation stage helps understand how the compatibility and legitimacy of the adopted legislation shapes its subsequent interpretation and enforcement in the adopting country. Their significance notwithstanding, compatibility and legitimacy are qualitative and relative concepts This makes them difficult to observe and measure directly and objectively and makes it necessary to employ proxies to approximate the extent of compatibility and legitimacy generated at the adoption stage and to evaluate its impact at the implementation stage.

At the adoption stage, the extent of compatibility and legitimacy likely to be generated may be gauged by the design, nature, and range of institutions engaged in the deliberation and enactment of the adopted legislation and their interaction with each other. Additionally, compatibility may be assessed by the extent of local information taken into consideration and applied as the legislation progresses through the deliberation and enactment phases, while the quality and extent of legitimacy may be ascertained by the authority and legality of the institutions engaged in the adoption process and their capacity for aggregating consent: public consent may be deemed to have been given as long as the legislation is adopted through a range of institutions that have the capacity and potential to elicit the actual or constructive consent of a sufficiently broad segment of the public.

At the implementation stage the impact of compatibility and legitimacy on the interpretation and enforcement of the adopted legislation may be observed by analysing the decisions of the enforcement authorities established by adopted legislation as well as the decisions of the general courts in response to the challenges brought before them in respect of the orders of the enforcement authorities. It is expected that legislation adopted through relatively more bottom-up, participatory, and inclusive institutions is not only likely to be better understood, applied, and utilised in their adopted contexts but also to engage more productively with the country's pre-existing legal system and thereby to gradually and steadily integrate into and become a part of it.

2

Adoption of Competition Laws in India and Pakistan

2.1 INTRODUCTION

India and Pakistan offer an excellent opportunity to explore the links between the adoption and implementation of competition legislation in South Asia. The two countries had first enacted anti-monopoly laws – the Monopolies and Restrictive Trade Practices Act in India and the Monopolies and Restrictive Trade Practices (Control and Prevention) Ordinance in Pakistan – in 1969 and 1970 respectively. By the early 2000s, however, both countries were engaged in consultations for replacing these anti-monopoly laws with modern competition legislation: India was the first to do so by enacting the Competition Act 2002 and Pakistan followed suit by promulgating the Competition Ordinance 2007.[1] In enacting modern competition legislations India and Pakistan in effect declared to their domestic audiences their commitment to achieving greater economic efficiency and consumer welfare[2] and to the international community, their willingness to align with international best practices in competition regulation in an effort to not only to join a rapidly growing international competition network[3] but also to become integrated in the global economy.

This chapter traces the process through which India and Pakistan adopted their competition legislations to understand the scheme and ambit of these legislations and to evaluate the extent of their compatibility with and legitimacy in their respective contexts. It appraises the pre-conditions of transfer in India and Pakistan focusing on the legal and political institutional landscapes and evaluates factors that motivated both countries to adopt modern competition legislation, the

[1] Hereafter 'the Indian Act' and 'the 2007 Ordinance' respectively.

[2] These goals are declared in the preambles of the Indian Act and the 2007 Ordinance.

[3] Until the mid-twentieth century there were less than ten competition regimes worldwide. However, after World War II, more and more countries adopted competition laws. Presently are over 110 competition regimes in place, of which over 80 were created after 1980.

transfer mechanisms they employed in the adoption, and the interplay of the legal and political institutions they engaged in this regard.

To this end, this chapter is organised as follows: Section 2.2 evaluates the legal and political context in India and Pakistan in which they adopted their anti-monopoly and competition legislations. Section 2.3 explores India and Pakistan's motivations for adopting competition laws, evaluates the mechanisms employed by them for the adoption,[4] and examines the nature and range of institutions engaged by them in this regard; Section 2.4 considers how India and Pakistan's adoption strategy has evolved over time and identifies the impact of the further institutions added into the mix in this process; Section 2.5 discusses how the adoption processes in the two countries have shaped the substance of their competition legislations, and Section 2.6 assesses the extent of the compatibility and legitimacy generated in the course of adoption in the two countries.

2.2 INDIA AND PAKISTAN: THE PRE-CONDITIONS OF TRANSFER

This section establishes the pre-conditions of transfer in India and Pakistan focusing on the Indian and Pakistani legal and political institutional landscape in a three-dimensional perspective, that is to say, evaluating not only the design and mandate of these institutions but also how these have evolved over time. To this end the section focuses on three distinct milestones, in the evolution of the legal and political institutions inherited by the two countries: when they became independent dominions on 14 August 1947;[5] when they adopted their first anti-monopoly legislation in 1969 and 1970 respectively; and in 2002 and 2007 when they adopted their respective modern competition legislations.

2.2.1 *1969: India Adopts its First Anti-monopoly Legislation*

In 1969, when India enacted the Monopolies and Restrictive Trade Practices Act, the Indian Constitution had been in force for nearly twenty years,[6] and the political

4 See Chapter 1, Section 1.2.2.

5 The independent states of India and Pakistan were carved out of the British Empire in pursuance of section 1 of the Indian Independence Act 1947<www.legislation.gov.uk/ukpga/1947/30/pdfs/ukpga_19470030_en.pdf> accessed 3 September 2021, prior to which both were governed by the legal and political institutions established under the Government of India Act 1935 <www.legislation.gov.uk/ukpga/1935/2/pdfs/ukpga_19350002_en.pdf> accessed 3 September 2021. Even after independence and until such time as the countries adopted their respective constitutions, they continued to be governed by the 1935 Act. They also inherited all British laws that had been in force in undivided India immediately prior to independence.

6 India adopted its Constitution on 16.11.1949 ('the Indian Constitution'). Although some Articles of the Constitution came into force on 26.11.1949, the Constitution became fully effective only from 26.01.1950. CL Anand, *Constitutional Law and History of Government of India* (8th ed, Universal Law Pub Co 2008) ch 2.

and legal institutional framework constituted under it had remained reasonably stable and operational throughout this time.[7]

Under the Indian Constitution, legislative powers were exercised by the parliament which comprised an upper house, 'the Council of States', and a lower house, 'the House of the People'.[8] Both houses had the authority to initiate a bill,[9] and a bill could only be passed into law with the agreement of both houses and with the assent of the president.[10] The federal legislature had the power to legislate in respect of all matters listed in the 'Union and Concurrent Legislative Lists'.[11] The executive power of the federation was vested in the president, who was assisted in his affairs by a 'Council of Ministers' headed by the prime minister.[12] The president also had the power to legislate by promulgating ordinances. However, the president could do so only if the parliament was not in session, and if he was satisfied that the situation warranted immediate legislative action. Ordinances promulgated by the president took effect as 'Acts of Parliament' but lapsed if they were not submitted to the parliament for approval within six weeks of its re-assembly.[13]

The Indian judicature was headed by the Supreme Court which heard disputes between the federation and the provinces or between one province and another. It also heard appeals from orders of the high courts sitting in their civil or criminal jurisdiction.[14] Each Indian state had a high court, which was subordinate to the Supreme Court and had the power to issue writs to any person or authority (including a governmental authority) operating within its jurisdiction.[15] Each high court was also mandated to supervise all subordinate courts and tribunals operating within its jurisdiction.[16] Judges of the Supreme Court and high courts were appointed in accordance with the qualifications and procedures stipulated in the Constitution and[17] the decisions of the Supreme Court were binding on all courts below it while those of the high courts were binding on all courts and tribunals below the high courts.[18]

The Indian Constitution did not expressly provide for regulation of monopolies. Therefore, in enacting the Monopolies and Restrictive Trade Practices Act the parliament relied on Articles 38 and 39(b) of the Indian Constitution read with

7 Indian Constitution, Article 1.
8 ibid Article 79.
9 ibid Articles 109–10. This includes all bills other than a money bill.
10 ibid Articles 107, 111.
11 ibid Articles 245 and 246.
12 ibid Articles 52–53, 76.
13 ibid Article 123.
14 ibid Articles 130, 132–34.
15 ibid Article 226.
16 ibid Article 227.
17 ibid Article 123, 217.
18 ibid Article 14.

items 42 and 52 of the Federal Legislative List. Article 38 empowered the federation to promote 'the welfare of the people by securing and protecting, as effectively as it may, a social order in which justice, social, economic and political, shall inform all institutions of the national life' while Article 39(b) affirmed that the federation was committed to directing its policy towards ensuring 'that the ownership and control of the material resources of the community are so distributed as best to subserve the common good'. Items 42 and 52 of the Federal Legislative List conferred on the federation the power to legislate in respect of 'inter-state trade and commerce' and 'industries, the control of which ... is declared by the Parliament by law to be expedient in public interest'. The Monopolies and Restrictive Trade Practices Act was substantially based on the UK Monopolies and Restrictive Practices (Inquiry and Control) Act 1948 and the jurisprudence that had developed around it.

2.2.2 1970 *Pakistan: Promulgating the Anti-monopoly Ordinance*

In 1970 when Pakistan promulgated the Monopolies and Restrictive Trade Practices (Control and Prevention) Ordinance, its institutional landscape was vastly different from that of India. Pakistan had framed its first Constitution in 1956, nine years after independence, broadly along the lines of the 1935 Act.[19] However, this Constitution was abrogated in October 1958 in the wake of a military takeover and all fundamental rights guaranteed under the Constitution were suspended.[20] In 1962, while still under military rule, Pakistan had framed its second Constitution which established a unicameral legislature, provided for a presidential form of government, and conferred extensive powers on the president. However, in 1969 this Constitution was also abolished pursuant to a second military takeover. As before, the military regime suspended the fundamental rights provided in the Constitution while directing the new regime to govern the country, as far as possible, in accordance with the abrogated Constitution.[21] Although Pakistan had established a Supreme Court as the apex court of the country to hear petitions on fundamental rights as well as appeals from the four provincial high courts, the powers of the judiciary with respect to enforcing fundamental rights and entertaining writs, were curtailed each time the Pakistani Constitution was suspended.

The abrogation of the 1962 Constitution meant that in 1970 when the then president of Pakistan promulgated the Monopolies and Restrictive Trade Practices

[19] See n.5.

[20] Upon taking over the governance of Pakistan, the military issued the Laws (Continuance in Force) Order 1958 which provided that the country should be governed as nearly as possible in accordance with the abrogated Constitution except for fundamental rights which remained suspended.

[21] These terms were stipulated in the Provisional Constitution Order 1969.

(Control and Prevention) Ordinance so in exercise of his powers *in accordance with* rather than *under* the Constitution. Further, given the absence of a specific article in the Constitution mandating the regulation of monopolies, in promulgating the anti-monopoly ordinance the president invoked the more general Article 131(2) which allowed the federation to legislate in respect of a matter necessary for the 'economic and financial stability' of the country.[22] Like its Indian counterpart, the Pakistani anti-monopoly ordinance was substantially based on the UK Monopolies and Restrictive Practices (Inquiry and Control) Act 1948 and the related jurisprudence.

2.2.3 *The Context at the Time of Adopting Modern Competition Legislation*

Despite the different paths that India and Pakistan had followed since their creation as independent states in 1947, at the time they adopted their modern competition legislations their institutional landscape appeared remarkably similar.

2.2.3.1 The Indian Legal and Political Landscape in 2002

When India enacted the Indian Act, its political and legal landscape was not very different from what it had been in 1969 when it had enacted the Monopolies and Restrictive Trade Practices Act.[23] The Indian Constitution had been in force for more than fifty years and the country's legal and political infrastructure had remained substantially unchanged.[24] Elections had by and large been held regularly at five-yearly intervals in accordance with the procedure stipulated in the Constitution and each time power had been transferred without any military intervention. The legislature, executive, and the judiciary continued to exercise their respective powers uninterruptedly and in accordance with the Constitution.[25]

2.2.3.2 The Pakistani Scenario in 2007

Unlike India, Pakistan had experienced considerable political and legal turmoil since 1970 when it had adopted the Monopolies and Restrictive Trade Practices

[22] Amber Darr, Khozem Haidermota, and Munib Akhtar, 'The Competition Commission Ordinance 2007: A Critical Analysis' CLD 2008 Journal 37.

[23] Although the Indian Act was notified on 14.01.2003 it is titled the Competition Act 2002.

[24] Between 1949 and 2002 the Indian Constitution was amended more than eighty times and the Indian government had exercised its right to declare an emergency on more than one occasion. However, as per the ruling of the Indian Supreme Court in *His Holiness Kesavananda Bharati Sripadagalvaru and others v State and Kerala and another* (*AIR* 1973 *SC* 1461), these amendments or emergencies did not alter the basic institutional structure of the country.

[25] With the exception of the Emergency (1975–77) which was a major interruption and broke the five-year election cycle.

(Control and Prevention) Ordinance. In 1971 Pakistan had lost its eastern wing[26] and had re-incarnated its western wing as an independent federation with four provinces. In 1973 Pakistan had framed its third Constitution.[27] Under this Constitution, the president was the head of state and the prime minister the head of the executive.[28] The parliament, comprising the upper house, Senate, and the lower house, National Assembly comprised the legislature,[29] however, the president had the power to dissolve the parliament.[30] Each house had the power to initiate a bill (except a money bill), however, this bill could only be made into law when passed by both houses and after receiving presidential assent.[31]

The federal legislature had the power to legislate on all matters listed in the Federal and the Concurrent Legislative Lists.[32] If legislation was required urgently and the parliament was not in session, the president had the power to promulgate an ordinance provided that it related to a matter listed on the Federal or Concurrent Legislative List. An ordinance promulgated in this manner lapsed after 120 days unless approved by the parliament within this period.[33] Interestingly, regulation of competition was not listed in either the Federal or the Concurrent Legislative List. However, Article 18 of the Constitution indirectly recognized the right of the State to regulate competition[34] and Article 151 empowered the State to regulate inter-provincial trade.[35]

The Pakistani Constitution also established the Supreme Court as the apex court of the country and high courts in each of Pakistan's four provinces. The Supreme Court had original jurisdiction in respect of disputes arising between governments and for the enforcement of fundamental rights, and appellate jurisdiction in respect of all decisions of the high courts.[36] The high courts also had original and appellate jurisdiction as well as the jurisdiction to issue writs against the government in

[26] In the aftermath of the 1970 general elections, Pakistan had partitioned with East Pakistan declaring independence as the People's Republic of Bangladesh and West Pakistan being renamed 'Pakistan'.

[27] The Constitution of the Islamic Republic of Pakistan 1973 ('the Pakistan Constitution') came into force on 14.08.1973 and remains in force till today.

[28] Pakistani Constitution, Articles 50, 90.

[29] ibid Articles 51, 59.

[30] ibid Article 58(2)(b).

[31] ibid Articles 70, 73.

[32] ibid Article 142.

[33] ibid Article 89.

[34] In terms of Article 18 of the Pakistani Constitution every citizen has the right to enter upon any lawful profession or occupation and to conduct any lawful trade or business. However, Article 18(b), clarifies that this right does not prevent the state from regulating trade, commerce, or industry in the interest of free competition.

[35] Article 151 states *inter alia* that whilst trade, commerce, and intercourse throughout Pakistan shall be free, the Parliament may by law impose such restrictions on the freedom of trade, commerce, or intercourse between one Province and another or within any part of Pakistan as may be required in the public interest.

[36] Pakistani Constitution, Articles 184–85.

appropriate cases.[37] Decisions of the Supreme Court were binding on all courts and those of the high courts on all courts and tribunals subordinate to them.[38] The Constitution also provided for the qualifications and mode of appointment of Supreme Court and high court judges.[39]

The Pakistani Constitution was suspended twice: from 1977 to 1981 and from 1999 to 2002. In both periods the country was brought under military rule, the legislature was dismissed, and the judiciary co-opted by the incoming military regime.[40] Even otherwise when the Constitution had been restored and the legislature allowed to operate as per the Constitution, the country continued to be governed by military chiefs turned presidents for three distinct periods from 1981 to 1985, a few months in 1988 and from 2002 to 2007. Throughout these periods the legislature and judiciary remained deferential to the military and on occasion even allowed the military president to amend the Constitution.[41]

The process of adopting a competition legislation for Pakistan was initiated in 2006 by a quasi-military government. Although the Supreme Court had initially endorsed the military takeover[42] and had subsequently supported the government established by the military chief, the relationship between the judiciary and the executive had become deeply strained over time. In March 2007, the military chief turned president had suspended the chief justice of Pakistan from his office on grounds of misconduct. The president's action had been challenged before the Supreme Court, and in July 2007, the Supreme Court had re-instated the chief justice.[43] This struggle between the president and the judiciary strained the relationship between all three organs of state with the tension reaching a peak towards October 2007 just as the competition legislation was introduced in the country.

2.3 INITIAL ADOPTION IN INDIA AND PAKISTAN: MOTIVATIONS, MECHANISMS, AND INSTITUTIONS

The similarity between the Indian and Pakistani institutional landscapes as the countries commenced the process of adopting their respective competition

37 ibid Article 199.

38 ibid Articles 189, 203.

39 ibid Articles 175–76, 193. In 1980 Pakistan amended its Constitution to provide for a Federal Shariat Court the limited mandate of examining whether a Pakistani statute or provision of law was 'repugnant to the injunctions of Islam'.

40 Throughout these periods the judiciary was restrained from hearing fundamental rights petitions and operated under an oath to support the military takeovers.

41 By this time the Pakistani Constitution had been amended seventeen times, of which the 8th and the 17th amendments were introduced by military chiefs turned presidents. The latter being made under the authority of the Supreme Court as given in *Syed Zafar Ali Shah v General Parvez Musharraf, Chief Executive and others* PLD 2000 SC 869.

42 ibid.

43 *Chief Justice of Pakistan, Mr. Justice Iftikhar Muhammad Chaudhry v The President of Pakistan through the Secretary and others* PLD 2010 SC 61.

legislations masked the very different trajectories along which these institutions had evolved over time and therefore the manner in which institutions in the two countries interacted with each other in the adoption process. This section compares the motivations and the interplay of the institutions at the deliberation and enactment phases in the two countries with the aim of identifying their adoption strategies.

2.3.1 *Motivations for Acquiring Modern Competition Legislation*

In deciding to adopt modern competition legislations both India and Pakistan were motivated by a combination of internal factors (such as the country's assessment of its economic and regulatory needs) and external factors (such as international economic developments and the recommendations of multi-lateral agencies). However, each country struck a different balance between these internal and external factors.

2.3.1.1 Domestic Self-reflection and Needs-Assessment in India and Pakistan

When India decided to revisit its anti-monopoly regime, it established a committee to determine whether it should amend its existing legislation or acquire an entirely new one. This move was in keeping with India's long tradition of establishing indigenous committees to evaluate its law reform proposals. The Monopolies and Restrictive Trade Practices Act 1969 was itself the culmination of recommendations made in the Hazari Committee Report 1965, the Mahalonobis Committee Report 1964, and the Report of the Monopoly Inquiry Committee.[44] In 1977, the Indian government had established the Sachar Committee to recommend measures to enhance the effectiveness of the 1969 Act,[45] and in 1984 the parliament had amended the Act in light of the recommendations of the Sachar Committee.[46] In 1991, the parliament had further amended the 1969 Act to bring it into alignment with India's economic liberalisation programme. By 1999, however, these amendments were deemed inadequate, and the Indian government established the Raghavan Committee with the mandate to propose the most appropriate competition law for the country.[47]

Pakistan, like India, had adopted its Monopolies and Restrictive Trade Practices (Control and Prevention) Ordinance 1970 primarily in response to domestic factors

[44] S Chakravarthy, 'Why India Adopted a New Competition Law' (CUTS International 2006) www.regulation.org.uk/library/india/CUTS-Why_India_Adopted_a_new_Competition_Law .pdf accessed 13 September 2021,

[45] Amitabh Kumar, 'The Evolution of Competition Law in India' in Vinod Dhall (ed) *Competition Law Today: Concepts, Issues, and the Law in Practice* (OUP 2007), 486–89.

[46] ibid 488.

[47] Chakravarthy (n.43) 19.

and in consultation with domestic institutions. In the 1950s Pakistan had seen rapid economic growth. By the early 1960s, however, nearly two-thirds of Pakistan's industrial assets, 80 per cent of its banking sector and 70 per cent of its insurance industry had become heavily concentrated in the hands of only twenty family groups. In response to these developments in 1963 the Pakistani government constituted an 'Anti-Cartel Laws Study Group' to study the trade, commerce, and industry of the country. This group reported the prevalence of monopolies, cartels, and vertically integrated businesses throughout the country and recommended the adoption of anti-monopoly legislation. On 28 June 1969 the government sought public comments on a draft anti-monopoly bill and on 26 February 1970 the president promulgated this bill as an Ordinance, which while not placed before parliament was subsequently given constitutional cover which allowed it to remain in force well beyond its ordinary constitutional life of 120 days.[48]

The 1970 Ordinance was amended four times, however, each time without public consultation:[49] in 1972, the government curtailed the scope of the 1970 Ordinance as part of its nationalisation process; in 1976 the government further curtailed its scope allegedly to promote and protect foreign private investment in Pakistan; finally in 1981, the government merged the anti-monopoly authority established under the 1970 Ordinance with the then newly formed Corporate Law Authority.[50] Therefore, by 2005 when Pakistan first considered the possibility of adopting a modern competition legislation, the domestic understanding of monopolies had shrunk considerably and the need to regulate them had receded considerably from the forefront of governmental priorities.

2.3.1.2 Impact of International Developments on Competition Legislation in the Two Countries

After joining the World Trade Organisation (WTO) in 1995[51] India had become increasingly pre-occupied with the idea of introducing a domestic competition regime both to safeguard the Indian economy from the threat of international cartels,[52] and for the country to remain relevant and attractive as a destination for foreign investment.

[48] Joseph Wilson, 'At the Crossroads: Making Competition Law Effective in Pakistan Symposium on Competition Law and Policy in Developing Countries' (2006) 26 Northwestern Journal of International Law & Business 565, 567–68.

[49] The 1970 Ordinance was amended twice in 1980 (by Ordinance No. XXVI of 1980 and Ordinance No. LVI of 1980) and once each in 1982 and 2002 (by Ordinance No. XIV of 1982; and in 2002 by Ordinance CI of 2002 respectively), however, there is no information or record of any public consultations for any of the amendments.

[50] Wilson, 'At the Crossroads' (n.47), 583.

[51] India joined the WTO on 01.01.1995. <www.wto.org/english/thewto_e/whatis_e/tif_e/org6_e.htm> accessed 22 June 2021.

[52] Report of the High Level Committee on Competition Policy & Law 2000 ('the Raghavan Report') <https://theindiancompetitionlaw.files.wordpress.com/2013/02/report_of_high_level_committee_on_competition_policy_law_svs_raghavan_committee.pdf> accessed 13 September 2021, para 1.22.

Pakistan had also joined the WTO at the same time as India.[53] However, just before formally acceding to the WTO, and perhaps partly due to developments in India, the Pakistani government had expressed an interest in bolstering laws relating to companies, securities, and exchange and so on, However, even at that time it had not considered reviewing the 1970 Ordinance.[54] By the late 1990s, due to its extensive interaction with the WTO and with multi-lateral agencies,[55] and its participation in international comparative competition studies,[56] Pakistan had realised that if it wanted to integrate successfully in an increasingly globalised world it needed to improve the competitiveness of its domestic markets.[57] Therefore, in the aftermath of the Doha Ministerial Conference in 2001, Pakistan sought assistance first from the United Nations Conference on Trade and Development (UNCTAD),[58] and later from the World Bank for developing a new competition law and policy framework.[59]

2.3.2 *Mechanisms and Institutions at the Adoption Stage in India and Pakistan*

The adoption stages in both India and Pakistan comprise two distinct phases: in the first phase the countries consider adopting the legislation – this may also include preparing the draft for submission to the government – and in the second they formally adopt the legislation in accordance with their respective legislative procedures.

53 See n.50.

54 ibid 589.

55 Eric David Manes, 'A Framework for a New Competition Policy and Law: Pakistan' (The International Bank for Reconstruction and Development 2007), paras 1.5, 1.6 ('the Manes Report'). Pakistan had recently completed the first-generation reforms under the guidance of and with technical assistance from the World Bank. By 2005, it was once again engaged with the World Bank for the second-generation reforms, which were geared inter alia towards improving Pakistan's 'international competitiveness in an increasingly globalised world'.

56 'Competition Regime in Pakistan: Waiting for a Shake-up' (CUTS 2002) <https://d4ynnvjs6l34j.cloudfront.net/9db88fd87a46d6405284ff195f7f38.pdf> accessed 13 September 2021.

57 Manes Report (n.54). Executive Summary, para (iii), (viii).

58 After the Doha Ministerial Conference in November 2001, Pakistan seriously considered revamping its anti-monopoly regime. Business Recorder 'Monopoly Trade Practices Law Being Revamped' 2004 <https://fp.brecorder.com/2004/04/20040428133601/> accessed 13 September 2021. However, its ambitions at this stage were limited to capacity building and technical assistance within the existing infrastructure with the help of a loan from the World Bank <https://documents1.worldbank.org/curated/en/857811627555757196/pdf/Announcement-of-World-Bank-Discusses-Roadmap-for-Assistance-to-Pakistan-Approves-Five-Hundred-Million-Dollars-to-Support-Ongoing-Reform-Program-on-June-11-2002.pdf> accessed 13 September 2021.

59 ibid. Acknowledgment.

2.3.2.1 The Deliberation Phase: Between the Raghavan and the World Bank-Led Committees

In response to its particular combination of internal and external factors, in 1999 the Indian government set up a nine-member 'High Level Committee on Competition Law and Policy' under the chairmanship of Mr S V S Raghavan, a retired senior Indian government official (hence the Raghavan Committee),[60] to advise whether amendments to the anti-monopoly and consumer legislations would suffice or if there was need for a new law.[61] Over the next two years the Raghavan Committee engaged with and obtained evidence from various chambers of industries and commerce, professional institutes, consumer organisations, experts, academics, and government officials.[62] The committee also consulted competition laws of nearly eighty countries – including those of the European Union, the United Kingdom, the United States, and Japan – and examined competition reports and texts authored by leading Indian and international competition experts. In 2000 the committee submitted its report to the government.[63]

Rather than establishing a committee as in the case of India, the Pakistani government requested the World Bank to form and lead a team to recommend a new competition law and policy framework for the country; to draft the appropriate competition legislation, and to design a new competition agency for enforcing it. The team set up by the World Bank in response to this request comprised World Bank officials, international consultants, and chartered accountants as well as Pakistani economists, lawyers, and academics. In arriving at its recommendations the team consulted 'perception indicators' and 'broad indicators from the market' in Pakistan[64] and drew upon its experience and understanding of competition regimes and models in developed and developing countries.[65] The team also engaged with the Ministry of Finance, the anti-monopoly authority, and a few international and

[60] Members of the Raghavan Committee included the chairman of a large consumer goods manufacturing company, a consumer activist, an economic journalist, a chartered accountant, an advocate, and a government secretary from the Department of Company Affairs dealing with competition law. The Hindu 'Competition Law for the New Millennium' <www.thehindu.com/2000/06/22/stories/0622000d.htm> accessed 13 September 2021.

[61] Raghavan Report (n.51), 1.2.2.

[62] Chakravarthy (n.43), 21.

[63] Raghavan Report (n.51).

[64] Manes Report (n.54), ch 1, paras 1.15–1.17.

[65] ibid para 2.2 n.8. In addition to the usual EU, UK, and the US models, the team also consulted competition laws of Brazil, Canada, Italy, India, Mexico, Republic of Korea, and Russia. The team also evaluated competition models from developing countries whose economic conditions matched those of Pakistan and which were at a similar stage of development, however, it did not consider the political and legal institutions or environment of these countries.

Pakistani experts other than those officially part of its team.[66] In May 2006 it organised a Growth and Competitiveness Conference in Lahore as well as some other public consultations.[67] By January 2007 the team had completed its deliberations, and had commissioned the Brussels-based law firm, Jones Day to prepare a draft competition law for Pakistan. Once finalised it submitted the report and the draft to the Pakistani Ministry of Finance.[68]

2.3.2.2 Formal Enactment of Competition Laws in India and Pakistan

India formally enacted the Indian Act 2002 on 14 January 2003 in accordance with the long-form legislative procedure prescribed in the Indian Constitution. The government introduced a bill in parliament, outlining the objects and reasons for its enactment. The parliament remitted the bill to the relevant standing committee for scrutiny, and the standing committee, after consulting with representatives of financial institutions, chambers of industry and commerce, consumer organisations, professional institutes, experts, academics, and relevant ministries of the government, presented its report to the parliament. In December 2002, after considering the recommendations of the standing committee, the parliament passed the bill with some modifications. The bill was then submitted to the president for his assent, which was granted on 13 January 2003.[69]

Pakistan also followed constitutional procedure in introducing its competition legislation however, instead of placing the draft bill before parliament, the Pakistani government submitted it directly to the military chief turned president, who in October 2007 promulgated it as an ordinance.[70] Legislation through ordinances is not unusual in Pakistan, however, the 2007 Ordinance was different in two respects: first, because it was not clear whether the president was competent to legislate in this regard given that competition was not listed in the Federal or Concurrent Legislative Lists[71] and second because it did not lapse at the expiry of the prescribed 120 days.[72] and remained in force due to a controversial Presidential order passed in

66 ibid. Acknowledgments.

67 ibid. Although the exact number of consultations held is not known, the report suggests that these were all held in the month of May and in the same city. There is no record of who attended these consultations or how these were advertised.

68 Joseph Wilson, 'Crossing the Crossroads: Making Competition Law Effective in Pakistan' (2011) 8 Loyola University Chicago International Law Review 105, 111. Also 'Voluntary Peer Review of Competition Law and Policy: Pakistan' (UNCTAD 2013). <http://unctad.org/en/PublicationsLibrary/ditcclp2013d4_overview_en.pdf> ch 1, 1, para 5, accessed 14 September 2021.

69 Chakravarthy (n.43), 22.

70 Voluntary Peer Review (n.67), ch 1A, 2, para 7.

71 See n.33 and text thereto.

72 For the president's power to promulgate Ordinances, see n.32 and text thereto. Laws made through ordinances in Pakistan include the Securities and Exchange Ordinance 1969, Companies Ordinance 1984, National Accountability Bureau Ordinance 1999, Insurance

response to the political developments in the country in the immediate aftermath of its promulgation.[73]

2.3.3 *Transfer Mechanisms and Interplay of Institutions in Adoption*

India and Pakistan employed different mechanisms and institutions in deliberating and enacting their respective competition legislations. The dominant mechanisms employed by each country and the institutions through which these were delivered shaped not only the substance the legislation but also its compatibility and legitimacy and thereby its potential to deliver results at the implementation stage.

2.3.3.1 India: A Case of *Socialisation*

India was motivated to adopt modern competition legislation to achieve domestic economic goals and as well as to gain international legitimacy. By the mid-1990s when India embraced economic liberalisation it had periodically reviewed its anti-monopoly legislation and understood that it needed a modern competition law to achieve greater economic efficiency and consumer welfare. Further, India's membership of the WTO and its participation in the Doha Ministerial Conference had helped it appreciate that a modern competition regime was necessary for its international legitimacy and for it to retain its competitive advantage in the global economy.

India adopted a consultative strategy to engineer the law reform necessary to realise its aspirations. The Raghavan Committee established to re-evaluate India's anti-monopoly regime[74] not only reviewed international competition models but also engaged with a broad range of domestic stakeholders and future users of the law to understand India's needs in this regard and to tailor its recommendations

Ordinance 2000, and National Reconciliation Ordinance 2007. The number of ordinances promulgated between 2002–07 was far greater than in any previous period: the president promulgated 134 ordinances during the National Assembly's five-year term as compared to eighty-eight bills presented to the Parliament during the same period. See *A Five-Year Report on Performance of Women Parliamentarians in the 12th National Assembly (2002–2007)* (Aurat Foundation Pakistan 2009).

[73] In November 2007 Pakistan's military chief turned president issued the Proclamation of Emergency and Provisional Constitutional Order No. 1 of 2007 declaring an emergency in the country and suspending the Constitution. Three weeks later, the president issued the Constitution (Amendment) Order 2007 amending the Constitution and validating and saving 'all actions taken and all Ordinances promulgated by him in the weeks leading up to the declaration of emergency'. The president's actions were in response to growing political unrest in the country and the need to 'save' the National Reconciliation Ordinance 2007 (NRO) promulgated on 5 October 2007 – three days after the 2007 Ordinance – to pardon political rivals turned allies. The 2007 Ordinance was saved simply for having been introduced simultaneously with the NRO rather than for any of its own attributes.

[74] See n.46 and text thereto.

accordingly. Despite these efforts, Raghavan Committee's investigation of international models was essentially an elite discourse and reflected bounded rather than rational learning to the extent that it was based almost entirely on textual analysis of preferred and readily available foreign models rather than through an objective or incisive empirical analysis of the outcomes that these models had achieved in their respective contexts. Its limitations notwithstanding, India's effort to understand and adapt foreign models before adopting them means that it acquired its competition legislation through *socialisation* albeit with elements of *emulation*[75] and *regulatory competition*.[76]

India's transfer strategy of *socialisation* strategy was further deepened by its engaging bottom-up, participatory, and inclusive institutions, drawn from the executive and the legislature, both in deliberating and enacting the Indian Act. The deliberation phase, led entirely by the executive acting through the Raghavan Committee, had first aggregated local knowledge by consulting a reasonably wide range of stakeholders from different sectors of the Indian economy, academia, and consumer groups. It had then analysed this local knowledge in light of international models and expert opinion before presenting its recommendations to the government. The government had then prepared a draft bill on the basis of the recommendations made in the Raghavan Report and in its own policy objectives and had then placed it before the parliament for enactment. The enactment phase had fallen exclusively within the purview of the legislature, which had further adapted the draft competition bill after another round of consultations led by its relevant standing committees (Table 2.1).

2.3.3.2 Pakistan: A Study in *Coercion*

In the case of Pakistan external influence, exerted primarily through the WTO and Pakistan's relationship with the World Bank, outweighed the faint domestic impulse to adopt a modern competition law. The relative weakness of Pakistan's domestic impulse was in part due to Pakistan not having periodically reviewed its anti-monopoly regime and, therefore, due to the government not fully understanding and appreciating the country's needs in this regard,[77] while its interest in adopting the law may have been spurred by India, Sri Lanka, and Nepal among other similarly situated developing countries having recently enacted some version of a competition legislation. Finally, and most importantly, Pakistan only actively engaged with the possibility of acquiring modern competition legislation after it

75 India's ongoing negotiations with the WTO are likely to have influenced it into adopting a competition legislation that conformed to international competition principles.

76 At the time it was considering adopting a modern competition law, India was aware of the possibility of its neighbours and other similarly situated developing countries doing the same and, therefore, of the need to remain regulatorily competitive.

77 See n.48.

TABLE 2.1. *Tracing the adoption processes in India and Pakistan*

Steps in the Process	India	Pakistan	Steps in the Process
PRE-CONDITIONS OF TRANSFER			
	Strong tradition of: • Parliamentary governance; • Constituting domestic committees for law reform; • Independent judiciary.	• Military chief turned president; • Young and fragile parliament; • Judiciary weakened by repeated military takeovers; • Strained relationship between executive, parliament, and judiciary.	
DELIBERATION PHASE			
Motivations	• Changes in domestic economic policy; • Realisation of changing external environment.	• Limited domestic realisation; • Persuasion on part of the World Bank	Motivations
Strategy	• Review of existing law; • Review of international models; • Extensive consultations with relevant stakeholders. • Law drafted internally.	• Advice by the World Bank team; • Internal consultations with the government; • Limited public consultations; • Law drafted by a Brussels firm.	Strategy
Institutions	• Drawn from the executive; • Domestically formed and led committee.	• Drawn from the executive; • Committee led by the World Bank	Institutions
ENACTMENT PHASE			
Strategy	• Draft tabled before parliament; • Referred to parliamentary standing committee; • Further input obtained from domestic stakeholders; • Passed by parliament.	• Draft submitted to the president; • Passed by the president without parliamentary or public consultation.	Strategy
Institutions	• Executive. • Legislature.	• Executive.	Institutions

had been persuaded by the World Bank that such a law was a necessary component of its first- and second-generation reforms and by its offer of financial and technical assistance to Pakistan for this purpose. While the influence of the WTO and the World Bank indicates that indirect *coercion* was the dominant factor in the transfer of competition legislation in Pakistan, the fact that Pakistan's preferred to adopt a law that reflected international best practices suggests that Pakistan sought this law more for its normative rather than its substantive value and to gain international legitimacy rather than for achieving domestic legitimacy or even economic efficiency, implies a strong element of *emulation*. Further the need to remain competitive with its developing world counterparts also hints at elements of *regulatory competition* in its adoption strategy.

The dominant element of *coercion* in Pakistan's adoption strategy was re-inforced by both the deliberation and enactment phases of the adoption stage being handled by top-down, exclusive institutions drawn only from the executive. The Pakistani executive had set the adoption process in motion when it had outsourced the deliberation and drafting of the competition legislation to a World Bank team, which by its very nature was more attuned to foreign models. Its engagement with Pakistani stakeholders was expected to contextualise these deliberations, however, these engagements were limited and select and did not materially influence the thinking of the core World Bank team. It is no surprise, therefore, the legislation drafted at the instruction of this team by a Brussels-based law firm was drawn almost entirely from international models and was only superficially adapted for the Pakistani context.[78] The World Bank team had submitted its report and the draft law to the Ministry of Finance, which instead of placing it before the legislature had submitted it to directly the president for promulgation.

2.4 ADOPTION CONTINUES: AMENDING THE INDIAN AND PAKISTANI COMPETITION LAWS

The adoption processes in India and Pakistan continued beyond the adoption of their respective competition legislations as both India and Pakistan amended their competition laws soon after initial adoption. In the course of these amendments, the countries not only engaged different transfer mechanisms and institutions and, thereby, not only but also re-adjusted the compatibility and legitimacy of the adopted legislations and thereby their potential to perform at the implementation stage.

2.4.1 *Amendments to the Indian Act*

Soon after its enactment, the Indian Act was challenged before the Indian Supreme Court on the ground that it did not conform with the principle of

[78] See n.66 and text thereto.

separation of powers and was, therefore, unconstitutional.[79] On 20 January 2005, the Supreme Court disposed of this challenge on a commitment provided by the government that it would take appropriate steps to separate the adjudicatory and regulatory functions of the Competition Commission of India (CCI) established in pursuance of the Act.[80] On 9 March 2006, in compliance of the order of the Supreme Court, the Indian government introduced the Competition (Amendment) Bill in parliament, which, among other amendments, provided for the establishment of an independent Competition Appellate Tribunal (Indian Tribunal) to hear appeals from the CCI's decisions. As before, the parliament referred the bill to the relevant standing committee, which recommended further amendments. On 9 August 2007, the government re-submitted the bill to the parliament and on 27 September 2007, after having received presidential assent, the bill was enacted as the Competition (Amendment) Act 2007.[81]

On 31 March 2017, India further amended the Indian Act, however, this time the amendments were introduced through the Finance Act 2017 which was passed by the parliament through a short-form procedure and without stakeholder consultations[82] and amended only sections 2(ba) and 53A of the Act to replace the Competition Appellate Tribunal with a 'National Company Law Appellate Tribunal' (NCLAT). The NCLAT had been established in 2016 initially only to hear appeals from Company Law Tribunals.[83] However, after this amendment it was given the additional mandate to hear with effect from 26 May 2017 competition appeals from CCI's interim and final orders.[84]

79 The petitioner in *Brahm Dutt v Union of India (2005) 2 Supreme Court Cases 431* challenged the Competition Commission of India (Selection of Chairperson and other Members of the Commission) Rules 2003 on the ground that the appointment procedure provided in these rules violated the principle of separation of powers provided in the Constitution and argued that given the CCI's adjudicatory powers, the procedure for appointment of its members should be the same as the procedure prescribed for the appointment of judges in the Constitution. In response the government argued that CCI was a specialist body that could not be operated by generalist judges. The government further argued that as long as the Supreme Court's and the high courts' power of judicial review remained in place, the government's power to appoint members to the CCI could not be challenged on the grounds of separation of powers. However, during the proceedings the government agreed to amend the Act to provide for a select committee to recommend CCI members as well as for a tribunal to hear appeals from the CCI's decisions (*Brahm Dutt Case*, pp 434–35).

80 ibid.

81 ibid. The amended Act was brought into force in stages: provisions relating to anti-competitive agreements and abuse of dominant position came into force on 20.05. 2009 by notifications no. S.O. 1241(E) and S.O. 1242(E) both dated 15.05.2009 and provisions relating to mergers or combinations were brought into force in 2011. By a further notification no. S.O. 1240(E), also dated 15.05.2009, the government established the Tribunal to hear appeals from the CCI's orders.

82 Indian Constitution, Articles 110 and 117.

83 National Company Law Appellate Tribunal <www.mca.gov.in/content/mca/global/en/about-us/affiliated-offices/nclat.html> accessed 14 September 2021.

84 ibid.

2.4.2 *Pakistan: Two Ordinances and an Act*

In time the efforts of the Pakistani executive to 'save' the life of the 2007 Ordinance proved insufficient. In early 2008, soon after Pakistan had held general elections and replaced the military chief turned president with a civilian president,[85] a petition was filed before the Supreme Court seeking the annulment of the declaration of emergency and all orders issued by the president in pursuance of the declaration, including the order saving among others the 2007 Ordinance.[86] In its decision in this petition the Supreme Court directed the government to place all saved ordinances, including the 2007 Ordinance, before the legislature within 120 days.[87] However, instead of doing so, the government promulgated a new Competition Ordinance on 26 November 2009, immediately before the expiry of the period stipulated by the Supreme Court.[88]

The government also did not place the 2009 Ordinance before the legislature and allowed it to lapse in March 2010. On 20 April 2010 the government promulgated yet another ordinance – the 2010 Ordinance – which would remain in force until early August 2010.[89] Immediately before the expiry of the 2010 Ordinance, the government placed a draft competition bill before the legislature[90] and on 13 October 2010 the legislature finally enacted the Competition Act 2010.[91] This Act was similar in substance to the Ordinances that had preceded it except that it provided for a Competition Appellate Tribunal – the Pakistani Tribunal – to hear appeals from orders of the CCP and limited the role of the Supreme Court to hearing appeals from orders of the Tribunal.[92]

2.4.3 *Evolution of Indian and Pakistani Adoption Strategies*

In drafting the 2007 amendments to the Indian Act, as at the time of initially enacting it, India appeared to continue its strategy of *socialisation*. Although the government did not set up a committee to consult with stakeholders before recommending amendments as it had done in first considering the Indian Act, it not only examined and adapted foreign models for segregating the CCI's regulatory and adjudicatory functions but also engaged with the legislature and the judiciary in

85 In November 2007, several judges of the superior courts in Pakistan refused to accede to the demand of military chief turned president to support his declaration of emergency and therefore, were dismissed from office. After considerable political struggle, the civilian government restored these judges to office, however the relationship between the judiciary and the executive remained strained for some time after.

86 See Section 2.3.2.2.

87 *Sindh High Court Bar Association v The Federation of Pakistan* PLD 2009 SC 879. Para 22(vii).

88 The Competition Ordinance 2009 (Ordinance No. XLVI of 2009).

89 The Competition Ordinance 2010 (Ordinance No. XVI of 2010).

90 This 2010 Ordinance lapsed in August 2010 without an Act to replace it. Wilson (n.67), 108–09.

91 Hereafter 'the Pakistani Act'.

92 Pakistani Act, sections 2(1)(p), 42–44.

this regard. The legislature aggregated local information through its elected representatives and standing committees and the Supreme Court utilised its institutional memory and expertise to appropriately adapt the proposed amendments for the Indian context. By 2017, however, when the government amended the provisions relating to the Indian Tribunal it appeared to have exchanged the *socialisation* strategy and the desire for international alignment with domestic expediency: instead of consulting international precedents, and socialising these for the Indian context, it took the decision to replace the Indian Tribunal with the NCLAT purely in response to the domestic need for re-organising and consolidating its independent tribunals. Further, in introducing this amendment through the Finance Act, which under the Indian Constitution may be passed without parliamentary scrutiny,[93] India narrowed the range of institutions engaging with the proposed amendment and exchanged any benefits that it may have derived from consultation for the speed and ease of legislation.

Pakistan, on the other hand, extended the mechanism of *coercion* and continued to avoid bottom-up, participatory, and inclusive institutions by adopting the 2009 and 2010 Ordinances, as it had adopted the 2007 Ordinance, by the order of the president without public consultations and parliamentary scrutiny[94] and by largely replicating the provisions of the 2007 Ordinance in the 2009 and 2010 Ordinances. In enacting the Pakistani Act, however, Pakistan engaged the parliament and through its standing committees, various stakeholders in the country, thereby moving towards a strategy of *socialisation* delivered through relatively more bottom-up, participatory, and inclusive institutions. However, this late attempt at *socialisation* could not displace the early effect of *coercion* and had a limited impact on the Act which remained similar in substance to the Ordinances that had preceded it. This may also partly be attributed to the fact that although the parliament was *designed* as a bottom-up, participatory, and inclusive institution, it lacked institutional capacity due to its chequered and interrupted history. It is likely that in introducing provisions for establishing the Pakistani Tribunal and prescribing an appellate trajectory substantially along the lines adopted by India in 2007 and the UK some years prior Pakistan was also engaging in *emulation* or and *regulatory competition*.

2.5 INDIAN AND PAKISTANI COMPETITION LEGISLATION: AN UNEXPECTED OUTCOME?

Although the very different mechanisms and institutions engaged by India and Pakistan for adopting their competition legislations suggest that the content of

93 Indian Constitution, Article 198.

94 The 2007 Ordinance and the 2009 Ordinance were almost identical and provided for appeals from the CCP's orders to be made directly to the Supreme Court. However, the 2010 Ordinance directed appeals from the CCP's orders to high courts.

Indian and the Pakistani Act must also be different, a comparison of the texts of these statutes reveals that this is not the case. This section explores factors in the adoption processes in the two countries that may have created this unexpected outcome.

2.5.1 Socialisation *and the Content of the Indian Act*

In India, the strategy of *socialisation* through an interplay of the executive, legislature, and the judiciary allowed an opportunity for a wide range of institutions to participate in the adoption process and for the draft competition legislation to be adapted for the Indian context in light of the information aggregated through these institutions.

This impact is evident from the evolution of the content of the Indian Act through the successive phases of the adoption stage. For instance, in the deliberation phase, the Raghavan Committee noted that 'the judiciary may be inexperienced in dealing with free market problems' and recommended the establishment of a single competition implementation authority,[95] sometimes referring to it as the 'Competition Law Tribunal' and at others as 'the Competition Commission of India'[96] and describing it varyingly as 'a specialised court/tribunal',[97] ' multi-member body', 'independent and insulated from political and budgetary controls of the government'.[98] The committee further recommended that the proposed authority be divided into investigative, prosecutorial, and adjudicative wings,[99] and be responsible for competition advocacy, adjudication, and implementation of its decisions.[100] The parliament incorporated the recommendations of the committee as endorsed by the government, in the Indian Act by providing for the establishment of the competition authority – CCI – as a single, multi-member, autonomous, statutory corporation with perpetual succession.[101] This authority was also to include at least one 'judicial member' who had either served or was qualified to serve as a judge of a high court. However, when the Indian Act was amended in 2007, in pursuance of the interaction between the government and the judiciary in the *Brahm Dutt* case,[102] the requirement of a judicial member was repealed, the CCI was re-designated as regulatory body only albeit with an adjudicatory function which was to be overseen and reviewed by the independent and quasi-judicial Indian Tribunal.[103]

The Raghavan Committee had also recommended that CCI be 'comprised of eminent and erudite persons of integrity from the fields of judiciary, economics, law,

95 Raghavan Report (n.51), para 6.1.2
96 ibid para 2.9.7.
97 ibid para 6.1.4.
98 ibid para 4.8.4 at 2 and 3.
99 ibid para 4.8.4 at 4, para 6.1.8.
100 ibid para 4.8.4.
101 Indian Act, section 7.
102 See n.78.
103 Amendment Act 2007 Section 17.

international trade, commerce, industry, accountancy, public affairs and administration' and had specifically warned against 'staffing [the institution] ... with civil servants on deputation'.[104] The Committee had, therefore, recommended a 'Collegium Selection Process', that would help weed out political favourites and allow competent and qualified persons to be appointed to the CCI.[105] It had further recommended that persons so appointed only be removed on the recommendation of the Supreme Court.[106] In enacting the Indian Act, the parliament, contrary to the recommendation of the Raghavan Committee, had allowed high court judges to be appointed to the CCI,[107] and had vested the power of appointment exclusively in the government.[108] While it is unclear whether the decision to disregard this recommendation came from the executive, or was introduced during parliamentary consultations, it had the effect of rendering the CCI and its members vulnerable to political influence. The parliament further compromised the CCI's independence by allowing the government to control its budget[109] and to supersede the CCI in certain circumstances.[110] Interestingly, when the Act was amended in 2007 it reverted to a number of recommendations made by the Raghavan Committee: it deleted the provision allowing high court judges to be appointed to the CCI;[111] inserted a provision requiring members to be appointed upon the recommendation of a 'Selection Committee', comprising the chief justice of India, secretaries of the Ministries of Corporate Affairs and Law and Justice, and two experts from fields related to competition law and policy;[112] and restricted the CCI from meeting its expenses from monies received by it as costs of proceedings.[113]

In certain matters the parliament followed the recommendations of the Raghavan Committee very closely. For instance the committee's insistence that consumer welfare be adopted as a guiding principle in competition enforcement

[104] Raghavan Report (n.51), para 4.8.6.

[105] ibid para 6.3.3, 6.3.4.

[106] ibid para 6.3.6.

[107] Indian Act, section 8(2).

[108] Indian Act, sections 8(1), 9. In terms of these sections the power to appoint members was vested in the government, and in terms of the Competition Commission of India (Selection of Chairperson and other Members of the Commission) Rules 2003 made in pursuance of the Act, the government was to constitute a committee 'for the selection of Chairperson and other Members of the Commission'. However, this provision, fell short of recommendations of the Raghavan Committee because the recommendations of the appointing committee were not binding on the government, and because the government had the power to amend the rules and thereby to do away with the committee altogether.

[109] Indian Act section 51(b) established a Competition Fund to pay salaries of CCI members and to meet its operating expenditures. The Competition Fund comprised of grants received by the CCI from the government as well as monies collected by it by way of costs or fees received by it in discharge of its functions under the law.

[110] Indian Act section 56.

[111] Amendment Act 2007, section 6.

[112] Amendment Act 2007, section 7.

[113] Amendment Act 2007, section 41.

in India was reflected in the preamble to the Act; its recommendation that the competition authority 'act as a [competition] watchdog', 'promote the introduction of required changes in the policy environment', 'perform a proactive advocacy function',[114] and check 'cartelisation, price-fixing and other abuses of market power',[115] were incorporated in the provisions relating to the CCI's advocacy and enforcement roles, and in the powers conferred upon it to investigate anti-competitive agreements and check abuses of dominant position. The committee's concerns regarding the future of India in a globalised economy were given expression in CCI powers in respect of international acts that impacted domestic Indian competition.[116] The committee's cautionary note that the 'premature implementation of Competition Law in [the area of mergers]', 'could act as a disincentive for ... mergers necessary to complete India's transition from a protected to a liberalized economy'[117] was addressed by the government delaying the bringing into force of the merger-related provisions.[118]

2.5.2 *The Effects of* Coercion *in Pakistan*

The adoption of its competition legislation through *coercion* and top-down and exclusive institutions had such a strong stabilising impact on the content of the Pakistani competition regime, that even the inclusion of the parliament in enacting the Pakistani Act could not displace it. This also suggests that bottom-up, participatory institutions can only dislodge the effects of *coercion* if they have historical depth and experience of aggregating local information and of working productively with the executive to adapt the content of the legislation for the domestic context.

The lingering effect of the early *coercion* in Pakistan is evident in the number of recommendations of the Manes Report that were retained in the 2007, 2009, and 2010 Ordinances as well as in the Pakistani Act. For instance, the Manes Report had envisaged Pakistan's national competition authority as a 'quasi-autonomous, quasi-judicial institution ... capable of applying severe penalties on private business in the case of violations of the law whilst remaining accountable to the government's competition policy, the law and the public ...'[119] It had further emphasised that the authority be a collegial body with a minimum of five and a maximum of seven members[120] and had recommended that orders of the authority be appealable to an 'internal Appellate Bench,' subject to judicial review to the Supreme Court.[121]

114 Raghavan Report (n.51), paras 1.1.9, 2.9.7.
115 ibid.
116 Indian Act, section 32.
117 Raghavan Report (n.51), para 4.7.8.
118 See n.80.
119 Manes Report (n.54), para 4.1.
120 ibid para 4.6.
121 ibid para 5.5.s

The 2007 Ordinance reflected nearly all these recommendations: it established the CCP as a collegial body corporate with perpetual succession and with not less than five and no more than seven members;[122] it also constituted an 'Appellate Bench' within the authority to hear appeals from orders of a single member or authorised officers;[123] and allowed appeals from orders passed by two or more members of the authority or of the Appellate Bench to be brought before the Pakistani Supreme Court.[124]

The 2007 Ordinance also reflected several recommendations of the Manes Report regarding the mandate of Competition Commission of Pakistan–CCP– including the recommendation that it be granted the power to check prohibited agreements, abuses of dominant position, deceptive marketing practices, and to regulate mergers and acquisitions.[125] The 2007 Ordinance provisions relating to competition enforcement were in accordance with the report's recommendation that the proposed authority treat enforcement as its highest priority and be given extensive investigation and sanctioning powers for this purpose,[126] while its provisions relating to advocacy reflected the recommendation that the authority it may also in advocacy as part of a two-pronged approach to improving competitiveness in the country.[127]

The Manes Report had also highlighted the importance of the 'quality of appointments' and the security of tenure of the appointed members for bolstering the authority's autonomy[128] and its ability to perform its functions in a robust manner.[129] To this end, the report had recommended that persons appointed to the authority be drawn from diverse but relevant professional backgrounds; be awarded appropriate remuneration packages, and if necessary, be removed through a transparent process.[130] However, the Manes Report did not prescribe a procedure for the appointment or removal of members of the authority.[131] The 2007 Ordinance incorporated the express recommendations of the Manes Report by stipulating that only persons known for their 'integrity, expertise, eminence and experience of not

122 2007 Ordinance, sections 12(2), 14(1).

123 2007 Ordinance, section 41.

124 2007 Ordinance, section 42.

125 Manes Report (n.54), ch 3 was reflected in sections 1(3), 3, 4 (read with sections 5, 7 and 9), 10 and 11 of the 2007 Ordinance.

126 2007 Ordinance chapter IV, particularly sections 31, 38, 39.

127 2007 Ordinance section 29. The Manes Report had also recommended that the Pakistani competition authority, exercise autonomy in its day-to-day work, follow due process, and remain accountable for its actions. However, these recommendations were not expressly included in the 2007 Ordinance. Manes Report (n.54), paras 3.2.3, 4.1, 4.12, 4.2, 4.8.

128 Manes Report (n.54), para 2.18, 4.4–4.7

129 ibid paras 4.2, 4.6.

130 ibid.

131 ibid paras 4.6, 6.38. While the Manes Report was silent as to the procedure for appointment of members, for removals it stated that the government may adopt the '[p]rocedure specified by Article 209 of the Constitution (ie.Supreme Judicial Council) [which] provides for a clear and transparency [*sic*] procedure'.

less than ten years in any relevant field including industry, commerce, economics, law accountancy or public administration' be appointed as the CCP's members (or chairperson).[132] However, also in accordance with the Manes Report, the 2007 Ordinance left it to the government to devise a scheme for the appointment[133] and removal of members.[134] In respect of removal of members the 2007 Ordinance included the additional stipulation that members be removed only after an inquiry conducted by an 'impartial person or body of persons"[135] however, it neither identified persons who may conduct such an enquiry nor stipulated a criteria for their selection. The Ordinance also left it to the government to prescribe rules for calling and conducting such inquiry.[136]

The 2007 Ordinance also departed from other recommendations of the Manes Report to confer more powers on the government and thereby undermined the independence of the CCP. For instance, even while declaring the CCP to be independent,[137] it gave the government control over CCP's budget; granted it the power to exempt certain categories of entities or agreements from the ambit of the Ordinance;[138] gave it the power to issue directives to the CCP;[139] authorised it to make rules for the CCP's governance and operations.[140] The 2007 Ordinance also allowed the CCP to utilise penalties to meet its operational expenditures thereby weakened its enforcement credibility.[141]

The fact that the majority of provisions of the 2007 Ordinance were in accordance with the Manes Report or supplied the gaps left by it and that these provisions remained unchanged in the 2009 and 2010 Ordinances and are still part of the Pakistani Act is indicative of the power of *coercion*. Although Pakistan engaged in *socialisation* in enacting the Pakistani Act (which led to the revocation of provisions

[132] 2007 Ordinance, section 14.

[133] 2007 Ordinance, section 14(5) stipulated that appointments to the CCP were to be made 'in such manner as may be prescribed'. The term 'prescribed' refers to rules that may be made under a primary legislation. Under section 55 of the Ordinance, the CCP had the power to make its own rules albeit with government approval. However, in terms of section 17 the government had the power to make rules regarding the salary, terms, and conditions of service of the CCP's chairman and members. Although the government made the Competition Commission (Salary, Terms and Conditions of Chairman and Members) Rules, 2009 these only stated that 'the government would appoint members in consultation with the chairman of the Commission' (Rule 3 sub rule 2).

[134] Ordinance 2007 section 14 (6).

[135] Ordinance 2007, section 19.

[136] ibid.

[137] 2007 Ordinance, section 12(3).

[138] 2007 Ordinance, section 52.

[139] 2007 Ordinance, section 54.

[140] See n.132. In terms of 2007 Ordinance, section 55 the CCP also had the power to make rules albeit with the approval of the government.

[141] 2007 Ordinance, section 20 stipulated that CCP was to fund its activities from the Commission Fund, which comprised inter alia the penalties collected by it.

allowing the CCP to utilise penalties towards meeting its expenditures[142] and to the insertion of provisions for establishing the Pakistani Tribunal and stipulating that appeals from orders of the Appellate Bench or of two or more members of CCP, lie directly to the Supreme Court) it not only failed to displace the earlier *coercion* nor deepened the understanding of competition principles amongst stakeholders.[143]

2.5.3 *The Effects of* Emulation *and* Regulatory Competition

A possible explanation for the remarkably similar substantive provisions of the Indian and Pakistani competition legislations that remained unchanged even as the laws progressed through the successive phases of the adoption stage and despite the countries engaging different transfer mechanisms and institutions (*socialisation* through bottom-up, participatory, and inclusive institutions in India and *coercion* through top-down and exclusive institutions in Pakistan) may lie in the countries having employed elements of *emulation* and *regulatory competition* in conjunction with their respective dominant strategies of *socialisation* and *coercion*. As has already been discussed, both India and Pakistan had engaged in *emulation* and *regulatory competition* due to their need for international legitimacy and their desire to remain competitive with similarly situated countries. It is also likely that both countries leveraged the pedigree, authoritativeness, and international acceptance of the substantive provisions of the competition legislation to convince members of the legislature or of the executive, as necessary, that it was in the country's interest to adopt these terms without amendment and to strengthen their domestic legitimacy. However, the fact that the countries remained unable to *socialise* and adapt these provisions for their contexts may be attributed to the lack of capacity in both and the absence of a meaningful discourse about internationally prevalent competition principles in their respective pre-existing legal systems. Arguably, the lack of discourse and its attendant lack of capacity was more pronounced in Pakistan in this period than in India where scholars had independently started commenting on competition law soon after the Raghavan Committee was constituted and certainly after its report had been made public.

2.6 COMPATIBILITY AND LEGITIMACY OF THE INDIAN AND PAKISTANI COMPETITION REGIMES

The transfer mechanisms and institutions engaged by India and Pakistan in adopting the Indian and Pakistani Acts respectively not only shaped their content but also

[142] Pakistani Act, section 20.
[143] Pakistani Act, sections 42, 44.

determined the extent of their compatibility with their respective contexts and their international and domestic legitimacy.

In adopting and later amending the Indian Act, India had engaged a wide range of bottom-up, participatory, and inclusive institutions drawn from all three branches of the state. These institutions had the capacity not only to aggregate knowledge from a relatively broad spectrum of domestic stakeholders but also to utilise this knowledge to appropriately 'Indian-ise' the competition blueprint for the Indian context. In sharp contrast, Pakistan's adoption, particularly of the 2007 Ordinance, was driven by the World Bank and executed through a limited number of exclusive and top-down institutions which had neither the capacity nor the inclination to aggregate local information or to meaningfully adapt international blueprints for Pakistan's local needs. The difference in the institutions engaged by the two countries in the adoption process meant that the Indian Act was likely to be relatively more compatible with the Indian context than the Pakistani Act would be for the Pakistani context. This compatibility (or lack thereof) was discernible from the very language of the two Acts: while the form of expression employed in the Indian Act is suited for the Indian context (sometimes at the cost of clarity as will be discussed in Chapter 5), that of the Pakistani Act closely mirrors the models on which it is based at the risk of being alien in its domestic context.

Further, the fact that the institutions engaged in the adoption and adaptation of the Indian Act were drawn from all three branches of the state, that is, the executive, the legislature, and the judiciary which were also able to interact with each other in the course of adoption allowed a relatively wide spectrum of stakeholders in India to be introduced to the proposed legislation and contributed to the domestic legitimacy of the legislation and made the CCP less concerned about asserting its international legitimacy by overt reliance on foreign competition materials and precedents in its decisions. In Pakistan, however, the institutions engaged in the adoption, particularly of the three Ordinances, were drawn exclusively from the executive and had only limited and curated interaction with other institutions in the country and with future end-users of the legislation. Pakistani stakeholders, therefore, remained largely uninformed about the rationale for adopting this legislation or its potential benefits for the economy, and were not in a position to meaningfully or even otherwise consent to its adoption. This meant that while these Ordinances had some formal and functional legitimacy in the country, the CCP was constrained to leverage its international legitimacy by overt and express reliance on foreign materials and precedents for establishing its domestic legitimacy.

The relatively higher compatibility and the legitimacy of the Indian Act makes it more likely that the Indian Act would be meaningfully enforced in the implementation stage rather than merely remaining a law in the books; that it would be understood and utilised by end-users and be applied by the CCI; and would not only enjoy a more productive relationship with the pre-existing legal authorities in the country but would also steadily integrate with the country's legal system. On the other hand, Pakistan's relatively weaker compatibility and legitimacy suggests that the CCP would face obstacles in enforcing the competition legislation: even if the CCP proved vigilant in applying the law to competition violations in the country, the users were not expected to understand or invoke the legislation or to approach the CCP with their grievances; the interactions between the CCP and the country's pre-existing legal system would likely be complicated and difficult; and the legislation would fail to integrate into the country's pre-existing legal system and would remain law on the books rather than transforming into a law in action.

3

The Spread of Competition Laws across South Asia

3.1 INTRODUCTION

South Asia, as demarcated for the purposes of the South Asian Association for Regional Co-operation (SAARC)[1] and the South Asian Free Trade Area (SAFTA)[2] includes Afghanistan, Bangladesh, Bhutan, India, Maldives, Nepal, Pakistan, and Sri Lanka.[3] These countries are not only at similar stages of economic development and have comparable relationships with multi-lateral agencies[4] but are also

1 South Asian Association for Regional Cooperation 'About SAARC' <www.saarc-sec.org/index.php/about-saarc/about-saarc> accessed 16 September 2021.

2 United Nations LDC Portal 'South Asian Free Trade Area' <www.un.org/ldcportal/south-asian-free-trade-area/> accessed 16 September 2021.

3 Some definitions of South Asia also include Myanmar, however, it is not included in the present study because being a member of ASEAN (Association of Southeast Asian Nations) rather than SAARC it more properly falls within the South-East Asian region. <https://asean.org/what-we-do/> accessed 16 September 2021.

4 The World Bank classifies Bangladesh, Bhutan, India, Nepal, Pakistan, and Sri Lanka as lower-middle-income countries and has recently added Nepal and Sri Lanka to this category: re-classifying Nepal upwards from the low-income category and Sri Lanka downwards from the upper-middle-income category. Maldives is classified as an upper-middle-income country, and Afghanistan as a low-income country. (The World Bank data <https://data.worldbank.org/country> accessed 25 November 2020; New World Bank country classifications by income level: 2020–21 <https://blogs.worldbank.org/opendata/new-world-bank-country-classifications-income-level-2020-2021> accessed 25 November 2020). Further, the United Nations classifies Afghanistan, Bangladesh, Bhutan, and Nepal as 'least developed countries' (United Nations Country Classifications: Data sources, country classifications and aggregation methodology). Maldives graduated from this category in 2011 and Bhutan is set to graduate in 2023. Bangladesh and Nepal were up for a review in 2021, however, as per data released on 1 July 2022 their classification remains unchanged. (Country classification: Data sources, country classifications and aggregation methodology <www.un.org/en/development/desa/policy/wesp/wesp_current/2014wesp_country_classification.pdf> accessed 25 November 2020) and New World Bank Country Classifications by income level 2022-2-23 <https://blogs.worldbank.org/opendata/new-world-bank-country-classifications-income-level-2022-2023> accessed 19 July 2022.

connected to each other through their geographies and parallel and sometimes overlapping histories.

Around the time that India and Pakistan adopted modern competition legislations in 2002 and 2007 respectively, the remaining South Asian countries were also taking steps towards adopting modern competition regimes for their own contexts. Among them Bangladesh, Nepal, Sri Lanka and more recently Maldives, have already enacted competition legislation, Bhutan has a competition policy and even Afghanistan was until recently evaluating its options in this regard. This chapter charts the progress of the competition regimes of the remaining six South Asian countries (the South Asian Six) along the deliberation-enactment-implementation continuum,[5] and analyses the motivations, mechanisms, and institutions engaged by each of them in this regard to evaluate the extent and quality of compatibility and legitimacy created or likely to be generated in the adoption process.

To this end this chapter is organised as follows: Section 3.2 examines the progress each of the South Asian Six have made along the deliberation-enactment-implementation continuum and describes where these are presently located; Section 3.3 examines the pre-conditions of transfer in each of these countries legal and political institutional landscape at the time they engaged with modern competition legislation and their motivations and strategies for engaging with these laws; Section 3.4 identifies the transfer mechanisms employed by each of these countries; Section 3.5 explores the compatibility and legitimacy generated or likely to be generated in the course of adoption for each of the South Asian Six and predicts their likely progress the implementation stage.

3.2 A COMPETITION TOUR OF THE SOUTH ASIAN SIX

Each of the South Asian Six have made progress towards adopting some version of a modern competition legislation. This section organises these countries according to the progress they have made towards adoption and examines the present state of their competition regimes to understand the overall picture of adoption of competition regimes in South Asia.

3.2.1 *Countries That Have Completed the Adoption Stage*

Four out of the South Asian Six – Sri Lanka, Nepal, Bangladesh, and Maldives – have already adopted competition legislation and have therefore completed both the deliberation and the enactment phase of the adoption stage.

[5] As developed in Chapter 2.

3.2.1.1 Sri Lanka and the Consumer Affairs Authority Act 2003

Sri Lanka was the first among the South Asian Six to adopt a competition legislation by enacting the Consumer Affairs Authority Act 2003 ('the Sri Lankan Act').[6] The Sri Lankan Act provides for the establishment of the Consumer Affairs Authority[7] and the Consumer Affairs Council,[8] that together have the mandate inter alia to promote effective competition, protect consumers, and regulate internal trade.[9] Both the Authority and the Council are semi-autonomous, collegiate bodies,[10] and the government has the power to appoint as well as remove their members.[11] The Sri Lankan Act, does not regulate mergers and acquisitions and focuses only on 'anti-competitive practices'.[12]

The Act confers wide-ranging regulatory, investigative, and advocational powers on the Authority[13] but limits its enforcement powers. For instance, in respect of anti-competitive practices,[14] the Authority's powers are primarily investigative and advisory.[15] If, upon completing its investigation, the Authority is of the view that there is a case to be tried, it may refer the matter to the Council for adjudication.[16] The Council has the power to terminate the anti-competitive practice or seek its

6 The Consumer Affairs Authority Act 2003 <http://caa.gov.lk/web/index.php?option=com_content&view=article&id=111&Itemid=560&lang=en> accessed 16 September 2021.

7 ibid section 2.

8 ibid section 39.

9 ibid Preamble.

10 ibid sections 3–5 for the Authority, and section 39 for the Council.

11 ibid. The power to appoint members of the Authority and of the Council and to remove members of the Authority (see Item 3 of the Schedule) vests in the government, however, the Act does not provide the mechanism for removal of members of the Council. In terms of section 49, the Authority may utilise sums recovered by it for its funding and for the payment of salaries of members of the Authority and the Council.

12 ibid section 35.

13 ibid section 7–12. The objects of the Authority as provided in section 7 include protection of consumers against marketing of hazardous goods or services; unfair and restrictive trade practices and ensuring adequate access to goods and services at competitive prices whilst in terms of section 8, it has the power to control or eliminate a range of anti-competitive practices, to conduct inquiries and investigations to establish such practices, to generate awareness about them and to promote good practices. The Authority is also given the power to regulate trade as per sections 9–12. Further, sections 26–32 deal exclusively with trading practices. Checking abuse of dominance is not listed in the powers or functions of the Authority.

14 For definition see ibid section 35.

15 The Authority has the power to entertain complaints from consumers (section 13); to enter into agreements with traders or manufacturers or their associations (section 14); to allow increase in prices of essential goods (section 18(2)); and to support the director general in referring cases of excessive pricing to the Council (section 19). In competition matters, the Authority may take cognisance of matters of its own accord or on receipt of a complaint (section 34) and may provide the parties an opportunity to be heard (section 36).

16 ibid sections 20–22, and 37–38 which allow a party to require the Authority to submit a matter to the Council.

modification, provided it is of the view that the practice is contrary to the 'public interest'.[17] Although the Act does not define 'public interest,' it requires the Council to 'take into account all matters which appear to [it] to be relevant' particularly those that may affect 'competition between persons supplying goods and providing services', 'the price and quality of such goods and services', and 'development of new techniques and products, and facilitating the entry of new competitors into existing markets' in making a judgment in this regard.[18] The Act is silent as to whether the orders of the Council may be appealed or as to the forum to which the appeal may lie.

3.2.1.2 Nepal's Competition Promotion and Market Protection Act 2063, 2007

Nepal enacted the Competition Promotion and Market Protection Act 2063 in January 2007 (hereafter 'the Nepalese Act').[19] The avowed aim of the Act is to make the 'national economy more open, liberal, market-oriented and competitive'; to enhance 'national productivity by developing the business capacity of producers or distributors'; and to maintain 'the economic interests and decency of the general public by doing away with possible unfair competition in trade practices'.[20]

In addition to the usual prohibitions on 'anti-competitive agreements',[21] 'abuse of dominant position',[22] and 'mergers or amalgamations with intent to control competition',[23] the Act specifically prohibits 'bid-rigging',[24] 'exclusive dealing',[25] 'market restriction',[26] tied-selling,[27] 'misleading advertisement',[28] and provides for the regulation of 'abuse of intellectual property'.[29] However, the Act limits its expansive ambit by exempting several industries, activities, and products (including cottage and small industries, the procurement of raw materials, export business, collective bargaining, research and development, management collaboration, collaboration for organisational and procedural improvements intended to enhance trade capacity

[17] ibid section 41(1).
[18] ibid section 41(2).
[19] The Competition Promotion and Market Protection Act 2063, 2007<http://admin.theiguides.org/Media/Documents/CompetitionPromotionMarketProtectionAct2007.pdf#:~:text=This%20Act%20may%20be%20called%20"Competition%20Promotion%20and,Nepal.%20This%20Act%20shall%20come%20into%20force%20immediately> accessed 16 September 2021.
[20] ibid Preamble.
[21] ibid section 3
[22] ibid section 4.
[23] ibid section 5.
[24] ibid section 6.
[25] ibid Section 7.
[26] ibid Section 8.
[27] ibid Section 9.
[28] ibid Section 10.
[29] ibid Section 31.

and agricultural products)[30] and by empowering the government to grant further exemptions if appropriate.[31]

The Act also provides for a Board, with powers of 'formulating policies', 'reviewing laws', and 'raising awareness' 'to enhance fair competition in market by protecting the market'.[32] In terms of the Act, the Board comprises senior government officials, and nominees from industry and consumer rights' organisations, that may be appointed and removed by the government.[33] The Act also requires the government to appoint a 'Market Protection Officer'.[34] In terms of the Act both the Board and the Market Protection Officer are authorised to receive complaints from the public[35] as well as to carry out investigations into alleged violations of the Act,[36] however, the power to adjudicate upon these matters vests exclusively in the courts.[37] Further only the Market Protection Officer has the power to bring a case before the court,[38] while the responsibility for handling the case vests entirely in a 'government attorney'.[39] The Act also allows a party aggrieved by a violation of the Act to directly approach the courts for compensation.[40]

3.2.1.3 Bangladesh Enacts the Competition Act 2012

Bangladesh enacted its Competition Act in June 2012 ('the Bangladeshi Act')[41] with the aim of enhancing economic development and eradicating anti-competitive practices.[42] This Act provides for the establishment of the 'Bangladesh Competition Commission' as an independent statutory body with perpetual succession,[43] comprising a chairperson and not more than four members. The Act requires members of the Commission to have at least fifteen-years experience in 'economics, matters relating to market, or public administration or similar subjects or legal profession or legal affairs activities in different public–private institutions or any other field deemed relevant by the government'. All members are to be appointed by

30 ibid Section 11.
31 ibid Section 29.
32 ibid Section 12(1).
33 ibid Section 12(3).
34 ibid Section 22.
35 ibid Section 23(1).
36 ibid sections 24 and 25.
37 ibid section 14. In terms of section 2(h), 'court' means the commercial bench of such a court as may be designated by the Government of Nepal in consultation with the Supreme Court.
38 ibid section 24.
39 ibid.
40 ibid section 29.
41 Competition Act 2012 <www.dpp.gov.bd/upload_file/gazettes/20533_10683.pdf> accessed 23 October 2020.
42 ibid Preamble.
43 ibid section 5.

the government in accordance with rules made for this purpose.[44] The government also has the power to remove members on specified grounds albeit after affording them an opportunity of being heard.[45]

The Commission has the power to review 'anti-competition agreements',[46] abuse of dominant position,[47] and mergers.[48] However, 'goods or services . . . controlled by the Government' may be excluded from the ambit of the Act if it is in the 'interest of the national security' to do so and if the goods and services are 'not open for private sector'.[49] The Act also authorises the Commission to adjudicate upon anti-competitive agreements, abuse of dominant position or mergers, while offences (including interfering in, contravening or failing to comply with an order of the Commission) under the Act are to be tried by a Magistrate. Persons allows persons aggrieved by the orders of the Commission may approach it for a review of its orders or to appeal against these to the government. It is not clear, however, whether there is a further right of appeal from the review orders of the Commission or of the appeal orders of the government.[50] Appeals from the orders of the magistrate[51] lie to the Court of Sessions, whose orders are to be final.[52]

3.2.1.4 Maldives' Competition Act 2020

Maldives adopted a competition legislation only recently: the Maldives parliament approved the Competition Act 2020 on 18 August 2020 (hereafter 'the Maldives Act') which was ratified by the president on 21 August 2021,[53] to come into effect on 1 March 2021. The Act is to be administered directly by the government through the relevant ministry and will apply to all commercial transactions 'carried out by enterprises' in the Maldives as well as those that are 'carried out overseas but that impact the competitiveness of any market in the Maldives'. The Act provides for checking anti-competitive agreements in relation to goods and services, excluding agreements within a single group of companies, and agreements with a public interest dimension. The Act also prohibits abuse of dominant position and mergers that result in 'substantial reduction in competitiveness in any market' but excludes mergers 'finalised between two government companies, and mergers that provide services which serve public economic interests' provided these have been approved by the minister in accordance with the Act. The Act also exempts mergers which

44 ibid section 7.
45 ibid section 9.
46 ibid section 15.
47 ibid section 16.
48 ibid sections 20–21.
49 ibid section 4.
50 ibid section 29.
51 ibid section 25.
52 ibid section 30.
53 Press Release <https://presidency.gov.mv/Press/Article/23615> accessed 16 September 2021.

though result in substantial reduction in competitiveness provide significant other economic benefits.[54]

The Act mandates the relevant ministry to establish a mechanism to address complaints regarding contraventions of the Act and allows parties aggrieved by decisions of the ministry to file appeals before the courts.[55]

3.2.2 *Countries still in the Adoption Stage*

Of the South Asian Six, Afghanistan and Bhutan have still to adopt a competition legislation. However, while Afghanistan has a draft competition act which indicates its intention to adopt such legislation, Bhutan believes that a competition policy is sufficient for its purposes.

3.2.2.1 Enactment Interrupted: Afghanistan and the Draft Competition Act

The draft Afghanistan Competition Act prepared as far back as 2011 (hereafter 'the draft Afghan Act')[56] aims to establish an independent 'Competition and Consumer Authority' (section 10) comprising five members, to be appointed by the government.[57] The government also has the power to remove members, albeit on specified grounds and after an inquiry.[58] The proposed Authority is embedded in the Ministry of Commerce[59] which has the power to supersede the Authority in specified circumstances.[60] The draft Act confers on the Authority the power to investigate and sanction anti-competitive agreements and abuse of dominant position, to regulate combinations, and to check hoarding.[61] The Act allows appeals from certain orders of the Authority to lie to a specially designated bench of the Commercial Court[62] and from certain other orders to lie to a especially designated Competition Court.[63] Appeals from orders of the Competition Court are to lie to the Supreme Court.[64]

3.2.2.2 Bhutan: To Enact or Not to Enact?

Bhutan claims not to need a competition legislation largely due to the smallness of its economy. In 2015, however, Bhutan adopted its first comprehensive competition

54 Competition Act <www.ctlstrategies.com/latest/competition-act/> accessed 19 October 2020.
55 ibid.
56 Draft Competition Act <https://documentcloud.adobe.com/link/review?uri=urn:aaid:scds:US:8e119aae-d5c9–4600-9c22–056aac34d4b6> accessed 17 September 2021.
57 ibid section 10.
58 ibid section 11.
59 Draft Competition Act <https://documentcloud.adobe.com/link/review?uri=urn:aaid:scds:US:8e119aae-d5c9–4600-9c22–056aac34d4b6> accessed 17 September 2021.
60 ibid section 46.
61 ibid section 3–9, 20–22.
62 ibid section 31.
63 ibid section 32.
64 ibid section 33.

policy[65] which envisaged establishment of a 'National Competition Council' to ensure that competition principles was followed across the government.[66] In 2020, Bhutan revised and updated this Policy (hereafter 'the Bhutanese Policy')[67] with the aim to allow Bhutanese citizens the right to practice any lawful trade and to foster private sector development through fair competition and by preventing commercial monopolies.[68] The Policy prohibits monopolies, abuse of dominant position, cartels, anti-competitive mergers, and deceptive marketing practices[69] and applies to government organisations and business entities.[70] The Policy excludes from its ambit economic activities that are in the interest of national security or have strategic importance.[71] The Office of Consumer Protection, established under the Bhutan Consumer Protection Act 2012,[72] has the power to review and monitor the implementation of the Policy.[73]

3.2.3 *Adoption of competition laws in the South Asian Perspective*

The review of the adoption of competition legislation across South Asia paints a very positive picture: six out of eight South Asian countries have completed the successive deliberation and the enactment phases of the adoption stage and have acquired some version of a modern competition legislation. Only Afghanistan and Bhutan are still to adopt a competition law and while Afghanistan has a draft legislation which may be enacted at a future date, Bhutan has not made any commitment in this regard (Figure 3.1).

However, a closer look at the competition legislation that these countries have adopted, or propose to adopt, reveals considerable variations amongst them. While some of these legislations provide for the establishment of independent, autonomous competition authorities, others fully embed competition enforcement in the country's pre-existing executive framework. Further, certain competition laws allow the competition authorities to take enforcement actions, while others envisage these authorities as intermediaries between the public and the courts. The greater number of these legislations vest the power of appointment and removal of members of their

65 Competition Policy 2015 <www.gnhc.gov.bt/en/wp-content/uploads/2017/05/Final-Draft-Competition-Policy-181114.pdf> accessed 17 September 2021.

66 ibid Article 14.

67 Competition Policy 2020 <www.gnhc.gov.bt/en/wp-content/uploads/2020/03/National-Competition-Policy-2020.pdf> accessed 17 September 2021.

68 ibid Article 3.

69 ibid Article 5.

70 ibid Article 2.

71 ibid Article 6.

72 Consumer Protection Act 2012 <http://extwprlegs1.fao.org/docs/pdf/bhu129924.pdf> accessed 19 September 2021.

73 ibid.

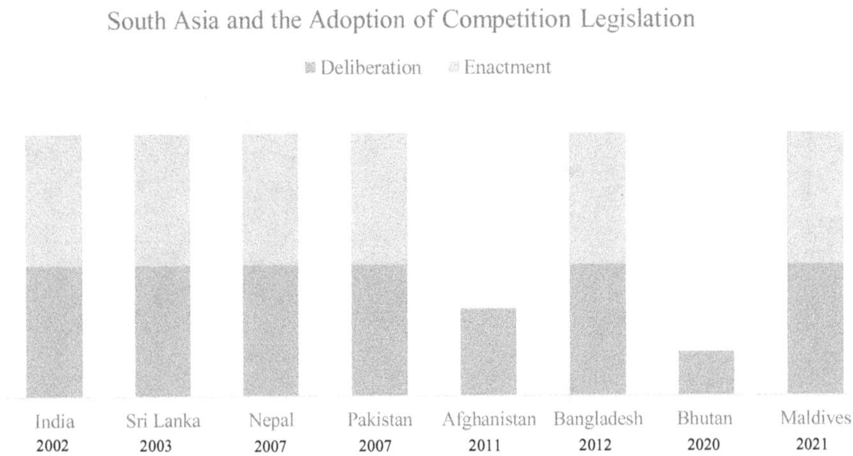

FIGURE 3.1. Adoption of competition legislation across South Asia (in descending chronological order)

competition authorities or boards entirely in the government, thereby giving the government exclusive control over their composition. These legislations also experiment with different competition enforcement pathways: the legislations in certain countries allow appeals from the orders of the competition authority to lie to independent, specialist tribunals, and from orders of the tribunals to lie to the general courts pre-existing in the country, while in others, the aggrieved party may only approach the government for redress (Table 3.1).

3.3 PRE-CONDITIONS OF TRANSFER AND THE ADOPTION PROCESS IN THE SOUTH ASIAN SIX

The variations in the substance of the competition legislation adopted by the South Asian Six and the enforcement authorities they create are largely attributable to the contexts and the adoption strategies that shaped them. This section groups the South Asian Six in accordance with their governance models and examines their individual pre-existing conditions of transfer, their respective motivations for adopting or engaging with adopting modern competition legislation, and the interplay of their institutions in the adoption process.

3.3.1 *Democracies and the Adoption of Competition Legislation*

Of the South Asian Six, Sri Lanka and Bangladesh are both former British colonies. Sri Lanka achieved dominion status under the Ceylon Independence Act 1947 and, since then, has adopted two constitutions – in 1972 and 1978. The 1978 Constitution

TABLE 3.1. *A comparative review of South Asian competition legislation*

COUNTRY (in the order of adoption)	Competition Authorities			Competition Enforcement Pathway
	Structure	Mandate	Composition	
India	• Comprising 2–6 members; • Independent; • Collegiate; • Government may also issue directives to supersede the authority.	• Specialist competition body with an advocacy and enforcement mandate including the power to investigate, take cognizance of, and sanction; anti-competitive agreements; abuse of dominance, and mergers. • Government has the power to exempt businesses and entities.	• Appointment of members on recommendation of a statutorily prescribed selection committee; • Removal by the government on specified grounds and upon conclusion of a supreme court enquiry.	**CCI issues order** ⬇ **Tribunal hears appeal** ⬇ **Supreme Court hears final appeal**
Sri Lanka	• Comprising minimum 10 members; • Chairman and 3 members to be government representatives; • Collegiate.	• Mandate includes investigating: trade, competition, and consumer issues (including hoarding).	Members to be appointed and removed by the government.	**Authority investigates** ⬇ **Consumer Affairs Council adjudicates** ⬇ **Appeal from order of the Council** **?**

Nepal	• No independent authority established; • Board set up comprising government officers and nominees.	• Formulating policies, reviewing laws, and raising awareness regarding: anti-competitive agreements; abuse of dominant position; mergers abuse of intellectual property. • Cottage & small industries, procurement of raw materials, export business, collective bargaining, research and development etc., excluded from the Act.	Government has exclusive power to appoint and remove members of the Board.	**policies and reviews laws, possibly complaints** ↓ **MPO files cases** ↓ **Commercial Court adjudicates** ↓ **Appeal from the order of the Commercial Court?** **?**
Pakistan	• Comprising 5–7 members; • 2 members may be government representatives; • Independent; • Collegiate.	• Specialist competition body with an advocacy and enforcement mandate including the power to investigate, take cognisance of, and sanction: anti-competitive agreements;	• Government to appoint in consultation with the Chairman • Government may remove on grounds specified in the Act and after an impartial inquiry (under rules made by the government) unless	**CCP issues order** ↓ **Tribunal hears appeal** ↓ **Supreme Court hears final appeal**

(continued)

TABLE 3.1. (*continued*)

COUNTRY (in the order of adoption)	Competition Authorities			Competition Enforcement Pathway
	Structure	Mandate	Composition	
		abuse of dominance; mergers. deceptive marketing practices. • Government has the power to exempt businesses and entities.	removal ordered by a competent court.	
Bangladesh	• Independent; • Chairman and 4 members; • Collegiate.	• Regulates: anti-competitive agreements, and; abuse of dominant position. • Public sector goods exempted in the interest of national security.	• Government to appoint in accordance with rules made for this purpose. • Government to remove members on specified grounds and after providing an opportunity of being heard.	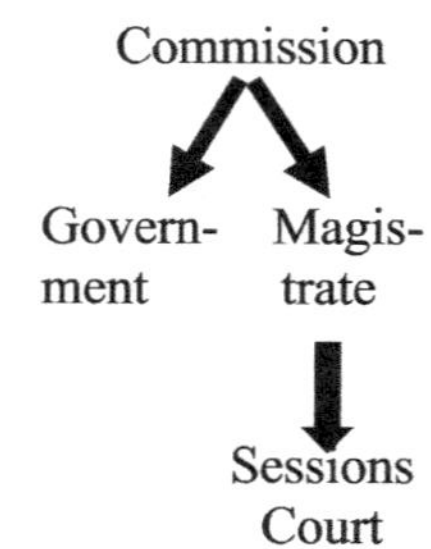
Maldives	No independent authority.	• To review anti-competitive agreements; abuse of dominance; mergers. Act does not apply to: government actions and those exempted under the Special Economic Zone Act.	Not applicable.	

		agreements within group of companies and with a public interest dimension; mergers with significant economic benefits.		
Afghanistan	• Competition and Consumer Authority; • Comprising 5 members; • Embedded in the Ministry of Commerce; • Minister of Commerce has power to supersede the Authority in specified circumstances.	• Authority had the power to review and regulate anti-competitive agreements; abuse of dominant position; combinations; hoarding.	• The government has the power to appoint members; • Government has the power to remove members albeit on specified grounds and after an inquiry.	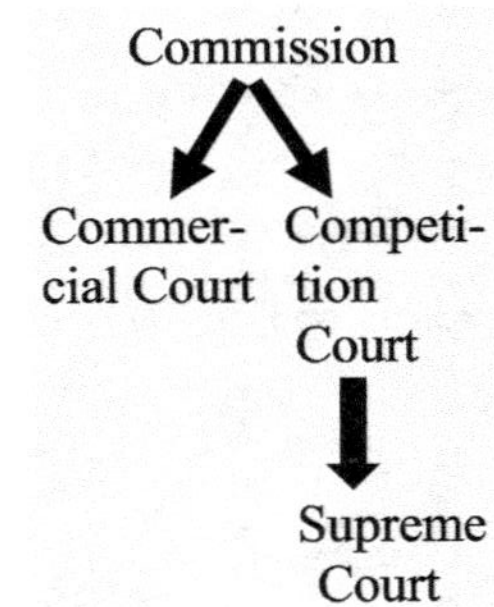
Bhutan	• No competition authority; • Office of Consumer Protection to implement the policy.	• Prohibits: monopolies; dominant position; cartels; anti-competitive mergers; deceptive marketing practices. • Economic activities in the national interest excluded.	Office of Consumer protection established under the Ministry of Economic Affairs and comprises government Officers.	No implementation trajectory specified.

has been amended twenty times but has never been suspended.[74] Bangladesh on the other hand was part of Pakistan until 1971 when it declared independence, prior to which it was part of India until 1947. Bangladesh adopted its first constitution in 1972 which has been amended eighteen times and was suspended once between 1982 and 1986.[75] In 1995 both Sri Lanka and Bangladesh joined the WTO.[76]

3.3.1.1 The Sri Lankan Context

Sri Lanka was motivated by both domestic needs and external pressure to consider a modern competition legislation. In 1977 Sri Lanka had embarked upon a programme of economic liberalisation and had enacted the Fair Trading Commission Act 1987 with the aim of curbing monopolies, preventing anti-competitive practices, and regulating mergers contrary to the public interest.[77] However, the Fair Trading Commission, established in pursuance of the Act, did not have the power to hear competition cases or to impose sanctions.[78] Soon after Sri Lanka joined the WTO, the WTO Secretariat carried out a trade review of its policies and practices and noted that it was necessary to further liberalise the Sri Lankan economy to ensure its competitiveness.[79] Sri Lanka first responded to this observation by supplementing its Fair Trading Act with sector-specific regulation, however, after a change of government in December 2001 and with the support of the World Bank and the United States,[80] it gradually moved towards an integrated and holistic trade and competition regulation regime, replacing the Fair Trading Act by the Consumer Affairs Authority Act 2003 (or the Sri Lankan Act as earlier defined).[81] It is not known whether and to what extent Sri Lanka consulted foreign competition legislation or domestic stakeholders in drafting the Sri Lankan Act. However, the fact that the Act was enacted through the parliament in accordance with the legislative procedures prescribed in the Sri Lankan constitution, suggests

[74] Sri Lanka <www.countries/countries/Asia/Sri_Lanka?lang=en> accessed 21 September 2021.

[75] Bangladesh <www.countries/countries/Asia/Bangladesh?lang=en> accessed 21 September 2021.

[76] WTO Members and Observers <www.wto.org/english/thewto_e/whatis_e/tif_e/org6_e.htm> accessed 21 September 2021.

[77] Fair Trading Commission Act 1987 <www.commonlii.org/lk/legis/num_act/ftca101987282/> accessed 2 November 2020.

[78] Apsara Thurairetnam, 'Competition Regimes: Sri Lanka' 161–62 <https://competitionregimes.com/pdf/AsiaPacific/30-Sri%20Lanka.pdf> accessed 2 November 2020.

[79] Trade Policy Review, Sri Lanka November 1995 <www.wto.org/english/tratop_e/tpr_e/tp017_e.htm> accessed 2 November 2020. Also see Consumer Affairs Authority Annual Report 2015, 21 <http://caa.gov.lk/web/images/AnnualReport/English/AR_2015_Eng.pdf> accessed 23 September 2021.

[80] Prime Minister Hon. Ranil Wickremesinghe, elected to office in 2001, was keen to carry out market reforms and was negotiating a free trade agreement with the United States. However, this initiative was abandoned in 2004 after the government was removed from office. See 'Parliament of Sri Lanka' <www.parliament.lk/en/prime-ministers> accessed 22 September 2021 and 'US ready to pursue FTA with Sri Lanka' <www.bilaterals.org/?us-ready-to-pursue-fta-with-sri> accessed 22 September 2021.

[81] See n.6.

that there was a degree of consultation with stakeholders with regard to the content of the legislation which further suggests they had at least constructively consented to the enactment.

3.3.1.2 Bangladesh's Efforts to Adopt an Enlightened Legislation

At the time of its independence from Pakistan in 1971, Bangladesh inherited the laws prevailing in Pakistan,[82] including Pakistan's Monopolies and Restrictive Trade Practices (Control and Prevention) Ordinance 1970.[83] However, Bangladesh's immediate economic priority at the time was enhancing its GDP rather than regulating monopolies,[84] and therefore, the Ordinance was not implemented.[85] Further Bangladesh espoused socialist policies shortly after independence which brought industrial production in the country nearly to a halt.[86] By 1973, the government gradually started revising its nationalisation policy and in 1979 replaced it with a nineteen-point program that emphasised greater productivity and efficiency. The government also returned many state-owned enterprises to the private sector.[87] The growth of the Bangladeshi economy from 1980 onwards was attributed to these policies.[88]

Soon after joining the WTO in 1995, Bangladesh once again considered the idea of regulating monopolies and to this end, adopting a modern competition policy. In a 2002 statement submitted at a regional meeting of the WTO Competition Working Group,[89] the Bangladesh Minister of Commerce noted that while there

82 Constitution of Bangladesh 1972, Article 149.

83 In pursuance of the Bangladesh Laws (Revision and Declaration) Act 1973, Bangladesh replaced the words 'Pakistan', 'Central Government', and 'rupees' throughout the Ordinance, with 'Bangladesh', 'Government', and 'Taka' respectively.

84 At the time of its independence in 1971, Bangladesh's population density was over 500 persons per km and was growing at 3 per cent annually. The country's cultivable land frontier was exhausted; only 6 per cent of the GDP originated from modern manufacturing (mostly jute and cotton textiles), and 85 per cent of the export earnings came from raw jute and jute goods which had weak international markets. Businessmen, mostly of Pakistani origin, had left the country, productive capacity and infrastructure had been damaged by war, and domestic savings had fallen to almost zero. See ODI Briefing Paper, 'Bangladesh Economic Performance and Prospects' (Overseas Development Institute 1990) <https://cdn.odi.org/media/documents/6760.pdf> accessed 22 September 2021.

85 Karen Ellis, Rohit Singh, Shaikh Eskander, Iftekharul Huq 'Assessing the Economic Impact of Competition: Findings from Bangladesh' (Overseas Development Institute 2010) <https://cdn.odi.org/media/documents/6058.pdf> accessed 22 September 2021.

86 Encyclopedia Britannica 'Economy of Bangladesh' <www.britannica.com/place/Bangladesh/Economy> accessed 20 October 2020.

87 ibid.

88 ODI Briefing Paper 'Bangladesh: Economic Performance and Prospects' (Overseas Development Institute 1990) <www.odi.org/sites/odi.org.uk/files/odi-assets/publications-opinion-files/6760.pdf> 1, accessed 20 October 2020.

89 In 2001 at the Doha Ministerial Conference, Ministers instructed the Working Group to focus inter alia on support for progressive re-inforcement of competition institutions in developing countries through capacity building. <www.wto.org/english/tratop_e/comp_e/history_e.htm> accessed 20 October 2020.

was growing awareness in Bangladesh of the need to 'control anti-competitive conduct by firms and multi-national companies' it was important to 'keep in the perspective the special needs of LDCs such as Bangladesh' especially the potential of 'enterprise behaviour' to give rise 'to problems in international trade relations', and to extract gains out of the economy.[90] The minister was particularly concerned about Bangladesh becoming 'trapped in an agreement which [it was] not fully prepared to negotiate and in which the dispute settlement mechanism would be mainly used against the weaker and upcoming countries'.[91] He therefore urged Bangladesh to take 'a cautious view to the whole issue of competition policy',[92] and emphasised the importance of building capacity before adopting competition legislation. He also urged that competition laws designed for countries such as Bangladesh 'not only be effective' but also 'equitable'.[93]

Throughout this period UNCTAD engaged extensively with Bangladesh to raise awareness of and build capacity for addressing competition issues.[94] By 2004, even though competition was no longer on the WTO agenda, a Bangladeshi thinktank, in partnership with an Indian thinktank and with support from the UK Department for International Development (DFID), launched a project to raise competition awareness in the country.[95] The project report, issued in 2005, noted that 'a healthy competition policy and Law [was] a necessity for the economic advancement of developing countries',[96] and that a survey carried out as part of the project showed that there was 'a consensus among stakeholders for an urgent need to regulate the market in terms of anti-competitive practices, to institute a mechanism to implement the law, and finally to develop the capacity of the stakeholders, empowering them to create an enabling environment where competition can flourish, benefiting both consumers and businesses'.[97] To this end, the report called for the establishment of 'a modern, independent, and transparent Competition Authority'[98] and for the enactment of an overarching competition law for Bangladesh, through

90 Statement of the Hon'ble Minister for Commerce, Mr Amir K Mahmud Chowdhury, MP, at the Regional Seminar on Competition Policy and Multilateral Negotiations, Hong Kong: April 2002 <www.iprsonline.org/resources/competition.html> accessed 21 October 2020.

91 ibid 3.

92 ibid 5.

93 ibid.

94 For instance, UNCTAD had delivered 'Training of Trainers' intensive courses in 2001 and 2002. UNCTAD 'Competition Policy for Development: A Report on UNCTAD's Capacity Building and Technical Assistance Programme' <https://unctad.org/system/files/official-document/ditcclp20042_en.pdf> accessed 22 October 2020.

95 'Promoting Competition Policy and Law in Bangladesh: A Civil Society Perspective' (CUTS International 2006) <https://cuts-ccier.org/pdf/BangladeshCAD.pdf> accessed 22 October 2020.

96 ibid 7.

97 ibid.

98 ibid 27.

consultations with all stakeholders.[99] Also the 2005 Poverty Reduction Strategy paper, prepared by Bangladesh in consultation with the International Monetary Fund (IMF) and the World Bank,[100] identified effective competition policy as an important factor in accelerating poverty reduction in the country,[101] and announced that it had sought technical assistance from the World Bank to draft a competition law.[102]

In 2008 Bangladesh produced its first draft competition law. However, this draft could not be enacted due to resistance by the business community that viewed is the law as a foreign intervention and an attempt on the part of the government to intimidate the community.[103] Despite these reservations, in June 2012 Bangladesh, with the support of the DFID and the International Finance Corporation (IFC), enacted a Competition Act (earlier defined as the Bangladeshi Act) as part of a wider programme of technical assistance for enhancing its investment climate.[104] Interestingly, however, contrary to the expectations created by the Bangladeshi stance before the WTO, the Act spoke only of economic development and sanctioning anti-competitive practices and made no reference to inclusivity or eradication of poverty.[105] The Act also had strong Indian overtones,[106] albeit

99 ibid 28.

100 IMF Country Report No. 05/410 'Bangladesh: Poverty Reduction Strategy Paper' (International Monetary Fund 2005).

101 ibid 20. Also see section 5.B.6.2 pp 72–73 which details a competition policy generally associated with developed countries and not a special adaptation, keeping in mind Bangladesh's status as a developing country.

102 Mark Dutz and R Shyam Khemani 'Competition Law and Policy: Challenges in South Asia' (The World Bank 2007), Acknowledgements.

103 Nazmul Haque Tonmoy, 'The Absence of Political Will to Implement Competition Policy in Bangladesh is a Major Obstruction of its Rapidly Growing Economy' (2018) 2(3) Comparative Law Working Papers 7. News reports published during this period drew support from the Indian Supreme Court's decision in favour of competition regulation. See, Financial Express 'Competition Commission: The Task Ahead' <https://thefinancialexpress.com.bd/views/columns/competition-commission-the-task-ahead> accessed 26 October 2020.

104 'IFC Helps Bangladesh Implement Mechanism to Make Regulations Efficient, Improving Governance' <https://ifcext.ifc.org/ifcext/pressroom/IFCPressRoom.nsf/0/27D09BF91AB7305E85257A97001879A2> accessed 23 October 2020. The first phase of the project was completed circa 2015 (Nathan 'End of Program Evaluation of Bangladesh Investment Climate Fund (BICF)' <www.nathaninc.com/end-of-program-evaluation-of-bangladesh-investment-climate-fund-bicf/www.nathaninc.com/end-of-program-evaluation-of-bangladesh-investment-climate-fund-bicf/> accessed 23 October 2020) and a second phase was launched in 2016. ('Enhancing Competitiveness in the Bangladesh Economy Continues to Form part of the FCO Agenda.' UKAid 'Bangladesh Investment Climate Fund, Phase 2' <https://devtracker.fcdo.gov.uk/projects/GB-1-204951/documents> accessed 23 October 2020).

105 n.41 Preamble.

106 See, for instance, the concept of 'combination' and of 'enterprise' in section 2 of the Bangladeshi Act and the concept of 'deemed' anti-competitive affect and of 'adverse affect on competition' in section 15 both of which it shares with the Indian Act. Also see n.103 which makes this comment about the 2008 draft as well.

intermixed with certain features that related specifically to the Bangladesh context.[107]

3.3.2 *Adopting Competition Laws in Former Monarchies*

Both Nepal and Maldives had been traditional monarchies before becoming independent constitutional monarchies in 1948 and 1968 respectively[108] Also, although the countries were never fully colonised, they had remained under British influence for significant periods of their histories.[109] Since its independence in 1948, Nepal had adopted seven constitutions the latest in 2015,[110] while Maldives had adopted three constitutions, the latest in 2008.[111] The modern constitutions of both countries prescribed separation of powers and vested the power of governance in the elected government while retaining the monarch as the titular head of state.[112] Nepal joined the WTO in 2004 while Maldives has been a member since 1995.[113]

3.3.2.1 The Context in Nepal

Shortly before joining the WTO in 2004, Nepalese thinktanks, in conjunction with an Indian thinktank and the DFID had already started investigating the state of competition in the Nepalese economy and participating in forums organised by UNCTAD to build domestic competition capacity.[114] Subsequently in its

[107] For instance, see Section 2.1(c) above particularly with reference to the enforcement pathway prescribed in the Bangladeshi Act.

[108] For Nepal see <www.constituteproject.org/countries/Asia/Nepal?lang=en> and 'Constitutional History of Nepal' <https://constitutionnet.org/country/nepal-country-constitutional-profile> accessed 22 September 2021; for Maldives see <www.constituteproject.org/countries/Asia/Maldives?lang=en> accessed 22 September 2021 and 'A Short Constitutional History of Maldives' <https://minivannewsarchive.com/politics/a-short-constitutional-history-of-the-maldives-73902> accessed 23 September 2021. While Nepal's constitutional history has been complicated due to war and internal strife, Maldives has been largely peaceful. For most of its long history, Maldives has been ruled by sultans, who from the sixteenth century onwards, have ruled under the direction and protection of successive European powers. From 1796, the archipelago became a protectorate of the British, a status that was formalised in 1887. In 1932, Maldives acquired its first constitution, however, it was only in 1968, after having obtained full political independence from the British in 1965, that Maldives abolished the sultanate and declared a new republic.

[109] For Nepal see <www.britishempire.co.uk/maproom/nepal.htm> accessed 22 September 2021 and for Maldives see <www.britishempire.co.uk/maproom/maldives.htm> accessed 22 September 2021.

[110] See n.108. The Nepalese constitution remained suspended from 1960 to 1962.

[111] ibid.

[112] Nepal Constitution 2015, Article 56 <www.constituteproject.org/constitution/Nepal_2016.pdf?lang=en> accessed 22 September 2021; Maldives Constitution 2008, Articles 5–7 <www.countries/constitution/Maldives_2008.pdf?lang=en> accessed 22 September 2021.

[113] See n.76.

[114] See generally Ratnakar Adhikari 'Discussion Paper on Competition Policy in Small Economies' (South Asia Watch on Trade, Economics and Environment (SAWTEE) and

discussions with the WTO, the Nepalese government made a voluntary commitment to adopt a competition law and in 2007, well after the subject of competition had been dropped from the WTO agenda,[115] Nepal followed through with this commitment and adopted the Nepalese Act.[116]

When the Act was enacted on 14 January 2007,[117] Nepal was governed directly by the King who had dissolved the parliament in 2002[118] and was only one day away from re-instating the parliament under the Interim Constitution 2007.[119] The parliament, therefore, had no role in the adoption of the Act. Certainly, some features of the Act, particularly the structure of the Board and the enforcement pathway, echo the approach adopted by Nepal in other comparable laws such as the Consumer Protection Act that was in force in the country at the time,[120] others reflect the recommendations made in deliberations between Nepalese and Indian thinktanks and multi-lateral agencies.[121]

3.3.2.2 Maldives and Competition Legislation for a Small Economy

The smaller, though wealthier and more developed Maldives seems to be an unlikely candidate for competition reform.[122] However, since its independence Maldives had maintained a close relationship with multi-lateral agencies and bodies which is likely to have motivated it to take action in this regard. After becoming a member of the World Bank in 1978 Maldives had long standing implemented

CUTS Centre for International Trade, Economics and Environment (CUTS-CITEE) 2002) <www.sawtee.org/publications/Discussion-Paper-3.pdf> accessed 29 October 2020; Ratnakar Adhikari 'Competition, Competitiveness and Development: Lessons From Developing Countries' UNCTAD/DITC/CLP/2004/1 (UNCTAD 2004) (<https://unctad.org/system/files/official-document/ditcclp20041_en.pdf>) accessed 29 October 2004. Also see the completion report of the Competition Advocacy and Education Programme conducted by SAWTEE in conjunction with DFID's Nepal Office <www.sawtee.org/programme/completed-programmes/competition-advocacy-and-education-programme-(caep).html> accessed 31 October 2020.

115 Apurva Kathiwada 'Nepal' 2 <https://cuts-ccier.org/pdf/23-Nepal.pdf> accessed 30 October 2020.

116 See n.19.

117 Nepali Date 2063-09-30.

118 'Nepal Parliament Dissolved' <http://news.bbc.co.uk/1/hi/world/south_asia/2003085.stm> accessed 23 September 2021.

119 The Interim Constitution of Nepal 2063 (2007) <www.satp.org/satporgtp/countries/nepal/document/papers/Interim_Constitution_2007.pdf> accessed 23 September 2021; Constitutional History of Nepal <https://constitutionnet.org/country/nepal-country-constitutional-profile> accessed 22 September 2021.

120 The Consumer Protection Act 1997 <www.lawcommission.gov.np/en/archives/category/documents/law-archives/statutes-acts-law-archives/consumer-protection-act-2054-1998> accessed 22 September 2021.

121 See n.114.

122 The World Bank in Maldives <www.worldbank.org/en/country/maldives/overview> accessed 19 October 2020.

thirty-two projects (with over $295 million in support) across many development areas;[123] the United Nations Development Programme (UNDP) also had a presence in Maldives since 1978 and had partnered with the government and non-governmental agencies in several projects relating to the environment, climate change, and governance.[124] In 1993 Maldives had become a member of the General Agreement on Tariffs and Trade (GATT) and in 1995 of the WTO[125] Since 1999 Maldives had also been worked closely with the IMF.[126] From 2000 onwards, Maldives had embarked upon a long-term plan to re-organise the Maldivian economy and political system. To this end in 2008 Maldives adopted a new constitution, which not only strengthened constitutional checks and balances in the country but also established the country's first Supreme Court.[127] In 2012 Maldives had implemented the Asian Development Bank's 'Inclusive Micro-, Small-, and Medium-Sized Enterprise Development Project' with a particular focus on enhancing its business environment and business support infrastructure[128] and had committed to adopting a competition law. In 2016 Maldives first circulated a draft competition bill for consultation. However, this bill was not enacted into law.[129] Multi-lateral agencies, nevertheless, kept the issue alive in the Maldivian reform agenda.[130]

It was finally in 2019 that the Maldives government, with the assistance of the United Nations Development Programme (UNDP), pulled together the various projects it was pursuing with different multi-lateral partners to create a holistic Strategic Action Plan 2019–23[131] in which it identified Maldives' economic, social,

[123] ibid.

[124] 'About UNDP in Maldives' <www.mv.undp.org/content/maldives/en/home/about-us.html> accessed 19 October 2020.

[125] See n.76.

[126] International Monetary Fund: Maldives <www.imf.org/en/Countries/MDV> accessed 19 October 2020.

[127] Maldives Constitution 2008, Article 145 <www.constituteproject.org/constitution/Maldives_2008.pdf?lang=en> accessed 23 September 2021.

[128] Maldives: Inclusive Micro-, Small-, and Medium-Sized Enterprise Development Project <www.adb.org/projects/43566-013/main#project-pds> accessed 19 October 2020.

[129] 2019 Investment Climate Statements: Maldives <www.state.gov/reports/2019-investment-climate-statements/maldives/> accessed 19 October 2020.

[130] IMF Country Report No. 19/102 'Technical Assistance Report: Public Investment Management Assessment' para 35 <www.imf.org/en/Publications/CR/Issues/2019/04/17/Maldives-Technical-Assistance-Report-Public-Investment-Management-Assessment-46814> accessed 19 October 2020. Also in 2016, Maldives had invited the IMF's Fiscal Affairs Department to visit the country for a Public Investment Management Assessment (PIMA) and in its 2017 report the IMF observed that the regulatory frameworks in place in Maldives provided for competition in some but not all public utility sectors.

[131] Strategic Action Plan <https://presidency.gov.mv/SAP/> accessed 19 October 2020. The plan was the culmination of extensive consultations with a wide range of stakeholders including government ministries, independent state institutions, state-owned enterprises, and civil society organisations. The compilation of the Plan was led by key ministries and was co-ordinated by the Policy Office of the President's Office together with support from the Ministry of National

and governance reform priorities, the steps needed to accomplish these,[132] and the mechanisms for their delivery.[133] As part of this plan, Maldives recommended the adoption of competition legislation by 2020 to 'facilitate a conducive business environment' and to 'ensure a business environment that is safe, fair and transparent with emphasis on strengthening consumer protection and promoting intellectual property rights'.[134] In September 2020 Maldives finally adopted the Maldives Act in pursuance of this agenda.[135]

3.3.3 *Competition in Hard Places: The Context in Afghanistan and Bhutan*

The two remaining South Asian Six – Afghanistan and Bhutan – have not adopted competition legislation, at least not yet. However, these countries are not only at very different stages of preparation in this regard – Afghanistan has already prepared a draft competition law while Bhutan contends that it does not need a competition law and a competition policy is sufficient for its purposes – but also have very different political and economic environments which are likely influence the future of competition. Bhutan, though not a parliamentary democracy, has enjoyed a reasonably stable political environment and has developed a development management system founded on the principle of Gross National Happiness (GNH).[136] Afghanistan's history on the other hand is a saga of decades of wars, civil strife, and constitutional instability: Afghanistan was a traditional monarchy until 1964 when it became a constitutional monarchy before being declared a Republic in 1973.[137] From 1978 until 2000 the Republic was embroiled in conflict, first with the Soviets and then with the Taliban.[138] In 2001, Afghanistan adopted an interim administrative framework under the Bonn Agreement brokered by the UN, which

Planning and Infrastructure and was completed over a five-month period. Prior to this in October 2000 Maldives it had engaged the International Trade Institute of Singapore (ITIS) to develop the Strategic Economic Plan (SEP). Interestingly, like the IMF PIMA report in 2017 (n.130), the ITIS had also identified lack of competition in the utilities sector (especially electricity and telecommunication) as a stumbling block in Maldives' the drive towards economic efficiency and had recommended the adoption of appropriate competition legislation. <https://sustainabledevelopment.un.org/content/documents/1416Maldives-strategic%20economic%20plan.pdf> accessed 19 October 2020.

132 ibid 10–12.

133 ibid 15.

134 ibid 86.

135 See n.53 and 54 and text thereto.

136 The World Bank in Bhutan <www.worldbank.org/en/country/bhutan/overview> accessed 14 October 2020.

137 'A Brief History of Afghanistan' <https://newint.org/features/2008/11/01/afghanistan-history> accessed 12 October 2020.

138 Afghan War 1978–92 <www.britannica.com/event/Afghan-War> accessed 12 October 2020.

was replaced in 2004 by the new Constitution of Afghanistan.[139] In 2016 Afghanistan also became a member of the WTO.[140] At the time of writing, Afghanistan had once again fallen into the hands of the Taliban and the fate of its constitution as well as its engagement with multi-lateral agencies was once again rendered uncertain.[141]

3.3.3.1 Afghanistan: Between the Draft and its Enactment

Afghanistan's 2004 Constitution had been in place for only about six years when it commenced deliberations for the adoption of a competition law. According to contemporaneous news reports, the Afghan government considered adopting this law due to fear on the part of the 'government and international organisations that as Afghanistan's markets opened, its valuable state assets would be vulnerable to oligarchs who would move quickly to secure monopolies over them'.[142] The deliberation phase in Afghanistan was funded by the DFID, that commissioned a UK thinktank to draft a competition regime for the country. This UK thinktank, in turn, engaged an Indian law firm to assist in deliberating and drafting appropriate competition legislation for the country. In drafting the law, the Indian law firm met with Afghan government officials to understand 'the kind of concepts Afghanistan needs' and incorporated these in the draft law modelled on UNCTAD and Organisation for Economic Co-operation and Development (OECD) templates.[143]

3.3.3.2 Bhutan: Too Small for Competition?

Bhutan's small economy is based on agriculture, forestry, and hydropower and is defined by its close relationship with India. Agriculture and forestry are primary sources of livelihood for more than half of Bhutan's population while hydropower comprises 40 per cent of its total exports and 25 per cent of its total revenue.[144] India is also the financier and buyer of Bhutan's hydropower projects and in 2008 agreed to build twelve new hydropower dams in Bhutan by 2020. In 2017 Bhutan signed a memorandum of understanding with Bangladesh and India to jointly construct a

139 J Alexander Thier, 'The Making of a Constitution in Afghanistan' State Reconstruction and International Engagement in Afghanistan, 30 May–1 June 2003, London School of Economics and Political Science and University of Bonn.

140 See n.76.

141 'Taliban Announces New Government in Afghanistan' <www.aljazeera.com/news/2021/9/7/taliban-announce-acting-ministers-of-new-government> accessed 23 September 2021.

142 'Indian Law Firm ELP Drafts Afghanistan's Competition Act' <www.legallyindia.com/content/indian-law-firm-elp-drafts-afghanistans-competition-act-20101210-1604> accessed 13 October 2020.

143 ibid.

144 'Bhutan Economy Profile' <www.indexmundi.com/bhutan/economy_profile.html> accessed 14 October 2020.

new hydropower plant for exporting electricity to Bangladesh.[145] Bhutan also shares a close economic relationship with India: 80 per cent of Bhutan's imports come from India; the Bhutanese currency is pegged to the Indian rupee, and India is also Bhutan's primary source of foreign aid.[146]

Given the close economic relationship between India and Bhutan it is not surprising that in 1992, just as India was opening up its economy, the Bhutanese government also initiated a process of de-monopolisation, generating greater competitiveness and enhancing consumer choice in the country by requiring companies supplying goods to the country, to engage with more than one dealer.[147] In the years that followed, the Bhutanese government adopted several policies and laws to create an enabling environment for the private sector including a Companies Act, Commercial Sale of Goods Regulation, Industrial Property Regulation, and De-monopolisation policy, and so on.[148] By 1999 Bhutan had also created sectoral regulators, for instance in the telecom sector,[149] and by 2001 it was contemplating consumer protection legislation to pursue the dual aims of promoting consumer welfare and competition in the country.[150] In 2012, Bhutan adopted a Consumer Protection Act,[151] (intended to be a hybrid consumer and competition instrument), on the basis of a report prepared by an Indian research organisation,[152] however, the Act that resulted from this exercise was more in the style of a sales of goods act than a competition law.[153] In 2015 Bhutan finally adopted its first competition policy drafted by an Indian consultant on the basis of a report commissioned by UNCTAD. In 2020 it updated this policy.[154]

[145] ibid.

[146] See n.136.

[147] 'Competition Policy in South Asian Countries' <https://cuts-ccier.org/pdf/Competition_Policy_in_South_Asian_Countries.pdf> accessed 14 October 2020, 2. Also see the very interesting story about Bhutan taming the Indian multi-national Hindustan Levers, in Pradeep Mehta (ed) 'Competition Regimes in the World: A Civil Society Report' chapter 5, 26 (CUTS 2006) <https://competitionregimes.com/publications/>

[148] Proceedings and Resolutions of the 75th Session of the National Assembly <www.nab.gov.bt/assets/uploads/docs/resolution/2014/75th_Session.pdf> accessed 15 October 2020.

[149] See n.147.

[150] ibid. During this period, the UNCTAD was also engaged in the promotion of consumer protection and competition in Bhutan. 'Capacity-building on Competition Law and Policy for Development: A Consolidated Report' (UN 2008) 23. See <https://unctad.org/system/files/official-document/ditcclp20077_en.pdf> accessed 29 November 2021.

[151] 'Consumer Protection Act 2012' <www.moea.gov.bt/wp-content/uploads/2017/07/Consumer-Protection-Act-of-Bhutan-2012.pdf> accessed 15 October 2020.

[152] 'Consumer Protection in Bhutan' <https://cuts-ccier.org/consumer-protection-in-bhutan/> accessed 15 October 2020. Also see Civil Society Report, ch 5 (n.147).

[153] ibid.

[154] The consultant Vinod Dhall had been a secretary in the Indian Ministry of Company Affairs. In July 2003 he had joined the CCI as an Officer on Special Duty and was later appointed as CCI's member-administration before resigning in 2008. 'Acting CCI Chairman Vinod Dhall Quits' <www.financialexpress.com/archive/acting-cci-chairman-vinod-dhall-quits/325038/> accessed 15 October 2020.

3.4 TRANSFER MECHANISMS AND PATTERNS ACROSS SOUTH ASIA

A review of the contexts and institutions engaged by the South Asian Six in adopting their competition legislations reveals that despite the variations in their histories, governance structures, and the size of their economies there are interesting parallels not only in the transfer mechanisms and institutions through which they adopted their competition legislation but also with the adoption processes of India and Pakistan.

Sri Lanka's primary motivation for adopting the Sri Lankan Act was external.[155] However, rather than simply resorting to *emulation* to adopt a competition law aligned with Western precedents, Sri Lanka engaged in *socialisation* of competition principles and adapted these to suit its context and its economic priorities. It also enacted the law through the parliament, which while often besieged by constitutional crises, has been functioning since 1948. In doing so, Sri Lanka, at least in theory, aggregated knowledge but also obtained the constructive consent of stakeholders. Interestingly, the Sri Lankan Act that results from this exercise, while uniquely Sri Lankan in scope and purpose, prioritises consumer protection and public interest, relegating competition regulation to an adjunct to these primary goals thereby reflecting domestic capacity and priorities rather than external recommendations.

Nepal, perhaps more so than Sri Lanka, was motivated, if not urged, by multilateral agencies to adopt a modern competition legislation. Like Sri Lanka, Nepal too engaged domestic institutions at the deliberation phase, however, unlike Sri Lanka, Nepal did not have a stable constitutional or parliamentary history and therefore was unable to meaningfully aggregate input and knowledge from the domestic context. In fact, at the time Nepal adopted its competition legislation it was governed directly by the King who was under no legal obligation to aggregate knowledge from stakeholders. However, the legislative exercise in Nepal was informed by reports of Nepalese thinktanks that had been prepared in consultation with their Indian counterparts and multi-lateral agencies. The Nepalese adoption strategy may therefore be deemed to be a mix of *coercion* and *socialisation* albeit delivered through top-down, exclusive institutions belonging entirely the executive (Table 3.2).

The mechanism of *coercion* appeared to be predominant in Bangladesh also. Bangladesh, like Sri Lanka and Nepal before it, had been motivated by the WTO and other multi-lateral agencies to adopt a competition law. However, unlike Nepal (but somewhat like Sri Lanka), it had resisted doing so for several years, in part because it was not convinced that a modern competition law was compatible with Bangladesh's more pressing economic needs of eliminating poverty and ensuring inclusive growth. During this period, non-governmental thinktanks operating in Bangladesh had liaised with Indian thinktanks to understand the competition

155 See n.79 and 80 and text thereto.

TABLE 3.2. *Strategies for adopting competition laws across South Asia*

Countries	Motivation	Mechanisms	Institutions
India	Internal with some international factors.	• *Dominant*: socialisation. • *Others*: emulation; regulatory competition.	• Bottom-up, participatory, inclusive; • Historic depth; • All three branches of state.
Sri Lanka	External more than internal.	• *Dominant*: coercion and socialisation. • *Others*: emulation.	• Bottom-up, participatory, inclusive; • Historic depth however, also political strife. • Executive and legislature engaged.
Nepal	External. No evidence of internal motivation.	• *Dominant*: coercion and socialisation. • *Others*: emulation.	• Primarily top-down and exclusive; • No historic depth; • Executive only.
Pakistan	External. Limited and weak evidence of internal demand.	• *Dominant*: Coercion; • *Others*: emulation, regulatory competition, and socialisation.	• Primarily top-down and exclusive; • Limited historic depth; • Mostly executive with limited engagement with Parliament.
Bangladesh	External. Limited and weak evidence of internal demand.	• *Dominant*: coercion and socialisation. • *Others*: emulation.	• Bottom-up, participatory, inclusive; • Limited historic depth; • Executive and legislature engaged. Limited engagement with judiciary also.
Maldives	External	• *Dominant*: coercion and socialisation. • *Others*: emulation.	• Bottom-up, participatory, inclusive; • Limited historic depth; • Executive and legislature engaged.
Afghanistan	External	*Dominant*: Coercion	• Top-down and exclusive • No historic depthlong standing political strife.
Bhutan	External	*Dominant*: Coercion *Others*: Socialisation.	• Top-down and exclusive.

regulation model most appropriate for Bangladesh and to create domestic awareness of the importance of competition regulation. It is not clear, however, whether these efforts had any impact on the content of the Bangladeshi Act, which despite being enacted by the parliament reflected the recommendations of the multi-lateral institutions rather than addressing the context specific concerns that had been expressed prior to its adoption. In a testament to the influence of the Indian think tanks the language of the Bangladeshi Act also mirrored that of the Indian Act. Maldives, like Bangladesh, had been working closely with multi-lateral agencies for the adoption of its competition law and the substantive provisions of the Maldives Act largely conformed to the Western competition principles on which they were based. However, Maldives had succeeded in generating greater acceptance for the proposed legislation by issuing the Strategic Action Plan prior to adopting the competition legislation and by outlining the rationale for doing so. Therefore, while Maldives may also be deemed to have adopted its competition law through a mix of *coercion* and *socialisation*, it is likely to have struck a better balance between the two, due in part to the nature of its relationship with multi-lateral agencies and its indigenous efforts in creating awareness.

Afghanistan and Bhutan, the two South Asian countries that have yet to adopt a competition law, have both been *coerced* by DFID and UNCTAD respectively to engage with competition principles. In both Afghanistan and Bhutan, the drafting of the competition law and policy respectively was outsourced to Indian consultants, albeit in Afghanistan indirectly through a UK-based thinktank. While in the case of Bhutan there is some evidence of *socialisation* in the linking of competition to the values of GNH, there is no evidence of a comparable attempt in Afghanistan.

This review also reveals two important commonalities among all South Asian countries: first, that with the exception of Bhutan, all South Asian countries have been motivated to adopt their competition legislations, due to their engagement with the WTO albeit to varying degrees. Second, that with the exception of India, even when these countries have adopted their competition legislations through their constitutional legislative institutions, these institutions have lacked the experience and the expertise meaningfully aggregate either local knowledge or consent. The combination of these two factors makes these countries particularly susceptible to *coercion* from multi-lateral agencies, and in respect of Bangladesh, Nepal, Bhutan, and Afghanistan, also from India. The effect of *coercion* is mitigated to some extent due to the opportunity to *socialise* and adapt the proposed legislation to the context provided by the engagement of domestic thinktanks (in Nepal and Bangladesh) and the enactment of competition laws through democratic institutions (in Bangladesh, Maldives, and Sri Lanka). However, the question remains whether this exercise also generates compatibility and legitimacy for the adopted laws and thereby facilitates their subsequent implementation.

3.5 COMPATIBILITY, LEGITIMACY, AND THE POTENTIAL FOR SUCCESS OF THE ADOPTED LEGISLATION

As in the case of India and Pakistan, the extent of compatibility and legitimacy of modern competition legislations in the South Asian Six may not be measured directly and may only be deduced from the mechanisms and institutions employed by these countries in the adoption process.[156] As discussed in Chapter 1, a law is more likely to be compatible with the context for which it is intended, if it is adopted through bottom-up, participatory, and inclusive institutions that have the capacity not only to aggregate local knowledge but also to utilise it in adapting the law to the context. The adoption through bottom-up, participatory, and inclusive institutions is also likely to generate greater legitimacy for the laws: although laws may enjoy formal legitimacy simply for having been introduced through institutions that have legality and authority in the country, a more substantive legitimacy is only possible if there is a degree of public consent, whether actual or constructive, to the law being adopted. The greater the compatibility and legitimacy of the adopted law, the greater its chances of being understood, accepted, and utilised in the adopting country and of enjoying a productive relationship with other elements in the legal system of the host country. This, in turn, is a critical factor in ensuring that the adopted law is translated from being a law in the books to law in action and steadily integrates into the host country's pre-existing legal system.

In order to understand the extent of compatibility and legitimacy generated in the course of adoption in Bangladesh, Maldives, Nepal, and Sri Lanka that have actually adopted competition legislation, it is important to consider the nature of their relationship with the WTO and other multi-lateral agencies; the branches of state that they engaged in the deliberation and enactment phases; and finally, the capacity of the institutions employed by them in the deliberation, rather than only in the enactment phase, to aggregate both tacit local information and consent. It is evident even from a cursory review of the adoption processes in Sri Lanka, Nepal, Bangladesh, and Maldives,[157] that as in Pakistan, the influence of the WTO and other multi-lateral agencies was a significant motivation in the adoption of competition laws.[158] It is further evident that Sri Lanka and Bangladesh, like India, have enacted their competition legislations through their parliaments, which are designed in terms of their constitutions, as bottom-up, participatory, and inclusive institutions, while Nepal adopted its legislation in a period when executive power was being exercised directly by the King. Given that compatibility and legitimacy derive from the institutions rather than the motivations through which laws are adopted, it may be argued that the competition legislation in Bangladesh, Maldives, and Sri Lanka, is likely to have the same degree of compatibility and legitimacy as the Indian Act has in the Indian context, while the extent of compatibility and legitimacy in Nepal is likely to be commensurate with that of Pakistan.

However, a closer look at the adoption processes in Bangladesh, Maldives, Nepal, and Sri Lanka suggests that such a conclusion is superficial because even though the

[156] See Chapter 2, Section 2.4.
[157] See Table 3.2.
[158] See Chapter 3.

impetus to adopt modern competition legislation came from external sources, the relationships between these countries and these external sources was not uniform: Among them, Maldives and Nepal appear more aligned with the vision of the multi-lateral agencies for their economies, while Sri Lanka and Bangladesh appear to insist on a competition legislation specifically tailored to their contexts. Further, in respect of the institutions engaged by these countries in the deliberation phase, only Maldives seems to have attempted a broad-based consultation by developing a holistic Strategic Action Plan prior to enacting its competition legislation. There is little evidence of a similar exercise in Sri Lanka, Nepal, or Bangladesh: there is no information of a governmental committee (like the Raghavan Committee in India), or a team formed and led by multi-lateral agencies (like the World Bank team in Pakistan), having been established in any of these countries to investigate the appropriateness of competition legislation and to inform the government and the parliament of its findings and recommendations. However, there is information that thinktanks based in each of these countries had produced some discussion and proposals for the legislation which are likely to have informed the substance of the adopted competition legislations. For all these countries, therefore, it may be argued that the deliberation phase generated limited compatibility and even lesser stakeholder consent and legitimacy.

Further although these countries engaged their parliaments in the enactment phase, the actual capacity of these parliaments to aggregate local knowledge and to apply it to the legislation proposed to be adopted, or to garner meaningful consent from stakeholders is limited due to their deference to the executive and multi-lateral agencies, their lack of historic depth and, their limited experience of legislating. In Nepal, the law was adopted before the parliament had even been re-instated and therefore the possibility of debates in parliament or through its committees does not arise. Even in Sri Lanka and Bangladesh the parliamentary system had been under considerable pressure due to long-standing civil strife and therefore was not equipped for or most likely even focused on fully engaging with the proposed legislation. Maldives, the most stable country from a governance point of view, had a long history of monarchy as well as an overt and accepted dependence on multi-lateral agencies for economic advice which it is not likely to have challenged.

This complex picture returns mixed results for compatibility and legitimacy of competition legislation in these countries. Although the input of the governments of these countries in respect of competition principles proposed by multi-lateral agencies creates some compatibility, and the adoption of these laws through the parliament confers authority and legality on them, these laws retain the unmistakeable stamp of their Western multi-lateral origins (especially the Bangladeshi and Maldives Act) and are only awkwardly *socialised* for context (for instance, the Nepalese Act). At times this manifests in the repetition in the content and the overall lack of conceptual clarity and at others in an ill-defined enforcement trajectory (for instance, in the Sri Lankan and the Nepalese Acts). Similarly, the legitimacy of the adopted competition legislations is undermined due to these having been enacted without a broad-based consultation with indigenous stakeholders beyond the limited formal debates in parliament. The absence of such consultation also suggests another missed opportunity to enhance the compatibility of the adopted laws with context.

The consequent superficial compatibility and legitimacy of the adopted competition legislation is likely to have a negative impact on the extent to which these laws may be understood, applied, and utilised in these countries and on the productivity of their interactions with the pre-existing legal system of the countries. This in turn is likely to adversely affect the extent to which these laws are translated from being laws on the books into laws in action and at the pace and extent to which they may become integrated in the pre-existing legal systems of the adopting countries. Although Afghanistan and Bhutan have not adopted competition laws, the conclusions regarding compatibility and legitimacy are equally likely to hold true for their draft law and policy respectively, given that both countries have engaged with competition legislation due to the persuasion of Western, multi-lateral agencies rather than in response to an internal demand and have had little (in the case of Bhutan) or no (in the case of Afghanistan) domestic input in the policy adopted by or the law proposed for them.

4

Enforcing Indian and Pakistani Competition Acts

An Overview of the Authorities and their Operations

4.1 INTRODUCTION

After formally adopting their respective competition laws, India and Pakistan were faced with the task of implementing them. The first step in this regard, for both countries, was to establish their national competition authorities. The Indian government adopted a measured approach in doing so: on 31 March 2003 it brought certain provisions of the Indian Act into force, and on 19 June 2003 it brought into force certain others. On 14 October 2003, the Indian government issued a notification for establishing the Competition Commission of India, the CCI.[1] However, even before the government had issued the notification establishing the CCI, a petition was filed before the Indian Supreme Court challenging the provisions relating to the CCI's composition.[2] The decision in this petition led to the amendment of the Act and to the reconstitution of the CCI.[3] Consequently, it was only in 2009 that the CCI was properly constituted and commenced operations, however

[1] The CCI was established by notification no SO 1198 (E) dated 14.10.2003.

[2] On 04.04.2003 in exercise of its powers under section 63 of the Act, the Indian government had notified the Competition Commission of India (Selection of Chairperson and other Members of the Commission) Rules 2003, which stipulated the mechanism for the appointment of the CCI chairperson and members. Soon thereafter, a petition was filed before the Supreme Court – *Brahm Dutt v Union of India (2005) 2 Supreme Court Cases 431* – which challenged these rules on the ground that the appointment procedure prescribed in them was in violation of the constitutional principle of separation of powers. The petition also argued that given the CCI's adjudicatory powers the CCI's members should be appointed according to the Constitutional procedure for appointment of judges.

[3] On 20.01.2005, the Indian Supreme Court disposed of the *Brahm Dutt* case, on the government's commitment that it would amend the Indian Act. On 09.03.2006, in compliance of the order of the Supreme Court, the Indian government introduced the Competition (Amendment) Bill in Parliament and on 09.08.2007 submitted a revised version. On 27.09.2007 the parliament enacted the Competition (Amendment) Act 2007.

only with respect to anti-competitive agreements and abuse of dominant postition.[4] Unlike its Indian counterpart, the Pakistan government acted with alacrity and certitude in operationalising the Pakistani competition regime: it brought all sections of the Pakistan Competition Ordinance 2007 into force at the same time and established the Competition Commission of Pakistan – the CCP – within six weeks of the promulgation of the 2007 Ordinance.[5] Consequently, while the CCP started issuing orders in respect of anti-competitive agreements, abuse of dominant position and mergers from 2008, the CCI's first orders were only issued in 2009 and then only in respect of anti-competitive agreements and abuses of dominance.

The different paths through which the CCI and the CCP had been established notwithstanding, they were (and are) the instruments through which the Indian and Pakistani competition legislations were translated from being laws on the books to laws in in action. The operations of the CCI and CCP also provide critical insight into the impact of the process through which competition legislation is adopted, on its subsequent implementation. Both the CCI and CCP derive their structure, composition, and mandate from the provisions of their competition legislations, which had been shaped through the transfer mechanisms and institutions employed by the countries at the adoption stage. In issuing their orders, both the CCI and CCP interpret and enforce provisions of their respective legislations, which orders therefore reflect not only the interplay of the structures, compositions, and mandates of the CCI and the CCP, but also reveal their understanding of their role in their respective economies. In this way, the decisions of the CCI and CCP are shaped not only by their internal dynamics but also the extent of the compatibility and legitimacy of the competition legislation under which they have been established. This chapter provides an overview of the operations of the CCI and the CCP with the aim of establishing the relationship between the adoption and implementation stages of the Indian and Pakistani competition laws.

To this end, this chapter is organised as follows: Section 4.2 introduces the CCI and the CCP as the first tier Indian and Pakistani competition authorities focusing on their structures, composition, and mandates, the types of orders they may issue, and the processes through which they arrive at their decisions; Section 4.3 traces the implementation trajectories envisaged by the Indian and Pakistani competition laws and identifies the potential points of interaction between the competition systems established under the adopted competition legislations and the pre-existing legal systems of the two

[4] On 15.05.2009 the Indian government issued notifications SO 1241(E) and SO 1242(E) bringing into force provisions relating to anti-competitive agreements and abuse of dominant position (sections 3 and 4 respectively). The sections of the Act relating to mergers were brought into force in 2011.

[5] In terms of 2007 Ordinance section 1(4) all sections of the 2007 Ordinance were brought simultaneously at the time of its promulgation on 02.10.2007. The CCP was established immediately after and became operational on 12.11.2007.

countries; Section 4.4 identifies, evaluates and compares these indicators to assess the success (or lack thereof) of the CCI and CCP in enforcing the competition. Finally, Section 4.5 examines the extent to which the CCI and CCP's performance may be traced back to the mechanisms and institutions employed by the countries in the adoption stage and their respective compatibility and legitimacy in their contexts.

4.2 THE INDIAN AND PAKISTANI COMPETITION ENFORCEMENT AUTHORITIES

Notwithstanding the differences in the motivations, mechanisms, and institutions through which India and Pakistan adopted their competition legislations, the competition authorities established by these legislations not only have similar structures, mandates, and compositions but also adopt comparable procedures for sanctioning infringements.

4.2.1 *CCI and CCP: their Structures, Mandates, and Compositions*

The structure of a competition authority refers to its organizational design – is it established as an independent body or is it embedded within the pre-existing system? Is it collegiate or hierarchical? Is it self-funded, or dependent on the government for funding? The mandate refers to the powers of the authority to take cognisance of infringements of the competition legislation and to issue orders in respect of these infringements while its composition refers to the requirements for appointing and removing members to the authority.

4.2.1.1 Structures: The Limits of Independence

The Indian Act and Pakistani Act (as well as the three Ordinances that preceded it) respectively provide for the CCI and the CCP to be established as autonomous, statutory collegiate bodies. The CCI comprises a chairperson and between two and six members,[6] while the CCP comprises a chairperson and between five and seven members.[7] Both the CCI and CCP are bound by policy directives issued by their respective governments,[8] and are required to meet their operational expenses with monies derived from the Commission Fund. In terms of the Indian Act, the Commission Fund comprises all government grants and fees received by the CCI and the interest accrued on these amounts,[9]while under the Paksitani Act in addition to government grants, fees and interest accrued thereon, the Commission

6 Indian Act sections 7(2), 8(1).
7 Pakistani Act sections 12(2), 14(1).
8 Indian Act section 55; Pakistani Act, section 56.
9 Indian Act sections 51.

Fund includes contributions from local and foreign donors or agencies, and a percentage of the fees and charges levied by other regulatory agencies in Pakistan.[10]

An important difference between the CCI and the CCP is that while the CCI was envisaged exclusively as a regulatory body with all appeals from its orders lying to the independently constituted Indian Tribunal and more recently to the NCLAT,[11] the CCP includes an 'Appellate Bench' to hear appeals from orders issued by single members or officers of the CCP.[12] In terms of the Pakistani Act appeals from all other orders of the CCP lie to the independent Pakistani Tribunal.[13]

4.2.1.2 Mandates and Powers of the Authorities

Both the CCI and the CCP have the power to take cognisance of agreements in respect of production, supply, distribution, storage, acquisition or control of goods or provision of services, that have a negative effect on competition[14] and abuse of dominant position[15] Both authorities also have the power to review mergers and acquisitions.[16] CCP also has additional powers to deal with deceptive marketing practices.[17] Both the CCI and the CCP have jurisdiction over all anti-competitive practices that distort competition in India or Pakistan regardless of where they may have originally occured.[18]

In both India and Pakistan, the government has the power to exempt certain entities or agreements from the operation of the competition legislations if it is required to do so in pursuance of international obligations or in the national or public interest.[19] Further, the Indian government has the power to supersede the CCI if it is of the opinion that the CCI is unable to discharge its functions or perform its duties; if it fails to comply with the directions given by the government which causes its financial position or its administration to suffer; or if it is necessary to do so in the public interest.[20] There is no provision in the Pakistani legislation

[10] Pakistani Act section 20. The Pakistani Act had amended the provision for the Commission Fund provided in the 2007 and 2009 Ordinances to exclude charges, fees and penalties levied by the CCP.

[11] Before it was amended in 2007, sections 23–25 of the Indian Act also provided for 'Benches'. However, these benches were to exercise the CCI's mandate rather than to hear appeals from its orders. In any event these sections were omitted when the Indian Act was amended in 2007.

[12] Pakistani Act section 41.

[13] ibid section 43.

[14] In terms of the Indian Act, section 3 these are referred to as 'anti-competitive agreements' and in terms of section 4 of the Pakistani Act, as 'prohibited agreements'. This book uses 'anti-competitive agreements' to refer to the Indian anti-competitive agreements and Pakistani prohibited agreements.

[15] Indian Act section 4; Pakistani Act section 3.

[16] In the Indian Act section 5, these are referred to as 'combinations' and in terms of section 11 of the Pakistani Act mergers also include acquisitions. Throughout this book combinations, mergers and acquisitions are referred to as 'mergers'.

[17] Pakistani Act section 10.

[18] Indian Act section 32; Pakistani Act section 1(3).

[19] Indian Act section 54; Pakistani Act section 54.

[20] Indian Act section 56.

which confers on the government the express power to supersede the CCP, however, it the Act stipulates that it is incumbent upon the CCP to comply with all policy directives issued by the government.[21]

4.2.1.3 Composition of the Authorities

Both the Indian and the Pakistani Acts provide for appointing persons of the highest calibre as members or Commissioners of the CCI and the CCP respectively. The Indian Act seeks to appoint to the CCI persons of 'ability, integrity and standing' having special knowledge or professional experience of minimum fifteen years in fields of international trade, business, commerce, law, finance, accountancy, management, industry, public affairs, administration, or any other area which the government deems useful for the CCI's purposes.[22] Similarly, the Pakistani Act seeks for the CCP, persons of 'integrity, expertise, eminence' and experience of a minimum of ten years in industry, commerce, economics, finance, law, accountancy, or public administration or holding such further qualifications as the government may prescribe.[23] In case of the CCP, the Pakistani legislation further stipulates that only two members may be government employees.[24] There is no comparable requirement in the Indian Act. In terms of the Indian Act members of the CCI may serve a term of five years while under the Pakistani legislation, members of the CCP may serve a term of three years. Both the Indian and Pakistani legislations allow members to be re-appointed until they have reached the age of retirement or if they are removed under the relevant provisions of the Acts.[25]

In terms of the Indian Act, as amended in 2007, members of the CCI may only be appointed at the recommendation of a 'selection committee' comprising among others the Chief Justice of the Indian Supreme Court and designated government representatives. This selection committee is required to recommend a panel of potential members to the government, who then selects members from the panel.[26] The Act further provides that a member may be removed by the government only on the grounds specified in the Act and after a Supreme Court inquiry into the reasons for the removal.[27] In terms of the Pakistani legislation, read with the rules made by the government in this regard, the government has exclusive discretion to appoint the CCP chairman. The government also appoints the members in consultation with the chairman.[28] The legislation further provides that members of the CCP may

[21] Pakistani Act section 56.
[22] Indian Act section 8(2).
[23] Pakistani Act section 14(5).
[24] ibid section 14(4).
[25] Indian Act section 10(1)(e); Pakistani Act section 17.
[26] Indian Act section 9(1), 8(1).
[27] ibid section 11.
[28] Pakistani Act section 14(5) r/w Competition Commission (Salary, Terms and Conditions of Chairman and Members) Rules 2009, Rule 3(2).

be removed by the order of the court or by the government on grounds specified in the Act, in accordance with rules made by the government and after an impartial inquiry.[29] At the time of writing the Pakistani government had not made rules for this purpose.[30]

4.2.2 *Types of Enforcement Orders that the CCI and CCP May Issue*

In terms of the Indian and Pakistani competition acts, the CCI and the CCP may issue a range of orders in respect of infringements and impose penalties or prescribe behavioral remedies as appropriate.[31]

For instance, in respect of anti-competitive agreements and abuse of dominant position, the CCI may direct a party to discontinue the agreement or practice and prohibit it from entering into such agreement or engaging in such practice in the future.[32] The CCI may also order the amendment of an anti-competitive agreement,[33] or division of a dominant entity[34] and may penalise parties for entering into anti-competitive agreements or for abusing their dominant position in the relevant market. The quantum of these penalties may be calculated as a percentage of the turnover (of the entity) or income (of the person or association as appropriate).[35] In certain circumstances and upon satisfaction of certain conditions, the CCI may impose a lesser penalty.[36] In respect of mergers and acquisitions, the CCI has the power to approve, restrain, or modify the schemes put forward by the parties.[37]

The CCP may issue orders in respect of anti-competitive agreements, abuse of dominant position, mergers and acquisitions, and deceptive marketing practices. In case of abuse of dominant position, the CCP may order a party to take measures to

[29] Pakistani Act section 19.

[30] The appointment and removal mechanism provided in the Pakistani competition legislation is the same as that provided in the Pakistan Telecommunication Authority Act 1996 section 3; Securities and Exchange Commission of Pakistan sections 5, 19; Regulation of Generation, Transmission and Distribution of Electric Power Act 1997 sections 3, 4; Pakistan Electronic Media Regulatory Authority Ordinance 2002 section 3; and Oil and Gas Regulatory Authority section 3.

[31] The CCI may issue orders in respect of anti-competitive agreements under: (i) section 26(2) of the Act when it dismisses a matter because there is no prima facie case; (ii) section 26(6) where the matter is dismissed after an investigation and hearing, and (iii) section 27 where the CCI finds a contravention after a hearing and imposes sanctions. Among these, only section 26(6) and 27 orders contain an in-depth examination and analysis of issues and therefore these are the only ones considered for this analysis.

[32] Indian Act section 27(a).

[33] ibid section 27(d).

[34] ibid section 28.

[35] ibid section 27(b).

[36] ibid section 46 r/w Competition Commission of India (Lesser Penalty) Regulations 2009.

[37] ibid section 31.

restore competition and to refrain from activities that led to the abuse.[38] In case of an anti-competitive agreement, the CCP may issue an order for its annulment or amendment and prohibit parties to the agreement from continuing with or entering into such agreement in the future.[39] The CCP may also impose penalties calculated either as fixed sums or as a percentage of turnover,[40] or if the circumstances warrant, it may grant leniency.[41] In approving a merger or acquisition, the CCP may approve it with or without conditions, order a further review, or undo or prohibit it altogether.[42]

4.2.3 *How do the CCI and CCP Decide? Issuing Orders at the Authorities*

A review of the Indian and Pakistani legislations suggests that the CCI and the CCP arrive at their decisions regarding anti-competitive practices through comparable processes. Both the CCI and CCP take cognisance of possible anti-competitive agreements and abuses of dominant position by (a) taking *suo motu* notice of a suspected violation;[43] (b) acting upon a complaint received from a person, entity,[44] or an association;[45] or (c) responding to a government reference.[46] This section outlines how the CCI and CCP proceed with and decide matters that come before them.

(i) *Decision making at the CCI.* In terms of the Indian Act irrespective of the source through which a matter arrives before the CCI, , the CCI's first responsibility is to form a *prima facie* view as to whether or not there is a case to be investigated.[47] If, after the examining the information before it, the CCI decides that there is no *prima facie* case, it may close the matter.[48] If, however, it forms the view that there is a *prima facie* case, it may refer the matter to the Director General

38 Pakistani Act section 31(1)(a).
39 ibid section 31(1)(b).
40 ibid section 38.
41 ibid section 39.
42 ibid section 31(1)(d).
43 Indian Act section 19(1); Pakistani Act section 30 r/w Regulation 16 of the Competition Commission (General Enforcement) Regulations 2007.
44 I refer to 'person' as defined in section 2(l) of the Indian Act and 'undertaking' as defined in section 2(1)(q) of the Pakistani legislation, as 'entity' throughout this work.
45 Indian Act section 19(1)(a); Pakistani Act section 30 r/w Regulation 17 of the General Enforcement Regulations (n.44).
46 Indian Act section 19(1)(b); Pakistani Act ibid. In the Indian Act the term 'government' means either the central or provincial government. Section 19(1)(b) also allows the CCI to entertain references initiated by a statutory authority. However, under the Pakistani Act 'government' means only the federal government, while statutory authorities are included in the definition of 'undertaking' provided in section 2(1)(q) of the Act.
47 Indian Act section 26(1).
48 ibid section 26(2).

Investigations (DG) and direct him to submit his report to the CCI within a specified time.[49] If the DG reports that there is a contravention of the Act, the CCI may share the investigation report with the parties and, if necessary, may order further enquiry.[50] If, however, the DG reports that there is no contravention, the CCI in its discretion may either still share the report with the parties and invite their comments and objections before finally deciding the matter or it simply close the matter.[51] This discretion is not available to the CCI in matters referred to it by the government or a statutory body in which case it is mandatory for CCI to share the report with the referring entity and to invite its comments before finally deciding the matter.[52] In all cases CCI may only finally decide a matter after hearing the comments and objections of the relevant parties and after examining the report of a further enquiry, if any.[53] Even in cases where the CCI proceeds to hear the matter on the basis of the DG's report, it is not bound to agree with the DG's conclusions and may close the matter or arrive at a different conclusion.[54] In the event that after a detailed hearing the CCI finds a contravention of the Act, it may issue such directions or impose such penalties on the entities as it deems appropriate.[55] The CCI also has the power to issue interim orders in the course of hearings before it.[56]

(ii) *CCP's process for decision-making.* Regardless of whether it takes *suo motu* notice of a violation of the competition legislation or responds to a complaint filed before it, the CCP is required to make an initial assessment as to whether or not there is a contravention of the Pakistani competition legislation.[57] If the CCP finds that the complaint is 'false and vexatious,' or if it forms the view that the facts do not warrant a further investigation', the CCP may close the matter.[58] If, however, it has reason to believe that there is sufficient evidence of a violation, it may either issue a show cause notice to the parties or initiate further investigation.[59] In issuing the show cause notice, it is incumbent upon

49 ibid section 2(g).
50 ibid sections 26(3), 26(8).
51 ibid section 26(3).
52 ibid section 26(5).
53 ibid sections 26(6), 27.
54 ibid,section 26(6).
55 ibid section 27.
56 ibid section 31.
57 General Enforcement Regulations (n.44), regulation 17(2).
58 ibid.
59 General Enforcement Regulations (n.44), regulations 17(2) 22. The Pakistani Act does not provide for a DG and the matter requiring further investigation is simply passed on to the CCP's investigation wing.

the CCP to inform the entity of the case against it, to invite it to state its case in writing, and to present it before the CCP either in person or through an authorised representative. The CCP may issue a final order after examining the submissions made by the entity and/or after providing it an opportunity of being heard. If the entity chooses not to submit to the CCP's jurisdiction, the CCP may decide the matter 'ex parte'.[60] The CCP also has the power to issue interim orders in the course of hearings before it.[61]

4.3 ACHIEVING THE BENCHMARKS OF SUCCESS IN THE INDIAN AND PAKISTANI CONTEXTS

In issuing their orders, the CCI and the CCP not only engage their structures, mandates, and compositions but also reflect the extent to which the competition legislation is understood, utilised, and applied in the country. However, in both India and Pakistan competition enforcement does not proceed along the linear pathway outlined in the statutes. This section outlines the competition enforcement pathways prescribed in the Indian and Pakistani Act, the possible sources of interference in this pathway and its implication for the 'success' of the competition enforcement in the Indian and Pakistani contexts.

4.3.1 *Enforcing Competition Laws: Pathways Prescribed for CCI and CCP*

As first-tier competition enforcement authorities the CCI and CCP may take cognisance of all infringements of their respective competition legislations and the manner in which they interpret and apply the provisions of the Acts is shaped by the interplay of their respective structures and compositions. In passing orders in respect of anti-competitive practices (whether anti-competitive agreements or abuses of dominance), the CCI and CCP define the scope of their respective legislations and declare the repercussions of infringing these. In doing so they perform an important advocacy function and create public awareness of the scope and authority of their respective competition legislations. In this way each order of these authorities not only impacts the compatibility and legitimacy of the competition legislations but also the extent to which the legislations are understood, applied, and utilised in theit countries and the pace at which they integrate into their pre-existing legal systems.

However, the CCI or CCP's understanding and application of provisions of their respective competition legislations is not final word on enforcement as both the Indian and the Pakistani Acts, provide for appeals from orders of the CCI or the CCP to lie to Indian and Pakistani Tribunals as the second-tier competition

60 ibid.

61 Pakistani Act section 32.

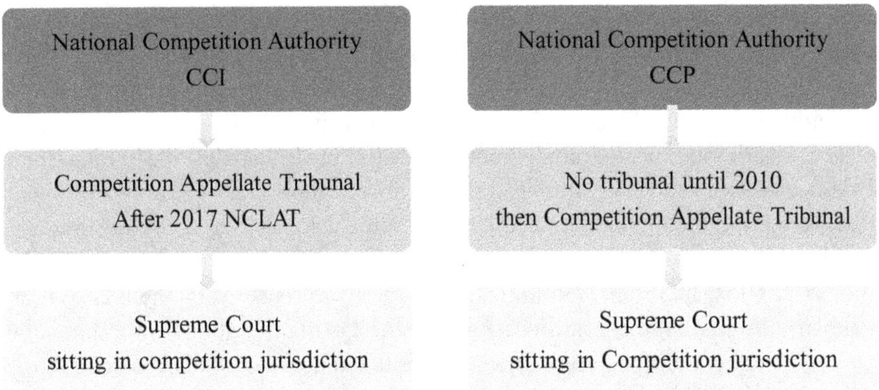

FIGURE 4.1. Competition enforcement pathways in India and Pakistan

enforcement authorities established under the Acts. Until 2017, the Indian Tribunal was envisaged as an independent, statutory body,[62] comprising one judicial and two technical members,[63] and had the power to hear appeals from all orders of the CCI.[64] In 2017, however, the Indian Act was amended to replace the specialist Indian Tribunal with the more generalist National Company Law Appellate Tribunal (NCLAT) established under section 410 of the Indian Companies Act 2013.[65] In Pakistan, prior to the enactment of the Pakistani Act, appeals from orders passed by more than one member of the CCP (under the 2007 and 2009 Ordinances) lay directly to the Supreme Court, and from orders issued under the 2010 Ordinance to the high court.[66] The Pakistani Tribunal was first provided for in the Pakistani Act as an independent statutory body, comprising one judicial member and two technical members who would have 'expertise in international trade, economics, law, finance and accountancy' (Figure 4.1).[67]

In both India and Pakistan, appeals from orders of the Tribunals lie to the Supreme Courts[68] which are apex courts established under the Indian and Pakistani constitutions. Judges appointed to these Supreme Courts are generalists, most often elevated after serving at the high courts for at least ten years. In both India and Pakistan, the Supreme Courts exercise their statutory competition jurisdiction

[62] Indian Act Chapter VIIIA (sections 53A–53U) inserted by the 2007 Amendment Act.

[63] ibid section 53C.

[64] Indian Act section 53D: members of the Indian Tribunal are required to have extensive experience of competition matters or of other disciplines relevant for the tribunal.

[65] Inserted vide Indian Finance Act 2017. National Company Law Appellate Tribunal <http://nclat.nic.in/about-nclat.html> accessed 22 June 2017. In terms of section 409 of the Indian Companies Act there is no requirement for a competition expert or specialist to be appointed to the NCLAT.

[66] 2007 and 2009 Ordinances, sections 41, 42; 2010 Ordinance section 42.

[67] Pakistani Act section 43.

[68] Indian Act section 53T; Pakistani Act section 44.

in addition to the constitutional and appellate jurisdiction conferred upon them under the respective Constitutions of the countries. In both countries orders of the Supreme Courts issued in exercise of their competition jurisdictions are final and may not be challenged before any courts or forums in the country.

The nearly identical enforcement pathways prescribed in the Indian and Pakistani Acts do not have similar histories of activation. The Indian government had established the Competition Appellate Tribunal in May 2009 almost simultaneously with making the CCI operational,[69] and other than minor interruptions the Indian Tribunal had remained functional until it was replaced by the NCLAT. In Pakistan, the first member and chairman of the Pakistani Tribunal was appointed only in July 2011 more than nine months after the enactment of the Pakistani Act.[70] The remaining technical members were not appointed for another year.[71] Further, the Pakistani Tribunal had only been functional for about five months when in April 2013 one member resigned and the other retired. It was only in 2015 after the lapse of another two years that the government appointed new members and re-constituted the Tribunal.[72]

4.3.2 *Interventions in the Competition Enforcement Pathways*

Competition matters do not always proceed along the linear implementation pathways prescribed in the Indian and Pakistani Acts largely due to intervention of the general courts pre-existing in the legal systems of these countries. In both India and Pakistan in addition to appealing orders or actions of the CCI or CCP to the Indian and Pakistani Tribunals (since 2017 to the NCLAT in India) and those of the Tribunals to the Indian or Pakistani Supreme Courts, entities aggrieved by the actions or orders of the CCI, CCP or the tribunals have the right to challenge these before the general courts on constitutional grounds by filing constitutional writ petitions before the high courts in their countries.[73] In filing these petitions aggrieved entities invoke the inherent and inalienable original jurisdiction of the general courts and may do so even while proceedings before the enforcement authorities are still pending. However, they must demonstrate that there is no

[69] The Indian government had established the Indian Tribunal by notification No SO 1240(E) dated 15.05.2009.

[70] Notification No F.15(1)/2010-A.V dated 27.07.2011. <http://pakistannewswire.net/retired-judge-appointed-chairman-competition-appellate-tribunal/> accessed 3 April 2017.

[71] Notification No F.21(1)/2011-Admn-III dated 29.05.2012.

[72] Pakistan appointed members of the Pakistani Tribunal on 10.04.2015, 28.05.2015, and 22.01.2016 respectively.

[73] High courts in both India and Pakistan have the jurisdiction to hear petitions on constitutional grounds, which cannot be ousted by any law in the country. Therefore, aggrieved entities have the right to invoke this jurisdiction even though high courts are excluded from the enforcement pathways provided in the Indian and Pakistani Acts.

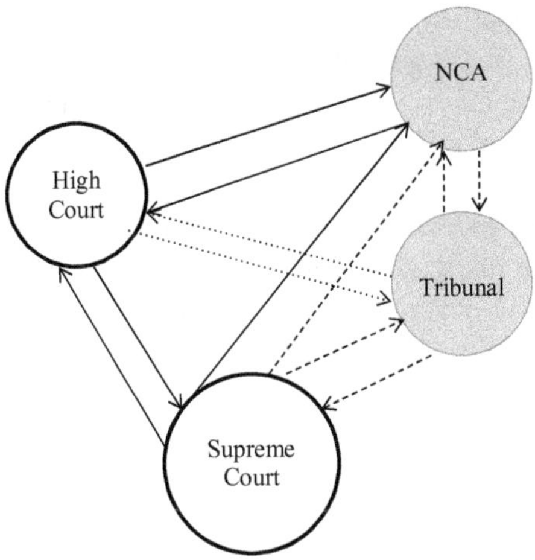

FIGURE 4.2. Interaction between the competition enforcement and the pre-existing systems

adequate, alternate remedy of appeal available to them against the actions or orders of the enforcement authorities. (Figure 4.2).[74]

Given that these petitions lie outside the competition enforcement pathways envisaged in the competition legislations in both India and Pakistan (see Figure 4.1) these may lead to unexpected consequences for competition enforcement in the two countries. In case the aggrieved parties invoke the constitutional jurisdictions of the high courts while proceedings are still pending before the CCI, or the CCP, or the Tribunals they most often also file an application for restraining the CCI or the CCP, or the Tribunal as the case may be, from continuing with the proceedings. In the event that the high courts grant a restraining order, the proceedings before the relevant competition authority are not only temporarily halted but also pulled out of the linear competition enforcement pathway prescribed in the Indian and Pakistani Acts. If the restraining or final order granted by the high courts is further appealed to the Supreme Court (sitting in its constitutional jurisdiction), and the Supreme Court imposes or continues the restraint, the temporary halt in

[74] In terms of Indian Constitution, Article 226 and the Pakistani Constitution, Article 199 the Indian and Pakistani high courts may: (a) direct a person carrying out a function in connection with the affairs of the state to refrain from doing anything he is not permitted to do or to do anything he is required to do by issuing a writ of *mandamus* and *prohibition*; (b) declare that any given act or proceeding performed by a person in connection with the affairs of the federation has been done without lawful authority and is without legal effect by issuing a writ of *certiorari*; (c) direct that a person held in custody within the jurisdiction of the court may be presented in court by a writ of *habeas corpus*; and (d) require a person holding public office to show the authority of law under which he claims to hold that office through a writ of *quo warranto*. The high courts also have powers to issue interim orders in any of these matters. Appeals from orders of the high courts in their writ. jurisdictions lie to the Supreme Courts in the two countries who may hear these appeals in their constitutional jurisdictions.

competition enforcement may be inordinately extended, depending on the speed with which the pre-existing legal system is equipped to deal with petitions.

This suggests that the intervention of the general courts has a considerable impact on competition enforcement. The precise nature of this impact depends on large part on the manner in which the courts respond to these competition-related challenges. Where the courts delay their decisions or pass orders which convolute and compound rather than resolve the issues brought before them, they not only obstruct the competition authorities in fulfilling their mandate, but in doing so also hinder the development of competition jurisprudence and thereby weaken both present and future competition enforcement in the country. However, in cases where the courts decide the petitions that come before them with alacrity and clarity, they not only clarify the due process norms and rules of natural justice as applicable to competition matters, but also provide guidance in respect of similar matters that may be brought before them in the future. As the general courts decide each successive competition matter they bring the competition legislation into greater alignment with the legal norms prevalent in the country and thereby contribute to the pace at which it integrates into the pre-existing legal system.

4.3.3 *The Pathways and the Benchmarks of Success*

The extent to which an adopted competition legislation integrates into the adopting country's pre-existing legal system is an important marker of its overall success. Whether and at what pace that is likely to happen in India and Pakistan depends on the extent to which their competition legislations are understood, utilised, and applied in their adopting countries and on the nature and quality of their interaction with their pre-existing legal systems. This in turn depends on the extent of compatibility and legitimacy the adopted legislations enjoy in their contexts: an adopted legislation that is more compatible with the context of the adopting country and enjoys greater legitimacy in it, is likely to be better understood and utilised by the stakeholders and enforcement authorities. The authorities established in pursuance of a more compatible and legitimate legislation are also likely to engage more productively with the country's pre-existing legal system and thereby to facilitate the steady integration of the adopted law into it.

In the Indian and Pakistani contexts, the extent of understanding, utilisation, and application of the adopted competition legislations and the extent of their compatibility and legitimacy in their respective contexts may be inferred and assessed by the number of matters that are brought, before the first-tier competition implementing authorities (ie the CCI or the CCP) in the first instance, the range of economic sectors to which these matters relate, and the number of matters that the CCI or CCP decide and dispose of. At the CCI and the CCP these matters are evaluated by competition specialists, however as matters proceed along the enforcement pathways prescribed in the Indian and Pakistani competition legislations, they are also examined by a combination of competition specialists and judicial members (at the Indian and Pakistani Tribunals)[75] and finally determined by generalist judges. In an ideal scenario as a matter proceeds along this pathway it becomes more harmonised with the country's pre-existing legal system so that when it is finally decided by the Supreme Court sitting in its competition jurisdiction, it becomes a part of the legal system of the country until such time as it may be distinguished by an equally competent forum. As more and more cases on different aspects of competition enforcment proceed along this pathway and are decided by the Supreme Courts, the competition legislations as a whole become more and more integrated into the pre-existing legal system of the country.

The nature and quality of the interactions between the adopted competition legislation and the pre-existing legal system of the country also relates to the extent of the compatibility and legitimacy of the adopted legislations. To understand these interactions in India and Pakistan the competition-related challenges filed before the high courts in their constitutional jurisdictions as well as the response of the courts to these challenges must be examined.[76] It may be argued that an adopted legislation that is more compatible with the pre-existing legal system of the adopting country and enjoys greater legitimacy in it, is likely to generate fewer challenges (or at least challenges on a smaller range of grounds) and is also likely to be better understood and better received by the general courts. However, given that courts sitting in their constitutional jurisdiction may only evaluate the constitutionality of actions and orders of competition authorities and are neither equipped nor empowered to comment on the correctness or otherwise of the application of competition principles[77] their decisions even when issued with clarity and alacrity are *directly* advance competition jurisprudence in the country. However, they do have an important *indirect* impact on competition enforcement: they bring the adopted legislation into conformity with country's legal system and validate its provisions and thereby, enhance its compatibility with the context, and its legitimacy in the country.

4.4 MEASURING THE PERFORMANCE AND INTERACTION OF COMPETITION STATUTES

Having established the benchmarks for assessing the performance and interactions of the Indian and Pakistani Acts, the next step is to measure these. This section argues that orders of competition authorities are the most appropriate source of data

75 Since 2017 in India, competition appeals are not evaluated by specialists even at the second tier as the NCLAT does not require competition specialist members.

76 Challenges to orders of the Tribunals are not included in this assessment due to limited data available for the Pakistani Tribunal.

77 See n.74 and 74 and text thereto.

for this purpose because they not only reflect the interplay of institutions and mechanisms at the adoption stage that shaped the provisions under which these authorities have been established but also offer an insight into the enforcement strategies adopted by these authorities for the implementation stage.

4.4.1 *Orders of CCI and CCP as Data for Evaluating Benchmarks of Success*

Orders of the Indian and Pakistani competition authorities, particularly of the first tier CCI and CCP, are an important source data for assessing the performance and interactions of the Indian and Pakistan competition legislations in their respective countries these orders are strong measures of the performance of the competition authorities in that they establish the number of cases decided by the CCI and CCP, and identify the sectors in which the authorities have intervened. The orders of the CCI and the CCP also form the best available evidence of the interaction between the competition legislations and the pre-existing legal system of the countries. Orders of the CCI and CCP in proceedings which had also given rise to petitions before the courts record the details of these petitions as well as the orders of the courts in respect of these challenges, or where the courts are still to pass orders, they record the status of these challenges. In this way, orders of the CCI and CCP provide important information about the range of grounds on which the proceedings before the CCI and CCP are challenged as well as rationale adopted by the courts in response to these grounds In in the absence of readily available court documents the orders of the CCI and the CCP form the only record of the interactions between the competition authorities and the courts.[78]

The performance and interadtion indicators derived from the orders of the CCI and the CCP also offer insight into the nature and extent of the compatibility and legitimacy of the competition legislations in their respective countries.

The orders of the CCI and the CCP are also particularly suited for the comparative analysis of the performance and interactions of the Indian and Pakistani Acts as the two competiion authorities arrive at these through comparable decision-making processes. It is important to clarify that the orders considered for this analysis are the final rather than interim orders of the CCI and the CCP. In the case of the CCI this means orders passed under sections 26(6) and 27 of the Indian Act, while in the case of CCP this means orders issued in pursuance of section 31 of the Pakistani Act.

[78] Given that high courts are dispersed across India and Pakistan and do not always maintain easily accessible judicial records, obtaining data directly from them is nearly impossible.

4.4.2 *The Relevant Indicators and their Significance*

The orders of the CCI and the CCP yield important information regarding the quality of their performance and interactions as well as how these have evolved over time. The following indicators derived from the orders are particularly relevant in this regard:

(i) *Total number of final orders passed and the sectors to which these relate*: the combination of these indicators reveals the extent and range of competition enforcement in India and Pakistan and serves as a proxy for the extent to which their competition legislations are understood, utilised, and applied in their contexts.

(ii) *Number of orders passed in proceedings initiated on the basis of complaints versus number of orders passed in proceedings initiated* suo motu:[79] Proceedings before the CCI or CCP may be initiated by a complaint; by the CCI or CCP themselves taking notice of a possible infringement; or on reference from a governmental authority. Of these, the first two mechanisms for initiating competition proceedings are of particular interest because while complaints indicate the extent to which members of the public understand and utilise the competition legislations, proceedings initiated by the CCI or CCP at their own initiative ie *suo motu*, reflect the authorities' understanding of the provisions of the Acts and their keenness to enforce them. A comparison of the number of orders passed in matters initiated by complaints versus *suo motu* also indicates the extent to which the Acts have been accepted in the contexts of their countries.

(iii) *Number of orders in which judicial precedents are cited and relied upon*: the number of orders in which the CCI and CCP cite or rely upon judicial precedents (whether domestic or international) or decisions of other competition authorities, indicates the CCI and CCP's strategy for interpreting the provisions of the Indian and Pakistani Acts. The nature and extent of this reliance also indicates the compatibility and legitimacy of these competition legislations: acts that enjoy greater compatibility and legitiamcy are less likely to rely on foreign materials to establish their meaning or assert their authority.

(iv) *Number of orders which prescribe sanctions*: in terms of the Indian and Pakistani Acts, the CCI and CCP may give directions to entities found acting in vioaltion of the competition legislations or impose penalties on them. The number of orders in which CCI and CCP sanction entities whether through penalties or directions indicate the extent to which the CCI and CCP have utilised and applied the competition legislations in

[79] The term 'complaint' includes 'information' (Indian Act section 19) and 'complaint' (Pakistani, Act section 30 read with General Enforcement Regulation 17 (n.44)).

the exercise of their mandates as well as the need of the authorities to assert their authority or the confidence they feel in their respective contexts. The number of sanctioning orders therefore also reflect the extnet of compatibility and legitiamcy of the competition legislations.

(v) *Number of orders which record petitions filed before courts*: the number of orders of the CCI or CCP which record petitions filed before the high courts while proceedings are still pending before the CCI and CCP, the grounds on which these petitions are filed, and the response of the courts to these petitions provide important insight into nature and quality of the interaction between the adopted competition legislations and the pre-existing legal systems of the countries and arguably a more productive interaction between the competition and pre-existing systems reflects the greater compatibilty and legitimacy of the competition legislations.

4.4.3 *Analysing the Indicators as per the Orders of the CCI and CCP*

The indicators may be observed and compared in the orders issued by the CCI and CCP in respect of abuse of dominant position and anti-competitive agreements in the years since the authorities have been in operation to understand the extent and quality of their performance and interactions in their respective contexts.

(i) *Total number of orders and the sectors to which these relate*. The provisions relating to anti-competitive agreements and abuse of dominant position in the Indian Act were only brought into force in 2009, while similar provisions in the Pakistani competition law had been in force since 2007.[80] Table 4.1 compares the orders of the CCI and CCP in respect of these two infringements in the from the time the two authorities became operational until 2021.

A yearwise comparison of this data reveals that while the CCP commenced enforcement robustly, the CCI had a more modest and cautious start. However, the comparison further reveals that after its initial burst of activity, the CCP's enforcement steadily declined, coming to a halt in 2014. Although enforced resumed in 2015, it never quite regained initial levels.[81] In contrast, after a slow start, the CCI's enforcement increased dramatically in the first few years of its operations and although the number of orders issued by CCI has been uneven in subsequent years, CCI's operations did not come to a halt at any time (Figure 4.3).

A sector-wise analysis of these orders suggests that the disparity in the total number of orders passed by the CCI and the CCP notwithstanding, both authorities have taken cognisance of competition infringements in at least eighteen sectors across

80 Reference to the Pakistani competition law is a reference to the 2007, 2009, and 2010 Ordinances and the Pakistani Act.

81 These figures are not a comment on the overall performance of the CCI or CCP, which is more multi-faceted.

TABLE 4.1. *CCI and CCP's final orders: anti-competitive agreements and abuses of dominance*

Year	CCI's Orders	CCP's Orders
2008	–	3
2009	0	9
2010	5	8
2011	33	8
2012	31	2
2013	21	4
2014	22	0
2015	28	1
2016	8	2
2017	18	3
2018	22	5
2019	10	3
2020	8	0
TOTAL	206	48

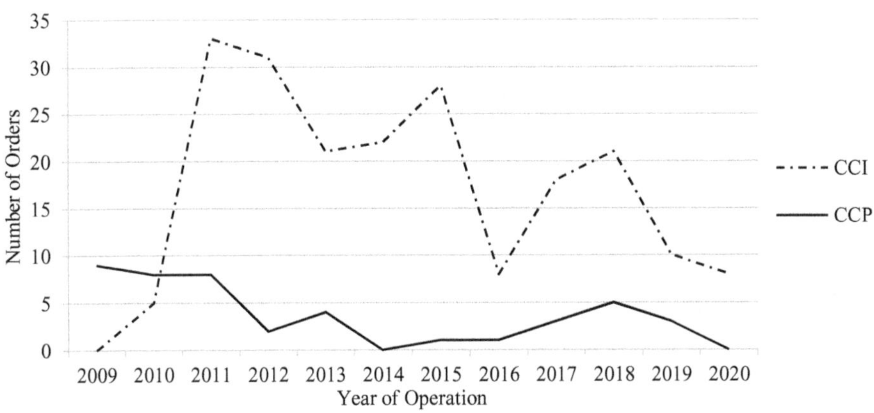

FIGURE 4.3. Comparison of total orders issued by the CCI and CCP (2007–20)

their economies, across their economies, including real estate, financial sector/capital markets, entertainment and media, health and pharmaceuticals, automobiles, information technology and telecom, petroleum and gas, railways and shipping, civil aviation, power and electricity, iron and steel, coal, food and beverage, professional services (including chartered accountants), education, and cement. However, the two authorities have not prioritised these sectors equally: for instance, while the CCI has passed the highest proportion of its total orders (nearly 16.2 per cent) in respect of entertainment and media only about 5.2 per cent of the CCP's orders are in this sector. Similarly, while the CCP has issued the highest proportion of its orders (nearly 13.2 per cent) in the food and beverage sector, only approximately 3.2 per cent of CCI's orders relate to this sector.

(ii) *Number of orders passed in proceedings initiated on the basis of complaints versus proceedings initiated* suo motu. The data suggests that while the number of cases transferred to the CCI or the CCP from their predecessor authorities and those initiated by them on the basis of references received from the governments are comparable,[82] there is considerable disparity in the numbers of cases initiated by them on the basis of complaints and *suo motu* on their own volition: the CCI has issued only 10.67 per cent of its total orders in *suo motu* cases while more than 62.5 per cent of the CCP's orders are in this category and the CCI has issued more than 73.78 per cent of its orders on the basis of complaints, while only 33.3 per cent of the CCP's orders have been initiated by complaints received from members of the public (Table 4.2).

It is further interesting to note that for both the CCI and the CCP the proportion of orders issued in response to complaints received versus orders in respect of *suo motu*

TABLE 4.2. *Year-wise breakdown of CCI and CCP's orders*

	Total Orders		*Suo Motu* Actions		Complaints	
Year	CCI	CCP	CCI	CCP	CCI	CCP[83]
2008	0	3	0	3	0	0
2009	0	9	0	5	0	4
2010	5	8	0	5	3	2
2011	33	8	1	5	24	3
2012	31	2	3	1	21	1
2013	21	4	0	3	17	0
2014	22	0	4	0	14	0
2015	26	1	2	1	23	0
2016	8	2	0	1	7	1
2017	18	3	2	1	15	2
2018	22	5	5	3	16	2
2019	10	3	3	2	7	1
2020	8	0	2	0	5	0
TOTAL	206	48	22	30	152	16
Percentage	100%	100%	10.67%	62.5%	73.78%	33.3%

82 Orders in cases transferred to them from their respective anti-monopoly authorities and those initiated on the basis of government references constitute approximately 15.65 per cent and 4.2 per cent of the CCI and CCP's total orders respectively.

83 This total does not include cases initiated by the CCP on the basis of informal complaints, that is, complaints which had not been filed in accordance with the procedure provided in the competition statute in force at the time.

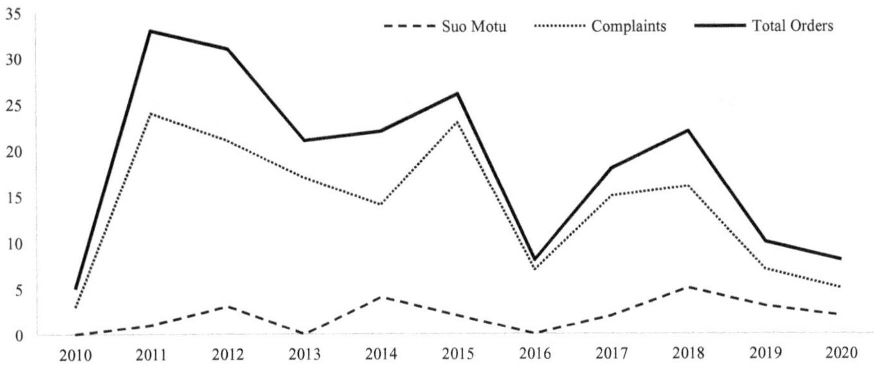

FIGURE 4.4. CCI orders in cases initiated through *suo motu* notices versus complaints

FIGURE 4.5. CCP orders in cases initiated through *suo motu* notices versus complaints

notices has not changed over time: in the case of the CCI, matters initiated on the basis of complaints remain consistently higher than matters initiated on the basis of *suo motu* notices, while in the case of the CCP orders in respect of matters initiated by *suo motu* notices consistently exceed matters initiated on the basis of complaints. Data further suggests that the decline in CCP orders in *suo motu* matters is attributable to a decline in its total orders rather than a shift towards matters initiated through complaints. Similarly, the decline in the CCI's orders in matters initiated on the basis of complaints is due to a decline in the total number of orders issued rather than a shift towards orders in *suo motu* cases (Figures 4.4 and 4.5).

(iii) *Number of orders in which judicial precedents and materials are cited*: A review of the orders of the CCI and CCP reveals that the CCP has relied more extensively and expressly on judicial precedents and materials (particuarly foreign materials and precedents) as compared to the CCI which appears to prefer interpreting the text of the Indian Act without overtly doing so (Table 4.3).

TABLE 4.3. *CCI and CCP reliance on judicial precedents and materials*

	Total Orders		Precedents or Materials Considered		Extent of Reliance on Foreign Materials	
Year	CCI	CCP	CCI	CCP	CCI	CCP
2008	0	3	0	3	0	3
2009	0	9	0	8	0	8
2010	5	8	1	6	1	6
2011	33	8	5	8	2	6
2012	31	2	4	2	3	2
2013	21	4	13	3	3	3
2014	22	0	11	0	3	0
2015	28	1	8	1	0	1
2016	8	2	3	2	2	2
2017	18	3	10	3	4	3
2018	22	5	12	4	5	2
2019	10	3	8	3	2	2
2020	8	0	5	0	0	0
TOTAL	**206**	**48**	80	**43**	**25**	**38**
Percentage	100%	100%	38.8%	80.9%	12.1%	79.16%

When they have relied on judicial precedents and materials, both the CCI and CCP have cited orders of their respective Supreme Courts and sometimes high courts, orders of the European Commission (EU Commission), the European Court of Justice (CJEU), and decisions and materials of United States anti-trust authorities. The CCI has also drawn upon materials and precedents from the Organisation for Economic Cooperation and Development (OECD), Brazil, United Kingdom (UK), Canada, Greece, Australia, and South Africa, while the CCP has cited decisions and materials from the OECD, UK, Singapore, Nordic countries, South Africa, Italy, Albania, Brazil, Hungary, Korea, and Turkey. However, the CCI has expressly referred to foreign materials and precedents in only 12.1 per cent of its orders, while the CCP has made express references to foreign precedents in 79.16 per cent of its orders. Over the years the CCI's express reliance on foreign precedents appears to have declined, and from 2013 onwards the CCI has increasingly relied upon its own earlier decisions. In the case of the CCP reliance on foreign precedents has remained consistently high, however, over time like the CCI, the CCP has increasingly relied on its own earlier decisions (Figure 4.6).

(iv) *Number of orders which prescribe sanctions.* Under their respective competition legislations, both the CCI and CCP may penalise entities engaging in anti-competitive practices, prescribe behavioural remedies for

TABLE 4.4. *CCI and CCP: Comparison of sanctions imposed*

	Total Orders		Penalties Only		Directions Only		Penalties + Directions	
Year	CCI	CCP	CCI	CCP	CCI	CCP	CCI	CCP
2008	0	3	0	0	0	2	0	1
2009	0	9	0	2	0	3	0	2
2010	5	8	0	0	0	2	0	4
2011	33	8	1	3	1	2	3	3
2012	31	2	2	0	3	0	10	2
2013	21	4	1	1	4	1	6	2
2014	22	0	0	0	3	0	13	0
2015	28	1	0	0	3	0	14	1
2016	8	2	0	1	0	0	3	1
2017	18	3	2	1	4	0	7	2
2018	22	5	7	3	1	0	8	0
2019	10	3	2	2	0	0	6	0
2020	8	0	0	0	3	0	1	0
TOTAL	206	48	15	13	22	10	71	18
	100%	100%	7.28%	27%	10.67%	20.8%	34.46%	37.5%

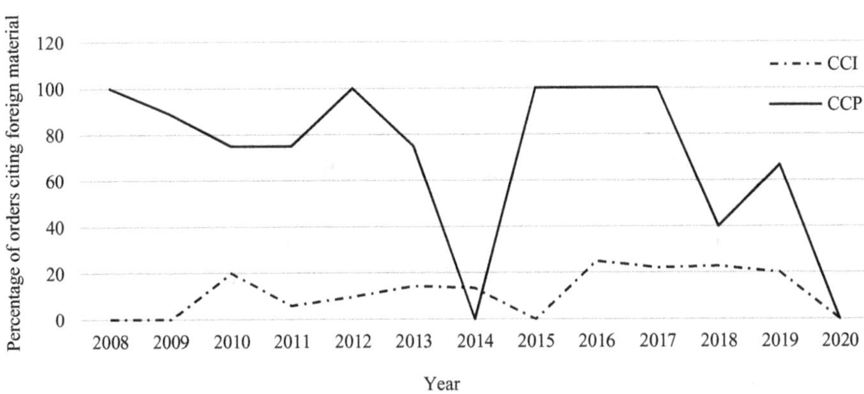

FIGURE 4.6. Comparison of orders of CCI and CCP citing foreign materials

them, or stipulate a combination of penalties and behavioural remedies. In the years since they were first made operational, the CCI and CCP have exercised all these powers, albeit to varying degrees (Table 4.4).

This data reveals that while the CCI sanctioned parties in 52.41 per cent of the cases in which it issued final orders, the CCP did so in 85.3 per cent of all such matters. The data further suggests that the preference of both the CCI and CCP for imposing penalties plus prescribing directions, the CCI doing so in 65.7 per cent of

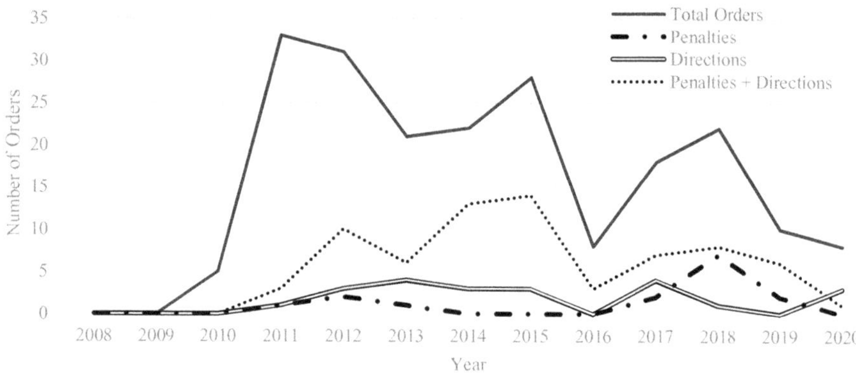

FIGURE 4.7. Trends in CCI's sanctioning strategy (2008–20)

all orders in which it imposes sanctions, and the CCP in 43.9 per cent of such orders.[84]

The year-wise trends for both the CCI and CCP suggest that the proportion of orders in which CCI has imposed sanctions has remained reasonably consistent over the years. It further appears that while the CCI has utilised all sanctioning strategies available to it, it has demonstrated a preference for different strategies at different times: for instance, between 2013 and 2019 it appears to have relied upon penalties plus directions as compared to either penalties or directions, while from 2019 onwards the number of cases in which it has imposed penalties (even with directions) appears to have declined as compared to orders in which it has issued directions only (Figure 4.7).

A year-wise trend of the CCP's orders also reveals that it has, like the CCI, utilised all sanctioning options available to it under Pakistani competition law. However, it appears that while the CCP issued directions in several cases prior to 2014 (even when these directions were given along with penalties), after 2014 it has almost entirely abandoned the practice, and in recent years has demonstrated a clear preference for imposing penalties even as compared to combining penalties with directions (Figure 4.8).

(v) *Number of orders which record petitions filed before courts.* Proceedings initiated before the CCI or CCP, or interim orders passed by them in the course of these proceedings, have been regularly challenged before Indian or Pakistani high courts on constitutional grounds. Although orders of the CCI and CCP that record these challenges are a reliable source of data for these challenges that are dispersed across high courts in India and Pakistan they only provide a partial

[84] The CCI has opted for penalties plus directions in seventy-one out of 108 (65.7 per cent) orders in which it imposed sanctions, while the CCP has done so in eighteen out of forty-one (43.9 per cent) of its orders.

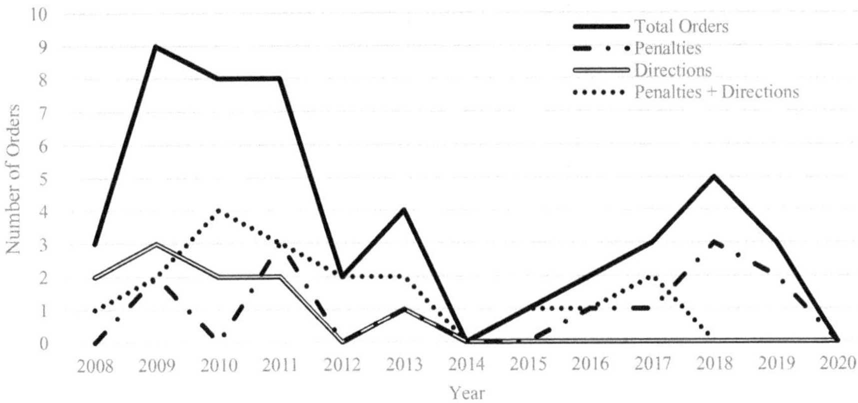

FIGURE 4.8. Trends in CCP's sanctioning strategy (2008–20)

picture in that they do not capture challenges filed in respect of proceedings are still pending before the CCI or the CCP at the time of writing, or orders in respect of these proceedings have not been posted on the official websites of the CCI or the CCP for some reason.

However, even this partial data provides important insights into the relationship between the competition authorities and the general courts in both India and Pakistan. It is evident, for instance, that more proceedings are challenged in India (47.9 per cent of all proceedings pending before the CCI) than in Pakistan (only 16.2 per cent of all proceedings pending before the CCP). However, it also appears that more proceedings before the CCP have given rise to multiple of challenges as compared to proceedings before the CCI (Table 4.5).[85]

Further, to the extent that the orders of the CCI and CCP record the decisions of the high courts in respect of these challenges, it appears that while the Indian courts restrained the CCI in 32.35 per cent challenges filed before them, several of these restraining orders were swiftly vacated and the CCI was allowed to proceed with the matters before it. Conversely, while the recorded number of restraining orders issued by Pakistani courts is low, almost none of these orders have been vacated. This is also borne out by the fact that while the Pakistani courts have only finally decided 17.2 per cent of the competition-related challenges brought before them the Indian courts have decided nearly 76.47 per cent of such matters (Table 4.6).

85 According to Table 4.6, 6 proceedings gave rise to twenty-nine challenges in Pakistan (multiplier of 4.8) while twenty-three proceedings gave rise to thirty-four challenges in India (multiplier of 1.47).

TABLE 4.5. *CCI and CCP orders recording challenges filed before general courts (2008–20)*

Year	Total Orders		Proceedings Challenged		Total Challenges[86]	
	CCI	CCP	CCI	CCP	CCI	CCP
2008	0	3	0	2	0	23
2009	0	9	1	3	1	5
2010	5	8	5	0	5	0
2011	33	8	3	0	3	0
2012	31	2	2	0	2	0
2013	21	4	4	1	5	1
2014	22	0	2	0	3	0
2015	28	1	0	0	0	0
2016	8	2	0	0	0	0
2017	18	3	2	0	8	0
2018	22	5	2	0	4	0
2019	10	3	2	0	3	0
2020	8	0	0	0	0	0
TOTAL	206	48	23	6	34	29
Percentage	100%	100%	47.9%	16.2%		

TABLE 4.6. *Response of courts to challenges filed from proceedings before proceedings before CCI and CCP*

Year	Total Challenges		Interim Orders of Courts		Final Orders of Courts	
	CCI	CCP	CCI	CCP	CCI	CCP
2008	0	23	0	4	0	2
2009	1	5	0	5	0	2
2010	5	0	0	0	6	0
2011	3	0	0	0	2	0
2012	2	0	1**	0	2	0
2013	5	1	1**	0	3	1
2014	3	0	1	0	2	0
2015	0	0	0	0	3	0
2016	0	0	0	0	0	0
2017	8	0	1	0	7	0
2018	4	0	3	0	1	0
2019	3	0	4	0	0	0
2020	0	0	0	0	0	0
TOTAL	34	29	11	9	26	5[87]
Percentage	100%	100%	32.35%	31.03%	76.47%	17.2%

** Interim orders replaced by final orders of the courts while proceedings before CCI were still pending.

[86] Some of these challenges are in respect of the same proceedings.

[87] On 26.10.2020 the Lahore High Court announced its decision in *LPG Association of Pakistan v Federation of Pakistan and others* disposing of more than ninety petitions pending before it, and on 16.09.2021, the Islamabad High Court decided *Islamabad Feeds (Private) Limited and others*

4.5 EVALUATING THE INDICATORS IN THE ADOPTION–IMPLEMENTATION CONTINUUM

The indicators derived from the orders of the CCI and CCP offer a rare insight into the compatibility and legitimacy of the Indian and Pakistani competition legislations by indicating the extent to which these are understood, utilised, and applied in their respective contexts as well as the quality of their interactions with the pre-existing legal systems in their countries. This in turn indicates the extent to and pace at which these adopted legislations are integrating into their country's legal system at the implementation stage and may therefore be regarded as successful.

The extent to which the Indian and Pakistani Acts are understood, utilised, and applied in their respective contexts may first be assessed on the basis of the number of orders that the CCI and CCP have issued since they commenced operations, and the sectors in which they have intervened.[88] It appears that although both the CCI and CCP have cast a reasonably wide net in terms of the range of sectors in which they have intervened, the numbers of their orders in respect of anti-competitive practices (which include anti-competitive agreements and abuse of dominant position) has remained somewhat erratic: while the CCI has gradually gained momentum after a slow start the CCP has lost pace despite a robust start even coming to a complete halt in 2014. Although the CCP has re-commenced enforcement since then, its total orders remain considerably lower than in its early years.

The numbers of orders of the CCI and CCP that have been issued in response to complaints filed before them as compared to orders issued in proceedings commenced *suo motu* by them, offers further insight into the extent to and manner in which the Indian and Pakistani competition legislations are utilised.[89] Where the number of orders issued in matters initiated by complaints outweigh the number of orders issued in matters in which the authorities have taken *suo motu notice*, as in the case of India, it may be argued that the Act is better understood, utilised and applied by members of the public while where orders in respect of matters initiated *suo motu* outweigh orders issued on the basis of complaints (as in the case of Pakistan) it may be argued that while the authority itself understands and is committed to utilising and applying the competition legislation, members of the public, appear neither to understand the import of the Act nor trust the ability the ability of the CCP to deliver, or both.

The link between complaints and the extent of the understanding, utilisation and application of the competition legislation by the public notwithstanding, a decline in the number of complaints received by the CCI over the years does not automatically indicate a fall in the overall understanding or utilisation of the legislation.

v Federation of Pakistan, etc. Both decisions have been appealed to the Supreme Court and at the of writing the CCP has not initiated recovery of fines in pursuance of either of these orders.

[88] Section 4.4.3 indicator 1.

[89] Section 4.4.3 indicator 2.

A review of the nature of complaints lodged before CCI over the years and the number of dismissals of complaints relative to the those that culminated in sanctions reveals that a significant proportion of complaints filed in the CCI's early years did not strictly relate to competition and, therefore, the decline in the number of complaints in successive years may be due to a better understanding of the remit of the legislation and the attendant decline of frivolous complaints.[90]

The interpretive strategies adopted by the CCI and CCP indicate their understanding of their roles and the direction in which they propose to proceed with the enforcement of their competition legislations. With regard to their interpretive strategies the fact that the CCI has relied less on precedents and materials as compared to the CCP and that it has preferred domestic rather than foreign sources. suggests that while the CCI views itself as a public-facing regulatory body that needs to make itself understood primarily to its complainants or to the entities complained about, the CCP sees itself as a judiciary-facing adjudicatory body and draws upon the authority of foreign precedents and materials to bolster its authority and to give legal cover to its opinions. The fact that the CCI relies more on domestic case law as compared to the CCP that draws extensively upon foreign authorities further suggests that while the CCI desires to assert its domestic legitimacy by expressing its alignment with India's pre-existing legal system, the CCP is keener to leverage its international legitimacy by associating with Western competition models and interpretations. Besides helping understand their substantive arguments, the interpretive strategies of the CCI and CCP also impact the extent to which their decisions, and by extension, the competition legislations they interpret, are likely to be understood and utilised by the public which in turn will bolster the future performance of the CCI and the CCP. The fact that over time, both the CCI and CCP increasingly cite their own orders suggests that both authorities have foreclosed fresh analysis of certain issues and have become more deeply entrenched their early interpretations.

Similarly the penal strategies adopted by the two authorities[91] offer an insight into how the CCI and CCP perceive their abilty to take strong enforcement action which in turn reflects their legitimacy in their contexts. The data reveals that both the CCI and CCP have utilised the entire range of sanctions available to them, which suggests that both have accepted their enforcement role and have understood and applied their mandate. However, the data also suggests that the CCI, in combining directions and penalties has preferred a balanced sanctioning strategy, which suggets that it sees its role as primarily corrective. The CCP on the other hand the CCP with its greater proclivity for penalties assumes a more punitive character. It may be argued that the CCI's relatively milder strategy in this regard is designed to safeguard its domestic legitimacy and to enhance public engagement with the

[90] In the early years orders passed under section 26(2) and 26(6) of the Indian Act outweighed orders under section 27.

[91] Section 4.4.3 indicator 4.

Indian Act and thereby to increase acceptance of the Act in the Indian context. Conversely, the more punitive strategy adopted by the CCP appears to be designed to assert its international legitimacy in the Pakistani context and to leverage it to gain domestic legitimacy. In the longer term this strategy is likely to have a contradictory effect: it may lead aggrieved parties to block the CCP's attempts to recover penalties and encourage future complainants to approach the CCP to seek redress for their grievances.

Finally, a comparison of the interactions between the CCI and CCP and India and Pakistan's general courts[92] reveals that although a comparable number of proceedings pending before the CCI and CCP have been challenged before the Indian and Pakistani general courts, the Indian courts have decided and disposed of more challenges filed before them than their Pakistani counterparts that have, until very recently, opted for restraining the CCP and keeping the petitions pending.[93] The more productive engagement between the CCI and the Indian courts reflects the relatively greater legitimacy of the Indian Act in its national context and has allowed the CCI to incrementally adapt its decisions to the requirements of India's pre-existing legal system, and thereby to increase the compatibility and legitimacy of the Act and the extent to which its provisions are understood and may be utilised by stakeholders in the coutnry. On the other hand, the lack of co-operation on the part of the Pakistani courts and the adopted competition systems seems to stem from the initially weak legitimacy of the Pakistani competition legislations which has not only deprived the CCP of much needed clarity and certainty in its operations and has thereby impeded the enforcement of the Pakistani competition legislation, but has also prevented the Pakistani Act from gaining a firm foothold in the country.

Two conclusions are evident from this assessment: first, that the Indian Act is gradually and steadily being transformed from a law in the books to a law in action and integrating into India's pre-existing legal system, while the Pakistani Act remains largely a law in the books alone and has achieved only a superficial connection with Pakistan's pre-existing legal system. Second, that a legislation which attains a higher degree of compatibility and legitimacy at the adoption stage, is more likely to be understood, utilised and applied in its context and enjoy a productive interaction with other elements in the pre-existing legal system of the host country and thereby acheives a higher degree of 'success' in the implementation stage as compared to a legislation, such as the Pakistani Act, which only achieves superficial compatiblity and legitimacy.

The compatibility and legitimacy generated through India's primary transfer mechanism of *socialisation*, which was delivered through the interplay of a wide range of bottom-up, participatory, and inclusive institutions, drawn from the executive, legislature, and the judiciary, that had the capacity to aggregate public opinion

[92] Section 4.4.3 indicator 5.
[93] See n.87.

and consent led to the '*Indianisation*' of the Act which in turn allowed the Act to be accepted and utilised as a valid part of the Indian legal system. However, this compatibility and legitimacy also seems to have rendered the CCI more cautious about preserving the space it had created for itself in the course of adoption. This manifests in the CCI's relatively conservative approach towards penal sanctions: at the deliberation stage, the Raghavan Committee had recommended that India's national competition authority recognise that the Indian economy was transitioning from a controlled to a liberal economy and, therefore, not be harsh in sanctioning violations. This principle appears to continue to guide the CCI's sanctioning strategy even today, and while it makes the CCI more acceptable to the Indian economy, it detracts from the effectiveness of competition enforcement in the country.

Conversely, Pakistan adopted its early competition legislation through *coercion* through a narrow range of exclusive, and top-down institutions and only introduced an element of *socialisation* in the adoption of the Pakistani Act by engaging in which it engaged more inclusive, bottom-up institutions that were designed to aggregate local information even if their actual experience of doing so was limited. However, just as the impact of *socialisation* in the Indian context is not all positive, the impact of *coercion* in the case of Pakistan is not all negative. The adoption of the Pakistani competition legislation through a narrow range of top-down, exclusive institutions allowed the Pakistani government to establish and operationalise the CCP within days of the promulgation of the 2007 Ordinance and thereby to achieve an early and decisive start to its competition enforcement.

However, the negative impact of *coercion* has been more far-reaching its positive effect. The compatibility and legitimacy deficit of the 2007, 2009, and 2010 Ordinances was only marginally rectified by the knowledge aggregated by the more bottom-up, participatory, and inclusive institutions engaged in the enactment of the Pakistani Act. Consequently, the compatibility and legitimacy of the Pakistani Act remained weak and manifested in the general reluctance of stakeholders to bring matters before the CCP either because they did not understand the underlying rationale for the legislation or because they did not recognise its legitimacy and in the CCP's continuing to operate largely on the basis of *suo motu* notices. The weakness in the compatibility and legitimacy of the Pakistani legislations also influenced the extent to which the CCP relied on case law and precedents, particularly foreign case law and precedents to establish its foreign antecedents and thereby to leverage its international legitimacy to gain domestic legitimacy. The CCP's penal strategy also seems to be designed for the CCP to assert itself in the domestic context in a further attempt to plug its legitimacy deficit. The fact that for a brief period the CCP issued directions only or accepted 'voluntary' commitments from the entities that had infringed competition law does not necessarily detract from the overall thrust of the CCP's penal strategy and is more likely to be a response to the CCP's inability to recover penalties due to restraining orders granted by the general courts.

However, it may also be interpreted as the CCP shrinking its enforcement until such time as its legitimacy is endorsed by the courts. Finally, the hesitant response of the Pakistani courts to the competition-related matters filed before them may be attributed at least in part to the fact that the Pakistani judiciary had been largely excluded from the deliberations at the adoption stage and that the superior judiciary's first brush with the competition legislation was when a package of ordinances introduced by a discredited military president were brought before it in the *Sindh High Court Bar Association* case, rather than with its aims or substantive provisions.

5

Anti-competitive Agreements and Interpretive Strategies in India and Pakistan

5.1 INTRODUCTION

The manner in which the CCI and CCP have interpreted the provisions of the Indian and Pakistani competition legislations in the first ten years of their operations is related to the compatibility and legitimacy generated for the legislations at the adoption stage. The greater compatibility and legitimacy generated for the Indian Act at the adoption stage allowed the CCI to rely on foreign precedents only when the legal questions involved in the case specifically required it to do so. However, the relatively weaker compatibility and legitimacy of the Pakistani Act, appeared to constrain the CCP to repeatedly invoke the close links between the Pakistani competition legislation and the EU and US competition models. Therefore, the interpretive strategies adopted by the CCI and CCP not only reflect the choice of strategy and interplay of institutions at the adoption stage but also play an important role in charting the enforcement trajectory of the competition legislations at the implementation stage.

To understand interpretive strategies employed by the CCI and CCP and their impact on the enforcement of the Indian and Pakistani competition legislations, this chapter examines the manner in which the CCI and CCP have interpreted the analytical tests for establishing anti-competitive agreements prescribed in their respective competition legislations. Given that these tests are embedded in the Indian and Pakistani legislations they have been shaped by the same transfer mechanisms and institutions that have shaped the legislations as a whole at the adoption stage. These tests also form the starting point for the CCI and CCP's assessment of anti-competitive agreements at the implementation stage. Therefore, an evaluation of the CCI and CCP's interpretation of these analytical tests not only helps understand thecompetition enforcement trajectory in India and Pakistan but also elaborates the links between the adoption and implementation stages of their respective competition legislations.

To this end Section 5.2 sets out the tests for anti-competitive agreements as provided in the Indian and Pakistani competition legislations and identifies aspects of these tests that reflect the influence of relevant provisions in the EU and US competition or antitrust legislation; Section 5.3 reviews and compares selected decisions of the CCI and CCP in respect of horizontal anti-competitive agreements (including cartels) while Section 5.4 focuses on vertical agreements. Finally, Section 5.5 explores the links, if any, between the CCI and CCP's interpretive strategies and the transfer mechanisms and institutions engaged by the countries at the adoption stage.

5.2 ESTABLISHING ANTI-COMPETITIVE AGREEMENTS IN INDIA AND PAKISTAN

The tests for establishing anti-competitive agreements provided in the Indian and Pakistani competition legislations are derived from the foreign models which have been adapted for the Indian and Pakistani contexts to varying degrees through the transfer mechanisms and institutions employed by the countries at the adoption stage. This section examines and compares these analytical tests in light of their international antecedents.

5.2.1 *The Test for Anti-competitive Agreements in the Indian Act*

Although the Indian Act does not define anti-competitive agreements, it states in section 3 that these include 'cartels'[1] as well as any other agreements, practices, or decisions[2] in respect of the 'production, supply, distribution, storage, acquisition or control of goods or provision of services' in India, that cause or are likely to cause an appreciable adverse effect on competition (AAEC) within India.[3] The Act prohibits 'enterprises', 'associations of enterprises', 'persons' or 'associations of persons' from entering into such agreements[4] and declares these to be automatically void.[5] Section 3(3) lists agreements or decisions that are *presumed* to have an AAEC including agreements or decisions to fix prices, limit or control production, divide markets, or enable bid-rigging, while section 3(4) enumerates agreements whose anti-competitive effect needs to be established by the CCI. These include tie-in arrangements, exclusive supply agreements, exclusive distribution agreements, refusals to

1 Indian Act section 2(c).
2 ibid section 3(3).
3 ibid section 3(1).
4 ibid.
5 ibid section 3(2).

deal, and agreements for resale price maintenance.[6] In terms of section 3(5) agreements that restrict the infringement of, or place reasonable restrictions for protecting rights granted under legislations listed in the sub-section are exempted from the operation of the section.[7]

Section 3 of the Indian Act is reminiscent of both section 1 of the Sherman Act 1890 and Article 101 of the Treaty of Functioning of Europe (TFEU). In assuming jurisdiction over all agreements that have or are likely to have AAEC in India and declaring them to be automatically void, section 3(1) echoes section 1 of the Sherman Act as well as Article 101(1) and 101(2) TFEU. However, in stipulating a requirement of 'appreciable' adverse effect on competition, the section reflects the EU's Notice on agreements of minor importance which do not appreciably restrict competition under Article 101(1) of the TFEU [2014] OJ C291/01 (the De Minimus notice), albeit, without providing comparable guidance for assessing appreciability.[8] Section 3 may equally be said to be a version of the US formula of 'substantial lessening of competition' employed in rule of reason analysis, which leaves it to the enforcement authorities to specify the necessary thresholds.[9]

The closed list of *presumed* anti-competitive practices enumerated in section 3(3)[10] is reminiscent of both the US per se rule and the 'by object' restriction stipulated in Article 101(1) TFEU.[11] To the extent that section 3(3) of the Act raises a *presumption* of anti-competitiveness in respect of certain agreements, it appears to be more in consonance with the scheme of Article 101 TFEU than with the per se rule, in that even though it does not specify whether the presumption is rebuttable, or list the pro-competitive factors that may be taken into account in rebutting the presumption[12] it provides an opportunity for arguments in rebuttal rather than

6 In terms of the proviso to the section, joint ventures that increase efficiency in production, supply, distribution, storage, acquisition or control of goods or provision of services are exempted from the section.

7 The laws listed in section 3(5) relate to intellectual property and include the Indian Copyright Act 1957, Patents Act 1970, Trade and Merchandise Marks Act 1958, Trademarks Act 1999, Geographical Indications of Goods Act 1999, Designs Act 2000, and the Semi-conductor Integrated Circuits Layout-Design Act 2000.

8 In its *De Minimis* notice – Notice on agreements of minor importance which do not appreciably restrict competition under Article 101(1) of the Treaty on the Functioning of the European Union (2014/C 291/01) – the EU Commission exempts agreements from the application of Article 101 if the market shares of the parties to the agreements meet the thresholds provided in the Notice.

9 Clayton Act, ch 323, 38 Stat 730 (1914) (codified as amended at 15 USC §§ 12, 13, 14–19, 21, 22–27 (2012)). id § 13 (price discrimination); id § 14 (tying and exclusive dealing); id § 18 (mergers).

10 Indian Act sections 3(3)(a) to (c).

11 Indian Act sections 3(3)(a) to (c) closely resemble Article 101(1)(a) to (c). Herbert J Hovenkamp, 'The Rule of Reason' (2018) 70 Florida Law Review 81, 98.

12 Although section 3(3) does not explicitly state this, the term 'presumption' suggests that if an agreement falls within the ambit of section 3(3), the burden of proof shifts to the defendant to prove that the agreement does not have AAEC in India.

outright declaring certain practices or agreements to be anti-competitive.[13] On the other hand, the requirement of establishing AAEC in respect of the non-exhaustive list of practices provided under section 3(4)[14] requires the balancing of anti-competitive and pro-competitive factors listed in section 19(3) of the Act, and appears to be in line with a US rule of reason analysis rather than the two-step analysis envisaged in Article 101 TFEU. Interestingly, however, the factors listed in section 19(3) closely resemble the conditions prescribed in Article 101(3) TFEU, although unlike Article 101(3), sections 3(4) or 19(3) of the Indian Act do not require the factors listed therein to be considered cumulatively.

The distinctive tests provided for anti-competitive agreements in sections 3(3) and 3(4) reflect the Act's differential treatment of horizontal agreements, that are presumed to be anti-competitive, and vertical agreements whose AAEC must be established. The Act's stance towards vertical agreements appears to be largely in consonance with the US and the EU approach traditional view of vertical agreements as only rarely anti-competitive.[15] The distinction between horizontal and vertical agreements is somewhat blurred in case of joint ventures which demonstrate specific pro-competitive effects. In terms of the proviso to section 3(3) these joint ventures may not be *presumed* to be anti-competitive but may be evaluated for AAEC. In doing so the Indian Act treats joint ventures more like section 3(4) vertical agreements distinct from other horizontal agreements under the Act. The distinctions are further confused by section 3(5) which while exempting from the application of the section, agreements placing 'reasonable' restrictions for the protection of rights under specific statutes listed in the section,[16] does not specify how reasonableness may be analysed or measured.

5.2.2 *Establishing Anti-competitive Agreements under Pakistani Competition Legislation*

The test for anti-competitive agreements under the Pakistani Act (and in the Ordinances preceding it) is spread over four sections: section 4 which stipulates the violation, and sections 5, 7, and 9 which provide for individual and block exemptions from the application of section 4. Section 4(1) defines the types of agreements and decisions that are considered anti-competitive under the Act; section 4(2) provides a non-exhaustive list of potentially anti-competitive agreements;[17] and section 4(3) declares that any agreement found to be anti-competitive

[13] Although section 3(3) does not explicitly state this, the term 'presumption' suggests that if an agreement falls within the ambit of section 3(3), the burden of proof shifts to the defendant to prove that the agreement does not in fact have AAEC in India. It is not clear, however, what factors the defendant may press in order to successfully rebut this presumption.

[14] Indian Act section 3(4)(a) to (e).

[15] See Hovenkamp (n.11) section IV and EU Commission Regulation No 330/2010.

[16] See n.7.

[17] These practices include price fixing, market partitioning, limiting quality or innovation, and collusive bidding.

under section 4(1) shall be automatically void. Section 5 allows for the possibility of individual exemptions while section 9 stipulates the criteria that an agreement or practice must fulfil in order to avail of the exemption. Section 7 enables the CCP to grant block exemptions on such terms as it may deem fit, however, unlike individual exemptions which may be obtained in respect of agreements already entered into, block exemptions may be granted prospectively if the CCP believes that a certain category of agreements or practices *are likely to* meet the criteria stipulated in section 9.[18]

These provisions of the Pakistani Act locate it squarely within the tradition and terminology of Article 101 TFEU. In prohibiting agreements that have the 'object or effect of preventing, restricting or reducing competition within the relevant market' section 4(1) replicates the language of Article 101 TFEU'; the categories of agreements listed in section 4(2) is nearly identical to the those referred to in Article 101(1) TFEU; and the criteria for exemptions provided in section 9 is comparable to that provided in Article 101(3) TFEU. Further, section 4(1), like Article 101(1) TFEU, does not distinguish between horizontal and vertical agreements; and section 4(2), declares that agreements entered into in violation of section 4 to be void just as Article 101(2) TFEU voids anti-competitive agreements under Article 101(1).

The CCP's power and discretion to grant block exemptions under section 7 of the Act appears to be in accordance with the EU's power to grant block exemptions.[19] However, section 9 which lists the conditions that must be fulfilled for block or individual exemptions is distinct form Article 101(3) in important respects. For instance, it does not require the conditions for an exemption to be established cumulatively and in fact introduces a balancing dimension[20] which is more reminiscent of the US rule of reason approach than of EU competition law.[21] In respect of individual exemptions, section 9 also does not clarify whether the exemption may be granted in independent proceedings that may be initiated by the party seeking the

18 Pakistani Act section 7(1). In terms of section 8(1)(b) it is incumbent upon the CCP to engage the public before granting any such exemption.

19 The EU Commission has issued a number of block exemptions in respect of horizontal and vertical agreements. See for instance, in respect of horizontal agreements, Commission Regulation (EU) No 1217/2010 of 14.12.2010 on the application of Article 101(3) of the Treaty on the Functioning of the European Union to certain categories of research and development agreements and Commission Regulation (EU) No 1218/2010 of 14.12.2010 on the application of Article 101(3) of the Treaty on the Functioning of the European Union to certain categories of specialisation agreements, and in respect of vertical agreements, Commission Regulation (EU) No 330/2010 of 20.04.2010 on the application of Article 101(3) of the Treaty on the Functioning of the European Union to categories of vertical agreements and concerted practices and Commission Regulation (EU) No 461/2010 of 27.05. 2010 on the application of Article 101(3) of the Treaty on the Functioning of the European Union to categories of vertical agreements and concerted practices in the motor vehicle sector.

20 Pakistani Act section 9(1)(c).

21 Michael A Carrier 'The Four-Step Rule of Reason' (Spring 2019) 33(2) Antitrust 51; Phillip E Areeda and Herbert Hovenkamp, *Antitrust Law: An Analysis of Antitrust Principles and Their Application* (2nd edn 2003) 1507(C), 385–86.

exemption, or whether an exemption application may be made in the course of a hearing under section 4.[22]

5.2.3 *How the Adoption Processes shaped the Tests for Anti-competitive Agreements*

The test for establishing anti-competitive agreements as provided in section 3 of the Indian Act combines, re-organises, and re-casts the tests for establishing anti-competitive agreements provided in the US and EU antitrust and competition laws. This suggests that rather than simply reproducing the best available, most authoritative international formula, India chose to study and adapt several authoritative formulas for the purposes of the Indian economy. This '*Indianisation*' of the test for anti-competitive agreements reflects India's dominant strategy of *socialisation*,[23] and its preference for 'learning', from the experience of countries where these competition principles had originated, even though the learning was bounded rather than rational, and did not result in the clearest possible articulation of the test for the Indian context.

The strong similarity between the scheme for evaluating and assessing anti-competitive agreements prescribed in the Pakistani Act and Article 101 TFEU, bears the unmistakable stamp of Pakistan's dominant transfer strategy of *coercion*.[24] Pakistan adopted its competition legislation at the recommendation of multi-lateral agencies and with their assistance – the government of Pakistan had initially been convinced of the need to upgrade its anti-monopoly legislation on the sidelines of the WTO Ministerial Conferences; the deliberation phase for the competition law had been spearheaded and managed by a team led by the World Bank, and the legislation itself was drafted by the Brussels-based law firm of Jones Day.[25] Given the high degree of similarity between the scheme for establishing anti-competitive agreements in the Pakistani Act and the EU competition law, suggests that Pakistan adopted the analytical test for anti-competitive agreements perhaps without fully understanding its import or how it works and without sufficient independent application of mind, or an attempt to learn from the model on which the test was based.

The fact that despite the difference in the dominant transfer strategies adopted by India and Pakistan, the tests for establishing anti-competitive agreements provided in their respective competition legislations are substantially and essentially similar, suggests that when it came to provisions relating to the mandate of the CCI and

[22] If exemptions can only be obtained in independent proceedings, then the scheme of section 4 read with section 9 departs from that of Article 101 in terms of which the defendant is required to establish the pro-competitive effects as part of the proceedings under Article 101(1).

[23] See Chapter 3.

[24] ibid.

[25] ibid.

the CCP, both countries opted for *emulation*. However, while India Indianised the language in which the test is stated, Pakistan reproduced it verbatim.[26]

The similarlity between the Indian and Pakistani tests for anti-competiive agreements also means that it is also makes it possible to compare the interpretation of these tests to understand whether the mechanisms of *socialisation-emulation* and *coercive-emulation* employed by India and Pakistan in adopting these tests continue to shape their interpretation at the implementation stage. Arguably, if the influence of the mechanisms and strategies employed at the adoption stage persists through to the implementation stage then, in the case of India, the CCI may be expected to adapt and *Indianise* foreign precedents for the Indian context and thereby continue to enhance the compatibility and legitiamcy of the competition legislation, while the CCP may be expected to rely upon EU decisions and materials in interpreting the analytical tests without adequately adapting these for the Pakistani context and in doing so, widening the gap between the adopted competitiion legislsation and the context for which it is intended.

5.3 CARTELS AND OTHER HORIZONTALS: THE FIRST DECADE OF THE CCI AND CCP

In the first ten years of their operations, both the CCI and CCP have focused more on cartels than any other type of anti-competitive practice. However, while the Indian Act *presumes* the AAEC of a cartel, the Pakistani Act leaves it to the CCP to decide whether a cartel is anti-competitive or not. This section examines selected decisions of the CCI and CCP in respect of different types of cartels, to understand how the authorities have interpreted and applied the relevant provisions of their Acts in this regard.[27]

5.3.1 *CCI and Agreements* Presumed *to Be Anti-competitive*

The questions, what is an agreement (for the purposes of section 3) and what does a 'presumption of AAEC' mean and entail are common to the CCI's orders relating to cartels, regardless of whether these are cartels for price fixing, limiting output, bid-rigging, and so on and underpin the review of the CCI's orders that follows.

5.3.1.1 The Confusion That Was the Indian Banking Association Case

The *Indian Banking Association* case was the CCI's first order in respect of any section 3 practice.[28] The issue before the CCI in this case was whether the banks' collective decision to impose a pre-payment penalty in respect of housing finance loans was anti-competitive. After reviewing the report of the DG and the evidence

[26] Ibid.

[27] This chapter only examines orders issued by the CCI under sections 26(6) and 27 of the Indian Act.

[28] *Neeraj Malhotra v Deustche Post Bank Home Finance Ltd & others* Case 5/2009 decided 02.12.2010. ('the *Indian Banking Association* case').

provided by the parties the CCI came to the conclusion that the banks had neither entered into an agreement nor acted in concert.[29] The CCI nevertheless proceeded to examine 'whether this practice causes effects of the nature mentioned under clauses (a) to (d) of sub section (3) of section 3 of the Act' or any 'appreciable adverse effect on competition' in India,[30] and found that the banks had sufficient economic justification for imposing a pre-payment penalty and, therefore, were not in violation of the section 3 of the Act.

The CCI's analysis is interesting for several reasons: first, the CCI does not just focus on the existence or otherwise of an agreement among the banks but also on the state of competition in the banking and housing industry;[31] second, the CCI refers to anti-competitive practices listed in section 3(3)(a)–(d) as anticompetitive *effects* and fails to distinguish between practices that are *presumed* to be anti-competitive and those whose anti-competitive effects must be established by the CCI with reference to the factors listed in section 19(3); and finally, it is interesting that the CCI does not clarfiy whether the section 3(3) presumption is or the person or authority that bears the responsibility to displace it.

Two CCI members dissented from CCI's main order. One of these, Member Prasad, examined the context in which the banks were operating but concluded that the banks *agreeing* to impose pre-payment penalty was an anti-competitive agreement within the meaning of section 3 of the Act. However, his conclusion rested more on a concern about and understanding of consumer interest rather than an incisive analysis of the law.[32] The other dissenting member, Member Parashar, engaged in a more rigorous analysis of the banks' 'meetings', 'common approach', and 'common decision' to impose a pre-payment penalty and concluded that these acts constituted an agreement for price fixing and limiting and controlling the provisions of services, which are *presumed* to have AAEC within the meaning of section 3(3)(a) and 3(3)(b) of the Act.[33] He also analysed the meaning of the presumption with reference to the jurisprudence of the Indian Supreme Court and concluded that it was rebuttable[34] by the defendant with reference to the factors listed in section 19(3).[35] Although member Parashar referred to both EU and US jurisprudence in arriving at his conclusion, the language he used was more closely aligned with that of US anti-trust.

5.3.1.2 An 'Agreement' Under the Indian Act

The term 'agreement' as defined in section 2(b) of the Act includes among others, understanding and arrangements whether formal or informal and whether or not

29 ibid para 17.
30 ibid para 18.
31 ibid para 15.1.
32 ibid R Prasad dissenting order.
33 ibid para 84.
34 ibid paras 96–97.
35 In this case the member concluded that the defendants had failed to rebut the presumption.

legally executed. Further, in terms of section 3 such an agreement may be entered into by an enterprise or association of enterprises or person or association of persons.[36] Over the years, the CCI has issued several orders in which it has treated decisions and practices of trade associations as agreements. For instance, the CCI found the 'joint decision making' of the association of film producers and distributors (in the *Producers and Distributors Forum* case)[37] and of the members of the Tamil Nadu Film Exhibitors Association (in the *Tamil Nadu Film Association* case)[38] and of the members of the Indian Cement Association (in the *Cement Manufacturers Association* case)[39] to be agreements for the purposes of this section. In the *CDA Goa* case, the CCI held that since the trade association was taking decisions 'relating to distribution and supply of pharma products' on behalf of its members, its practices and decisions fell within the ambit of section 3;[40] and in the *Jute Mills Association* case, it held that the 'action in concert' of members of the Gunny Trade and Jute Mills Associations to 'determine and control prices' was tantamount to a 'tacit agreement' contrary to section 3.[41] In certain cases (the *Paper Merchants Association* case, for instance),[42] the CCI found that the byelaws of the trade association rather than its decisions or actions constituted an anti-competitive agreement.[43]

The CCI's approach towards finding an agreement in cases of collusive bidding or bid-rigging is different of necessity because these agreements do not ordinarily involve trade associations. For instance, in the *PES Installations* case, the CCI looked to circumstantial evidence to establish collusion among the parties and found that the 'identical typographical mistakes in price format' reflected 'mutual contribution' and 'meeting of minds' on the part of the bidders.[44] Similarly in the *Aluminium Phosphide* case, the CCI found that the fact that the bidders had quoted

[36] See Indian Act section 2(h) for definition of 'enterprise'.

[37] *FICCI v United Producers/Distributors Forum & others* Case 1/2009 decided 25.5.2011 ('*Producers and Distributors Forum* case') para 23.5.

[38] *Reliance Big Entertainment Limited v Tamil Nadu Film Exhibitors Association & others* Case 25/2010 decided 16.02.2012 ('the *Tamil Nadu Film Exhibitors Association* case'), para 41.

[39] *Builders Association of India v Cement Manufacturers Association & others* Case 29/2010 decided 20.06.2012 ('the *Cement Manufacturers Association* case'), paras 6.5.3, 6.5.4, 6.5.19, 6.5.38, 6.5.50.

[40] *Varca Druggist & Chemist and others v Chemists & Druggists Association Goa and others* MRTP Case No. C-127/2009/DGIR (4/28), decided 11.06.2012 ('the *CDA Goa* case'), para 27.12.

[41] *Indian Sugar Mills Association & Others v Indian Jute Mills Association & others* Case 38/2011 decided 03.04.2014 ('*Jute Mills Association* case'), para 165.

[42] *Vijay Gupta v Paper Merchants Association Delhi & others* Case 7/2010 decided 24.03.2011 ('*Paper Merchants Association* case'), para 4.7.

[43] In certain other cases, the CCI's assessment of what constitutes 'an agreement' remained limited, almost cursory. See for instance *Uniglobe Mod Travels Pvt Limited v Travel Agents Federation of India & others* Case 3/2009 decided 04.10.2011 ('*Travel Agents Federation of India* case'), paras 68.1.1, 68.1.2, 68.4.5.

[44] *A Foundation for Common Cause & People Awareness v PES Installations (Pvt) Limited* Case 43/2010 decided 16.4.2012 ('*the PES Installations* case'), paras 6.2, 6.45, 6.46.

identical rates despite very different manufacturing and transportation costs was evidence of co-ordinated behaviour contrary to section 3,[45] and in the *Orissa Concrete* case, the CCI accepted the DG's view that the quotation of similar rates, the use of the same handwriting to fill out all tender documents, combined with the failure of the parties to provide a reasonable justification for these, was sufficient proof of collusion on their part.[46]

5.3.1.3 Interpreting the Presumption of AAEC

Like the concept of agreement, the CCI's understanding of the presumption of AAEC – the stage at which it comes into play and whether and how it may be rebutted – has also evolved considerably over time. For instance, in the *Producers and Distributors* case the presumption was established once the CCI found that the parties were engaged in price fixing (by fixing the revenue ratio) and limiting and controlling production (by boycotting multiplexes).[47] The CCI claimed that the presumption was rebuttable (without providing a legal justification for the claim),[48] and indicated that the rebuttal would have to be made with reference to the 'factors of AAEC given in section 19(3)'.[49] Although the CCI suggested that the primary onus for the rebuttal was on the defendants[50] it took into account the DG's examination of section 19(3) factors[51] in concluding that the presumption had not been rebutted and the parties were, therefore, in contravention of section 3 of the Act.[52]

However, this clarity of analysis is not always evident in subsequent cases. In the *CDA Goa* case the CCI noted that once a violation of section 3(3) has been established, the presumption regarding AAEC is triggered and the onus shifts to the infringing party to rebut the presumption with reference to section 19(3) factors.[53] However, after noting that the defendants had failed to discharge the burden to rebut the presumption,[54] the CCI evaluated evidence brought by the DG, however, not to decide whether the presumption could be rebutted as in the *Producers and Distributors* case, but to support its finding of AAEC.[55]

45 *Re Aluminum Phosphide Tablets Manufacturers* Suo motu Case 2/2011 decided 23.04.2012 ('the *Aluminum Phosphide* case'), paras 7.21, 7.22, 7.29, 7.32, 7.40.
46 *Shri B.P Khare v Orissa Concrete and Allied Industries & others* Ref Case 5/2011 decided 21.02.2013 ('the *Orissa Concrete* case') para 34.
47 *Producers and Distributors* case (n.37) para 23.9.
48 ibid para 23.10.
49 ibid.
50 ibid paras 23.51, 23.53.
51 ibid paras 23.54–23.57.
52 ibid para 24.
53 *CDA Goa* case (n.40), para 27.29.
54 ibid.
55 ibid para 27.31.

This confusion persisted in CCI's order in the *Travel Agents Association of India* case[56] and the *Cement Manufacturers Association* case[57] where after asserting the presumption and then rejecting the rebuttal offered by the defendants, the CCI examined section 19(3) factors not to investigate whether there was evidence of a rebuttal but to establish AAEC.

This apparent confusion regarding the nature of the presumption and the steps that the CCI took to establish AAEC in light of the presumption, gave way to a new clarity in the CCI's subsequent orders. For instance, in the *Jute Mills Association* case, the CCI observed that the argument that the CCI is required to establish AAEC for agreements falling within the ambit of section 3(3) 'is fallacious.'[58] It also referred to the defendants' attempt to shift the statutory burden of proof onto the CCI in this regard as 'wholly untenable'[59] and did not evaluate section 19(3) factors to conclude that the defendants had acted in contravention of section 3 of the Act.[60] CCI adopted a similar approach in the *Paper Merchants Association* case[61] and the *Tamil Nadu Film Exhibitors Association* case.[62]

In bid-rigging cases, the CCI's focus remained almost entirely on establishing collusion in bidding rather than on considering the presumption of AAEC. In the *PES Installations* case the CCI made no reference to the presumption of AAEC let alone to section 19(3) factors and the need for their evaluation.[63] In the *Aluminium Phosphide* case the defendants specifically raised the objection that the CCI had erred in failing to analyse section 19(3) factors.[64] However, the CCI rejected the objection on the basis that since a contravention of section 3 (3)(b) and 3(3)(d) had been established, 'the AAEC [was] presumed per se' and the presumption could only be rebutted by the defendants' through 'cogent evidence'.[65] Interestingly, despite rejecting the legal requirement for doing so, the CCI still evaluated section 19(3) factors before concluding that the defendants had contravened section 3 of the Act.[66] The CCI followed a similar approach in the *Orissa Concrete* case.[67]

56 *Travel Agents Federation of India* case (n.43) paras 68.2.1, 68.2.4, 68.2.5, 68.9.2.
57 *Cement Manufacturers Association* case (n.39) paras 6.10.7, 6.10.8, 6.10.11.
58 n.41 para 173.
59 ibid.
60 ibid. Regardless, however, the CCI noted the DG's evaluation of section 19(3) factors in this regard.
61 n.42 para 4.10.
62 n.38 para 45.
63 n.44 paras 6.60–6.64.
64 n.45 para 7.6.
65 ibid para 7.42.
66 ibid paras 7.43, 7.45.
67 n.46 paras 35, 36, 38, 42.

5.3.2 *Interpretive Challenges for the CCP*

Like its Indian counterpart, the CCP has also tackled several cartels in the years it has been in operation. This section examines how the CCP has interpreted the terms 'agreement' and 'by object' as well as its overall strategy for establishing cartels under the Pakistani Act.[68]

5.3.2.1 Defining the 'Agreement'

In its earliest orders, the CCP appeared sure-footed in defining anti-competitive agreements. For instance, in the *Pakistan Banking Association* case,[69] it found that an advertisement issued by the Pakistan Banking Association regarding the Enhanced Savings Account scheme constituted a decision of the association and was, therefore, an agreement for the purposes of the Act.[70] Similarly, in the *Institute of Chartered Accountants of Pakistan* case it found a circular conveying a decision of the Institute's Council to be an agreement,[71] while in the *Karachi Stock Exchange* case, it held that the decisions of the three stock exchanges constituted an arrangement among them and their respective members, and were therefore, agreements under the Act.[72]

In bid-rigging cases the CCP focused on conduct which 'may amount to a concerted practice', and on situations in which parties knowingly adopt or adhere to collusive practices which facilitate co-ordination.[73] CCP also considered 'coincidences' and 'indicia' to point in the direction of an agreement if there were 'no other plausible explanation' for them..[74] Factors the CCP took into consideration in this regard included failure to contest 'wrongful' disqualification and failure to provide basic documents required of a bid,[75] formation of a joint venture for the purposes of bidding, voluntary price reduction, absence of consideration for an agreement, membership of the same corporate group and close business dealings among bidders (evidenced by a common business address and use of common business facilities).[76]

68 Pakistani Act section 2(1)(b).

69 File 2/sec-4/CCP/07 decided 10.04.2008.

70 ibid para 46.

71 File 3/Sec-4/CCP/08 decided 04.12.2008. para 3. The CCP relied on this decision in subsequent cases, see for instance, *Pakistan Vanaspati Manufacturers Association* case File 1(15)/PVMA-ISB decided 30.06.2011 ('the *Vanaspati Association* case'), para 34.

72 File 1/Dir(Inv.) KSE/CCP/08), decided 18.03.2009.

73 *Dredging Companies* case, File 3(17)/L.O/CCP/2009 decided 23.07.2010 paras 40, 42.

74 ibid para 41.

75 ibid para 43.

76 *PESCO Tender Order/Amin Brothers Engineering et al* case, File 13/PESCO/CMTA/CCP/2010 decided 13.05.2011 ('*the PESCO Tender Order* case'), paras 47–48, 51–52.

In certain cases, such as the *1-Link* case,[77] where the CCP was presented with a formally executed agreement, it did not have to establish the existence of the agreement, and, therefore, moved directly to an evaluation of whether such an agreement had the object or effect of restricting competition in Pakistan.

5.3.2.2 Between the 'Object' and the 'Effect'

For an agreement to be found anti-competitive under section 4 of the Pakistani Act, it must either have an anti-competitive object or effect. In the *Pakistan Banking Association* case, the CCP found that the agreement among the banks to collectively decide rates of profits and other terms and conditions regarding deposit accounts was in violation of section 4 of the Act. In reaching this conclusion, the CCP relied almost exclusively on EU and US precedents[78] rather than considering the objectives of the agreement or the context in which it was executed. It also did not provide an opportunity for the defendants to argue for an exemption under section 5 (read with section 9) of the Act (thereby excluding an Article 101(3) TFEU style analysis of possible pro-competitive effects of the agreement).[79] The CCP also rejected the possibility of applying an EU style *de minimis* rule.[80]

In the *Institute of Chartered Accountants of Pakistan* case, the CCP found the practice of prescribing a minimum fee to be tantamount to price fixing and, therefore, per se anti-competitive[81] or anti-competitive by object.[82] Similarly, in the *Karachi Stock Exchange* case the CCP categorised the exchanges' decision to fix a price floor, as a 'per se violation'[83] and concluded that it had the object of restraining competition.[84] In the *1-Link* case, the CCP drew a distinction between prices fixed by a joint venture for the purposes of 'creating significant and beneficial efficiencies that could not otherwise be accomplished'[85] and other 'horizontal price fixing agreements'.[86] It held that while the former 'may be considered under a rule of reason' and would be eligible for consideration of an exemption under the Act,[87] the latter were to be viewed 'as having the object of preventing, restricting and reducing competition' and, therefore, not eligible for an exemption.[88] Interestingly,

77 *1-Link Guarantee Limited & Member Banks* case ('*the 1-Link* case') File 1/24/ATM Charges/C&TA/CCP/2011 decided 28.06.2012.
78 n.69 paras 48–50.
79 ibid.
80 ibid.
81 n.71 para 12.
82 ibid paras 21 and 35.
83 n.72 paras 44–45, 48–49, 52–53.
84 Even though the order argues that the object of the agreement is to be determined by understanding the objective intent of the parties, it makes little attempt to do so.
85 n.77 para 62.
86 ibid para 91.
87 ibid para 62.
88 ibid para 97.

however, even in respect of agreements where the CCP deemed a rule of reason inquiry to be warranted, it moved directly to considering the exemption without actually engaging in such analysis.[89]

In cases of collusive bidding, the CCP appeared uncertain about the analytical test to apply. In the *Dredging Companies* case[90] the CCP examined the treatment of collusive bidding in various jurisdictions,[91] and came to the conclusion that 'bidding consortia are to be treated on case-to-case basis applying the rule of reason and should not be treated as per se illegal i.e. agreements that always have anti-competitive objects and effects'.[92] However, rather than actually undertaking a rule of reason analysis, the CCP decided the case on an evaluation of the relevant market, specifications of the project that had been bid for, and the legal status of the parties to the agreement. Within a year of this order the CCP reconsidered its position when in the *PESCO Tender Order* case it held that 'collusive bidding remains in the restraint by object category before the Commission' as the 'anti-competitive effects of these actions have consistently been established over a hundred years of competition jurisprudence and no economic evidence has been established that shows pro-competitive benefits of these actions'.[93] Interestingly, the CCP did not distinguish the *Dredging Companies* case,[94] and did not cite any precedent in support of its arguments.

In contrast to its treatment of bid-rigging, the CCP found all instances of market allocation to be anti-competitive per se or by object. However, a closer reading of two of its decisions in this regard – one in the *GCC Medical Centres* case[95] and the other in the *LDI* case[96] – reveals disparity in the CCP's reasoning. In the *GCC Medical Centres* case, the CCP noted the existence of two anti-competitive agreements, one for price fixing and the other for market allocation. However, rather than categorising these agreements as horizontal or vertical or as anti-competitive by object or by effect, the CCP simply analysed the texts of the agreements, described the allegedly anti-competitive practice and concluded that the agreements were in violation of section 4 of the Pakistani Act by reference to foreign literature and precedents. In respect of the price fixing agreement, the CCP accepted the justifications offered by the defendants,[97] while in respect of the market allocation agreement, it penalised the defendant on the ground that division

89 ibid para 64.
90 n.73 para 47.
91 n.73 paras 48–52, 56–57.
92 n.73 para 59.
93 n.76 para 30.
94 n.73.
95 *GCC Approved Medical Centres* File 2(2)/JD(L)/POEPA/CCP/2011, decided 29.06.2012 ('the *GCC Medical Centres* case'), paras 100–05.
96 *LDI Operators* case File 5(114)/Reg/ADG-SCP/LHC/CCP/13 decided 30.04.2013 ('the *LDI* case') to the extent that it relates to price fixing (paras 93–108).
97 n.95 para 94.

of markets was restrictive of consumer choice and therefore exploitative of consumers.[98] It was only in quantifying the penalty for these contraventions that the CCP noted that 'respondents have engaged into an arrangement . . . which is per se illegal'.[99] The CCP adopted a different approach in the *LDI* case, in which after it had declared quota/market allocation as 'a per se' violation under EU competition law, and had expressly acknowledged that it was not required to conduct economic analysis for a per se violation,[100] it carried out perhaps its first (if not only) quasi economic analysis of an anti-competitive agreement.[101]

5.3.2.3 CCP's Analytical Steps for Horizontal Agreements

The CCP typically commenced its analysis of horizontal agreements by establishing the existence of an agreement. In the majority of its orders, this finding was immediately followed by a strong invocation of the Pakistani Act's foreign antecedents. For instance, in the *Pakistan Banking Association* case, before applying section 4 of the Act to the alleged anti-competitive agreement, the CCP traced the links of the provision to Article 81 of the EU Treaty and reproduced the analytical test as stated in Article 81, noting in particular that the terms 'object' and 'effect' were disjunctive, that is, if an agreement is deemed to have an anti-competitive object there was no need to inquire into its effect.[102] The CCP then cited a range of EU and US precedents in support of its arguments to establish the international context,[103] before moving on to examining the alleged agreement between the banks, however, even this analysis was carried out largely with reference to foreign precedents rather than the likely economic impact of the agreement in the context in which it was intended to operate.

The CCP similarly invoked its foreign pedigree in the *ICAP* case:[104] it noted that section 4 was 'similar to Article 81 of the Treaty of Rome'[105] and was also 'in congruity with section 1 of the Sherman Antitrust Act of the United States'.[106] Then relying almost exclusively on US decisions, the CCP came to the conclusion that ICAP's actions were tantamount to a per se or by object restriction of competition and therefore in violation of section 4 of the Act.[107] In the *Karachi Stock Exchange* case, the CCP combined the EU understanding of 'by object'[108] with

98 ibid paras 100, 102, 105.
99 ibid para 107.
100 n.96 paras 119–20. Interestingly, in finding a per se violation the CCP drew support from the EU Guidelines on Application of Article 81.
101 n.96 paras 144–60.
102 n.69 para 48.
103 ibid paras 49, 50.
104 n.71.
105 ibid para 11.
106 ibid.
107 ibid paras 12, 13, 14.
108 n.72 para 42.

the US concept of 'naked restraints'[109] and thereby found the stock exchanges' decision to fix a price floor, to be a 'per se violation'[110] of the Act and having the object of restraining competition.

The CCP repeated its reasoning in the *Karachi Stock Exchange* case in a several subsequent orders such as in the *All Pakistan Newspaper Society* case,[111] the *All Pakistan Cement Manufacturers Association* case,[112] the *Dredging Companies* case,[113] and the *PESCO Tender Order* case.[114] Over time, however, the CCP's reasoning in this regard grew more cursory,[115] such that when it issued its decision in the *1-Link* case, the CCP simply addressed the facts before it rather than recounting the history of its connection with the EU and US regimes.[116] The CCP, however, continued to cite foreign precedents in support of its arguments.

This seeming uniformity in the CCP's approach towards horizontal agreements was punctuated with interesting exceptions. For instance, in the *PESCO Tender Order* case,[117] after a discursive review of the Pakistani Act's fundamental connection with EU and US regimes, the CCP noted that '(t)his similarity with the EU Law does not mean that Pakistan must only look at EU case law and principles … we have over time developed our own jurisprudence and are not bound by any particular international jurisprudence.[118] The CCP then leveraged this declaration of independence to hold that collusive bidding was a by-object restraint of competition albeit with the support of precedents from a range of international jurisdictions, and without distinguishing the *Dredging Companies* case.[119] Another departure from its uniform approach is evident in the *Vansapati Association* case,[120] in which responding to an argument that it was incumbent upon the CCP to examine the

[109] ibid.

[110] ibid paras 44, 45, 48, 49, 52, 53.

[111] File 06/Sec 3/CCP/08 decided 23.04.2009.

[112] File 4/2/Sec 4/CCP/2008 decided 27.08.2009.

[113] n.73.

[114] n.76.

[115] See, for instance, *Jamshoro Joint Venture Limited and LPG Association of Pakistan* File 3/LPG/DIR(INV)/M&TA/CCP/2009 decided 14.12.2009; *Takaful Pakistan Ltd and Travel Agents' Association of Pakistan* File 9/M(A&R)/CAA-TAAP/CCP/2007 decided 29.01.2010; *Pakistan Poultry Association* File CCP/Cartels/04/2010 decided 16.08.2010; *Pakistan Jute Mills Association and its member mills* File CCP/Cartels/03/2010 decided 03.02.2011; *Pakistan Ship's Agents' Association* File 08/APPMA/CMTA/CCP/10/1709 decided 22.06.2011, and *LDI Operators* case (n.96).

[116] n.77. The CCP stated in its order that the difference between EU and US competition/antitrust law was only of 'semantics' and that the EU law encompassed 'the principles developed in the US jurisdiction within its statute' (para 25). The CCP also stated that the 'EU classification of "object" and "effect" echoes the broad principles developed by the US courts in the "per se" and "rule of reason" doctrines' and the 'various terms developed in the US and the EU, therefore, have the same underlying principles' (para 27).

[117] n.76.

[118] n.76 para 28.

[119] n.76 para 30.

[120] n.71.

legal and economic context in which the agreement had been executed, the CCP held that establishing the legal and economic context of the agreement was the responsibility of the defendant and not that of the CCP.[121]

5.3.3 *Evolution of CCI's and CCP's Approach towards Anti-competitive Agreements*

The CCI's more recent decisions demonstrate increasing clarity and uniformity in its approach towards horizontal anti-competitive agreements. While the CCI has interpreted and explained the analytical test for anti-competitive agreements in a number of its decisions,[122] in an almost equal, if not greater number of other decisions it has applied a somewhat truncated version of the test to the facts before it without any reference to the provisions of the Indian Act.[123]

In the majority of its decisions, the CCI has applied the test uniformly, without reference to its US or EU antecedents and without expressly citing international case law. The CCI has focused on establishing the existence of an agreement and has *presumed* AAEC, eschewing the urge to examine section 19(3) factors to establish it. For instance, in the *Malayalam Movie Artists* case, the CCI focused on finding a tacit understanding between the members of the association, and then directly imposed a penalty on the parties for their anti-competitive conduct.[124] Similarly in the *Dry Battery Cell* case[125] and the *EPS Systems* case,[126] the CCI moved

[121] ibid para 53(b).

[122] For instance *Indian Foundation of Transport Research & Training v Sh. Bal Malkait Singh & others* Case 61/2012 decided 16.02.2015; *Sheth & Co. & others* Suo Motu Case 4/2013 decided 10.06.2015; *Cartelization in Public Sector Insurance Companies* Suo Motu Case 2/2014 decided 10.07.2015; *Shri Ghanshyam Das Vij v Bajaj Corporation Limited & others* Case 68/2013 decided 12.01.2015; *Express Industry Council of India v Jet Airways (India) Limited & others* Case 30/2013 decided 17.11.2015; the *Cement Manufacturers Association* case (n39); *Re Alleged Cartelization by Cement Manufacturers v Shree Cement Limited and others* RTPE 52/2006 decided 31.08.2016.

[123] For instance *Swastik Stevedores Private Limited v Dumper Owner's Association & others* Case 42/2012 decided 21.01.2015; *Rohit Medical Store v Macleods Pharmaceutical Limited & others* Case 78/2012 decided 29.01.2015; *Shri Jyoti Swaroop Arora v Tulip Infratech Limited & others* Case 59/2011 decided 03.02.2015; *Bio Med Private Limited v Union of India & others* Case 26/2013 decided 04.06.2015; *Kerala Cine Exhibitors Association v Kerala Film Exhibitors Federation & others* Case 45/2012 decided 23.06.2015; *Kannada Gratiakara Koota Shri Ganesh Chetan v Karnataka Film Chamber of Commerce & others* Case 58/2012 decided 27.07.2015; *Crown Theatre v Kerala Film Exhibitions Federation* Case 16/2014 decided 08.09.2015; and *Shivam Enterprises v Kiratpur Sahib Truck Operators Transport Society Limited & others* Case 43/2013 decided 04.02.2015.

[124] *Shri T G.Vinayakumar v Association of Malayalam Movie Artists and others* Case No. 98/2014 decided 24.03.2017 ('the *Malayalam Movie Artists* case'), paras 7.51–7.72, 7.91.

[125] *In Re: Cartelisation in respect of zinc carbon dry cell batteries market in India* Suo Motu Case No 02 of 2016 decided 19.04.2018 ('the *Dry Battery Cell* case').

[126] *In Re: Cartelisation in the supply of Electric Power Steering Systems* Suo Motu Case No 07 (01) of 2014 decided 09.08.2019 ('the *EPS Systems* case').

immediately from establishing the existence of the cartel to considering the application of leniency (in the *Dry Battery Cell* case)[127] and the quantum of penalty (in the *EPS Systems* case).[128]

Like the CCI, the CCP also appears to have moved away from detailed discussions regarding its international antecedents. However, the CCP still appears hesitant to set out an analytical test for anti-competitive agreements that is fully anchored in the language of section 4 and continues to hinge its findings either on a single foreign decision that fits the particular facts of the case before it[129] or on its own earlier decisions.[130]

5.4 VERTICAL AGREEMENTS UNDER THE INDIAN AND PAKISTANI ACTS

In addition to horizontal agreements under section 3(3) of the Indian Act, the CCI has also examined a number of vertical agreements under section 3(4) in terms of which it is incumbent upon the CCI to establish AAEC with reference to section 19(3) factors. However, a review of some of the CCI's key decisions under section 3(4) reflects a lack of consistency if not confusion as to the type of agreements that may be included in this section as well as how these may be analysed.

The CCI first discussed a section 3(4) violation in the *Global Automobiles* case[131] in which it was alleged that the agreements between defendant automobile companies and their distributors were unduly restrictive and therefore anti-competitive. In deciding this case, the CCI listed five requirements for establishing a contravention of section 3(4): there must be an agreement; the parties to such agreement must be at different stages or levels of the production chain; the parties must be in different markets; the agreement should be for one or more of the practices listed in clauses (a) to (e) of section 3(4), and the agreement should cause or be likely to cause AAEC.[132] The CCI further stated that in ascertaining AAEC of such an agreement, the 'existence of the first three factors listed in section 19(3) would normally indicate no AAEC as they are in the nature of efficiency justifications',[133] however, it also cautioned that the absence of the last three factors alone could

[127] n.125 paras 9.24, 9.28, 9.30.

[128] n.126 paras 24–25.

[129] *Pakistan Poultry Association* File 42/PPA/C & TA/CCP/2015 decided 29.02.2016 ('the *Poultry* case').

[130] *Pakistan Automobile Manufacturers Authorized Dealers Association & Member Undertakings* File 1/101/PAMADA/C & TA/CCP/2013 decided 10.04.2015 ('the *PAMADA* case').

[131] *Automobile Dealers Association v Global Automobiles & others* Case 33/2011 decided 03.07.2012 ('*Global Automobiles* case').

[132] ibid para 12.4.

[133] ibid para 12.9.

neither determine AAEC nor establish efficiency. On this basis the CCI concluded, that in most cases it would be prudent to examine all section 19(3) factors to arrive at the agreement's net impact on competition.[134] On the facts of the case, although the CCI found an agreement as well as evidence of anti-competitive practices[135] it held that the parties to the agreement had only an 'insignificant presence in the market' and, therefore, were not capable of causing AAEC. In doing so the CCI explicitly drew support from the EU *de minimus* rule stating that 'this is probably the reason that in EU, vertical agreements are not given much of a thought unless both parties possess at least 30% market share in respective markets'.[136]

The CCI followed a similar approach in the *Apple* case[137] in which it held that although Apple and Airtel/Vodafone had entered into a tying-in agreement which was proscribed under section 3(4),[138] the agreement did not cause AAEC because 'for a vertical agreement to be anti-competitive requires the monopolization claim to hold, and given the minuscule market share of the tying party the monopolization claim will be contrived'.[139] The CCI nevertheless evaluated section 19(3) factors before concluding that the defendants had not infringed section 3(4).[140] The CCI also noted that the defendants did not have an 'intention' to foreclose competitors.[141]

The 'intent to foreclose' argument appeared once again in the *Hockey India* case,[142] in which the restrictions placed by Hockey India on the free movement of hockey players were alleged to be in violation of section 3(4).[143] Although the CCI found the agreement between Hockey India and the players to be a vertical agreement,[144] it cited its decision in the *Apple* case[145] to argue that for a vertical agreement to be anti-competitive the entitty imposing the vertical restriction should be in a dominant position and should have the intention to foreclose competition in the market.[146] On the specific facts of the case, the CCI found the restrictions imposed by Hockey India to be 'proportionate' to its objectives and, therefore, not in contravention of section 3(4).[147] By re-emphasizing the element of intent which it

[134] ibid.
[135] ibid para 12.5.
[136] ibid paras 12.10, 12.13.
[137] *Shri Sonam Sharma v Apple Inc. USA & others* Case 24/2011 decided 19.03.2013 ('the *Apple* case').
[138] ibid paras 63, 65, 69.
[139] ibid para 70.
[140] ibid para 80.
[141] ibid paras 70, 74.
[142] *Shri Dhanraj Pillay & others v Hockey India* Case 73/2011 decided 31.05.2013 ('the *Hockey India* case').
[143] ibid para 10.13.1.
[144] ibid para 10.13.2
[145] n. 137.
[146] ibid para 10.13.2.
[147] ibid para 10.13.6.

had earlier referred to in the *Apple* case,[148] and by introducing the element of proportionality the anti-competitive effects of an agreement the CCI not only conflated an abuse of dominance analysis with a vertical agreement analysis but also re-defined the very idea of anti-competitive effect.

In the *Honda Siel* case[149] the CCI examined agreements between Original Equipment Manufacturers (OEMs) and their Original Equipment Suppliers (OESs) and distributors and re-affirmed and clarified several important principles relating to section 3(4) agreements which also formed the basis of several of its subsequent decisions.[150] For instance, the CCI underscored that parties to a vertical agreement must be part of the same production chain; it explicitly recognised the single economic entity doctrine as enunciated in EU law (in relation to the agreements between the OEMs and their overseas OESs) but relied upon US jurisprudence to establish the parameters of the doctrine.[151] The CCI also re-asserted the significance of section 19(3) factors in establishing AAEC, and defined the trigger for and scope of the section 3(5) exemption.[152] Finally, although the CCI acknowledged the possibility of selective distribution networks (in relation to agreements between OEMs and their authorised dealers), after examining guidelines and decisions from more advanced competition regimes,[153] it concluded that there was no justification for allowing such networks to operate in the present case.[154] The CCI also identified more 'Indianised' aspects of anti-competitive vertical agreements: for instance, in respect of agreements between OEMs and their foreign OESs that were not part of the same group, the CCI required evidence of a 'conspiracy' in addition to the finding of an agreement,[155] while in respect of agreements between OEMs and their local distributors (which the CCI found to be anti-competitive) the CCI relied upon the unexplained concept of 'greater public good'.[156]

[148] n.137.

[149] *Shri Shamsher Kataria v Honda Siel Cars India Limited & others* Case 3/2011 decided 25.08.2014. ('the *Honda Siel* case').

[150] For instance, *ESYS Information Technologies Pvt Ltd v. Intel Corporation (Intel Inc.) & others* Case 48/2011 decided 16.01.2014; *Magnus Graphics v Nilpeter India Pvt Ltd & others* Case 65/2013 decided 02.12.2014, and Case 52/2013 *Financial Software and Systems Pvt Limited v ACI Worldwide Solutions Private Limited and others* decided 13.01.2015.

[151] n.149 para 20.6.3.

[152] ibid para 20.6.7.

[153] ibid paras 20.6.24–20.6.42. The CCI also drew an analogy between section 19(3) and Article 101 (3) TFEU and referred to the Guidelines on the Application of Article 81(3), EU Vertical Block Exemption Regulations (with specific reference to hardcore restraints), the practice and decisions of Brazilian and South African competition authorities, the French Competition Authority's sectoral inquiry of motor vehicle and to several EU and US decisions.

[154] ibid para 20.6.23.

[155] ibid para 20.6.6.

[156] ibid paras 20.6.26, 20.6.28.

The CCI's most interesting, indeed controversial decision in respect of vertical agreements was in the *Hiranandani Hospital* case,[157] in which the CCI found an agreement between a hospital and a stem cell bank to be in violation of section 3(4). The CCI arrived at this conclusion by reading section 3 of the Act in light of the Act's overall purpose (which it said was to protect freedom of trade and consumers' interests), and by arguing that doing so allowed it to consider the impact of *any* agreement that fell within the ambit of section 3(1) even if it could not be clearly categorised as a section 3(3) or 3(4) agreement.[158] The CCI found the agreement between the hospital and the stem cell bank to be 'anti-competitive' on the basis that exclusive contracts between a hospital and stem cell bank restricted consumer choice, dampened innovation, and foreclosed competition in the stem cell market.[159] Further, although the CCI engaged in a spirited examination of section 19(3) factors, it stopped short of an economic analysis and ignored the 'appreciability' argument which had informed its earlier decisions.[160] Two members issued dissenting orders in this matter: Member Gauri arguing that there was no vertical agreement in this matter because 'the hospital was a platform'; there was no 'final consumable product', and no tie-in because 93 per cent of the patients had the choice of availing only maternity services offered by the hospital,[161] and Member Tayal arguing that section 3(1) could not be 'interpreted de-hors of section 3(3) and section 3(4) of the Act', and that the provisions of section 3(4) may be applied only when there is an agreement between two undertakings operating at different stages of the production chain.[162]

In its recent decisions, the CCI has clarified the principles for evaluating vertical agreements, not only in respect of traditional brick and mortar sectors but also in the digital space, however, the CCI has still avoided a detailed analysis of section 19(3) factors as well as rigorous economic analysis. For instance, in the *Hyundai* case[163] in which it considered allegations relating to exclusive supply agreements, retail price maintenance, and at least three different types of tie-ins, the CCI analysed the facts and the relevant clauses of the agreement and affirmed its decisions in the *Honda Siel* case[164] and the *Apple* case,[165] to establish retail price

[157] *Mr Ramakant Kini v Dr LH Hiranandani Hospital, Powai, Mumbai* Case 39/2012 decided 05.02.2014 ('*Hiranandani Hospital* case'). The CCI followed this reasoning in several later cases, including *PK Krishnan v Paul Madavana Alkem Laboratories & others* Case 28/2014 decided 01.12.2015 and *Maruti & Company v Karnataka Chemists & Druggists Association & others* Case 71/2013 decided 28.07.2016.

[158] ibid para 15.

[159] ibid para 20.

[160] ibid. Also n.131, n.137.

[161] ibid Dissenting Order, Member Gauri para 61, 67.

[162] ibid Dissenting Order, Member Tayal para 4, 14.

[163] *Fx Enterprise Solutions India Pvt Ltd v Hyundai Motor India Limited* Case Nos 36 & 82 of 2014 decided 14.06.2017 ('the *Hyundai* case').

[164] n.149.

[165] n.137.

maintenance.[166] However, instead of examining possible pro-competitive justifications listed in section 19(3) the CCI moved directly to sanctioning Hyundai.[167] Similarly in the *KAFF Appliances* case,[168] the CCI explored the elements of anti-competitive vertical agreements in the digital space and found evidence of price prescription. However, instead of establishing whether the price prescription led to AAEC, the CCI moved directly to considering the justifications offered by KAFF.[169] Its decisions in the *Hyundai* case and the *KAFF Appliances* case reflect the CCI's reasoning in the *Hiranandani Hospital* case,[170] despite its decision having been overturned by Indian Tribunal.[171] In the *Hyundai* case for instance, the CCI held that for two products to be tied together it is not necessary that the products form part of a single product chain or result in an observable end-product,[172] while in the *KAFF Appliances* case it held that a platform is part of a vertical supply chain.[173]

Unlike the CCI, the CCP evaluates vertical agreements in the same way as it does horizontal agreements. Although the CCP first discussed anti-competitive vertical agreements in the *Karachi Stock Exchange* case,[174] it did not apply this discussion to the facts of the case, and it was only in the *Wateen* case which dealt with an exclusive services agreement between a telephone company and a residential authority that it focused specifically on vertical agreements.[175] Even in this case, however, instead of exploring the concept of vertical agreements or the context in which the particular agreement in the caes was operating, the CCP concluded that the agreement was anti-competitive after simply interpreting the clauses of the agreement.[176] The *Vanaspati Association* case offered another opportunity for the CCP to consider vertical agreements between the Vanaspati Manufacturers' Association and transporters' associations.[177] However, instead of evaluating the object or effect of these agreements the CCP simply held that 'no determination with respect to this issue [could] be made unless all parties concerned are probed on this account'.[178]

[166] n.163 paras 76, 94, 104, 108, 114.
[167] n.133 para 116 onwards.
[168] *In Re: Jasper Infotech Private Limited (Snapdeal) v KAFF Appliances (India) Pvt Ltd (Kaff)* Case No 61 of 2014 decided 15.01.2019 ('the *KAFF Appliances* case').
[169] ibid see paras 56–63, 69–70.
[170] n.157 and the text thereto.
[171] *Dr LH Hiranandani Hospital v CCI and another* Appeal 19/2014 decided 18.12.2015.
[172] n.163 para 99.
[173] n.168 paras 36–37. More interestingly, the echoes of the *Hiranandani Hospital* case may also be heard in the CCI's decisions in respect of horizontal agreements. For instance, in the *Malayalam Movie Artists* case the CCI notes that the scope of section 3 of the Act is much wider than sections 3(3) and that even if an agreement does not fall within these two sub-sections it may be deemed to be anti-competitive if it has AAEC. n.124 para 7.93.
[174] n.72 paras 43–45.
[175] *Wateen Telecom (Pvt) Limited and Defence Housing Authority* case, Case 09/Reg/Comp/CAP/CCP/2010 decided 22.03.2011. ('the *Wateen* case').
[176] ibid para 29.
[177] n.71 para 51.
[178] ibid para 54.

The CCP issued a somewhat more detailed decision in respect of vertical agreements in the *Engro Vopak Terminal Limited* case,[179] which related to a concessionary agreement between a port authority and a terminal operating company for the handling and storage of liquid chemicals. Although the CCP concluded that the agreement was anti-competitive because it granted exclusive rights to a private entity and was likely to foreclose competition in the relevant market,[180] it did not categorise the agreement as either horizontal or vertical, did not address whether the agreement was anti-competitive by object or effect, and did not engage in any economic analysis in arriving at its conclusion. Instead, as it had in the *Wateen* case,[181] the CCP relied entirely on a literal interpretation and analysis of the concessionary agreement to establish a violation of section 4 of the Act.[182]

More recently the CCP examined vertical agreements in the *Reliance Paints* case,[183] and the *NFC Employees Society* case,[184] however, once again it failed to clarify the law in this regard. In the *Reliance Paints* case, the CCP addressed both exclusive dealing and resale price maintenance. However, rather than categorising the agreements as horizontal or vertical or clarifying that the parties to the agreements operated at different levels of the market, the CCP simply discussed the anti-competitiveness of exclusivity agreements,[185] providing the only clue as to its understanding of the nature of the agreements by its reference to the EU Notice on Vertical Restraints.[186] In the *NFC Employees* case[187] the CCP once again avoided categorising the agreement as either horizontal or vertical, did not confirm whether the was anti-competitive by object or by effect (although it did refer to the enquiry report which identified it as a by object infringement);, or needed to be assessed under the per se rule or rule of reason.[188] In fact the the CCP stated that the relevant clauses had 'the object as well as the effect of reducing, restricting and preventing competition in the relevant market' and even when it noted that the agreement was detrimental to the 'overall competitive process in the market' it did not elaborate on the observation.[189]

More worryingly, in all its decisions in respect of vertical agreements, as it had been in the case of horizontal agreements, the CCP appears to be hesitant to fully anchor the test for anti-competitive vertical agreements in the language of section 4 or the

179 *Port Qasim Authority and Engro Vopak Terminal Limited* case Files 6/LP/CMTA/CCP/2010 & 2/(192)/AGR/Exm./Reg/CCP/2010 decided 29.06.2011.

180 ibid paras 2, 55.

181 n.175.

182 ibid para 57.

183 *Reliance Paints* File no 31/RP/C&TA/CCP/2015 decided 30.03.2018 ('the *Reliance Paints* case').

184 *NFC Employees Co-operative Housing Society* File no 80/NFCEHS/C&TA/CCP/2016 decided 27.11.2018 ('the *NFC Employees* case').

185 n.183 paras 27, 31.

186 ibid para 34.

187 n.184 para 27.

188 ibid paras 28–29.

189 ibid para 33.

economic context of Pakistan and prefers instead to link its findings either to a specific foreign decision that fits the particular facts of the case before it,[190] or to its own earlier decisions[191] and continues to adopt a formalistic and increasingly summary strategy for deciding matters.

5.5 RELATING CCI AND CCP'S INTERPRETIVE STRATEGIES TO THEIR ADOPTION PROCESSES

The CCI and CCP's interpretive strategies, as evident in the case of anti-competitive agreements, may be traced to the mechanisms and institutions through which India and Pakistan adopted the Indian and Pakistani Acts. This section explores the manner and extent to which the adoption processes in the two countries have shaped the respective interpretive strategies of the CCI and CCP.

5.5.1 *Reliance on Models From Which Analytical Tests Were Derived*

The extent to which the CCI and CCP rely on precedents from their parent competition models in interpreting and applying the analytical tests for anti-competitive agreements offers an important insight into the link between the adoption and implementation stages of the Indian and Pakistani Acts. Given that the Indian Act is adapted from a range of international models, it may be expected that in interpreting the analytical test for anti-competitive agreements the CCI may also draw inspiration from a variety of international models, whereas given the strong nexus between the Pakistani and EU competition regimes the CCP may be expected to rely primarily on EU precedents. Further, given India's dominant transfer mechanism of *socialisation* which underscores its desire to *learn* from foreign systems rather than simply to *emulate* them, the CCI may also be expected to *adapt* any precedents it relies upon for the Indian context, whereas given Pakistan's dominant transfer mechanism of *coercion* which underpins its motivation to gain international legitimacy and to leverage it in the domestic context, the CCP may be expected to cite foreign precedents as much for their normative value as for their substantive appropriateness.

The CCI's orders in respect of horizontal and vertical agreements meet expectations on both counts. The CCI's express reliance on foreign materials and precedents is limited and the precedents and materials it has cited are derived from a range of jurisdictions. However, in addition to *expressly* citing foreign cases and materials, the CCI has also *implicitly* relied on foreign precedents and materials and has integrated these into its analysis. This strategy affirms the CCI's inclination to *learn* from and to apply these precedents rather reproducing these merely for their

[190] For instance, the *Poultry* case, n.129.

[191] Examples include the *PAMADA* case, n.130 and *Pakistan Engineering Council* case (File 2(32)/ Comp Cell/CCP/2015 decided 20.04.2016.

normative value. At the implicit level the CCI's orders appear to lean towards an EU style of reasoning: several of its orders examine allegedly anti-competitive agreement in their economic and legal context and in light of their objectives; the CCI acknowledges and applies the *de minimis rule* where relevant; and engages in an Article 101(3) style analysis of pro-competitive factors, even in respect of *presumed* anti-competitive agreements.

In contrast, the CCP's interpretive strategy deviates from expectations. While in its early orders the CCP relies extensively on foreign precedents and materials, it cites EU and US cases in almost equal measure rather than relying exclusively on EU precedents and also relies upon precedents from other jurisdictions albeit not as frequently. However, rather than adopting the EU analytical approach and semantics wholesale, the CCP most often alternates between the EU and the US approaches, often conflating the two. Therefore, while the EU's impact is evident in several of its orders in which the CCP asserts that it is incumbent upon it to examine 'the object or effect' of an agreement and that the 'object' and 'effect' are disjunctive concepts, the US influence may be seen when the CCP interprets 'object' to mean 'per se'; when, in a majority of its orders, it does not consider the context of the agreement; when it refers to an effect-based enquiry as a rule of reason enquiry; and when it does not allow a *de minimis* style exception in any of its orders. Further, the CCP's very explicit recourse to foreign precedents not merely as aids in interpretation in its analysis of anti-competitive agreements, but also as an assertion of the close ties between the Pakistani Act and foreign authoritative models Pakistani Act, underscores its need foreign authoritative models for both international and domestic legitimacy.

5.5.2 *Continued Recourse to Transfer Mechanisms Employed in the Adoption Process*

In interpreting the analytical tests for anti-competitive agreements, both the CCI and CCP appear to continue with the transfer mechanisms used by India and Pakistan respectively at the adoption stage: the CCI continues to *socialise* foreign precedents and materials for the domestic Indian context, while the CCP prefers to *emulate* foreign precedents and materials especially when it relies on these to establish its authority (and, by extension of the Pakistani competition legislation). Although the CCP does engage in some *socialisation* it appears to superimpose meaning on the express wording of the Pakistani Act, rather than engaging directly wtih and clarifying it.

5.5.3 *Impact of Adoption Processes on the Evolution of CCI and CCP's Interpretive Strategies*

Over time, the CCI's interpretation of the section 3 analytical test has become more consistent and predictable. In the majority of its orders the CCI begins by considering whether there is an agreement. If an agreement is established, it considers whether the agreement is horizontal or vertical with reference to the economic and legal context within which the agreement operates. In case of horizontal agreements, the CCI most often requires the defendant to rebut the presumption of AAEC with reference to factors listed in section 19(3), whereas in respect of vertical agreements it considers the effect by taking into account possible pro-competitive factors. The CCI also applies the *de minimis rule* to exclude certain agreements from the ambit section 3. However, the CCI does not consider itself bound by this consistency where it forms the view that the sector[192] or the practice[193] merits a flexible or novel approach.

In contrast, the CCP's approach tends to lose its consistency and structure over time and the CCP appears to remain more anchored in EU and US precedents rather than focusing on the express wording of the provisions of the Pakistani Act. In its earliest orders the CCP first categorised an agreement either as anti-competitive by object (which it conflated with the per se rule), or by effect (which it used interchangeably with the rule of reason) and then analysed it, albeit often exclusively with reference to EU and US precedents.[194] Over time, however, the CCP has either omitted the categorisation step altogether[195] or has simply placed the agreement or practice within a category without providing a basis for doing so.[196] Also, the CCP has applied different tests to similar agreements or practices at different times not due to changing economic conditions or its evolving understanding of the economic factors underlying these agreements, but rather on the basis of a single precedent that, in its view, fit the facts of the case before it.

Despite the considerable disparities between them, there are at least two similarities between the CCI and CCP's interpretive strategies: first, the analytical tests as applied by both authorities are almost unrecognisable in a strictly EU or US sense. However, while in India the analytical test has been almost entirely 'Indianised' linguistically as well as in application, the analytical test in Pakistan remains suspended between the express provisions of the Pakistani competition legislation and the international precedents the CCP relies upon in interpreting and applying it. Second, and perhaps more damagingly, both the CCI and CCP have interpreted the analytical tests in an entirely formalistic manner rather than anchoring these in an economic analysis of the alleged anti-competitive agreements and practices even when the law and the practice under review has warranted such an analysis

The CCI's recourse to *socialisation* in interpreting the Indian Act at the implementation stage is directly correlated with India's use of *socialisation* through a wide range of bottom-up, participatory, and inclusive institutions at the adoption

[192] For example n.122 (cement); n.137 (IT sector), and n.149 (automobiles).
[193] n.157 and text thereto.
[194] For example, n.69, 72, 73, 77 and text thereto.
[195] n.73 and 111 and texts thereto.
[196] n.76.

TABLE 5.1. *Essential features of CCI and CCP's interpretive strategies for anti-competitive agreements*

Factors	CCI	CCP
Express reliance on foreign precedents	Limited.	Extensive.
Continued recourse to dominant transfer mechanism	Yes. Evident in CCIs *socialisation* of precedents derived from a range of sources.	Yes. CCP continues to *emulate* foreign precedents. Some *socialisation* also evident.
Reference to the statute	Extensive.	Limited.
Economic analysis	Limited to non-existent.	Limited to non-existent.
Evolution of strategy	Greater opening up to international influence.	Greater focus on CCP's own decisions.

stage. At the adoption stage, India through the mechanism of *socialisation* had succeeded in creating an 'Indianised' analytical test for establishing anti-competitive agreements, which while combining elements from EU and US regimes does not fully align with either and which is stated sufficiently precisely in the Indian Act to be interpretable by the CCI without extensive recourse to foreign competition jurisprudence and materials. It is no surprise therefore that the CCI also anchors its evaluation of anti-competitive agreements at the implementation stage in the wording of the analytical test as expressed in section 3 of the Act, and resorts to foreign precedents and materials only when necessary and then also adapts and *socialises* these for local context.[197] However, this strategy has the negative effect, particularly in these early years of the CCI's operations, of generating a certain Indian-ised hubris towards competition enforcement and of isolating it from international developments in this regard.

Similarly, the CCP's preference for *emulation* in the interpretation of its analytical test for anti-competitive agreements may also be traced to Pakistan's adopting its competition legislation primarily through *coercion*. Adoption by *coercion* had succeeded in transferring the *words* of competition principles but had failed to generate a deep understanding of their meanings in the Pakistani context. The lingering

[197] The CCI cites foreign, particularly EU case law only exceptionally: for instance n.39 (the *Cement Manufacturers Association* case) & n.122 (*Alleged Cartelization of Cement Manufacturers* case); n.38 (the *Tamil Nadu Film Exhibitors Association* case); n.137 (*Apple* case); n.149 (*Honda Siel* case). In all these cases the CCI was entering new sectors which had already been addressed internationally or the agreements it was examining were particularly complex.

impact of *coercion* is evident in the CCP's preference for foreign precedents over the express words of its competition statute, and the absence of a meaningful attempt on its part to correlate foreign jurisprudence and the words of the Pakistani legislation.[198] Although this combination of *coercion* and *emulation* in adopting the legislation made the CCP more pre-occupied with asserting its international legitimacy by tracing its lineage to the EU and US competition/anti-trust systems from which it was derived, it also had the positive effect of aligning the CCP, even in its earliest orders, with the international approach towards competition enforcement.

198 India, despite its preference for *socialisation*, demonstrates a similar confusion in its early orders which may be attributed to bounded rationality in its pursuit of *socialisation*.

6

Understanding Penalties in the Context of the Adoption Process

6.1 INTRODUCTION

Sanctions, designed not only to punish entities for their anti-competitive practices but also to deter them from engaging in similar practices in the future, are central to competition enforcement: the majority of competition legislations confer on national competition or other authorities the power to prescribe monetary or behavioural sanctions (or both), and governments as well as the public evaluate the performance of competition or other relevant authorities by reference to their ability to impose strong sanctions and, in case of monetary sanctions, their success in recovering them. The signifcance of sanctions is also evident in India and Pakistan: the Indian and Pakistani competition legislations confer on the CCI and CCP, a range of monetary and non-monetary sanctioning options in respect of findings of anti-competitive agreements and abuses of dominant position, and in the years since they became operational, the CCI and CCP have exercised these powers to varying degrees.

Interestingly, notwithstanding the emphasis particularly on monetary sanctions or penalties in the Indian and Pakistani competition legislations, these are not discussed at any length in the Raghavan Report or the Manes Report that had proposed modern competition regimes for India and Pakistan respectively in the first place.[1] This means that the penal provisions in the Indian and Pakistani competition legislations have been introduced without any discussion with the stakeholders. It also means that the scheme and language of the penal provisions is more in alignment with the foreign models on which they are based rather than the

[1] Report of the High Level Committee on Competition Policy & Law 2000 ('the Raghavan Report') <https://theindiancompetitionlaw.files.wordpress.com/2013/02/report_of_high_level_committee_on_competition_policy_law_svs_raghavan_committee.pdf> accessed 13 September 2021; Eric David Manes, 'A Framework for a New Competition Policy and Law: Pakistan' (The International Bank for Reconstruction and Development 2007) ('the Manes Report').

exigencies of the contexts for which these are intended. The compatibility and legitimacy deficit resulting from introducing penal provisions without consultation with domestic stakeholders has affected not only the way in which the CCI and CCP have exercised their penalising powers but also the quantum of penalties they have succeeded in recovering. Even more interestingly, it appears that the penal strategies adopted by the CCI and the CCP further clarify the links between the adoption and implementation stages of competition legislation in the two countries. This chapter traces the evolution of the CCI and CCP's penal strategies and argues that the processes through which India and Pakistan adopted their respective competition legislations have a twofold impact on the penal strateiges: first, the *direct* impact which stems from the extent of compatibility and legitimacy generated for the Indian and Pakistani competition legislations through the adoption process, and second, the *indirect* impact which is linked to the adoption process lays the groundwork for the establishment of the competition enforcement infrastructure envisaged in the two competition legislations.

This chapter explores these issues as follows: Section 6.2 explores the manner in which the adoption processes in India and Pakistan are likely to impact the penal strategies of the CCI and the CCP at the implementation stage; Section 6.3 evaluates the *direct* impact of the adoption process by reviewing the penalties that the CCI and CCP have imposed over the years and understanding their connection with the compatibility and legitimacy generated for these legislations through the adoption process; Section 6.4 examines the *indirect* impact by examining the steps that the Indian and Pakistani governments have taken towards establishing the competition enforcement infrastructure envisaged in the Indian and Pakistani competition legislations, and the impact of this infrastructure on the CCI and CCP's exercise of their penalising powers; Section 6.5 examines possible approaches for strengthening the penal strategies of the CCI and CCP and, therefore, competition enforcement in India and Pakistan.

6.2 ADOPTION PROCESS AND PENALTIES: UNDERSTANDING THE TWO-PRONGED IMPACT

The processes through which India and Pakistan adopted their modern competition legislation differed not only in the dominant mechanisms through which the transfer took place but also in the nature and range of institutions engaged by the countries for the purpose. This section re-visits the Indian and Pakistani adoption processes and examines the ways in which the unique combination of mechanisms and institutions engaged by the two countries in adopting their respective competition legislations are likely to impact the CCI and CCP's penal strategies.

India had adopted the Indian Act through *socialisation* and had engaged bottom-up, participatory, and inclusive institutions from all three branches of the Indian state in both the deliberation and the enactment phases. These included the

Raghavan Committee which had been established by the executive to consider and recommend the parameters of the proposed competition legislation, standing committees of the Indian parliament that had informed the initial enactment of the Indian Act in 2002 and its amendment in 2007, and the Supreme Court of India. Each of these institutions had the capacity to aggregate and evaluate information from stakeholders across the country and to adapt the proposed competition legislation in light of this information. Consequently, India was able to 'Indianise' its competition legislation and thereby to enhance its compatibility with and legitimacy in the Indian context. In contrast, Pakistan had adopted its competition legislations through *coercion* by the WTO and the World Bank and with limited domestic participation: although the World Bank team that had led the deliberations included representatives from Pakistan, it only held two or three public consultations over a brief six-month period and commissioned a Brussels-based law firm to draft the Pakistani competition legislation. Consequently, Pakistan was not able to generate a broad-based understanding of and acceptance for the competition legislation and the legislation remained more aligned with its international antecedents than with Pakistan's context and priorities.[2]

In influencing the compatibility and legitimacy quotient of the adopted competition legislations, the adoption processes in both India and Pakistan have *directly* impacted the penal strategies of the CCI and CCP. However, this correlation is neither simple nor binary and must be explored with care. Indeed, the data suggests that the somewhat higher compatibility and legitimacy of the legislation, as in India, does not automatically translate into an aggressive penal strategy, and the relatively limited compatibility and legitimacy of the Pakistani legislation does not necessarily lead to weak and hesitant competition enforcement. Further, the adoption processes in both countries have also *indirectly* impact the penal strategies of the CCI and CCP by the extent to which these have succeeded in laying the groundwork for the establishment of the competition enforcement systems envisaged in the adopted legislations: while the legitimacy of the competition legislation in India appears to have been conducive to the establishment and operation of the competition enforcement system, the relatively weaker legitimacy in Pakistan has obstructed the setting up and the functioning of its competition enforcement system. In both cases the establishment or otherwise of competition enforcement systems has further impacted the penal strategies adopted by the CCI and the CCP.

6.3 DIRECT IMPACT: CCI AND CCP'S APPROACH TOWARDS PENALTIES IN THEIR ORDERS

Imposing penalties is one among several sanctioning options available to the CCI and CCP under the Indian and Pakistani competition legislations, and in exercising

[2] The adoption processes for both India and Pakistan have been discussed at length in Chapter 2.

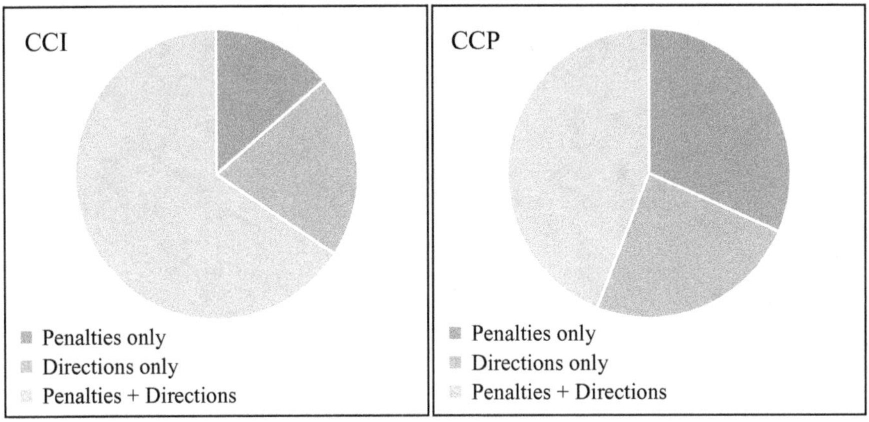

FIGURE 6.1. Penal strategies as per orders of the CCI (2009–20) and the CCP (2008–20)

their powers in this regard both the CCI and the CCP have considrable discretion to fix the quantum within the scheme of the penal provisions of their respective legislations. In terms of section 27(b) of the Indian Act, the CCI may impose a penalty 'not more than ten per cent of the average of the turnover for the last three preceding financial years, upon each of such person or enterprises which are parties to such agreements or abuse',[3] while under the Pakistani Act[4] the CCP may impose a penalty in an 'amount not exceeding seventy-five million rupees or an amount not exceeding ten percent of the annual turnover of the undertaking'.[5]

In the years they have been operational, both the CCI and CCP have made extensive use of their powers to impose penalties in respect of anti-competitive practices (which include anti-competitive agreements and abuses of dominance). However, while the CCI has almost always combined penalties with behavioural directions, even if simply directing the relevant parties to cease and desist from their anti-competiitve behaviour, the CCP has imposed penalties in isolation almost as much it has combined them with directions (Figure 6.1).

A closer look at these orders reveals that in the eighty-five orders in which the CCI imposed penalties, it imposed a lump sum penalty only in two orders, both issued in its first year of its operations.[6] In the remaining eighty-three orders, the CCI

3 Indian Act section 27(b) and proviso. In respect of cartels the CCI may impose a penalty 'of up to three times of its profit for each year of the continuance of such agreement or ten percent of its turnover for each year of the continuance of such agreement, whichever is higher'.

4 The 2007, 2009, and 2010 Ordinances preceding the Pakistani Act also contained the same provisions.

5 Pakistani Act section 38(2)(a).

6 See *FICCI v United Producers/Distributors Forum & others* Case 1/2009 decided 25.5.2011 ('*Producers and Distributors Forum* case') and *Uniglobe Mod Travels Pvt Limited v Travel Agents Federation of India & others* Case 3/2009 decided 04.10.2011 ('*Travel Agents Federation of India* case').

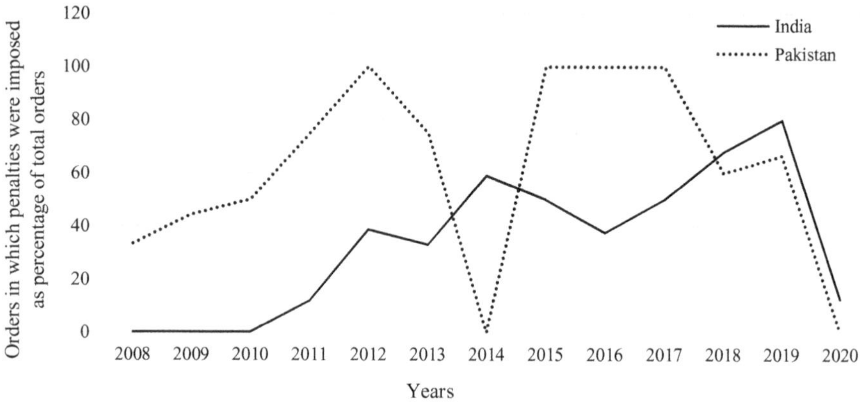

FIGURE 6.2. Evolution of CCI and CCP's penalising strategies

expressed penalties as a percentage (ranging from 2 per cent to 10 per cent) of the average turnover (in case of companies) or average income or receipts (in case of associations and natural persons) calculated usually for three preceding years.[7] From 2018 onwards, the CCI refined its penal formula calculating penalties as a percentage of *relevant* turnover or income. In the majority of its orders, the CCI justified the rate at which it fixed the penalty by linking it to the severity of the infringement. In stark contrast, the CCP expressed its penalties as lump sums in all but six of its orders, in which it stipulated these as a percentage of the turnover[8] and did not justify the quantum of penalties whether expressed as percentages of turnover or as lump sums in any of its orders. Overall, it appears that until 2018 the CCP imposed penalties in a greater proportion of its orders than the CCI, however, after 2018, the CCI and CCP imposed penalties in a comparable number of orders (Figure 6.2).[9]

The divergence in the CCI and CCP's approaches towards imposing penalties may be directly traced to the processes through which India and Pakistan had adopted their respective competition legislations and the compatibility and legitimacy generated in the course of adoption. In India, the engagement of a wide range of institutions in the deliberation and the enactment phases not only allowed the competition legislation to be adapted for the Indian context, but also for Indian

[7] Only very rarely the CCI imposed penalties at a rate lower than 2 per cent or as a multiple of net profits.

[8] Even in these instances the CCP relied on turnovers for one or two years only. See for instance *All Pakistan Cement Manufacturers Association* case File 4/2/ Sec 4/CCP/2008 decided 27.08.2009; *Jamshoro Joint Venture Limited and LPG Association of Pakistan* case File 3/ LPG/DIR(INV)/M&TA/CCP/2009 decided 14.12.2009; *Pakistan Poultry Association* File CCP/Cartels/04/2010 decided 16.08.2010; *Urea Manufacturers* F No 01/UREA/C&TA/CCP/ 2010 decided 29.03.2013; *LDI Operators* case File 5(114)/Reg/ADG-SCP/LHC/CCP/13 decided 30.04.2013; *Pakistan Flour Mills Association* F No 89/PFMA/C &TA/CCP/2016 decided 13.12.2019.

[9] This is with the exception of 2014 in which the CCP did not issue any enforcement orders.

stakeholders to become aware of and understand the rationale and import of the legislation (even if not specifically of the penal provisions). The engagement of the judiciary particularly, bolstered the compatibility of the legislation with India's pre-existing legal system and provided it with an important stamp of domestic legitimacy. Further, the fact that even before the CCI was made fully operational India had allowed a skeletal version of the CCI to engage in competition advocacy not only helped a wide range of stakeholders to become familiar with the Act but also helped the CCI to develop an understanding of the response its proposed enforcement actions were likely to receive. As a result of these efforts when the CCI was finally constituted and operationalised in 2009, it was more aware of and attuned with the domestic context and enjoyed a reasonable degree of legitimacy in it. However, this alignment with the domestic context it also made the CCI reluctant to pursuing an aggressive penal strategy and thereby to jeopardise the space it had so painstakingly carved for itself in the Indian legal context. In contrast, the introduction of competition legislation in Pakistan through top-down, exclusive institutions, drawn primarily from the executive which did not engage in broad-based discussions with stakeholders, prevented Pakistani stakeholders from understanding the rationale and objectives of the competition legislation and the legislation from acquiring greater compatibility and legitimacy in the country. The CCP that came into being through this process was isolated from the very entities it was mandated to regulate, and was almost entirely aligned with the foreign authorities with which it claimed a relationship. The confidence it gained from its international antecedents allowed the CCP to pursue a somewhat aggressive penal strategy in its early enforcement actions and thereby not only to sanction anti-competitive practices but also to leverage to leverage its international legitimacy to gain domestic legitimacy, in Pakistan.

The CCI's relatively conservative approach in imposing sanctions is also partially attributed to *socialisation*, which impressed upon the CCI the need to take local conditions into account in enforcing the Indian Act and therefore to be cautious in imposing penalties. In the deliberation phase, the Raghavan Committee had urged that the authority established to enforce the legislation in India recognise that the Indian economy was transitioning from a controlled to a liberal economy and therefore not be harsh in sanctioning violations as doing so would be detrimental to economic growth in the country. Similarly, the CCP's preference for imposing lump sum rather than pro-rated penalties may at least partly be traced to *coercion*, particularly to the World Bank's emphasis in the deliberation phase on penalties being the most appropriate sanctioning strategy. As to why CCP decided the quantum of penalties without reference to turnover it may be argued that it would have been dififcult to obtain the necessary data in this regard.. However, this seems unlikely given that the majority of the CCP's orders addressed violations by companies that are required by law to file and publish their financial reports it appears more likely that the CCP made a conscious decision to disengage penalties from turnover and thereby to expand the scope of its discretion in this regard.

6.4 INDIRECT IMPACT: THE ROLE OF COMPETITION ENFORCEMENT SYSTEMS

Both the Indian and Pakistani Acts envisage a three-tier competition enforcement system in their respective contexts. At the base of this system are the national competition authorities, the CCI and the CCP, at the second tier are the Indian and Pakistani Tribunals that are mandated to hear appeals from the orders of the CCI and CCP, and at the third and final tier are the Supreme Courts of the two countries. This section examines the indirect impact of the adoption process on the CCI and CCP's penal strategies by first tracing the connection between the adoption process and the establishment of competition enforcement systems in the two countries and then evaluating the role of the competition enforcement systems in shaping the CCI and CCP's penal strategies.

6.4.1 *Establishing the Competition Enforcement Systems in India and Pakistan*

The early engagement of the parliament and the executive in India in the adoption of its competition legislation generated among ts state institutions a greater awareness, understanding, and ownership not only of the contents of the alacrity with which Indian Act but also of the proposed strategy for enforcing it which in turn contributed to the Indian government established and operationalised the Indian Tribunal. Although the impetus for establishing the Tribunal had come from the Supreme Court's decision in the *Brahm Dutt* case,[10] the idea of establishing it had been presented to the Supreme Court by the government itself in the form of an undertaking in which it had committed to amend the Indian Act to segregate the CCI's regulatory and judicial functions. The government had also drafted the relevant provisions of the 2007 Amendment Act and the legislature had enacted it after appropriate deliberations. It was in pursuance of these provisions that the executive established the Indian Tribunal almost immediately after operationalising the CCI.[11] On 20 May 2009, the government appointed a former Judge of Supreme Court, Dr Justice Arijit Pasayat, as the Tribunal's first chairperson and for the next eight years, except for a brief period of under one year in which the Tribunal had a chairperson but no members, the Tribunal regularly heard and decided appeals from final and interim orders of the CCI.

In 2017 the Indian government and the legislature further amended the Indian Act to replace the specialist Indian Tribunal by the NCLAT which had been constituted in 2016 exclusively to hear appeals from orders under the Companies Act 2013 and the Insolvency and Bankruptcy Code 2016.[12] Interestingly, the government

[10] *Brahm Dutt v Union of India* (2005) 2 Supreme Court Cases 431.

[11] Notification SO1240 (E) dated 15.05.2009.

[12] NCLAT had been established in pursuance of Companies Act 2013 section 410.

introduced this amendment to the Indian Act through a Finance Act[13] which is intended to 'give effect to the financial proposals of the Central Government' rather than to substantively amend legislation and may be passed by the legislature only after summary scrutiny. In introducing an amendment to the Indian Act in this manner, the government was not only able to move swiftly in changing in the competition enforcement system in the country, but also completely avoided the obligation of providing reasons for the proposed change and its impact on the effectiveness of competition enforcement in the country.[14] The significance of this change notwithstanding, it does not detract from the Indian Tribunal's early role in developing and clarifying the provisions of the Indian Act and in shaping the trajectory of competition enforcement in India. At the time of writing it was too early to say whether the NCLAT would follow in its footsteps or chart a trajectory of its own which reflects its broader corporate expertise.

The engagement of the legislature and the executive in establishing the Pakistani Tribunal is rather different. The 2007 and 2009 Ordinances, both of which had been promulgated by executive orders without the engagement of the legislature, did not provide for a Pakistani Tribunal. In terms of both these Ordinances, appeals from orders passed by a single member or authorised officer of the CCP, were to lie to the CCP's internal appellate bench, while appeals from all other orders of the CCP and those of its internal appellate bench lay to the Supreme Court.[15] The competition enforcement system prescribed in these Ordinances was challenged in various petitions before the courts, and even though the Supreme Court did not finally decide any of these petitions, the grounds on which the competition enforcement system was challenged are generally accepted to be correct[16] and perhaps it is because of this critique that the government amended the competition enforcement system in the 2010 Ordinance, so that appeals from tinterim and final orders, passed by more than one CCP member or by its internal appellate bench, were to lie first to the high courts, rather than directly to the Supreme Court and the orders of the high courts were to be appealed to the Supreme Court.[17]

13 Indian Finance Act 2017 section 171.

14 Indian Constitution Article 109.

15 2007 and 2009 Ordinances sections 41 and 42. Although some appeals were filed before the Supreme Court during this period, none of these were finally decided most likely due to the endemic delay at the Supreme Court along with the uncertain status of competition legislation. One example is the appeal filed before the Supreme Court by the Institute of Chartered Accountants of Pakistan (CA 274/2009 (*Institute of Chartered Accountants of Pakistan v Competition Commission of Pakistan*) against the order of the CCP's Appellate Bench dated 11.03.2009 by which it had dismissed ICAP's appeal against the CCP's single-member order dated 28.11.2008 (File No 3/Sec-4/CCP/08 *The Institute of Chartered Accountants of Pakistan*). While the Supreme Court admitted ICAP's appeal by its order dated 19.03.2009 and restrained the CCP from enforcing its final order it did not finally decide the appeal.

16 Under the Pakistani Constitution Article 185, the Supreme Court does not have the jurisdiction to hear appeals directly from orders of a regulatory body without an intervening appeal before a tribunal or high court.

17 2010 Ordinance section 42.

The idea of the Pakistani Tribunal was first introduced through the Pakistani Act which replaced the 2010 Ordinance. In terms of the Act, appeals from orders issued by more than one of CCP's officers or members, were to lie to the specialist Pakistani Tribunal, and appeals from the orders of the Tribunal to the Supreme Court.[18] Interestingly, the provisions relating to the Tribunal were the only new provisions in the Act, which was otherwise substantially the same as the Ordinances that had preceded it which suggests that the Pakistani executive and the legislature did not reflect on the substantive provisions of the Pakistani Act and did not displace the effect of the original *coercion*. It may be argued that the legislature was reluctant to interfere with the substantive provisions of the competition law as these had gained a degree of domestic acceptance and legitimacy in the nearly three years that it had been in force, largely due to the aggressive CCP's penal strategy in this period however, it may equally be argued that this reluctance was due to the powers of persuasion of the multilateral agencies that had introduced the law in the country in the first place.

This lack of meaningful engagement on the part of the executive and the legislature even in the enactment of the Pakistani Act meant that the executive neither fully appreciated the need for competition enforcement in the country nor its responsibility to facilitate enforcement by establishing the Tribunal. Consequently, even though the Pakistani Act – and thereby the provisions for establishing the Tribunal – came into force in October 2010, the government appointed its first member and chairman on in July 2011,[19] and allowed a further year to elapse before appointing the Tribunal's technical members.[20] In April 2013 after functioning for only about five months and deciding only one appeal,[21] the operation of the Tribunal was brought to a halt due to one of its members resigning and the other retiring after reaching the age of superannuation. The Pakistani government took another two years to reconstitute the Tribunal by appointing two new members.[22] Consequently, it was nearly five years after the enactment of the Pakistani Act that the Tribunal finally had quorum to make rules for its conduct and proceedings and thereby to properly recommence operations (Figures 6.3 and 6.4).[23]

The Indian and Pakistani Tribunals, once established and operationalised, formed a critical first step in activating the competition enforcement systems in the two countries, and generating a dialogue and a feedback loop between the different tiers of the system. This feedback loop was significant in that it was expected not only help rationalise the CCI and CCP's penal strategies and to contribute to the recovery of

[18] Pakistani Act section 43. Under the Pakistani Constitution Articles 175(2) and 212(3), appeals from orders of specialist tribunals may only lie to the Supreme Court directly if authorised by statute.

[19] Notification No F15(1)/2010-AV dated 27.07.2011.

[20] Notification No F21(1)/2011-Admn-III dated 29.05.2012.

[21] See Box 6.3.

[22] These appointments were made vide Pakistani government notifications dated 10.04.2015, 28.05.2015, and 22.01.2016.

[23] Competition Appellate Tribunal Rules 2015 made by SRO 749(1)/2015 dated 31.07.2015.

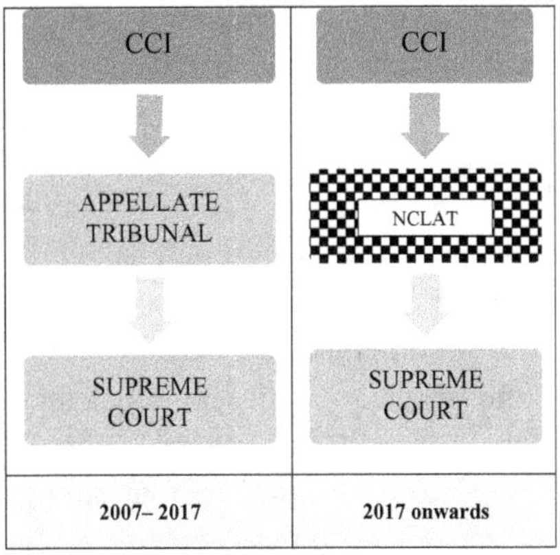

FIGURE 6.3. Evolution of competition enforcement system in India

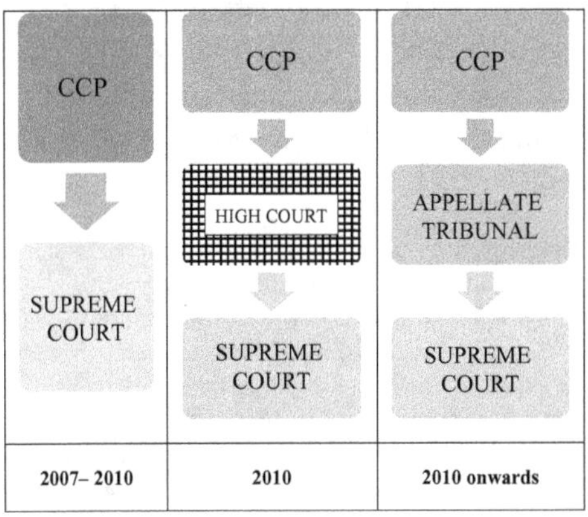

FIGURE 6.4. Evolution of competition enforcement system in Pakistan

penalties imposed by them, but also to develop competition jurisprudence in the two countries and thereby to facilitate the steady integration of the adopted competition legislations into their pre-existing legal systems.

6.4.2 *Tribunals and the Recovery of Penalties*

For the CCI and CCP to be effective in bringing about pro-competitive reform in their respective countries it is important that they are able to recover the penalties they impose.[24] Under law, both the CCI and CCP are required to deposit their

[24] This analysis does not make any assessment of the appropriateness of the quantum of penalties imposed by the CCI or CCP in any of the cases.

recovered penalties to their respective national exchequers: in terms of section 47 of the Indian Act all penalties realised by the CCI are to be credited to the Consolidated Fund of India and in terms of section 40(8) of the Pakistani Act all penalties and fines recovered by the CCP are to be credited to the Public Accounts of the Federation.[25] On a narrow view of enforcement, a well-functioning Tribunal which in hearing appeals from orders of the first-tier enforcement authorities restrains them from recovering the penalties imposed by them, may be seen as an obstacle in successful competition enforcement. However, a more holistic perspective, suggests that while the operation of the Tribunal may delay the recovery, its ability to review the orders of the first-tier authorities helps refine the rationale of first-tier authority's penalising decisions and thereby strengthens its penal strategy which over time leads to more effective enforcement.

In India, where a large number of orders of the CCI are appealed to the Tribunal, the Tribunal's response has varied according to the facts of the case. In certain cases the Tribunal has upheld the CCI's final orders and dismissed the appeal(s)[26] while in others it has allowed the appeal, set aside the CCI's order, and quashed the penalty.[27] In some of its orders the Tribunal has upheld the CCI's order but revised the amount of penalty imposed by it,[28] whereas in others still, it has remanded the

[25] This provision was not present in the 2007 Ordinance in terms of which the penalties were required to be paid into the Commission Fund.

[26] For example, see orders of the Tribunal in *Travel Agents Association of India v Uniglobe Mod Travels (P) Ltd & others* Appeal 24/2011 and *IATA Agents Association of India v Uniglobe Mod Travels (P) Ltd & others* Appeal 8/2012 both dated 10.07.2013; *Nandu Ahuja, Sunil Arjan Lulla, Jyoti Deshpande v CCI & another* Appeals 11/2013, 12/2013, 13/2013 dated 17.01.2014; *Nandu Ahuja, Sunil Arjan Lulla, Jyoti Deshpande v CCI & another* Appeals 1/2012, 2/2012, 3/2012 dated 05.08.2013; *Film Distributors Association (Kerala) v CCI and others* Appeal 61/2015 dated 03.07.2015; *Jose C Mundadan v CCI and others* Appeal 55/2015 dated 17.08.2015; *Jose C Mundadan v CCI and others* Appeal 56/2015 dated 27.04.2016; *Coal India Limited and another v CCI and others* Appeal 80/2014 dated 09.12.2016; *Kerala Film Exhibitors Association and another v CCI and others* Appeal 100/2015 dated 04.02.2016.

[27] For instance, the Tribunal allowed the following appeals against the CCI's orders: *Telugu Film Chamber of Commerce v Cinergy Independent Film Service Pvt Ltd and others* Appeal 15/2013 decided 14.10.2015; *All India Organization of Chemists & Druggists (AIOCD) and others v CCI and others* Appeals 21/2013, 6/2014, and 7/2014 decided 09.12.2016; *Tamil Nadu Film Exhibitors Association v CCI and another* Appeal 14/2014 decided 28.04.2015; *Dr LH Hiranandani Hospital v CCI and another* Appeal 19/2014 decided 18.12.2015; *Indian Jute Mills Association v CCI and others* Appeals 73/2014, 77/2014, 78/2014, 83/2014, 84/2014, 85/2014, 86/2014, 87/2014, 88/2014 and 8/2015, 9/2015, 10/2015, 11/2015, 12/2015, 13/2015, 14/2015 and 15/2015 decided 01.07.2016; *Alkem Laboratories Limited v CCI and other* 9/2016, 14/2016 and 15/2016 decided 10.05.2016; *Director, Karak Pharmaceuticals Pvt Ltd v CCI and others* Appeal 42/2014 decided 07.12.2015; *Shib Sankar Nag Sarkar and another v CCI and others* Appeal 34/2014 decided 10.05.2016; *Bengal Chemist & Druggists Association and others v CCI and another* Appeal 37/2014 decided 10.05.2016.

[28] For instance, the Tribunal reduced the penalty by 10 per cent in *Gulf Oil Corporation Ltd v Competition Commission of India & others* Appeals 82/2012, 83/2012, 84/2012, 85/2012, 86/2012, 87/2012, 88/2012, 89/2012 and 90/2012 decided 18.04.2013; modified the penalty from 5 per cent to 3 per cent of the turnover in *MDD Medical Systems India Private Limited v CCI and others* Appeals 93/2012, 94/2012 and 95/2012 decided 25.02.2013; affirmed the order but revised the penalties in *Excel*

matter to the CCI for re-hearing.[29] Occasionally, appellants before the Tribunal have voluntarily withdrawn their appeals to directly approach the CCI,[30] while at times the Tribunal has dismissed appeals on technicalities.[31] In at least one instance, in which even though the Tribunal did not agree with the CCI's justification for imposing the penalty, it chose not to interfere with the CCI's order on the basis that the amounts involved were insignificant.[32]

Interestingly, the impact of the Tribunal's operation is not immediately evident in the quantum of penalties realised by the CCI. As per the CCI's Annual Report 2018-19, from the commencement of its operations until 31 March 2019 the CCI had imposed penalties in 177 cases in the cumulative sum of Indian rupees 13,881 crore (or INR 138,810,000,000.00 or Indian rupees one hundred and thirty-nine billion, eight hundred and million only). However, until 2019 the CCI had only realised penalties in the sum of Indian rupees 126.92 crore (INR 1,269,200,000.00 or Indian rupees one billion, two hundred and sixty-nine million, two hundred thousand only) and had refunded Indian rupees 66.53 crores (INR 665,300,000.00 or Indian rupees six hundred and sixty-five

Crop Care Limited v CCI & others Appeals 79/2012, 80/2012 and 81/2012 decided 29.10.2013; revised the penalty from 10 per cent to 1 per cent in *Bengal Chemist & Druggists Association and others v CCI and another* Appeal 37/2014 decided 10.05.2016; and reduced the penalty from 2 per cent to 1 per cent in *National Insurance Company Ltd v CCI* Appeals 94/2015, 95/2015, 96/2015 and 97/2015 decided 09.12.2016.

29 For instance, the first respondent appealed the CCI's order in *Vijay Gupta v Paper Merchants Association Delhi & others* (Case 7/2010) and the Tribunal by its order dated 29.08.2011 remanded the matter to the CCI which issued a supplementary order on 10.01.2013; in an appeal from the CCI's order in *Belaire Owners' Association v DLF Limited HUDA & others* (Case 19/2010) the Tribunal by its order dated 29.03.2012 directed the CCI to order modification of the agreements between DLF and apartment owners; by its order dated 20.12.2013 in *International Cylinder (Pvt) Ltd v CCI* Appeals 21/2012 to 65/2012 decided 20.12.2013 directed the CCI to re-hear the case on the issue of penalty. When the CCI passed a further order which was also appealed in *ECP Industries Ltd v CCI* Appeal 47/2015 and the Tribunal by its order dated 01.03.2016 once again directed the CCI to re-hear the matter on penalty; and by its order dated 09.12.2016 in *Toyota Kirloskar Motor Private Limited v CCI and others* Appeals 60/2014, 61/2014 and 62/2014 revised the criteria for penalties and remanded the case to the CCI for re-calculation of the quantum of penalties.

30 For instance, see the Tribunal's order dated 10.01.2013 in *Kansan News Pvt Ltd v Fastway Transmissions Pvt Ltd & others* Appeal 137/2012.

31 For instance, the Tribunal dismissed nine Appeals against the CCI's order dated 16.02.2012 in *Sunshine Pictures Private Limited v Eros International Media Limited v Central Circuit Cine Association Indore & others* (Cases 52 & 56/2010) for non-payment of court fees. The parties filed a further appeal, *Film Distribution Association, Kerala v Eros International Media Ltd & others* (68/2012); the Tribunal refused an interim injunction and then by its order dated 03.01.2013 dismissed the appeal for parties' failure to comply with the Tribunal's direction to deposit the amount of the penalty while the appeals were being heard.

32 The Tribunal took this view in appeals filed against the CCI's order dated *Reliance Big Entertainment Limited v Karnataka Film Chamber of Commerce* (Cases no 25, 41, 45, 47, 48, 50, 58, 69/2010).

million, three hundred thousand only). This means that from 2009 until 2019 the CCI had recovered a mere 0.91 per cent of the total penalties imposed by it and had refunded 52 per cent of the recovered amount, leaving its total recovered amount at approximately 0.45 per cent of total penalties imposed.[33] This somewhat bleak picture suggests that at the very least the activation of the competition enforcement system delayed (if not entirely stalled) rather than facilitating the recovery of penalties.

However, limiting recoveries is not the only impact of the operation of the Indian Tribunal as the Tribunal's orders have also played an important role in rationalising the CCI's penal strategies, particularly its methodology for fixing the quantum of penalties. For instance, by its order in *Excel Crop Care Limited v CCI & others*[34] the Tribunal reduced the penalty of 9 per cent of the average of three years turnover of each of the contravening entities (as imposed by the CCI)to one-tenth of the amount on the basis that the CCI had not only failed to provide a justification for fixing the penalty at 9 per cent but had also arbitrarily selected the base turnover.[35] Similarly, in its order in *Toyota Kirloskar Motor Private Limited v CCI and others*[36] the Tribunal revised the criteria applied by the CCI for determining the quantum of the penalty imposed and required the CCI to re-calculate it on the basis of 'relevant' turnover. The Tribunal also noted that it was not in favour of heavy penalties and recommended that the CCI approach penalties in the spirit of a 'transitory reform process'.[37] In certain other cases, the Tribunal quashed the penalty imposed by the CCI on the grounds that it had en imposed without providing the respondent an opportunity of being heard in violation of the principles of natural justice.[38] Of these orders, the Tribunal's order in the *Excel Crop Care* appeal[39] is of particular significance, not only because it was challenged before the Supreme Court by both the appellants and the CCI and therefore represents the analysis of all three tiers of India's competition enforcement system, but more so because it has formed the basis for the CCI's calculations of penalties in almost all subsequent cases.

[33] CCI's Annual Report 2018–19 Table D1.

[34] Appeals 79/2012, 80/2012 and 81/2012 decided 29.10.2013 brought against the CCI's order in *Re Aluminum Phosphide Tablets Manufacturers* Suo Motu Case 2/2011 dated 23.04.2012.

[35] n.34 paras 43–70, particularly para 69.

[36] Appeals 60/2014, 61/2014, and 62/2014 decided 09.12.2016 brought against the CCI's order in *Shri Shamsher Kataria v Honda Siel Cars India Limited & others* Case 3/2011 decided 25.08.2014.

[37] ibid paras 167–68.

[38] Order of Tribunal in *President All Kerala Chemists and Druggists and another v CCI and others* Appeals 5/2016 dated 10.05.2016 para 34.

[39] n.34.

Box 6.1 The decision of the Indian Supreme Court in the *Excel Crop Care* appeal

Background

In its final order in the *suo motu* case of *Aluminium Phosphide Tablets Manufacturers* the CCI had found Excel Crop Care Limited, Sandhya Organics Chemicals (Pvt) Limited, and United Phosphorus Limited to have engaged in collusive bidding and had penalised each of them in a sum equal to 9 per cent of their average turnovers for the three preceding years.[40]

Appeal to the Tribunal

All three companies appealed the CCI's order before the Indian Tribunal and the Tribunal, by its joint order,[41] affirmed the CCI's decision to the extent that in jointly boycotting the 2011 tender[42] and in quoting identical prices in tenders over several years[43] the companies had acted in pursuance of a 'common design'[44] and had thereby contravened the provisions of the Indian Act.[45] However, in respect of the quantum of the penalty the Tribunal found that the CCI had not provided any 'discussion whatsoever nor any justification' for the penalty of 9 per cent on average of three years' turnover.[46] The Tribunal therefore directed the CCI to re-calculate the penalties[47] by following the steps provided in the Indian Act,[48] and after taking into account all relevant factors.[49] Both the CCI and the appellants challenged the order of the Tribunal before the Supreme Court of India.

The Supreme Court Order[50]

The Supreme Court decided both appeals through a single order dated 8 May 2017 in which it confirmed that the CCI was within its rights to hold an inquiry into the bid rigging,[51] and that the DG had the power to investigate the boycott of the 2011 tender.[52] The Supreme Court also fully endorsed the Tribunal's analysis and findings.[53]

On the issue of the reduction of penalties, the Supreme Court held that the core question was 'whether penalty under Section 27(b) of the Act has to be on "total/entire

40 *Re Aluminium Phosphide Tablets Manufacturers* Suo motu Case no. 2/2011 decided 29.10.2013.
41 n.34.
42 ibid para 36 pp 34–35; para 40 p 37.
43 ibid pp 34, 37.
44 ibid pp 35, 37.
45 ibid para 41.
46 ibid para 43.
47 ibid para 67.
48 ibid paras 51–52.
49 ibid para 63.
50 *Excel Crop Care Limited v CCI* 2017 8 SCC 47.
51 ibid para 34.
52 ibid para 36.
53 ibid para 50.

turnover" of the company covering all the products or if it is relatable to "relevant turnover", viz., relating to the product in question in respect whereof provisions of the Act are contravened'.[54] The Supreme Court noted that section 27 itself did not clarify this issue,[55] however, after a detailed discussion in which it also referred to foreign jurisprudence, the Supreme Court concluded that 'adopting the criteria of "relevant turnover" for calculating the penalty will be more in tune with the ethos of the Act and the legal principles which surround matters pertaining to imposition of penalties'.[56] The Supreme Court, therefore, declared that it did not 'find any error in the approach of the order of the COMPAT [the Tribunal] interpreting Section 27 (b)'.[57]

As regards the CCI's arguments that penalties were designed to act as deterrents to anti-competitive practices, the Supreme Court held that nevertheless 'the penalty cannot be disproportionate to the violation and it should not lead to shocking results'. The Supreme Court also held that the aim of deterrence cannot justify an interpretation of the law that may lead to 'the death of the entity' itself and emphasised the importance of the doctrine of proportionality, which it stated was based on equality and rationality and was a 'constitutionally protected right, which can be traced to Article 14 as well as Article 21 of the Constitution.'[58]

The various iterations of the Pakistani competition legislation, the lack of certainty regarding its legal status, and the Pakistani government's ambivalence towards establishing and maintaining the competition enforcement system, meant that prior to the legislation being amended to provide for the Pakistani Tribunal, parties aggrieved by the CCP's orders could either challenge these before the CCP's internal appellate bench (this option was available only to orders passed by single members or authorised officers of the CCP) or to bring appeals directly to the Supreme Court.[59] In this period, therefore, nearly all the CCP's penalty-imposing orders were challenged before the general courts on constitutional grounds rather than appealed on their merits before the appellate bench or the Supreme Court. One of the first such petitions was brought against the CCP's final order in the *APCMA* case.[60] Although the *APCMA* case had provoked considerable litigation while it was still pending before the CCP,[61] the matter appeared to have been

[54] ibid para 56.
[55] ibid para 71.
[56] ibid para 74.
[57] ibid.
[58] ibid.
[59] See n.15 and 17 and text thereto.
[60] *In the matter of Show Cause Notices issued All Pakistan Cement Manufacturers Association and its Member Undertakings* F. No. 4/2/ Sec 4/CCP/200UU8 decided 27.08.2009 ('the APCMA case').
[61] See Preface for details.

resolved when the courts allowed the CCP to issue a final order in the matter. However, just as the CCP announced its final order the Lahore High Court once again restrained it from taking any adverse action against the defendants, thereby not only preventing the CCP from enforcing its order and from realising the penalties from the defendants, but also keeping it embroiled in constitutional battles and thereby diverting its already limited resources from competition enforcement to fighting for its legal survival.[62]

The petitions in the *APCMA* case gave rise to other petitions against many of the CCP's final orders. The majority of these petitions argued that that the CCP had not been properly and constitutionally constituted and lacked the quorum required to pass the final order. These petitions also alleged that the orders passed by the CCP were not in accordance with the competition legislation in force in the country; that the CCP had passed the orders with *mala fide* intent and by exercising powers beyond its jurisdiction;[63] the competition legislation could not be applied to agreements entered into before its coming into force;[64] and that certain actions of the CCP were tantamount to judicial review of subordinate legislation and, therefore, contrary to the law.[65] Some petitions also urged that the CCP's orders were contrary to government policy in the sector to which these referred and, therefore, exposed the petitioners to possible adverse governmental action,[66] and that the CCP had not fully appreciated the facts in arriving at its conclusions.[67] Barring a few petitions decided on technical grounds,[68] the general courts most often simply admitted these petitions and restrained the CCP from recovering penalties by enforcing the orders it had already passed without addressing the considerable constitutional and jurisdictional issues that these raised.[69]

[62] ibid, Lahore High Court's order dated 31.08.2009.

[63] Including petitions filed before the Islamabad High Court by *Wateen Telecom Limited* Writ Petitions (WP 1134/2011) and *Defence Housing Authority Lahore* (WP 1465/2011) and before the Lahore High Court by *Allied Bank Limited* (WP 21290/2012).

[64] Including petition filed before the Sindh High Court by *Engro Vopak Terminal Limited* (CP D-2491/2011).

[65] Including petition filed before the Lahore High Court by *Institute of Chartered Accountants* (WP 4412/2013).

[66] Including petition filed before the Sindh High Court by *Pakistan Ship's Agents Association* (CP D-2494/2011).

[67] Including petitions filed before the Lahore High Court by *GCC Approved Medical Centres* (WP 20280/2012). The LHC's order in this petition was subsequently relied upon by petitioners in *Canal View Diagnostic Centre* (WP 20729/2012), *GCC Approved Medical Diagnostic Centre & others* (WP 20729/2102), and *Urgent Medical Diagnostic Centre & others* (WP 21106/2012) and was used as a basis of further injunctions granted by the LHC by its order dated 04.01.2013.

[68] For instance, petitions filed by the APCMA before the Islamabad High Court and by Attock Cement Limited before the Sindh High Court were both dismissed on technical grounds.

[69] On 26.10.2020, eleven years after the petitions were first filed before it, the Lahore High Court by its order in *LPG Association of Pakistan v. Federation of Pakistan* W.P. No. 9518 of 2009 finally decided ninety-three petitions in sectors as diverse as accountancy, automobiles,

Given that the petitions challenging the final orders of the CCP had been filed due to an absence of an independent and authoritative appellate forum rather than in response to genuine constitutional concerns, the number of petitions before the general courts was expected to decline once the Pakistani Tribunal had been established. However, the uncertain start of the Tribunal in 2013 meant that the practice of filing petitions in lieu of appeals lingered until 2015 when the Tribunal was finally made operational. In the next few years the Tribunal decided approximately sixteen appeals: dismissing two appeals on technical grounds;[70] deciding eight in favour of the CCP[71] and six against it.[72] In at least two instances, parties aggrieved by the Tribunal's orders[73] filed appeals before the Pakistani Supreme Court whilst the CCP challenged all orders in which the Tribunal had found against it. Unfortunately, however, beyond this period there is very little information regarding appeals filed before the Tribunal or its decisions in respect of these appeals. Also, at the time of writing the Supreme Court was yet to decide any of the appeals filed from orders of the Tribunal.

The government's hesitation and delay in establishing the Pakistani Tribunal and the consequent diversion of matters to the general courts in their

cement, dairy, developers, education, fertiliser, healthcare, food, oil and refineries, paints, power, real estate, sugar, and telecom. Shortly after, the Islamabad High Court also disposed of a petition by its order dated 16.09.2021 in *Islamabad Feeds (Private) Limited and others v Federation of Pakistan*. However, both these orders are presently under appeal before the Pakistani Supreme Court.

70 For instance, the Tribunal dismissed *Nauman Anwar Butt v DHL* Appeal 2/2016 by order dated 21.12.2016 and *University of South Asia v CCP* Appeal No. 10/2016 by order dated 28.09.2016.

71 The Tribunal's orders in favour of the CCP include its orders in *Tara Crop Sciences (Pvt) Limited v CCP and other* Appeal 2/2015 decided 30.11.2016; *Al- Rahim Foods (Pvt) Limited v CCP and others* Appeal 3/2016 decided 25.01.2017; *HASCOL Petroleum Ltd v CCP and others* Appeal 7/2016 decided 21.12.2016; *Pakistan Poultry Association v CCP* Appeal 9/2016 decided 28.09.2016; *Saleem Habib Godial v CCP* Appeal 1/2016 decided 29.03.2017; *Toyota Sahara Motors v CCP* Appeal 1/2016 decided 29.03.2017; *Bahria Town (Pvt) Limited v CCP* Appeal 3/2017 decided 10.05.2017; *PTCL v CCP* Appeal 4/2017 decided 10.05.2017.

72 The Tribunal passed orders against the CCP in *1-Link Guarantee Ltd and others v CCP and others* Appeal 1-26/2012 decided 20.03.2013 (*1-Link* order); *Reckitt Benckiser Pakistan Ltd v CCP* decided 26.11.2015; *Al- Rahim Foods (Pvt) Limited v CCP and others* Appeal 3/2016 decided 25.01.2017; *Synthetic Fibre Development v CCP* Appeal 12/2016 decided 07.06.2017; *Institute of Business Management v CCP* Appeal 5/2016 decided 07.06.2017; *WAH Engineering College v CCP* Appeal 6/2016 decided 07.06.2017; and *University of Faisalabad v CCP* Appeal 4/2016 decided 07.06.2017.

73 Orders of the Tribunal in *Tara Crop Sciences (Pvt) Limited v CCP and other* Appeal 2/2015 and *Pakistan Poultry Association v CCP* Appeal 9/2016 were appealed to the Supreme Court by the aggrieved parties. Both the CCP and the appellant appealed the order of the Tribunal in *Al-Rahim Foods (Pvt) Limited v CCP* Appeal No. 3/2016.

constitutional jurisdiction has played a large role in the CCP's inability to recover penalties. At the time of writing despite the orders of the Lahore and Islamabad High Courts the CCP had still not commenced recovery proceedings in pursuance of its enforcement ordrs, most likely because it is waiting for the decision of the Supreme Court in respect of these petitions.[74] This means that the only penalties the CCP has recovered to date are those paid voluntarily by the parties. The CCP's sense of helplessness and frustration in not being able to recover penalties is evident from the CCP chairperson's messages in its Annual Reports 2013 and 2014. In the 2013 Annual Report, the chairperson noted that although the CCP had imposed penalties in the sum of PKR Rs 25 billion, it had not been able to realise any of these. The chairperson had therefore called upon the government to operationalise the Tribunal and had requested the courts to at least offer the CCP an opportunity of being heard before granting *ex parte* injunctions restraining it from recovering penalties.[75] Similarly, in the 2014 Annual Report, the chairman noted that over 300 petitions filed against its orders were still pending before the courts, and once again called on the government to operationalise the Tribunal.[76] Interestingly, this gridlock between the CCP and the government finds no reference in the CCP's Annual Reports after 2014, which together with its reduced competition enforcement actions and an increase in orders passed in respect of deceptive marketing practices suggests a shift in the CCP's enforcement priorities and its increased focus on advocacy.

In addition to obstructing the CCP from realising the penalties it had imposed, the government's failure to operationalise the competition enforcement system also meant that the CCP received no support from the second- and third-tier competition enforcement authorities in rationalising and strengthening its penal strategy. With the Pakistani Tribunal having been fully functional since 2015 and the high courts finally deciding some of the petitions filed before them, there is reason to hope that all tiers of the competition enforcement system may gradually engage with each other. However, this hope is not without the lingering fear that the government's initial delay in setting up the competition enforcement system may have irrevocably damaged not only the CCP's confidence for strong enforcement actions but also its legitimacy which in turn may have caused it to redirect its attention towards other less controversial directions (such as competition advocacy), at the cost of meaningful competition enforcement in the country.[77]

74 n.69.

75 Annual Report 2013, chairperson's message.

76 Annual Report 2014, chairman's message.

77 Even a cursory review of the CCP's Annual Reports 2015, 2016, and 2017 reveals that the number of orders in respect of deceptive marketing practices far exceed any other orders passed

6.4.3 *Beyond Penalties: Competition Enforcement Systems and Competition Jurisprudence*

Once an appellate tribunal is functional it does much more than simply ruling on the appropriateness of the penalties imposed by the first-tier competition enforcement authorities. For instance, from the earliest days of its operations, the Indian Tribunal received appeals from the CCI's interim and final orders on a range of procedural and substantive issues and through its orders either clarified the CCI's processes and operations,[78] or provided a basis for the matter to be escalated to the Supreme Court, which sitting in its competition jurisdiction was able to guide both the CCI and the Tribunal in these matters.

The instances in which matters were escalated to the Supreme Court have proved particularly significant for competition enforcement. In engaging the first-, third-, and final-tier competition authorities the final orders in these matters have not only tested and strengthened the competition enforcement system but have also facilitated the integration of competition principles in the country's pre-existing legal system. An important example in this regard is the Indian Supreme Court's decision in the *SAIL* case which clarified procedures for the CCI and for the Indian Tribunal in several important respects.[79]

by the CCP in these years. Even in the few competition cases that the CCP has decided it has imposed penalties only in the *Pakistan Automobile Manufacturers Authorized Dealers Association & Member Undertakings* File 1/101/PAMADA/C & TA/CCP/2013 decided 10.04.2015; *Pakistan Poultry Association* File 42/PPA/C & TA/CCP/2015 decided 29.02.2016; and *Pakistan Engineering Council* File 2(32)/Comp Cell/CCP/2015 decided 20.04.2016. In all these orders the CCP neither clarified the basis on which it had fixed the quantum of penalty nor the correlation between the quantum and either the turnover of these entities or the enormity of their contraventions.

78 For instance, the All India Organisation of Chemists and Druggists Association appealed the CCI's interim order in *Santuka Associates Pvt Ltd Cuttack v All India Organization of Chemists and Druggists* Case 20/2011 in terms of which it had been fined for failing to provide information to the DG without a reasonable explanation. By its order dated 27.04.2015 the Tribunal ruled on the issue of the CCI's orders being signed by members who were not present at the hearing and on the period for which the CCI may penalise for failure to comply with orders of the DG. Similarly, deciding an appeal against the CCI's interim order in *Financial Software and Systems Pvt Limited v ACI Worldwide Solutions Private Limited and others* Case 52/2013 in terms of which the CCI had granted interim relief to the complainant and had issued a restraining order against the defendants, the Tribunal by its order dated 06.05.2014 allowed the appeal and directed the DG to complete the investigation expeditiously and the CCI to pass a final order within the time stipulated in the order.

79 *Competition Commission of India v Steel Authority of India Limited* (2010) 10 SCC 744.

Box 6.2 The decision of the Indian Supreme Court in the *SAIL case*

Background

In October 2009 the CCI initiated proceedings against the Steel Authority of India Limited (SAIL) upon receipt of an 'information' or complaint from Jindal Steel and Power Limited (Jindal), which alleged that SAIL had abused its dominant position in the relevant market by entering into an exclusive agreement with Indian Railways for the supply of rails. By an interim order dated 10 November 2009 the CCI sought comments from SAIL. However, rather than providing its comments within the stipulated time, SAIL sought a six-week extension from the CCI. By its order dated 8 December 2009 the CCI denied SAIL's request for extension and directed the DG to investigate the allegations against SAIL and SAIL to supply its comments to the DG in the course of this investigation.[80]

Appeal to the Tribunal

SAIL appealed the CCI's order dated 8 December 2009 before the Indian Tribunal and on 11 January 2010 the Tribunal issued an interim order restraining the DG from continuing with its investigation against SAIL. When it received this order, the CCI sought permission from the Tribunal to join the proceedings on the basis that its order of 8 December 2009 was merely a direction for investigation and therefore not appealable before the Tribunal. On 15 February 2010 the Tribunal dismissed the CCI's request to join the proceedings[81] and rejected its contention that an appeal could not be brought against its direction to the DG.[82] On the question of whether the CCI had allowed SAIL sufficient time to file its comments, the Tribunal held that while the CCI was not under an obligation to invite comments from the defendants,[83] once it had done so, it could not 'abandon the opportunity granted midway'.[84] Therefore, the Tribunal directed the CCI to re-hear SAIL's application for extension of time and to provide reasons for its decision not only in this instance but in all future orders.[85] Throughout its order the Tribunal supported its arguments and conclusions with references to earlier decisions of the Indian superior courts.

The Decision of the Supreme Court

The CCI appealed the order of the Tribunal before the Indian Supreme Court,[86] and on 9 September 2010 the Supreme Court issued a detailed order which clarified

[80] *Steel Authority of India Limited v Jindal Steel & Power Limited* Appeal 1/2009 decided 15.02.2010 para 2.
[81] ibid para 29.
[82] ibid para 18.
[83] ibid para 34.
[84] ibid.
[85] ibid para 37.
[86] See n.79.

several important procedural points both for the CCI and the Tribunal. The Supreme Court disagreed with the Tribunal both on the question of the maintainability of the appeal and the issue of joining the CCI as a party to the appeal. In respect of maintainability, the Supreme Court held that the orders stating CCI's prima facie view or its directions to the DG were not appealable and confirmed that appeals could only be filed in respect of orders listed in section 53(A)(1)(a) of the Indian Act On the issue of joining the CCI in the proceedings the Supreme Court held that the CCI is a necessary and proper party to all proceedings that may be brought before the Tribunal against its orders or actions.[87] The Supreme Court also noted that although the CCI had no statutory obligation to issue a notice or grant a hearing to the defendants before referring a case for investigation, it was incumbent upon it to record its reasons for such referral. The Supreme Court further held that it was also incumbent upon the CCI and the DG to conclude all investigations and inquiries expeditiously so as not to adversely affect the parties to the proceedings. The Supreme Court also clarified that it was permissible for the CCI to issue an interim order during an inquiry or investigation provided that such an order was in compliance with section 33 of the Indian Act. The Supreme Court also required that the CCI issue a final order within sixty days of issuing an interim order.[88] The Supreme Court, as the Tribunal before it, drew upon Indian authorities and invoked norms of due process prevalent in the Indian legal system in arriving at its conclusions in respect of each of these issues.

On the other side of the border in Pakistan neither the Pakistani Tribunal nor the Supreme Court were able to support the CCP in its performance or in developing competition jurisprudence in the country, not becuase they were reluctant to do so but largely due to the government's failure to establish the Tribunal and thereby to operationalise the competition enforcement system in Pakistan. According to the Law and Justice Commission of Pakistan Report 2015, when the Tribunal commenced operations in early 2015 there were forty-nine appeals pending before it. During that year, five new appeals were instituted while only one appeal was decided, therefore, at the end of 2015 fifty-three appeals remained pending before the Tribunal.[89] Further, according to a news report published in August 2017, the Tribunal had disposed of forty-four out of ninety-five appeals pending before it against orders of the CCP.[90] The news report also clarified that appeals against orders of the CCP that had previously been filed before the Supreme Court had also

87 ibid pp 8–9.
88 ibid.
89 National Judicial (Policy Making) Committee 'Administrative Tribunals and Special Courts Annual Report 2015' (c) Law and Justice Commission of Pakistan, chapter 16.
90 'Tribunal takes up 95 appeals for reviewing CCP orders' <https://fp.brecorder.com/2017/08/20170830213730/> accessed 5 September 2020.

been transferred to the Tribunal.[91] Unfortunately, however, there is limited information about the operations of the Tribunal: the Tribunal neither maintains an official website nor publishes its statistics and the few of its orders that are available in the public domain, including those that have been reported in Pakistani law journals, are in respect of deceptive marketing practices rather than anti-competitive matters.[92] In the one reported order against a final order of the CCP in respect of anti-competitive agreements, the Tribunal appears to have accepted and endorsed the CCP's findings without any evaluation or analysis.[93]

Although some of the orders of the Pakistani Tribunal have been appealed before the Supreme Court,[94] and have raised some very important issues that, if decided, would have not only clarified the substantive provisions of the Pakistani Act but also the norms of procedure required to be followed by the CCP,[95] the Supreme Court has yet to decide any of these.[96] An important example in this regard is the CCP's appeal to the Supreme Court against the Tribunal's decision in the *1-Link* case[97] which remains undecided even after nearly ten years.

Box 6.3 The incomplete story of the Pakistani *1-Link case*

The Case before the CCP

This matter proceeded from an allegation that several Pakistani banks had engaged in price-fixing contrary to section 4 of the Pakistani Act by fixing charges for a range of services, including ATM cash withdrawals, Utility Bills Payment Services (UBPS), and Interbank Fund Transfers (IBFT). In deciding this matter the CCP, relied upon a US precedent which fit the facts of the case,[98] and drew a distinction between prices fixed by a *joint venture* for the purposes of 'creating significant and beneficial efficiencies that could not otherwise be accomplished'[99] (ie agreements for UBPS

[91] Under the 2007 and 2009 Ordinances except for certain appeals that lay to its internal appellate bench, appeals from orders of the CCP lay directly to the Supreme Court.

[92] Orders of the Pakistani Tribunal in respect of deceptive marketing practices include *Raja Asir Munir and another v DHL Pakistan (Pvt) Limited and 2 others* 2018 C L D 725; *Colgate Palmolive (Pakistan) Limited v CCP and another* 2019 C L D 254; *Ghulam Fareed and 8 others v CCP and another* 2019 C L D 279; *Pakistan State Oil Limited v CCP* 2019 C L D 538; *Engro Foods (Pvt) Ltd and 2 others v CCP* 2019 C L D 981.

[93] *Pakistan Poultry Association v CCP* 2018 C L D 759 para 9.

[94] See for instance appeals referred to in n.73 none of which have been decided to date.

[95] For instance, *Competition Commission of Pakistan v NIB Bank* CA 551/2013 (the *1-Link* appeal).

[96] In Pakistan the reluctance of the Supreme Court to engage with competition appeals is generally attributed to the endemic delay in Pakistani courts, however, the fact that it engaged more with general matters than with competition matters suggests that it did not prioritise competition matters. See Chapter 7 for more on this.

[97] See *1-Link* order n.72.

[98] *In re 1-Link Guarantee Ltd* File 1/24/ATM Charges/C&TA/CCP/2011 decided 28.06.2012, para 63.

[99] ibid para 62.

and IBFT) which it stated 'may be considered under a rule of reason' and may be eligible for an exemption under section 5 (read with section 9),[100] and other 'horizontal price fixing agreements' (ie for ATM cash withdrawal)[101] which it found to have 'the object of preventing, restricting and reducing competition' and, therefore, were not eligible to be considered for an exemption.[102]

Appeal Before the Pakistani Tribunal

Aggrieved by the CCP's order, the banks appealed to the Pakistani Tribunal to re-examine whether 1-Link and the banks in its network had violated section 4 of the Pakistani Act in entering into the range of agreements addressed in the CCP's order. The banks also argued that in the event that the Tribunal found evidence of a cartel, may consider whether there were any mitigating circumstances that could 'make it reasonable to condone the cartelisation'.[103] Rather than engaging with the core issue brought before it, the Tribunal noted that the 'rigid application of competition law causes more harm than good'[104] and that a lenient and flexible application of the competition legislation did not mean that the 'CCP should compromise when a violation of the Act has occurred or that cartelisation by way of price fixing should be spared just because the collusive conduct is *de minimus* in either scope or effect'.[105] The Tribunal then set aside the order of the CCP on consideration of the 'broad and real context' in which it operated.[106] In stating these views, the Tribunal did not engage with the reasoning detailed in the CCP's order and did not consider any precedents, whether of the CCP, of foreign competition authorities, or of the Pakistani courts.

CCP Goes to the Supreme Court

The CCP appealed the Tribunal's order to the Pakistani Supreme Court. It argued that the Tribunal's judgment was contrary to the settled law on the subject; that the Tribunal had ignored the evidence on record and had misinterpreted the express provisions of the Pakistani Act in relation to price-fixing agreements; and that the Tribunal was not justified in setting aside the CCP's order which was not only well-reasoned but also had been passed in accordance with the norms of due process and the requirements of the Act. On this basis the CCP asked the Supreme Court to set aside the Tribunal's order, however, the Supreme Court is yet to decide this appeal.

100 ibid.
101 ibid para 91.
102 ibid.
103 *1-Link* order n.72 para 8.
104 ibid.
105 ibid para 9.
106 ibid paras 15, 18.

6.5 ADOPTION PROCESSES, PENAL STRATEGIES AND COMPETITION ENFORCEMENT

The mechanisms and institutions through which India and Pakistan adopted their competition legislations and the compatibility and legitimacy generated for these legislations in the adoption process due to the unique interplay of mechanisms and institutions pre-existing in each country, directly impacted the early penal strategies adopted by the CCI and CCP. Interestingly, the comparatively greater compatibility and legitimacy of the Indian Act rather than enabling the CCI to pursue an aggressive penal strategy, made it more cautious, perhaps due to its need for maintaining and safeguarding the space it had so painstakingly carved out for itself in the course of adoption. Conversely, the somewhat weaker compatibility and legitimacy of the Pakistani competition legislation set the CCP free of the need to negotiate its space with other elements pre-existing in the Pakistani legal system and allowed it to pursue an aggressive penal strategy and to chart a course that it perceived to be in alignment with its international antecedents. This aggressive penal strategy in turn helped the CCP leverage its international legitimacy to gain a foothold in the Pakistani context.

Notwithstanding the importance of the *direct* impact of the adoption process on the CCI and CCP's penal strategies, it is its *indirect* impact that is of greater though less observed significance. This indirect impact stems from the extent to which the different branches of the Indian or Pakistani state engaged with each other in the course of adoption either generally or specifically in introducing the provisions for the Tribunals in their competition legislations which in turn affected the support they provided in the establishment of the Tribunals and thereby activating the competition enforcement systems in their respective contexts.

A functioning competition enforcement system brings important benefits: it has the potential to support the first-tier competition authorities in developing a more rational approach towards penalties and in enforcement more generally. This is likely to reduce the chances of these orders being challenged simply on the basis of the quantum of penalties, or if these are challenged for these to be resolved more expeditiously. A well-functioning competition enforcement system also engages the successive tiers competition authorities and brings the competition enforcement system into internal alignment which further faciitates their interaction with each other. Most importantly, as competition principles interpreted and applied in the orders of first-tier competition authorities are evaluated at each successive stage of the competition enforcement system first by competition specialists and generalist judges at the Tribunal and second by generalist judges well-versed in the norms of the country's pre-existing legal system, these orders not only allow the competition law to become more compatible with and gain greater legitimacy in the country, but also to steadily integrate into its pre-existing legal system. It is also likely that these orders succeed in bringing forth a more competitive economy.

The point that particularly bears emphasising is that the low percentages of penalties realised by the CCI and CCP are not in themselves meaningful or accurate indicators of the progress of competition enforcement in India and Pakistan, and that it is important to evaluate these recoveries against the development of competition jurisprudence in the countries and the manner and extent to which all tiers of the competition enforcement systems have engaged with each other in the process.

In the case of India, even in matters where the CCI has not realised penalties so far, it has commenced an important conversation with the Indian Tribunal and the Indian Supreme Court and has rationalised its penal strategies in light of the feedback and guidance provided by either or both of them. Conversely, the CCP has been deprived of these benefits: not only is the Pakistani Tribunal still in the early stages of its operation and has made no comment about the penalties imposed by the CCP but also the Pakistani Supreme Court is yet to decide any competition appeals filed before it and to render its opinion in this regard. Therefore, while in India the disadvantage of limited recoveries is offset by the strengthening of India's competition enforcement system, there is no such corresponding development in Pakistan. Going forward, it is likely that the interaction between the CCI, the Indian Tribunal, and the Supreme Court as inter-connected segments of the Indian competition enforcement system will contribute to the overall development of competition jurisprudence in the country, the enhancement of the compatibility and legitimacy of the adopted competition legislation. This in turn will escalate the pace at which competition principles integrate into and become part of the Indian legal context and bolster the extent to which the competition legislation is understood, utilised, and applied in the country to foster a competition culture and ultimately a more competitive economy. On the other hand, the erratic, superficial, and limited engagement between the CCP, the Pakistani Tribunal, and the Pakistani Supreme Court suggests that Pakistan has still some way to go before its adopted competition legislation is fully recognised and utilised as a legitimate and essential legal instrument and in the creation of a competitive economy.

7

Pre-existing Legal Systems and Competition Enforcement

7.1 INTRODUCTION

The Indian and Pakistani Acts provide for three-tiered, linear competition enforcement systems. If these systems work as envisaged in the competition legislations then only the specialist members of the first tier competition authorities, the CCI and CCP, will take cognisance of and evlauate anti-competitive practices as defined in the Indian and Pakistani Acts and in doing so will interpret and enforce the provisions of these Acts. Appeals from orders of the CCI or CCP will lie to the Indian and Pakistani Tribunals, also established under the Indian and Pakistani Acts, where these orders will be examined jointly by competition and judicial experts. Finally, appeals from orders of the Tribunals will lie to the Supreme Courts of the countries, where generalist judges sitting in their competition appellate jurisdiction, will assess these orders against norms prevalent in the country's pre-existing legal system. It may be expected that as successive competition matters will proceed from the first to the third tiers of the competition enforcement system a dialogue between the authorities will emerge which in time will would not only bring these authorities into greater alignment with each other but also allow the competition enforcement systems, to be shaped by the principles and norms of the pre-existing legal systems which will facilitate the gradual integration of the competition law into these systems .

In actual fact, however, competition matters do not proceed along the linear competition enforcement pathways envisaged in the competition legislations and frequently depart from it to interact with the general courts in the two countries. The manner in which the general courts react to these competition matters determines when and whether the matters are returned to the competition enforcement pathways to finally move towards their conclusions. However, in focusing on the relationship of the three competition authorities with each other without reference to possible interference from the general courts pre-existing in the countries, the

Indian and Pakistani Acts underplay the significance or impact of such interventions. In doing so these Acts suggest that interventions from the general courts are either likely to be infrequent or even if not infrequent, are likely to be easily addressed so that they cause little or no disruption to the competition enforcement systems. This chapter explores this implicit assumption by examining the extent and nature of interactions between the competition enforcement systems established in pursuance of the adopted competition legislations and pre-existing legal systems in India and Pakistan. It argues that not only are the interactions between the Indian and Pakistani Acts and the pre-existing legal systems in the two countries largely shaped by the strategies, mechanisms, and institutions through which the countries had initially adopted their respective competition legislations, but also that the nature and quality of these interactions has a discernible and significant impact on competition enforcement in these countries.

To this end the chapter is organised as follows: Section 7.2 maps the competition enforcement pathways established under the Indian and Pakistani Acts and identifies the likely points of interaction between the competition enforcement systems and pre-existing legal systems in these countries; Section 7.3 examines and compares interactions that emanate from interim orders of the CCI and CCP and explores reasons for the divergence between the two; Section 7.4 compares the interactions in India and Pakistan with the aim of understanding these in the context of the strategies, mechanisms, and institutions through which they had adopted their respective competition legislations; Section 7.5 considers the effects of these interactions on the enforcement and evolution of the competition legislations and the pace at and extent to which these legislations are likely to integrate into the pre-existing legal systems of their countries.

7.2 MAPPING THE 'INTERACTIONS' IN THE INDIAN AND PAKISTANI CONTEXTS

The interaction between adopted competition legislations in India and Pakistan and their pre-existing legal systems takes place through the competition authorities established under the Indian and Pakistani Acts – the CCI, the CCP, and the Indian and Pakistani Tribunals – and the pre-existing general courts established under their respective Constitutions. In both India and Pakistan general courts mean the high courts, hearing and deciding petitions in their inherent constitutional jurisdiction and the Supreme Courts hearing appeals from these matters also in their constitutional rather than competition jurisdictions.

The competition enforcement pathways envisaged under the Indian and Pakistani Acts begins with the national competition authorities, the CCI and CCP, proceed to the Indian and Pakistani Tribunals that are mandated to hear appeals from decisions of the CCI and CCP, and culminate in the Indian and Pakistani Supreme Courts

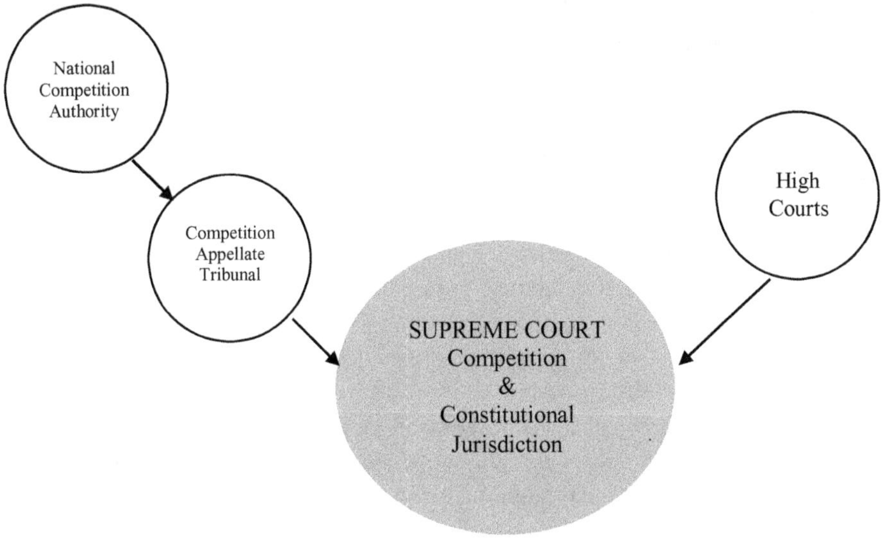

FIGURE 7.1. Competition enforcement and the constitutional pathways

sitting in their specially conferred competition appellate jurisdictions.[1] According to this pathway, the competition enforcement systems and the pre-existing legal systems interact at one point only: when the Supreme Court sitting in its competition appellate jurisdiction hears appeals from orders of the Tribunals and then too on limited grounds arising from the appealed orders (Figure 7.1).[2]

In both India and Pakistan, in addition to their competition appellate jurisdiction, the Supreme Courts also exercise constitutional and general appellate jurisdictions, and the competition enforcement systems also come into contact with the pre-existing systems when the high courts hear writ petitions from persons aggrieved by the actions or orders of the tier (the CCI and the CCP) and second tier (Indian and Pakistani Tribunals) competition authorities in exercise of their inherent constitutional jurisdictions.[3]

Aggrieved parties may file petitions against proceedings pending before the CCI, the CCP, or the Indian and Pakistani Tribunals before the high courts under Article 226 of

1 Under the Indian and Pakistani Constitution, the Supreme Courts are the apex constitutional courts of the countries. However, Article 138(2) of the Indian Constitution and Article 175(2) of the Pakistani Constitution allow the jurisdictions of their respective Supreme Courts to be enlarged by statute. It is in pursuance of these provisions that section 53T of the Indian Act and section 44 of the Pakistani Act confer on the Indian and Pakistani Supreme Courts the jurisdiction to hear appeals from orders of the Indian and Pakistani Tribunals respectively.

2 This competition enforcement pathway is the same as the competition enforcement system. the different terminology is used to indicate the direction along which matters proceed within the system.

3 In accordance with the rules of procedure in force in the two countries, these petitions may be filed before the high court that has jurisdiction in the territory in which the aggrieved party has its registered office or carries on a substantial part of its business.

the Indian Constitution and Article 199 of the Pakistani Constitution. These nearly identical Articles allow persons aggrieved by the orders or actions of the government or of any natural or legal persons performing functions in connection with governmental affairs, to challenge these orders or actions before the relevant court on the ground that these infringe one or more of the fundamental rights guaranteed under the Indian or Pakistani Constitutions.[4] If, upon hearing a petition, the general court is satisfied that fundamental rights have been violated, it may, in exercise of its inherent constitutional jurisdiction, issue one or more of the following writs: (a) *writ of mandamus and prohibition* directing a person carrying out a function in connection with the affairs of the federation to refrain from doing anything he is not permitted to do or to do anything he is required to do; (b) *writ of certiorari* declaring that any act or proceeding performed by a person in connection with the affairs of the federation has been done without lawful authority and is without legal effect; (c) *writ of habeas corpus* directing that a person held in custody within the jurisdiction of the court may be presented in court; (d) *writ of quo warranto* requiring a person holding public office to show the authority of law under which he claims to hold that office. The high court may also issue interim restraining orders while these petitions remain pending.[5] The orders of both the CCI and the CCP qualify as functions in connection with the affairs of the Union or federation (in the case of India and Pakistan respectively) and the high courts in both countries have the power to issue one or more of these writs as may be appropriate (Figure 7.2).

The possibility of challenging the orders and actions of the first- and second-tier competition authorities before the general courts gives rise to two further possible points of interaction between the competition enforcement and constitutional systems: one between the first-tier competition authorities, ie the CCI and CCP and the high courts and the other between the second-tier competition authorities, ie the Indian and Pakistani Tribunals, and the high courts. There is no direct point of interaction with the Supreme Courts and they only hear appeals from orders of the high courts in these petitions. Although both these points of interaction are of interest, this chapter focuses only on the first (between the CCI and CCP and the high courts) due to the very limited available data for the Pakistani Tribunal which prevents a comparative analysis with orders from the Indian Tribunal.[6]

The interaction between the first-tier competition authorities, the CCI and CCP, and the general courts in India and Pakistan is initiated when a person files a

[4] These mean any of rights conferred under Articles 12–35 of the Indian Constitution, or Articles 8–28 of the Pakistani Constitution.

[5] See Article 226 read with Article 32 of the Indian Constitution and Article 199 read with Article 184(3) of the Pakistani Constitution.

[6] The exclusive focus on the first interaction is not a shortcoming of this work as both these sets of interactions are likely to follow similar patterns, and insights in respect of one are also likely to be instructive in understanding the other.

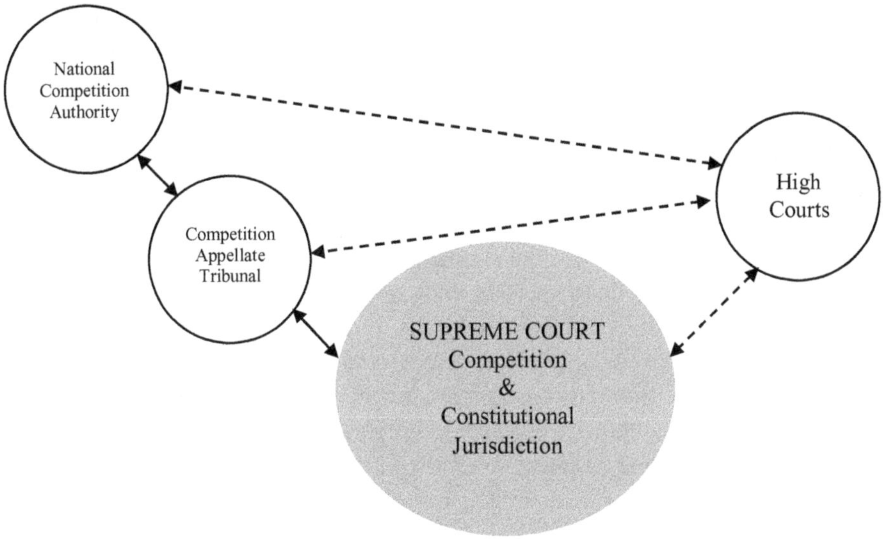

FIGURE 7.2. Points of interaction between competition enforcement and pre-existing legal systems

petition before a general court alleging a violation of its constitutional rights in the proceedings before the CCI or CCP, as the case may be. In hearing this petition in exercise of its inherent constitutional jurisdiction the court has the option to either immediately decide the matter by passing a final order or to allow further time for hearing and issue an interim restraining order for such time as the petition remains pending before it. If the general court issues an order deciding and disposing of the petition the matter may either be returned to the CCI or the CCP, where it may proceed along the competition enforcement pathway, or the order of the general court may be appealed to the Supreme Court in its constitutional jurisdiction, whereby it still remains in the constitutional system and the competition system remains suspended most in compliance with a restraining order issued by the high courts. The Supreme Court, sitting in its constitutional jurisdiction, also has the option to decide the matter and to either return it to the high court for further action, thereby retaining it within the pre-existing legal system, or to the CCI or CCP directly from where it may proceed along the competition enforcement pathway. If, instead of issuing an order deciding and disposing of the petition, the general court issues an interim restraining order the matter may still be returned to the CCI and CCP, albeit with restrictions on how they may proceed. The CCI or the CCP as the case may be, then have the option to comply with the interim order of the general court or appeal it to the Supreme Court in its constitutional jurisdiction. In either case the matter remains in the pre-existing legal system and is not returned to the competition enforcement system until such time as it is finally decided by the general courts.

This discussion suggests that as important as the number of orders or actions of the CCI or the CCP that are challenged before the general courts, is the response of the general courts to these challenges. While filing a petition is a constitutional right, the response of the courts is a reflection of judicial discretion and capacity and impacts the nature, quality, and speed of competition enforcement in India or Pakistan, and the pace at and extent to which the Indian and Pakistani Acts integrate into their respective pre-existing legal systems. If the general court issues a final decision disposing of the petition before it – regardless of whether it decides in favour of the competition authority or the aggrieved party – and if the parties refrain from appealing the order in the constitutional jurisdiction, the matter is returned to the competition authority and proceeds along the competition enforcement pathway, albeit in the manner directed by the courts. In such a situation, the interaction between the competition enforcement systems and pre-existing systems supports competition enforcement by providing guidance and clarity and thereby enhancing its compatibility with the context and its legitimacy in it. If, however, the general court issues an interim order simply restraining or restricting the competition authority, it not only fails to provide clarity and guidance but also suspends competition enforcement. The longer such a restraining order remains in place the greater the erosion not only of the effectiveness of competition enforcement but also the legitimacy of the entire competition enforcement system.

7.3 'INTERACTIONS' IN INDIA AND PAKISTAN

Parties aggrieved by orders or actions of the CCI and CCP in both India and Pakistan have filed petitions before the general courts. While in India these petitions have generally been filed against interim orders of the CCI, in Pakistan challenges have historically been brought against final as well as interim orders of the CCP. This section compares the challenges brought against the interim orders of the CCI and CCP[7] and explores reasons for the divergence between the Indian and Pakistani experience.[8]

7.3.1 *Interaction between CCI and the General Courts*

In the majority of petitions filed against the CCI's interim orders, aggrieved parties sought from the general courts writs of *mandamus and prohibition*, *certiorari* and

[7] In Pakistan petitions were also filed against final orders of the CCP because the Pakistani Tribunal had not been established. This has been more fully discussed in Chapter 6.

[8] Petitions against orders of the CCI and the CCP were filed in high courts throughout the two countries and there is no central record of these petitions. Luckily, however, several petitions including the decisions of the general courts in them have been recorded in the subsequent the orders of the CCI and CCP in these matters. While it is likely that this information may not be entirely accurate or complete as a review of CCI and CCP's Annual Reports suggests that there may be petitions pending before high courts in addition to the ones noted in this chapter. However, the information derived from the orders of the CCI and the CCP suffices in providing an insight into the nature and impact of these interactions.

quo warranto, ie they requested the courts to direct that the CCI should refrain from doing something it was not permitted to do or to do something it was required to do; declare that an act or proceeding performed by the CCI had been performed without lawful authority and was therefore, without legal effect; or require the CCI to show the legal authority for its actions.[9]

One ground repeatedly raised before the general courts was that the CCI did not have the jurisdiction to hear matters that had been commenced before its predecessor anti-monopoly authority, particularly if the anti-monopoly authority had initiated an investigation but failed to complete it. In response, several general courts unequivocally declared this ground to be without merit and directed the petitioners to submit to the CCI's jurisdiction.[10] A further related point raised before the general courts was that the CCI did not have the authority to exercise its jurisdiction in respect of practices that had commenced before the relevant provisions of the Indian Act had been brought into force. In responding to all petitions in which this ground was raised, the general courts clarified that the CCI did indeed have the jurisdiction to examine conduct that had commenced prior to the relevant provisions coming into force, provided such conduct had continued even after the coming into force of these provisions.[11] In at least one case, the aggrieved party challenged the CCI's power to issue a show-cause notice on the ground that doing so was tantamount to the CCI pre-judging the case. In this matter the general court clarified that the CCI had the jurisdiction and the responsibility to form a preliminary view of a case and therefore the show cause notice was valid.[12] In certain other cases, parties challenged the CCI's jurisdiction to initiate investigations, however, the general courts did not entertain these petitions or others filed on similar grounds.[13]

[9] Indian Constitution, Article 226.

[10] Petitions on this ground include *Interglobe Aviation Limited v Secretary CCI* WP 6805/2010 decided by the Delhi High Court on 06.10.2010 and *Gujarat Guardian Limited v CCI and others* WP 7766/2010 also decided by Delhi High Court on 23.11.2010.

[11] For instance, in *MP Merhotra v Kingfisher Airlines Limited & others* Case 4/2009, Kingfisher had challenged the CCI's demand for information before the Bombay High Court. The BHC dismissed this petition on 31.03.2010 after which Kingfisher challenged BHC's order to the Supreme Court. The Supreme Court admitted Kingfisher's petition but did not restrain the CCI from continuing with its proceedings and in due course, the CCI imposed a fine on Kingfisher for abuse of dominant position. Kingfisher then appealed the CCI's order before the Indian Tribunal, which set aside the CCI's order and asked it to reconsider the matter. After reconsidering the matter the CCI through its order dated 09.01.2012 imposed a further fine on Kingfisher. Kingfisher once again appealed to the Tribunal and on 29.08.2012 in *Kingfisher Airlines Limited v CCI and others* Appeal 15/2012 the Tribunal set aside the CCI's latest order.

[12] See for example *Amir Khan Productions (Pvt) Limited v Union of* India WP 358/2010 decided by the Bombay High Court on 18.08.2010 (CCI Annual Report 2010–11).

[13] For example, see references to petitions in the CCI's orders in (a) *Federation of Indian Airlines & others* Case RTPE 3/2008 decided 02.12.2010, para 8 and (b) *Shri Shamsher Kataria v Honda Siel Cars Limited India & others (Hyundai)* Case 3/2011 decided 27.07.2015, paras 1.5, 7.4.4. Also see orders of the high courts in (a) *Arun Kumar Bajoria v CCI and another* WP (C) 2471/2016, in which the petitioner challenged directions issued by the CCI on the grounds that the CCI lacked jurisdiction to issue these and the Delhi High Court by its order dated 21.03.2016 held

In a few of its orders, in which the CCI records petitions filed in relation to the order, the CCI has recorded only the response of the general courts rather than the grounds on which the petitions had been filed. Regardless however, a review of the responses of the high courts as recorded in these orders suggests that the courts' responses have varied according to the facts and circumstances of the case. In certain matters, the court expressly endorsed the CCI while in others it directed the CCI to take certain actions; in some cases, the courts restrained the CCI from pursuing one or more of the parties to the proceedings, and, in very rare instances, they restrained the CCI from continuing with the proceedings altogether. Importantly, in matters where the courts restrained the CCI from proceeding altogether they did so for a limited period only.[14]

In certain proceedings pending before the CCI the complainant itself approached the courts. For instance, in one matter the complainant approached the court for interim relief against the defendants, while the matter was still pending before the

that the CCI was competent to decide its own jurisdiction and dismissed the petition and (b) *Telefonaktiebolaget LM Ericsson v CCI & others* WP 1006/2014 in which the petitioner argued that the CCI could not investigate its affairs as these were governed by the Patents Act, but the Delhi High Court by its order dated 16.04.2016 recognised the CCI's jurisdiction and allowed it to continue with its investigation.

[14] For instance, see references to petitions in the CCI's orders in (a) *Vedant Bio Sciences v Chemists & Druggists Association of Baroda* Case C-87/2009 decided 05.09.2012, paras 11–15. In this case the CCI's proceedings were challenged on two occasions: on the first, the Gujarat High Court did not restrain the CCI, however, on the second, the GHC restrained the CCI from requiring petitioner's officers to produce evidence until such time as the GHC had finally decided the matter. The GHC did not restrain the CCI from continuing with the proceedings against the remaining parties; (b) *Peeveear Medical Agencies Kerala v All India Organization of Chemists & Druggists* Case 30/2011 decided 09.12.2013, para 12.5.12. This order refers to WP 2882/2012 in which Karnataka High Court had issued a restraining order against CCI; (c) *Sandhya Drug Agency v Assam Drug Dealers Association & others* Case 41/2011 decided 09.12.2013, paras 11 & 12. This order records a petition filed before Gauhati High Court which initially restrained the CCI but soon vacated the injunction and allowed the CCI to continue with the proceedings; (d) *Collective Boycott/refusal to deal by the Chemists and Druggist Association Goa etc* Suo Motu Case 5/2013 decided 27.10.2014. This order records that while the Bombay High Court restrained the CCI from hearing the issue of individual culpability of officers of associations/companies, it did not restrain the CCI from proceeding against the associations/companies themselves; (e) *Shri Shamsher Kataria v Honda Siel Cars India Limited & others* Case 3/2011 decided 25.08.2014, para 22.9. This order refers to WP 2734/2013 in which the Delhi High Court issued an order restraining the CCI from giving effect to its order for ten days; and (f) *Durga City Cable Network v In2 Cable (India) Limited & others* Case 23/2010 decided 10.08.2011, paras 8 & 17 which records the Delhi High Court's refusal to restrain the CCI from proceeding with the matter in a petition filed before it. The following orders of the high courts, not yet recorded in orders of the CCI, are also significant in this regard: (a) order of Madras High Court dated 04.02.2015 in *Hyundai Motors India Limited & BMW India Pvt Limited v CCI and another* WP 31808 and 31809/2012, in which the MHC refused to restrain the CCI and dismissed the petitions. The order was confirmed in appeal also before the MHC through an order dated 23.07.2018 in *Hyundai Motor India Limited v CCI and others* WA 340/2015 and (b) order of Delhi High Court dated 10.10.2014 in *DLF Home Developers Limited v CCI & another* WP 6361 and 4362/2014.

CCI, however, the court dismissed the petition and directed the complainant to approach the CCI instead.[15] In another matter the complainant asked the court to direct the CCI to hear an application on an urgent basis[16] and in at least one recent case, rather than waiting for the court to issue an order in a petition brought against its proceedings, the CCI voluntarily gave an undertaking that it would not to take adverse action against the defendants while the petitions remained pending before the court.[17]

Overall, the responses of the general courts to petitions from proceedings pending before the CCI suggest that in issuing more final rather than interim orders, the courts have dealt decisively with the objections raised against the CCI, and in deciding these petitions relatively soon after these were filed they have also dealt with these with reasonable alacrity.[18] It is also evident that decisions of the courts throughout India have formed valuable precedents for the CCI in subsequent proceedings. For instance, the CCI has cited Delhi High Court's decision in the *Interglobe* and the *Gujarat Guardian* petitions[19] in several later orders, including its orders in *Varca Druggist & Chemist and others v Chemists & Druggists Association Goa*;[20] *In re Cartelization by Cement Manufacturers* case,[21] and *Re Alleged Cartelization by Cement Manufacturers v Shree Cement Limited and others.*[22] Similarly, the CCI has cited the order of the Bombay High Court in the *Kingfisher* case[23] in a number of its subsequent orders, including its order in *Chemists & Druggists Association Goa* case;[24] *In re Cartelization by Cement Manufacturers* case;[25] *Shree Cement* case;[26] *Shri Sonam Sharma v Apple Inc. USA*

[15] *Reliance Big Entertainment Limited v Karnataka Film Chamber of Commerce* Cases 25, 41, 45, 47, 48, 50, 58, 69/2010 decided 16.2.2010, para 2.1.20.

[16] *Santuka Associates Pvt Limited v All India Organization of Chemists and Druggists & others* Case 20/2011 decided 19.02.2013, para 3.

[17] For example, in *Google Inc & others v CCI & another* WP 7084/2014 the petitioners asked the high court to set aside the CCI's order directing an investigation into its affairs and its order rejecting Google's review application. The petitioner also asked the court to restrain the CCI from continuing with its proceedings. By its order dated 27.04.2015, the Delhi High Court directed the CCI to reconsider the application for review and the CCI itself gave an undertaking that it would not take any adverse action against the petitioners while the review application remained pending.

[18] See Chapter 4, Tables 4.5 and 4.6.

[19] n.10.

[20] Case MRTP C-127/2009/DG1R4/28 decided 11.06.2012, para 26.9.

[21] Case RTPE 52/2006 decided 03.07.2012, para 104.

[22] Case RTPE 52/2006 decided 31.08.2016, para 51.

[23] *MP Merhotra v Kingfisher Airlines Limited & others* Case 4/2009 decided 09.01.2012. Also see n.11.

[24] See n.20, para 26.11.

[25] See n.21, para 106.

[26] See n.22, para 55.

& others;[27] *In re Alleged cartelisation by steel producers;*[28] *Shri Sunil Bansal & others v Jaiprakash Associates Ltd and others;*[29] and *Builders Association of India v Cement Manufacturers Association and others.*[30]

7.3.2 *CCP's Interim Orders and Challenges before the General Courts in Pakistan*

Unlike India where petitions were primarily filed against orders issued by the CCI in the course of proceedings, in Pakistan petitions were filed to challenge show-cause notices and interim orders issued by the CCP as well as to challenge its final orders. However, for the purpose of comparison with India, this section only considers petitions filed against the CCP's show-cause notices or interim orders.[31] These petitions may be further divided into two groups: the first comprising petitions filed in the period when the 2007 Ordinance was in force ('the first group of petitions') and the second comprising petitions filed after the 2009 and 2010 Ordinances were brought into force and includes the period up to and after the enactment of the Pakistani Act ('the second group of petitions'). In both the first and second group of petitions, parties approached the general courts to seek writs directing the CCP to refrain from doing what it was not permitted to do or to do what it is required to do (writs of *mandamus and prohibition*); writs declaring that the CCP's given act or proceeding was without lawful authority and without legal effect (writs of *certiorari*); or writs requiring the CCP or its officers to show the authority under which they claimed to hold office (writs of *quo warranto*).[32]

In the first group of petitions, the grounds on which parties sought these writs included that the show-cause notice issued by the CCP was not in accordance with the law; certain sections of the 2007 Ordinance, and, therefore, the CCP's actions in exercise of its powers under these sections, were ultra vires the Pakistani Constitution[33] and contrary to the fundamental rights guaranteed under it;[34] the subject of competition was not listed in the Pakistani Constitution's Federal Legislative List and, therefore, the president was not competent to promulgate the

[27] Case 24/2011 decided 19.3.2013, para 14.
[28] Case RTPE 9/2008 decided 09.01.2014, para 107.
[29] Cases 72/2011, 16/2012, 34/2012, 53/2012, 45/2013 decided 26.10.2015, para 14.
[30] Case 29/2010 decided 31.08.2016, para 163.
[31] See n.7.
[32] Pakistani Constitution, Article 199.
[33] The petitions most often cited 2007 Ordinance, sections 41 and 42 in this regard.
[34] For instance, interim orders of the Sindh High Court in *Karachi Stock Exchange & another v Federation of Pakistan and others* CP 786/2008 dated 30.04.2008 and modified on 05.06.2008 and the *Pakistan Banking Association* case CP 938/2008 dated 07.11.2008. The CCP appealed both these orders to the Supreme Court and the Supreme Court by its orders dated 13.11.2008 in CPs 759 and 760/2008 and 23.10.2008 in CP 715/2008, set aside the restraining orders issued by the SHC on the CCP's undertaking that it will not recover any fines from the petitioners while the petitions remained pending.

2007 Ordinance; and that the CCP did not have the jurisdiction under the 2007 Ordinance to initiate proceedings against the petitioners.[35] In the majority of instances, the courts simply accepted the petitions for hearing and issued interim orders restraining the CCP from proceeding until the next date of hearing, without scrutinising the grounds on which these had been filed. On subsequent hearings the court simply extended the restraining order until the next hearing and allowed the status quo to continue still without scrutinising the grounds on which the petitions had been filed. A ground raised repeatedly in the second group of petitions, particularly in the period in which the 2007 Ordinance had lapsed and the Pakistani Act was still to be enacted (ie in the period in which the 2009 and 2010 Ordinances were in force), was that the CCP did not have the legal competence to issue show-cause notices until such time as the legislature had ratified the Ordinances in compliance with the Pakistani Supreme Court's order in *Sindh High Court Bar Association v Federation of Pakistan*.[36]

Perhaps the most important petition in the first group of petitions was filed by the Liquefied Petroleum Gas Association of Pakistan (LPGAP) in which the LPGAP challenged the show-cause notice issued by the CCP to the LPGAP and its members and sought a restraining order from the court. The high court allowed the petition and restrained the CCP from acting on its show-cause notice. The CCP challenged the high court's decision before the Supreme Court and the Supreme Court set aside the restraining order of the high court and directed the CCP to first decide the issue of jurisdiction. The Supreme Court also directed the CCP to 'voluntarily' commit to the court that it would not take any adverse action against LPGAP until such time as the petition remained pending. This meant that although the CCP could continue hearing the matter to issue a final order, it could not recover the penalty it had imposed

35 The Lahore High Court granted injunctions to several cement companies on these grounds in relation to the *All-Pakistan Cement Manufacturers Association* case (File 4/2/ Sec 4/CCP/2008 decided 27.08.2009). See for instance the LHC's order in WP 15616/2009 dated 10.08.2009 (Pioneer Cement Limited) and several other orders all dated 11.08.2009 in WP 15624/ 2009 (All Pakistan Cement Manufacturing Association); WP 15640/2009 (Askari Cement Limited); WP 15622/2009 (Attock Cement Limited); WP 15639/2009 (Bestway Cement Limited); WP 15631/ 2009 (Cherat Cement Limited); WP 15670/2009 (Dandot Cement Limited); WP 15623/2009 (Dewan Cement Limited); WP 15630/2009 (DG Khan Cement); WP 15669/2009 (Fauji Cement Limited); WP 15629/2009 (Fecto Cement Limited); WP 15619/2009 (Flying Cement Limited); WP 15688/2009 (Kohat Cement Limited); WP 15620/2009 (Lafarge Cement Limited); WP 15637/2009 (Lucky Cement Limited); WP 15618/2009 (Maple Leaf Cement Company Limited); and WP 15638/2009 (Mustehkam Cement Limited).

36 PLD 2009 SC 879. See Chapter 2 for a detailed discussion in this regard. The Sindh High Court granted an injunction on 14.01.2010 in CP D-110/2010 (filed by Mirpurkhas Sugar Mills) on the ground that the CCP was not competent to act against the company until the Pakistani Act had been enacted.

as doing so would be tantamount to taking 'an adverse action' contrary to the undertaking it had given to the Supreme Court.[37] In October 2020, nearly eleven years after the petitions were filed the Lahore High Court finally decided the LPGAP petition along with ninety-two others in sectors as diverse as accountancy, automobiles, cement, dairy, developers, education, fertiliser, healthcare, food, oil and refineries, paints, power, real estate, sugar, and telecom.[38] However, both the CCP and the original petitioners appealed the order before the Pakistani Supreme Court and remain pending at the time of writing.

Another important petition from the first group of petitions that also qualifies as a second group petition relates to the CCP's proceedings against the All Pakistan Cement Manufacturers' Association (APCMA). On 28 October 2008 the CCP had issued a show-cause notice to APCMA and its members which the parties had then challenged before the Islamabad High Court. Although at first the court by its order dated 10 November 2008 restrained the CCP from passing a final order against the defendants, by a further order dated 5 December 2008 it dismissed the petitions as 'premature' and allowed the CCP to continue with the hearings. Given this reprieve from the high court, the CCP scheduled a hearing for APCMA and its members for 3 August 2009. In the meantime, however, the parties approached the Lahore High Court and obtained yet another injunction against the CCP. The Lahore High Court vacated this second injunction on 24 August 2009 and allowed the CCP to continue with its hearings which culminated in the CCP issuing its final order on 27 August 2009.[39] However, on 31 August 2009, before the CCP could take any steps to enforce its order, the Lahore High Court issued yet another interim order, this time restraining the CCP from taking any adverse action against APCMA and its members.[40] The petitions filed in the APCMA matter have also been decided by the Lahore High Court's October 2020 order in the LPGAP petitions, and the member cement companies of the APCMA have also challenged the Lahore High Court's order to the Supreme Court where it presently remains pending.[41]

[37] The Lahore High Court issued the restraining order in LPGAP's petition WP 9518/2009 on 27.05.2009. The CCP filed CP 1022/2009 before the Supreme Court and the Supreme Court by its order dated 26.05.2009 set aside the LHC's restraining order and remanded the matter to the LHC on the basis of the CCP's undertaking. Here, after a further order dated 05.08.2009, the petition remained pending until October 2020.

[38] *LPG Association of Pakistan v Federation of Pakistan and others* 2021 C L D 214. Shortly after, the Islamabad High Court also issued an order dated 16 September 2021 in *Islamabad Feeds (Private) Limited and others v Federation of Pakistan*. This too has been appealed to the Supreme Court.

[39] The CCP's order dated 27.08.2009 in File 4/2/ sec 4/CCP/2008, paras 11–13.

[40] The petition challenging the final order of the CCP in this case is discussed in detail in Chapter 6. Also see the Preface for the complete story.

[41] At the time of writing this the Supreme Court has not admitted any of these appeals for hearing.

The nature and quality of the interactions between the CCP and the general courts in Pakistan has had a considerable impact on subsequent proceedings before the CCP, however, unlike India, this impact has been largely obstructive rather than supportive. Instead of clarifying the CCP's position and thereby providing it guidance in issuing its subsequent orders, the orders of the high courts provided grounds for other parties aggrieved by the actions and orders of the CCP to launch further petitions against the CCP. For example, when the CCP initiated proceedings against the Pakistan Sugar Mills Association (PSMA) and its members the PSMA and its members relied on Sindh High Court's interim order in the *Mirpurkhas Sugar Mills* petition[42] to obtain further restraining orders against the CCP.[43] Similarly, the Lahore High Court's decision in the *LPGAP* case[44] opened floodgates of interim injunctions against show-cause notices issued by the CCP. Often, the high courts granted these injunctions at the first hearing mostly because 'other constitutional petitions raising similar issues have already been heard by [the] Court' and without any scrutiny of the grounds on which the petition had been filed.[45] Although the CCP challenged a number of such interim injunctions before the Supreme Court, the Supreme Court mostly preferred to mediate between the CCP and the high courts rather than taking decisive action and allowed the CCP to continue with the proceedings while restraining it (or asking it 'voluntarily' restrain)

[42] n.36.

[43] These include Sindh High Court's orders dated 19.01.2010 in CP D-149/2010 (Pakistani Sugar Mills Association), order dated 20.01.2010 in CP D-164/2010 (Al Abbas Sugar Mills Limited), order dated 26.01.2010 in CP D-196/2010 (Pangrio Sugar Mills), and order dated 12.02.2010 in CP 360/2010 (Sakrand Sugar Mills Limited). These also include the Lahore High Court's orders dated 21.01.2010 in WP 1176/2010 (Chishtia Sugar Mills Limited), WP 1175/2010 (Gojra Samundari Sugar Limited), WP 1122/2010 (Shahtaj Sugar Mills Limited), WP 1173/2010 (Sheikhoo Sugar Mills Limited); orders dated 11.02.2010 in WP 2654/2010 (National Sugar Limited) and WP 2556/2010 (Pattoki Sugar Mills Limited); and order dated 12.02.2010 in WP 2761/2010 (Shakarganj Mills Limited). The CCP challenged these orders before the Supreme Court, for instance CPs nos 521/2010, 522/2010, 523/2010, 524/2010, and 525/2010 and CPs 1065/2010, 1066/2010, and 1067/2010. However, the CCP was unable to explain its delay in filing these appeals and, therefore, the Supreme Court dismissed these without granting any relief to the CCP, only directing the high courts to hear the petitions expeditiously.

[44] n.37 and text thereto.

[45] A petitioner from the electronics sector (name not provided) made this statement in WP 3530/2010. The Lahore High Court by its order dated 23.02.2010 allowed an injunction on this basis and also relied on the decision in its orders in subsequent petitions including WP 22575/2011 (Transfopower Industries) decided 12.10.2011; WP 23640/2011 (AB Ampere (Pvt) Limited) decided 21.10.2011; WP 23743/2011 (Pak Electron) decided 25.10.2011; and WP 27488/2011 (KBK Electronics) decided 08.12.2011. By its orders dated 16.06.2011, the court also granted injunctions against the CCP in WP 13496/2011 (Creative Engineering), WP 13497/2011 (M.R Electric); WP 13498/2011 (Redco Pakistan Limited), WP 13499/2011 (Amin Brothers Limited), and Nam International (WP 13500/2011). Also, Sindh High Court by its orders dated 07.06.12 and 13.08.12 in CP D 2125/2012 (Schneider Electric Pakistan) and CP D 2871/2012 (Medical Diagnostics Centre and others) restrained the CCP from taking coercive action against the petitioners and suspended the operation of the show cause notice.

from taking any adverse action against the petitioners, while directing the high courts to hear and expeditiously decide the pending petitions.[46]

7.3.3 *The Divergence in the Indian and Pakistani Experience: Are Court Systems Responsible?*

Notwithstanding that only a comparably small proportion of orders of the CCI and CCP were challenged in writ petitions before the general courts in India and Pakistan and sought nearly identical writs from the courts, the interactions between the competition enforcement systems (as represented by the CCI and CCP respectively) and the pre-existing legal systems of the countries (as represented by their general courts) differ on two important counts: first, the grounds on which the aggrieved parties brought these petitions, and second, the manner in which the courts responded to these challenges.

The grounds on which parties to proceedings pending before the CCI invoked the inherent constitutional jurisdiction of the Indian general courts are primarily procedural in nature. For instance, the petitions call into question the CCI's authority to take notice of certain allegedly anti-competitive practices or the manner in which the CCI takes such notice. On the other hand, grounds on which aggrieved parties in Pakistan approached the Pakistani general courts are both procedural and substantive. While the procedural grounds raised in petitions filed before the Pakistani courts are comparable to those raised before the Indian courts, the substantive grounds are linked to the circumstances in and mechanisms through which the Pakistani competition legislations were promulgated. Some of the most repeated substantive grounds in the Pakistani petitions include calling into question the constitutionality of the Pakistani competition legislation; the validity and legitimacy of the CCP; and the legality of its power to initiate and pursue proceedings against the petitioning entities. It is further interesting to note that in the Pakistani context substantive grounds appear more frequently than procedural grounds in petitions filed from proceedings of the CCP.

An important aspect of the response of the general courts to petitions filed before them is the speed with which they delivered their response. The Indian general courts have mostly responded to the petitions stemming from proceedings pending before the CCI with reasonable alacrity and clarity and have utilised a relatively wide range of legal tools available to them rather than simply restraining the CCI indefinitely from continuing with the proceedings. In doing so the Indian general courts have supported the CCI's operations and have helped bring the competition enforcement system into alignment internally with its successive tiers as well as

[46] The CCP filed appeals before the Supreme Court (CPs 1938,1939, 1988, 1989, 2008, and 2009/2011) against orders of the high court in petitions filed by Transfopower Industries, AB Ampere, and Pak Electron among others. However, by its order dated 22.12.2011 the Supreme Court refused to interfere with the interlocutory orders and merely directed the high courts to hear and dispose of the petitions expeditiously.

externally with India's pre-existing legal system by enhancing its compatibility and legitimacy in the Indian context. In comparison, the response of the Pakistani general courts to the petitions filed before them appears largely hesitant, and has the effect of impeding rather than facilitating the operation of the CCP. The most common response of the Pakistani general courts to the petitions coming before them has been to issue a restraining order at the very first hearing often without providing the CCP an opportunity to present its case. In nearly all matters in which they have issued *ex parte* restraining orders, the courts have simply extended the restraint at subsequent hearings rather than engaging with the petition on its merits. The reluctance of the Pakistani general courts to decide the petitions on their merits and their tendency to easily restrain the CCP led to more and more petitions being brought before the courts and more damagingly, left the CCP in a state of legal uncertainty which cast a long shadow not only on the CCP's ability to enforce its orders but also made it hesitant about initiating proceedings against the most powerful business actors in the country who had easy recourse to the general courts. In 2020, after avoiding competition petititions for nearly eleven years the general courts took the first decisive steps in issuing an orders in the *LPG Association of Pakistan v.Federation of Pakistan and others* (2021 C L D 214) and in *Islamabad Feeds (Private) Limited and others v. Federation of Pakistan*, however, these matters are still pending before the Supreme Court and it is likely that the time lost due to the intitial delay has adversely and to some extent irreversibly impacted the CCP's domestic legitimacy which may continue to hinder meaningful competition enforcement in the country.

It is often argued that the delay on the part of the Pakistani general courts in responding to the competition matters is simply another manifestation of the general problem of endemic delay in the Pakistani legal system. However, the problem of delay is not unique to Pakistan and it is undisputable that both the Indian and Pakistani legal systems keep cases pending for inordinately long periods of time is.[47] According to the Annual Reports of the Indian and Pakistani Supreme Courts, regardless of the number of cases instituted or disposed of by the Supreme Courts in a given year, the number of cases pending before them remains relatively constant over time.[48] Given that the Indian and Pakistani Supreme Courts are the apex judicial bodies and responsible for monitoring the operations of the high courts in their respective countries, the delay at the Supreme Court level is likely to be replicated in the high courts (Figure 7.3).

[47] 'Pending Cases & Absence of Judges: Indian Judiciary Delays Justice, Denies Equity' https://thelogicalindian.com/story-feed/awareness/indian-justice-system-delay-19973, and 'What causes Judicial Delays in Pakistan' <https://crssblog.com/what-causes-judicial-delays-in-pakistan> both accessed 30 August 2020.

[48] This observation is based on data provided in the most recent available reports of the Indian and Pakistani Supreme Courts: Annual Reports of the Supreme Court of India 2017–18 and the Annual Report of the Supreme Court of Pakistan 2017–18. There is no expectation that these numbers would have declined significantly in subsequent years.

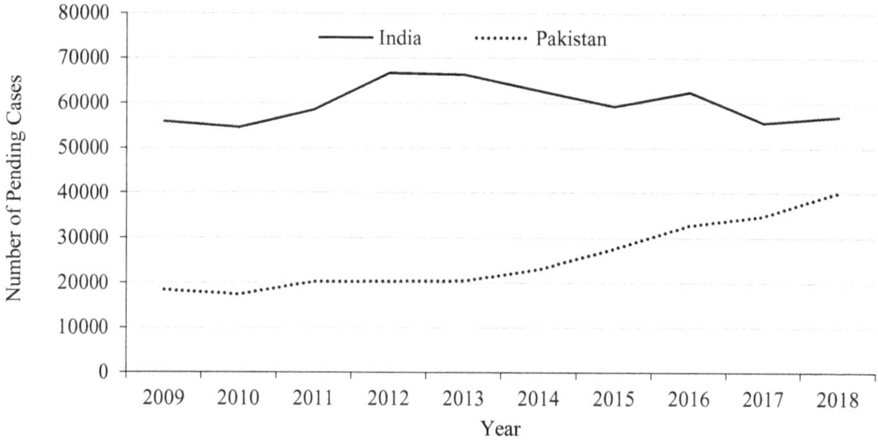

FIGURE 7.3. Comparison of cases pending before the Supreme Courts of India and Pakistan (2009–18)

If, as is commonly suggested, the delayed response of the Pakistani general courts to competition-related petitions filed before them is due to the endemic delay inherent in Pakistan's pre-existing legal system, then such a delay in disposing of competition matters would also have been evident in India which suffers from the same problem, and Indian general courts would not have disposed of a higher proportion of competition-related challenges filed before them than their Pakistani counterparts. The disparity in the rates of disposal of competition-related petitions in the two countries suggests it is important to look beyond the endemic delay argument to discover another more plausible explanation for the attitude of the courts towards competition petitions in the two countries.

7.4 ADOPTION PROCESSES: ANOTHER EXPLANATION FOR THE INTERACTIONS

An important explanation for the differing responses of the Indian and Pakistani general courts to competition-related petitions filed before them lies in the very different processes through which the countries had adopted the competition legislations and the institutions they had engaged in this regard. It has already been discussed (in Chapter 2) that in India the adoption was carried out through a reasonably wide range of bottom-up, participatory and inclusive institutions, while Pakistan relied almost exclusively on a limited number of top-down, exclusive institutions. This section builds on this discussion to examine the extent to which India and Pakistan engaged their respective judiciary along with the executive and the legislature at the adoption stage and evaluates how this may have affected the subsequent interactions between the competition enforcement and pre-existing legal systems in the two countries.

7.4.1 *Engagement of the Judiciary in the Indian and Pakistani Adoption Processes*

The judiciary's understanding of the context and aims of the competition legislation is commensurate with the phase of the adoption process at which it engages with the competition legislation and on the nature and extent of this engagement. In turn the level of the judiciary's understanding of the competition legislation influences its attitude towards it and its interest in deciding petitions arising from or in relation to it.

The Indian judiciary first engaged with the Indian Act when the *Brahm Dutt* petition challenging the constitutionality of the Indian Act was brought before the Supreme Court immediately after the first round of deliberation and enactment at the adoption stage had been completed but before the commencement of the implementation stage of the Indian Act.[49] The petition required the Supreme Court to evaluate the scheme of the Act particularly the provisions relating to the competition authority acting as an adjudicatory body. in light of the Indian Constitution and tasked the Supreme Court to direct the government to appropriately amend the Act to ensure its compliance with the principle of separation of powers enshrined in the Indian Constitution.

Although the Indian Supreme Court disposed of this appeal on the basis of an undertaking given by the government its early engagement with the Act had a three-pronged effect: in requiring the government to amend the Indian Act to bring it in conformity with the Indian Constitution, the Supreme Court generated a second round of deliberation and enactment which helped enhance the Indian Act's compatibility with India's pre-existing legal system; in considering the scheme and substance of the Indian Act the Supreme Court generated awareness not only in the public but also within the superior judiciary of the rationale of the Act and the manner in which it was to be enforced; and, most importantly, by allowing the Act to continue its operations (albeit after necessary amendments) the Supreme Court endorsed and bolstered its domestic legitimacy. The enhanced compatibility and legitimacy of the Act subsequently contributed to a more productive interaction between the Act and the general courts.

In Pakistan, as in India, the judiciary engaged with the competition legislation after it had been through the first round of deliberation and enactment. In the case of Pakistan, however, this engagement came more than a year after the competition legislation had entered the implementation stage. Although the World Bank team, that had led the deliberation of the 2007 Ordinance, had met with one or two judges in the course of its discussions it had done so in their private rather than institutional capacity.[50] The judiciary as an institution first formally engaged with the competition legislation when

[49] *Brahm Dutt v Union of India* (2005) 2 Supreme Court Cases 431. See Chapter 2, Section 2.4.2, particularly n.79 for details.

[50] See Chapter 2, Section 2.3.2.1.

the validity of the 2007 Ordinance was challenged before the Supreme Court.[51] However, unlike the *Brahm Dutt* petition in India, the petition brought before the Supreme Court of Pakistan did not address the scheme or provisions of the Pakistani competition legislation but only the circumstances and instruments through which it had been promulgated and saved. The core aim of the petition was to seek the annulment of the declaration of emergency which had allowed the 2007 Ordinance among several other ordinances to remain valid beyond the 120 days permitted by the Pakistani Constitution.[52] Consequently, in deciding this petition the Supreme Court addressed the 2007 Ordinance in the broader constitutional perspective only rather than on its substantive merits or demerits.

Another factor that further complicated the attitude of the Pakistani judiciary towards the 2007 Ordinance (and by extension, towards the competition legislation that followed) was that at the time of its promulgation the Pakistani judiciary was locked in an unprecedented battle with the executive and was also facing disturbance in its own ranks: the superior judiciary in Pakistan had refused to endorse the November 2007 declaration of emergency and barring a few exceptions, had opted to resign from office instead. In 2008 the judges that had resigned in protest against the emergency were restored to office, however, the relationship between the judiciary and the executive remained strained for some time especially as the elected government resisted compliance with the order of the Supreme Court in the *Sindh High Court Bar Association* matter.[53]

The strained relationship between the executive and the judiciary in Pakistan and the failure of the government to provide permanent legal cover to the 2007 Ordinance had a negative effect on subsequent interactions between the CCP and the Pakistani general courts in at least three ways: first, the judiciary remained oblivious to the rationale for a competition law, of the core principles of competition, and the enforcement pathway envisaged in the 2007 Ordinance; second, although the engagement with the judiciary did provide an opportunity for further deliberation, the judiciary did not avail of this opportunity and therefore did not meaningfully enhance the compatibility and legitimacy of the competition legislation; and finally, and most damagingly, the judiciary remained hesitant to take decisive action in respect of competition matters either because it was reluctant to legitimise actions that were in any way connected with the declaration of emergency or because it simply wanted the government to resolve the legal foundations of its competition legislation before it decided these matters. The fact that the courts continued to restrain the CCP at the very first hearing of the petition even after the enactment of the Pakistani Act suggests that the initial hesitation had only

[51] *Sindh High Court Bar Association v The Federation of Pakistan* PLD 2009 SC 879.

[52] Also see Chapter 2, Section 2.4.1, particularly n.86.

[53] n.51. Also see Chapter 2, Section 2.3.2.2 particularly n.72. The elected government was reluctant to enact the National Reconciliation Ordinance 2007 because it feared defeat in parliament. This was also a factor in the delay in enacting the Competition Act.

compounded over time even when the reasons that had given rise to it in the first place, had long ceased to exist.[54]

7.4.2 *The Interplay of the Executive and the Legislature in the Adoption Process*

In addition to the engagement of the judiciary in the adoption process, the interactions between the adopted competition legislations and the pre-existing legal systems of India and Pakistan have also been shaped by the extent to which the legislature and the executive have assumed ownership of these legislations and have taken an interest in and accepted responsibility for establishing the necessary infrastructure for the competition enforcement systems envisaged in the competition legislation.

This sense of ownership is generated by the engagement of a wide range of institutions from different branches of the state in the adoption process and is an aspect that the domestic legitimacy of the adopted legislation enjoys in its country. The adoption of the Indian Act through bottom-up, participatory, and inclusive institutions drawn from the executive, legislature, and, in the second round, also of the judiciary, meant that each branch of state accepted its own responsibility towards implementing the Indian Act which was an important factor in ensuring that the CCI and the Indian Tribunal were operationalised simultaneously.[55] The timely establishment of the Indian Tribunal ensured that parties aggrieved by actions or orders of the CCI had recourse to an independent, specialist appellate body. The Tribunal being operational not only reduced the numbers of constitutional petitions filed before general courts but also narrowed the grounds on which these were filed, as constitutional petitions are only maintainable if the aggrieved parties do not have an 'an adequate alternate remedy' available to them.[56] This also meant that matters brought before the general courts were largely within their competence and expertise further which facilitated their timely and clear resolution. This also meant that

54 The judicial practice of issuing restraining orders at first hearings and then allowing these orders to continue for long periods of time is commonplace in Pakistan. However, the fact the CCP remained largely unsuccessful in displacing these restraining orders in any court in Pakistan hints at the overall hesitation of the courts to engage with competition matters.

55 See Chapter 2, Section 2.4.2, n.80 and Chapter 6, Section 7.4.1.

56 In *Commissioner of Income Tax v Chhabil Dass Agrawal*[(2014) 1 SCC 603 the Indian Supreme Court reiterated the established legal position that when a statutory forum is created by law for the redressal of grievances, then subject to certain exceptions, the high court does not have the power to entertain a writ petition by ignoring such statutory dispensation. The Supreme Court further stated that although it is within the discretion of the high court to grant relief under Article 226 of the Indian Constitution despite existence of an alternative remedy, the high court must not exercise this jurisdiction if there is an adequate efficacious alternative remedy available to the petitioner and he has approached the high court without availing it. However, the Supreme Court conceded that the high court may make an exception if the petitioner makes out an exceptional case warranting such interference or if there are sufficient grounds to invoke the extraordinary jurisdiction under Article 226 of the Indian Constitution.

even if aggrieved parties invoked the jurisdiction of the general courts in matters that the general courts could not properly entertain, the general courts had the option and the clarity to direct the parties to file these before the Indian Tribunal.

Unlike India, Pakistan had first introduced its competition legislation through top-down, exclusive institutions drawn only from the executive. While doing so had the advantage of the legislation being promulgated swiftly and without interference particularly from the legislature, it also meant that the adopted legislation was not sufficiently adapted for the Pakistani context and lacked necessary domestic legitimacy. It also meant that there was limited institutional ownership of the competition legislation in the country: the Pakistani legislature only became aware of the rationale for and provisions of the competition legislation when it was finally placed before it in August 2010, after the legislation had already been in force for nearly three years. At this stage the legislature was neither interested in assuming ownership of the legislation nor in ensuring that the competition enforcement system envisaged in the legislation was fully and swiftly established. Further, even though the executive had been exclusively responsible for introducing competition legislation in the country, the fact that a particular government had taken the decision to do so in isolation from other organs of the state dampened the interest and ownership of the executive when a different government came into power. Therefore, even the executive did not feel any urgency to establish the necessary infrastructure to enforce the legislation.

The considerable delay on the part of the Pakistani government in operationalising the Tribunal led to a disconnect between the first and second tiers of the competition enforcement system in Pakistan and the subsequently established Pakistani Tribunal not only failed to engage meaningfully with the orders of the CCP but also remained deferential to it. This in turn prevented the third tier competition enforcement authority the Supreme Court – from playing its proper role as an appellate forum. The absence of an appropriate appellate remedy in the early years of competition enforcement meant that parties aggrieved by the CCP's orders had no choice but to file petitions before the general courts whether they had a genuine grievance or simply wished to stall the CCP in particularly in the enforcement of its orders. This meant that at times these parties were constrained to manipulate the grounds on which the petitions were filed simply to meet the requirements of the constitutional jurisdiction of the courts. This not only increased the number of constitutional objections to the competition legislation and obfuscated the issues of real merit, but also increased manifold the number of petitions pending before the courts. Given that in Pakistan, like in India, general courts must entertain constitutional petitions if aggrieved parties do not have an adequate alternate remedy meant that the courts had no option but to admit these petitions because the Pakistani Tribunal had not been established and there was no option to redirect the petitions elsewhere.[57] The combination of a large number of petitions,

[57] As per decisions of the Pakistan Supreme Court in *Anjuman e Ahmedya v Deputy Commissioner* PLD 1966 Supreme Court 639, recently affirmed in *Rana Aftab Ahmed Khan*

some of which had been filed on spurious constitutional grounds, overwhelmed the courts and further contributed to the their hesitation to take decisive action in respect of the petitions filed before them.[58] As a result, no issues of real merit reached the Supreme Court and those that did had to be returned to the Tribunal for its consideration once it had been established and operationalised.

7.4.3 *The Adoption Process and the Divergence in Interactions*

The above discussion suggests that the adoption process impacts the interaction between the competition enforcement systems and the pre-existing legal systems of the adopting countries in complex and unexpected ways. It appears that obtaining feedback from a wider range of state institutions, particularly the judiciary, in deliberating the proposed legislation, and adapting the proposed legislation in light of the feedback received particularly from the judiciary, not only brings the legislation into alignment with the countries' pre-existing legal systems and enhances its compatibility with the context but also generates broader-based acceptance and ownership for the legislation and thereby increases its domestic legitimacy.

For instance, in the case of India, the proposed competition legislation was deliberated and drafted primarily by the executive, however, rather than acting alone the executive consulted a wide range of stakeholders in this exercise. As the legislation progressed through the enactment phase it was first adapted in light of the feedback provided by the legislature and its standing committees (which also engaged with public stakeholders), and then according to the objections raised by the judiciary in respect of the structure and composition of the competition authorities proposed to be established by the Indian Act. Although this engagement with a wide range of institutions delayed the enforcement of the Indian Act from 2003 (when it was first enacted) to 2009 (when the CCI and the Tribunal were made operational), it provided the basis for a smoother, more productive interaction between the adopted competition legislation and the country's pre-existing legal system. Given its early familiarity with and endorsement of the scheme and substance of the Indian Act, the judiciary in most instances was able to respond to the petitions filed before it on their merits rather than becoming embroiled in questions relating to the constitutionality of the Indian Act. Further, given its direct role in preparing the draft Act, the executive was also committed to establishing the competition enforcement system as envisaged in the Act and not only enjoyed the support of the legislature in doing so but also remained accountable to it.

The importance of a wide ranging and focused engagement with the proposed competition legislation is evident also in its absence in the Pakistani context. In

v Muhammad Ajmal and another PLD 2010 SC 1066 a person can invoke the writ jurisdiction of the Courts if it does not have an adequate alternate remedy available to it.

58 The first decision to be issued in any petition was in 2020, nearly eleven years after the petition had first been filed. However, this decision is under multiple appeals before the Supreme Court. See n.38.

Pakistan, as in India, the deliberation (including the drafting of the competition legislation) were led by the executive. However, unlike India, the Pakistani executive largely acted in isolation from other institutions and stakeholders and in fact outsourced the deliberation to a World Bank-led team and the drafting exercise to a European law firm. Also although the Pakistani legislature and judiciary also like its Indian counterparts engaged with the competition legislation, the legislature did so after the competition legislation had already been in force for three years and the judiciary only did so superficially and formally and that too only with the 2007 Ordinance. While the executive's disproportionately larger role in the Pakistani adoption process had the important advantage of bringing the competition legislation into force without delay,[59] it also had the distinct disadvantage of weakening the compatibility and legitimacy of the adopted competition legislation, which in turn led to its constitutionality being called into question before the general courts and significantly complicating the interaction between the competition enforcement system and the country's pre-existing legal system. The imbalance of power between the executive and the legislature also meant that the executive remained largely unaccountable for its acts and omissions.

7.5 COMPETITION ENFORCEMENT SYSTEMS, INTERACTIONS, AND ENFORCEMENT

Clear, productive, and supportive interactions between the adopted competition legislation, as represented by the competition enforcement systems, and the pre-existing legal systems in the adopting countries, as represented by their general courts, are important, if not necessary, for the successful enforcement of the adopted laws. A productive interaction between the adopted legislation and pre-existing legal system gradually enhances its compatibility and legitimacy in the adopting country. This in turn, allows the adopted legislation to be more fully understood, utilised, and applied in its country and facilitates its steady integration into the country's pre-existing legal system.

It is also important to understand that the interactions between the adopted and pre-existing systems are not accidental and are in fact shaped by the mechanisms, strategies, and institutions through which the countries adopt their competition legislations. The impact of the adoption process is two-fold: the first limb of the impact stems from the extent to which the judiciary formally engages with the adoption process which shapes its perception and understanding of the competition

[59] There is a generally held belief among officers of the CCP that the author had discussions with in the course of writing this book, that had the Competition Ordinance 2007 been presented to the parliament, it would not have been ratified, and that it was in the interest of competition enforcement in the country that the law was introduced through an ordinance and then saved through a constitutional amendment. While the author accepts the view of the CCP officials, she is more interested in evaluating the impact of the government's strategy rather than judging its expediency.

legislation which in turn influences its response to matters relating to or arising from this legislation. The second limb of the impact derives from the nature and extent of the engagement of the executive and the legislature in the course of adoption which affects their subsequent commitment to establishing the competition enforcement systems envisaged in the competition legislations. A country such as India, which employs the more inclusive, bottom-up mechanism of *socialisation* for adopting the Indian Act, succeeds in developing a productive interaction between the competition enforcement and pre-existing legal systems while a country like Pakistan, that adopts its competition legislation through top-down, exclusive *coercion*, which leaves out the judiciary, legislature, and in some ways, even the executive from the process, not only adversely affects the response of the general courts to competition related challenges filed before them but also the commitment of the executive to make available the necessary resources for establishing the competition enforcement system and the legislature to hold it accountable for failing to do so.

Further, the extent of compatibility and legitimacy generated in the course of adoption creates a virtuous cycle: the compatibility and legitimacy generated for the competition legislation at the adoption stage facilitates the interaction between the competition enforcement system and the general courts at the implementation stage and the quality of the interactions between the two systems. Over time these interactions bring the competition enforcement system into alignment wtih the pre-existing legal system and thereby further bolster their compatibility and legitimacy in their domestic contexts.

This is evident in the Indian context, where the timely setting up and operationalising of the Indian Tribunal meant that there was an opportunity for aggrieved parties to have the CCI's orders examined by an independent appellate forum and thereby to clarify important procedural and substantive issues. In the event that the orders of the Tribunal were appealed before the Supreme Court, it also had the opportunity to provide its generalist expertise which led to clarity in competition enforcement across all tiers of the competition enforcement system and brought them into alignment with each other. For instance, the order of the Tribunal in the *Excel Crop Care* case[60] and before that in the *SAIL* case,[61] provided the CCI an important opportunity to seek and obtain clarity from the Supreme Court with regard to its penal strategy and procedure. Having obtained this clarity, the CCI was able to respond appropriately to similar objections in subsequent cases and thereby to deter repetition of these grounds before appellate fora or before the general courts.[62]

The orders of the Tribunal and of the Supreme Court hearing appeals from these orders narrowed the possible grounds on which the CCI's interim orders or

[60] See Chapter 6, Box 6.1.

[61] See Chapter 6, Box 6.2.

[62] The decisions of the Supreme Court in the *SAIL* and the *Excel Crop Care* are among the two most often cited orders of the CCI.

proceedings could be challenged before the general courts in their inherent constitutional jurisdictions, and aligned the CCI's procedures with the norms prevailing in India's pre-existing legal system. This played an important role in reducing the number of frivolous petitions filed before the general courts and allowed the courts to deal with such petitions as came before them more effectively and expeditiously, thereby providing increasing clarity to the CCI. In this way, each order of the Supreme Court, whether in its competition or constitutional jurisdiction, enhanced the compatibility and legitimacy of the Indian Act and facilitated its integration into the country's pre-existing legal system.

Conversely, the absence of a functional Tribunal in the early crucial years of Pakistan's competition enforcement, directed towards the general courts all challenges in respect of proceedings pending before or even concluded by the CCP and led to the Pakistani competition legislation itself being challenged on a number of the grounds including that the competition enforcement system envisaged in the 2007, 2009, and 2010 Ordinances was contrary to the country's pre-existing legal system. The large number of petitions that reached the general courts and the range of constitutional grounds on which these petitions were filed compounded the difficulty of the general courts and perhaps contributed to their reluctance to respond to these petitions. The failure of the general courts to engage with competition matters even if just to confirm at best the constitutionality of the CCP and of the legislation under which it was established, not only prevented the CCP from enforcing its orders but also halted the development of competition jurisprudence in the country. This in turn meant that the compatibility and legitimacy of the Pakistani legislation, remained as weak and superficial as it was when the legislation was first adopted if not further deteriorating over time.

The interactions between the CCP and the courts were expected to improve when the Pakistani Act was enacted and later when the government first operationalised the Tribunal: some of the constitutional objections to the Act were automatically resolved, and parties aggrieved by the CCP's orders now had the option of approaching the Tribunal and, therefore, addressing the orders of the CCP on their merits. It was further expected that the more productive interaction with the general courts would in turn bolster the compatibility and legitimacy of the Pakistani Act as well as the extent to which it was understood, utilised, and applied in the country and recognised as a part of the Pakistani legal system. Unfortunately however, the actual impact of the establishment of the Tribunal remains difficult to ascertain given that the Tribunal does not publish its orders and the few of its orders that are available deal either with deceptive marketing practices or only superficially with anti-competitive practices. So far, the Pakistani Supreme Court has not issued orders in any of the several appeals from orders of the Pakistani Tribunal and, more recently, in respect of orders of the Lahore and Islamabad High Courts that have been appealed before it.

8

Implementing Competition Laws across South Asia

8.1 INTRODUCTION

Since 2002 four South Asian countries besides India and Pakistan have also enacted modern competition legislations while the remaining two have taken steps to express their commitment to, or at least their interest in, competition. The four that have already adopted competition legislations – Sri Lanka, Nepal, Bangladesh, and Maldives – employed comparable transfer mechanisms and institutions in their adoption processes despite the considerable differences in their histories and governance structures, and the very different sizes of their economies. Much like Pakistan these four countries were primarily motivated to adopt modern competition legislations by their engagement with the WTO and other multi-lateral agencies. However, instead of resorting to top-down exclusive institutions as in the case of Pakistan, Sri Lanka, Bangladesh, and Maldives, mirrored India in enacting their respective competition legislations through their parliaments, which are designed under their constitutions, as bottom-up, participatory, and inclusive institutions. Nepal, like Pakistan, adopted its legislation in a period when its parliament had been dissolved and power was vested in and exercised directly by the president; of the two remaining South Asian countries, Bhutan has demonstrated its continuing commitment to competition by recently revising and updating its 2015 competition policy[1] even though it does not at present consider it necessary to adopt or enforce a legislation, while Afghanistan's interest is evident from it having prepared a draft competition bill shortly after adopting a modern constitution, however, given the political turbulence in the country since 2021, it is unlikely that the draft bill will be enacted into law any time in the near future.

The aim of this chapter is to understand the overall state of competition enforcement in South Asia by examining the progress made by the remaining six South Asian countries in implementing their competition legislations or otherwise promoting

[1] Chapter 3, Section 3.2.2.2 (b) and 3.3.3.2(b).

competition in their contexts. To this end this chapter proceeds on the premise that as in the case of India or Pakistan, each country's success at the implementation stage is correlated to the institutions and mechanisms through which the countries deliberated and adopted the legislation or policy, and the extent and quality of compatibility and legitimacy generated by the interplay of institutions and mechanisms at the adoption stage. In respect of countries that have adopted competition legislation but are still to enforce it, this chapter draws upon the Indian and Pakistani experience to understand not only how the legislation is likely to be enforced but also to offer suggestions to these countries for facilitating future enforcement.

This chapter is organised as follows: Section 8.2 revisits the Indian and Pakistani experience at the implementation stage to highlight how it has been shaped by the compatibility and legitimacy generated for the Indian and Pakistani Acts at the adoption stage; Section 8.3 outlines the progress each of the South Asian Six have made towards promoting competition and correlates it to the extent of compatibility and legitimacy of their enacted or proposed competition legislation or policy as well as identifying the gaps in their enforcement; Section 8.4 draws upon the Indian and Pakistani enforcement experience to predict how these countries are likely to fill the gaps in their enforcement and to identify strategies that may employ in this regard; Section 8.5 sets out the overall state of competition enforcement in South Asia.

8.2 REVISITING THE INDIAN AND PAKISTANI EXPERIENCE

Evaluating the Indian and Pakistani competition enforcement in a comparative perspective revealed not only the significance of compatibility and legitimacy for a more 'successful' enforcement of the adopted legislation but also offered important insight into how compatibility and legitimacy generated at the adoption stage may be maintained and even enhanced in the implementation stage. This section revisits the key aspects of this discussion.

8.2.1 *The Adoption Stage and Generation of Compatibility and Legitimacy*

India and Pakistan adopted their respective competition legislations in remarkably different legal and political landscapes. While India was a stable democracy at the time of adopting the Indian Act and had a strong tradition of separation of powers and of instituting committees for studying and proposing law reform, Pakistan was under quasi-military rule when it promulgated the 2007 Ordinance in which the executive enjoyed disproportionately greater power than the other organs of state and was exclusively responsible for liaising with multi-lateral agencies that had led much of Pakistan's economic law reform in preceding years.[2]

[2] Chapter 3, Section 3.3.1.1 and 3.3.2.1.

The countries also employed different transfer mechanisms and engaged different institutions in adopting their respective legislations. India adopted its competition regime by adapting foreign models for the Indian context through two rounds of *socialisation* (albeit with some shades of *emulation*)[3] delivered by a range of domestic, bottom-up, participatory and inclusive institutions drawn from each of its three organs of state. The institutions engaged in the first round of deliberation and enactment of the Indian Act included the independent Raghavan Committee that evaluated foreign competition models and aggregated local information from stakeholders over three years cumulatively as well as parliamentary standing committees that engaged legislators and stakeholders. while in the second round, India's superior judiciary played an important role in bringing the Indian Act into alignment with India's pre-existing legal system.[4] In contrast, Pakistan adopted the 2007 Ordinance through *coercion* (albeit also with traces of *emulation*),[5] delivered through top-down, exclusive institutions drawn only from executive. These institutions lacked both capacity and incentive for aggregating local information and, therefore, relied almost exclusively on the World Bank team to decide the most appropriate competition legislation for the Pakistani context, limiting their own input to prescribing the mechanisms for appointment and removal of the members of the proposed competition authority.[6] Pakistan adopted the 2009 and 2010 Ordinances with the same top-down, exclusive institutions and engaged the legislature only in enacting the Pakistani Act. Although the legislature had the capacity, at least in theory, to aggregate local information and to appropriately adapt the competition legislation for context, it enacted the Pakistani Act with only one amendment regarding the establishment of the Pakistani Tribunal while retaining all substantive provisions of the preceding Ordinances.[7]

The impact of the adoption processes in both India and Pakistan is most evident in the provisions of their respective legislations relating to the structure and composition of the competition authorities they purport to establish. The strategy of *socialisation* in India allowed the relevant provisions of the Indian Act to be adapted for alignment with the constitutional norms prevalent in India's pre-existing legal system,[8] while that of *coercion* in Pakistan led to the CCP being structured almost entirely as per the suggestions of the World Bank team with the

3 ibid Section 3.3.3.1.

4 Chapter 2, Section 2.4.1.

5 ibid Section 2.3.2.2.

6 The appointment and removal mechanisms prescribed in the 2007 Ordinance and retained in the Pakistani Act are nearly identical to five different Pakistani regulatory laws enacted shortly before or contemporaneously with the Ordinance. See for instance, the Pakistan Telecommunication Authority Act 1996 (sections 3(2) and 3(5)); Securities and Exchange Commission of Pakistan Act 1997 (sections 5 and 19); Regulation of Generation, Transmission, and Distribution of Electric Power Act 1997 (sections 3(1) and 4(1)); Pakistan Electronic Media Regulatory Authority Ordinance 2002 (sections 3(2) and 3(5)); and Oil and Gas Regulatory Authority Ordinance 2002 (sections 3(8) and 3(11)).

7 Chapter 2, Section 2.4.2.

8 ibid Section 2.5.1.

exception of the CCP's composition which was left to the discretion of the Pakistan government.[9] More importantly, however, India's strategy of *socialisation* through bottom-up, participatory, and inclusive institutions that engaged with all three branches of the state as well as with members of the public generated understanding and ownership across these institutions, thereby bolstering the compatibility and legitimacy of the Indian Act.[10] Conversely, in the Pakistani context, *coercion* and the attendant limited engagement with only top-down, exclusive institutions drawn from the executive, culminated in the adoption of a competition legislation that was more attuned to international best practices than to the domestic context, and whose legitimacy was routinely called into question until such time as the Pakistani Act was finally enacted through bottom-up, participatory, and inclusive institutions.[11]

8.2.2 *Impact of Compatibility and Legitimacy on the Implementation Stage*

Competition enforcement in both India and Pakistan is shaped by the extent of compatibility and legitimacy generated for the competition legislation at the adoption stage. In turn the quality and nature of enforcement impacts the compatibility and legitimacy of the competition legislation at the implementation stage, either enhancing it or, in failing to do so, gradually deteriorating it.[12] The adoption of the Indian Act through *socialisation* and a range of bottom-up, participatory, and inclusive institutions had generated greater compatibility and legitimacy than the adoption of competition legislation in Pakistan by *coercion* through a limited number of top-down, exclusive institutions. The relatively greater compatibility and legitimacy of the Indian Act allowed it to be better understood, applied, and utilised in the Indian context. Each competition matter that was finally decided by the Indian Supreme Court enhanced the compatibility and legitimacy of the Act and facilitated the gradual integration of the Indian Act into India's pre-existing legal system. In contrast, the relative lack of compatibility and legitimacy in Pakistan led not only to the competition legislation being under-utilised in the country but also created friction between the adopted legislation and the Pakistani legal system. Over time these obstacles in enforcement diminished the already limited compatibility and legitimacy of the competition legislation and forced it to remain an outsider to Pakistan's pre-existing legal system.

The compatibility between the Indian Act and its context and the relative lack of compatibility of the Pakistani legislation with the Pakistani legal system is reflected in the CCI's and CCP's overall performance: once the CCI commenced operations

9 ibid Section 2.5.2 and n.6.
10 ibid Section 2.5.1.
11 ibid Section 2.5.2.
12 For the quality and nature of enforcement see Chapter 4, Section 4.4.3.

in 2009, it received a steady stream of complaints from the public and gradually developed a consistent approach for addressing these complaints. On the contrary, the CCP hardly received any complaints or references, especially in its early years, and initiated the majority of actions *suo motu* at its own volition. In time, the CCP's performance declined, coming to a complete halt in 2014. When the CCP re-commenced enforcement actions post 2014 the numbers of its *suo motu* actions was sharply reduced and the CCP largely restricted itself to responding to complaints, which continued to remain low.[13]

Similarly, the disparity in the legitimacy of the Indian and Pakistani legislations manifested itself in various ways. It was particularly evident in the extent to which the organs of state in either country understood the basis for competition enforcement and owned their responsibility for establishing and operationalising the competition enforcement systems.[14] It was also evident in the extent to, and manner in which the CCI and the CCP relied on and utilised international precedents in enforcing provisions of their competition legislations.[15] Given the relatively stronger legitimacy of the Indian Act, the CCI, even in its earlier orders only expressly referred to or applied foreign decisions and materials when it was necessary for it to do so to support its arguments[16] while the weaker legitimacy of the CCP constrained it to cite especially EU and US antecedents, not merely to evaluate competition issues but also to establish its international pedigree and thereby to leverage its international legitimacy to gain domestic legitimacy.[17] The nature of the CCI and CCP's interactions with their respective pre-existing legal systems is a further manifestation of the legitimacy of the competition legislations:[18] the relative higher legitimacy in India appears to have generated a more supportive response from the general courts to the challenges filed before them in respect of proceedings pending before the CCI while the weaker legitimacy in Pakistan has resulted in reluctance on the part of the general courts to address and deal decisively with the competition-related challenges.[19] The CCI's relatively lenient approach towards penalties may similarly be attributed to its desire to maintain its legitimacy in the domestic context, while Pakistan's relatively aggressive penal strategy, particularly in its early years, suggests the need to assert its international legitimacy and thereby perhaps to compensate for its weaker legitimacy.[20] Finally, the relatively greater number of complaints filed before the CCI may be attributed to its relatively stronger legitimacy in the Indian context while CCP's preference for *suo motu*

[13] ibid Section 4.4.2.
[14] Chapter 7, Section 7.4.
[15] Chapter 5.
[16] Chapter 5, Sections 5.3 and 5.4.
[17] ibid.
[18] Chapter 7.
[19] ibid Sections 7.4 and 7.5.
[20] Chapter 6, Section 6.5.

action may be traced to its weak legitimacy and as yet another attempt on its part to leverage its international legitimacy.[21]

8.2.3 *Compatibility and Legitimacy and the 'Hiatus' between Adoption and Implementation*

Their rather different starts notwithstanding, the Indian and Pakistani competition regimes had in common the fact that their operations were at least partially suspended for considerable periods of time, albeit for different reasons and at different stages of the adoption–implementation continuum. This period of suspension – the hiatus stage – is often omitted from an analysis of the implementation of competition legislation in the two countries for the obvious reason that no enforcement actions are recorded in this period. However, a closer review of the activities of the CCI and CCP in the hiatus stage suggests that both authorities utilised the opportunity presented by the break in enforcement to raise greater competition awareness among the stakeholders in their countries. This section takes a closer look at the hiatus stage in India and Pakistan and examines its impact, if any, on the compatibility and legitimacy, and future implementation of their respective competition legislations.

The CCI entered a nearly six-year-long hiatus stage even before it was fully operational when the Indian Act was challenged before the Supreme Court in the *Brahm Dutt* case.[22] At this time, the Indian government had only brought into force some of the provisions of the Indian Act which included provisions for establishing the CCI and authorising it to engage in competition advocacy, but not provisions relating to the appointment of its members or any of its enforcement powers in respect of anti-competitive practices.[23] This six-year-period only ended when the Indian government appointed the CCI's members in accordance with the procedure provided in the 2007 Amendment Act[24] and brought into force the provisions relating to CCI's enforcement powers under the Act.[25] For the six years in which it remained in the hiatus stage the CCI existed with a single member/chairperson whose sole mandate in pursuance of section 49(3) of the Act was to take 'suitable measures as may be prescribed for the promotion of competition advocacy, creating awareness and imparting training about competition issues'. This single member/

[21] Chapter 4, Section 4.4.2.

[22] Chapter 2, Section 2.4.1.

[23] By SO 715(E) dated 19.06.2003 the Indian government brought in force several sections of the Indian Act including section 7 (Establishing the Commission) and section 49 (Competition Advocacy). Other sections brought into force by this notification were challenged in the *Brahm Dutt* case and were amended by the 2007 Amendment Act. Also see Chapter 4, n.1.

[24] CCI Annual Report 2009–10, Chairperson's Statement.

[25] Indian Act, sections 3 and 4 relating to anti-competitive agreements and abuse of dominant position respectively were brought into force by SO 1241(E) and SO 1242(E) both dated 15.05.2009.

chairperson exercised his powers to organise a range of seminars and workshops with business associations, professional institutions, government ministries and departments, and educational establishments throughout India.[26] Although this extensive advocacy could not amend the provisions of the Indian Act and thereby increase its compatibility with context, it raised public awareness and understanding of these provisions and thereby enhanced its legitimacy. Consequently, by the time the Act was operationalised in 2009, members of the public were more prepared and more willing to engage with it. As has already been discussed the more cases that were brought before the CCI and appealed to the Tribunal and ultimately to the Supreme Court, the more the law was clarified and brought into alignment with each other as well as the country's pre-existing legal system.

The CCP entered its hiatus stage several years after first becoming operational. The CCP had been established and operationalised almost immediately after the promulgation of the 2007 Ordinance.[27] Its situation remained stable even when the 2007 Ordinance was replaced first by the 2009 and then the 2010 Ordinance and later by the Pakistani Act. Throughout this period, the CCP prioritised enforcement over advocacy[28] only partially shifting its attention towards advocacy when its legal status became uncertain in the wake of the order of the Supreme Court in the *Sindh High Court Bar Association* case.[29] However, in 2013 the CCP entered an eighteen-month hiatus stage when the term of the CCP's second chairperson came to an end and the government instead of appointing a new chairperson to replace her, left the CCP in the care of an acting chairperson. During this period the CCP did not issue any enforcement orders and focused almost entirely on competition advocacy[30] engaging with the public to create awareness and with government departments to help ensure that their policies, if not actually pro-competitive, were not anti-competitive either.[31] It is a testament to the CCP's efforts during this period that it won the World Bank's 2013 Competition Advocacy Contest in the category of 'Successfully promoting pro-competition market reforms, opening of markets, and infusion of competition principles in other sectoral policies.'[32] Therefore, the CCP's advocacy efforts significantly bolstered the international and domestic legitimacy of the Pakistani competition legislation which in turn, helped the CCP restart its enforcement actions with complaints and references rather than resorting to its initial strategy of initiating *suo motu* actions.

[26] Amitabh Kumar, 'The Evolution of Competition Law in India' in Vinod Dhall (ed) *Competition Law Today: Concepts, Issues and the Law in Practice* (OUP 2007), 497.

[27] Provisions brought into force included enforcement powers with respect to anti-competitive agreements (section 4) and abuse of dominant position (section 3), powers to approve or reject mergers (section 11), and its powers to engage in competition advocacy (section 29).

[28] CCP Annual Report 2011, 'Meeting the Chairperson', vii.

[29] CCP Annual Report 2012, 'Message by the Chairperson', 7. Also Chapter 2, Section 2.4.2.

[30] CCP Annual Report 2014, Acting Chairman's Message, 6–7.

[31] ibid 6.

[32] ibid 7.

8.3 THE IMPLEMENTATION EXPERIENCE OF THE REMAINING SOUTH ASIAN COUNTRIES

Unlike India and Pakistan, the other South Asian countries – the South Asian Six – have made limited progress towards meaningfully implementing their competition legislations or otherwise preparing the ground for future competition enforcement. This section examines the progress made by these countries and relates it to their adoption processes and the compatibility and legitimacy generated through them.

8.3.1 *Adoption Processes and Compatibility and Legitimacy in the South Asian Six*

The South Asian Six had engaged with competition legislation in distinct legal and political landscapes. Sri Lanka and Bangladesh are both former British colonies: Sri Lanka had become a British dominion in 1947, adopted its first constitution in 1972, and replaced it in 1978 with its present constitution, while Bangladesh had gained independence first from the British as East Pakistan and then from Pakistan in 1971 and had adopted its first constitution in 1972.[33] Nepal and Maldives were both traditional monarchies before becoming constitutional monarchies and later republics.[34] Nepal adopted seven constitutions until it adopted the present constitution in 2015, while Maldives adopted three constitutions, the latest in 2008.[35] Bhutan and Afghanistan were both traditional monarchies. However, while Bhutan peacefully transitioned to a constitutional monarchy in 2008, Afghanistan's history has been more chequered: it was a constitutional monarchy from 1964 to 1973, a republic from 1973 to 1978, and in a state of war first with the Soviets and then with the Taliban from 1978 until 2000. In 2004 Afghanistan adopted a new Constitution; however, in 2020 it once again fell into the hands of the Taliban.[36]Their disparate histories notwithstanding, these countries are all members of the WTO: Sri Lanka, Bangladesh, and Maldives since 1995; Nepal since 2004, and Afghanistan from 2016. Bhutan is the only South Asian country which is presently not a WTO member, but it too has established a working party to support it in obtaining membership.[37]

Among the South Asian Six Sri Lanka was the first to adopt modern competition legislation on the persuasion of the WTO, the World Bank, and the United States

[33] Chapter 3, Section 3.3.1.

[34] In April 2008 Nepal elected a Constituent Assembly and in May the same year the newly elected Constituent Assembly declared Nepal a Federal Democratic Republic, abolishing the 240-year-old monarchy. Nepal today has a president as head of state and a prime minister as head of government. Ministry of Foreign Affairs 'History of Nepal' <https://mofa.gov.np/about-nepal/history-of-nepal> accessed 31 October 2020.

[35] ibid Section 3.2.

[36] ibid Section 3.3.

[37] World Trade Organisation, Members and Observers <https://www.wto.org/english/thewto_e/whatis_e/tif_e/org6_e.htm> accessed 31 October 2021.

and as part of its programme of economic liberalisation.[38] The Sri Lankan Act which continues in force today provides for a two-tier, non-exclusive, competition enforcement system comprising the Consumer Affairs Authority and the Consumer Affairs Council whose members are to be appointed and removed by the government.[39] Nepal, despite considerable political turmoil and uncertainty, was next to adopt modern competition legislation in early 2007 largely due to external persuasion.[40] Shortly before Nepal joined the WTO, Nepalese thinktanks had started engaging with multi-lateral agencies and foreign thinktanks to consider an appropriate competition legislation for the country, however, there is no information and indeed little likelihood of meaningful engagement between these thinktanks and the parliament or other stakeholders in the enactment phase.[41] The Nepalese Act, like the Sri Lankan Act, does not provide for a specialist competition authority. However, unlike the Sri Lankan Act, which establishes a non-exclusive authority, the Nepalese Act opts for a Board which it sets up as part of the government. The Act also provides for a Market Protection Officer with the mandate of filing complaints before the Nepalese general courts that remain exclusively responsible for enforcing the Nepalese Act as well as for hearing claims for compensation that may be brought by private parties in pursuance of the Act.[42]

Bangladesh adopted a modern competition legislation five years after Nepal[43] largely due to its engagement with the WTO and other multi-lateral agencies.[44] Although Bangladesh had finalised the first draft of its legislation in 2008 it only enacted it in 2012 under a wider programme of technical assistance from the World Bank.[45] Unlike the Sri Lankan and Nepalese Acts, the Bangladeshi Act provides for an exclusive and independent competition authority–the Bangladesh Competition Commission–, however, it provides that the members of the authority may be

38 Chapter 3, Section 3.3.1.1. Although there is no information about the deliberation phase of the Sri Lankan Act it is known that it was enacted through the parliament in accordance with the legislative procedures prescribed in the Sri Lankan constitution.

39 ibid Section 3.2.1.1.

40 Chapter 3, Section 3.3.2.1.

41 In January 2007 when it enacted the Nepalese Competition Act, Nepal was undergoing a period of political turmoil: although Nepal had witnessed considerable tension between the monarchy and democratic forces throughout its history, a People's Movement launched in 2006 demanded the transfer of power from the monarchy to a democratically elected government. At the time the Nepalese Act was passed, Nepal was governed by an interim constitution which had been brought into force only weeks before its adoption and power still vested in the monarchy and the prime minister appointed by it. It is therefore unlikely that there was any meaningful engagement with the parliament in the enactment phase. See 'History of Nepal', n.34.

42 Chapter 3, Section 3.2.1.2.

43 ibid Section 3.3.1.2.

44 Bangladesh was still part of Pakistan when Pakistan had adopted the Monopoly Control Ordinance 1970 and had retained it after independence. However, given its considerable economic difficulties it had not prioritised the enforcement of this Ordinance.

45 Chapter 3, Section 3.3.1.2.

appointed and removed exclusively by the government. The Act vests in the Bangladeshi government the power to review the orders of the Commission, however, it does not state whether the orders of the Commission or the government may be appealed before the general courts. Unlike regulatory infringements that may be examined by the Commission, offences under the Act are to be tried by a magistrate and may be appealed to the Court of Session whose orders are to be final.[46] Maldives is the last and most recent country to enact a modern competition legislation and it too has done so under external influence. Maldives has maintained a close relationship with multi-lateral agencies and bodies since its independence, and from 2000 onwards it has also embarked upon a long-term plan to reorganise the Maldivian economy and political system with their assistance and support. Maldives finally adopted the competition legislation as part of its Strategic Action Plan for economic reform developed with the support of UNDP.[47] The Maldives Act does not envisage an independent competition authority and entrusts its enforcement to the relevant ministry of the government. However, the Act allows parties aggrieved by the decisions of the ministry to bring appeals before the general courts.[48]

Of the remaining two South Asian Six, Bhutan has adopted a competition policy and Afghanistan has prepared a draft Act which is yet to be enacted. Bhutan's preference for a policy rather than a legislation may be attributed to its small, relatively undiversified economy[49] which is defined and indeed circumscribed by its close relationship with India. Therefore, in 1992 as India embarked upon its Liberalisation, Privatisation and Globalisation programme the Bhutanese government also took measures to create a more competitive economy. One of the measures it proposed in this regard was a hybrid consumer and competition legislation. However, the Consumer Protection Act it finally adopted was more a sale of goods than a competition act[50] and therefore, the question of competition remained unaddressed. It was only in 2015 that Bhutan adopted its first competition policy based on a report commissioned by UNCTAD and prepared by an Indian consultant. Bhutan revised this policy in 2020 and entrusted the Office of Consumer Protection established in pursuance of the Consumer Protection Act to implement it.[51] Afghanistan's competition story, despite having failed to reach its denoument in the enactment of a competition legislation, is true to the type seen across South Asia. As in other South Asian countries, Afghanistan was convinced of its need for a modern competition legislation by multi-lateral agencies. These agencies working

[46] ibid Section 3.2.1.4.
[47] Chapter 3, Section 3.2.2.2.
[48] ibid.
[49] Bhutan's economy is essentially comprised by the agriculture, forestry, and hydropower sectors.
[50] Chapter 3, Section 3.3.3.2.
[51] Chapter 3, Section 3.2.2.2.

with the Afghani government commissioned an Indian law firm to draft the Afghani Act.[52] The draft proposes a 'Competition and Consumer Authority' which though described as independent is embedded in the Afghani Ministry of Commerce which has the power to appoint and remove members of the authority and to supersede it in specified circumstances.[53]

Their diverse pre-conditions of transfer notwithstanding, each of the South Asian Six to varying degrees derived their motivation to adopt modern competition legislation due to their engagement with the WTO and other multi-lateral agencies. Further, in all these countries the deliberation phase was led by their governments, albeit with varying level of support of multi-lateral agencies, however, Maldives was the only country in which the government engaged in a broad-based consultation with stakeholders prior to enacting its competition legislation. Although there is some information of thinktanks in Sri Lanka, Nepal, and Bangladesh engaging in discussions regarding appropriate competition principles for their countries prior to the enactment of the competition legislations, it is not clear whether and to what extent these discussions were taken into account in the enactment of these legislations. In Sri Lanka, Bangladesh, and Maldives the competition legislation was enacted through parliament, however, there is no information of any engagement betwen parliamentary standing committees and stakeholders. Stakeholder consultation is also unlikely to have taken place in Nepal which enacted its competition legislation by the order of its monarch[54] or in Bhutan and Afghanistan, both of which largely outsourced the deliberation to Indian consultants.

A review of the complex interplay of transfer mechanisms and institutions engaged by these countries in the adoption process returns equally complex results for the extent of compatibility and legitimacy generated in these processes: while the input of the governments of these countries in the deliberation phase creates some compatibility between the proposed legislations and the context for which these are intended, this compatibility is superficial. For instance, both the Bangladeshi and Maldives Act retain the unmistakeable stamp of their Western multi-lateral origins while the lack of conceptual clarity in the Sri Lankan and Nepalese Acts reflects the unconvincing attempts of their institutions to adapt the law for their contexts. Equally, while the enactment of these legislations through the parliament (in Sri Lanka, Bangladesh, and Maldives) or by the monarch (in Nepal) confers a degree of formal authority and legality on these legislations, in all but Maldives which published a strategic plan ahead of the enactment, their substantive legitimacy remains weak due to the absence of broad-based consultations with domestic stakeholders. Although Afghanistan and Bhutan have not adopted competition

[52] ibid Section 3.3.3.1.

[53] ibid Section 3.2.2.1.

[54] n.41.

legislations, the extent of the compatibility and legitimacy of the draft Afghani Act or the Bhutan policy is also likely to be weak given their external motivations for engaging with competition legislation and, more importantly, their outsourcing of the deliberation entirely to externally situated experts.

8.3.2 *Implementing Competition Legislation in the South Asian Six*

Of the South Asian Six, three out of the four that have adopted modern competition legislations, i.e., Sri Lanka, Nepal, and Bangladesh have established the first-tier competition authorities envisaged in these legislations, however these authorities are yet to issue any competition-related orders while one, Maldives, has only recently brought its Act into force. Interestingly even though Bhutan and Afghanistan they have not adopted modern competition legislations have also taken some steps to promote a competition culture. This section examines the progress made by each of these countries at the implementation stage, or at the very least in laying the ground for this stage.

8.3.2.1 Sri Lanka: Consumer Welfare at the Cost of Competition

The Sri Lankan Act focuses as much on protecting consumers and regulating internal trade as it does on promoting effective competition in the country.[55] Even within the ambit of competition the Act focuses inordinately on anti-competitive agreements as compared to abuse of dominant position and excludes mergers altogether.[56] In fact the Act is often described as resembling 'a consumer welfare law rather than a competition law'.[57]

The Sri Lankan Act's lack of focus on competition is also reflected in the operations of the Consumer Affairs Authority established in pursuance of the Act.[58] Although the Authority lists 'Promotion of Competition' as one of the services

55 The Sri Lankan Act, Preamble.

56 Sri Lankan Act, section 35. The provision relating to anti-competitive practices was first stipulated in the Fair Trading Commission Act 1987 which preceded the Sri Lankan Act. As per its decision in *Ceylon Oxygen Ltd. v Fair Trading Commission* (SLR-Year-1997-Vol 2p 372) the Sri Lankan Court of Appeal refused to recognise predatory pricing, discriminatory rebates, and exclusive dealings as anti-competitive practices for the purposes of the 1987 Act, therefore, it is unlikely that in the absence of an express statutory clarification, the same provision in the Sri Lankan Act would be interpreted differently.

57 Dianarthy Suthakar 'Beyond "More Economics-Based Approach": A Legal Perspective on Competition in Sri Lanka' 11th International Research Conference 2018, General Sir John Kotelawala Defence University, 25. <http://ir.kdu.ac.lk/bitstream/handle/345/2568/Law%20new_4.pdf?sequence=1&isAllowed=y> accessed 5 November 2020.

58 Consumer Affairs Authority <http://caa.gov.lk/web/index.php?lang=en> accessed 31 October 2021.

it provides; has appointed a director for this purpose;[59] and requires 'traders' to file with it, quarterly information regarding their production, imports, quantity, sales quantity, and value,[60] it is not clear whether and to what end it utilises this information. Further, while the Authority's Annual Reports suggest that the Authority has regularly conducted competition-related investigations even referring some of these to the Council for adjudication;[61] has launched various competition awareness programmes; conducted market research, and calculated market shares of a range of manufacturers[62] there are no details available for the scope or impact of any of these efforts or of any orders that the Council may have passed in respect of any matters referred to it by the Authority.[63]

The Authority's lack of commitment to competition enforcement has not gone unnoticed. An UNCTAD Investment Policy Review of Sri Lanka noted that the fate of competition regulation in Sri Lanka was uncertain, because the regulatory machinery put in place by the Sri Lankan Act was too heavily dependent on governmental discretion and support and, therefore, not able to respond vigilantly or professionally to complaints regarding anti-competitive behaviour.[64] The review further noted that '[r]ecent governments ha[d] been less than fully committed to competition' and had promoted a non-competitive environment by allowing several privatisations that strengthened market positions in a range of sectors, fixing minimum prices in others and overall remaining timid in encouraging private competition.[65] A more recent World Bank Trade and Competitiveness Report noted that the competitiveness of the Sri Lankan economy was far from ideal: it stated that the

59 Consumer Affairs Authority, 'Promotion of Competition' <http://caa.gov.lk/web/index.php?option=com_content&view=article&id=117&Itemid=566&lang=en> accessed 31 October 2021.

60 Sri Lankan Act, section 57. Consumer Affairs Authority 'Production/ Imports/Quantity, Sales Quantity/Value' <http://caa.gov.lk/web/index.php?option=com_content&view=article&id=177&Itemid=526&lang=en> accessed 31 October 2021.

61 Sri Lankan Act, section 39.

62 Annual Report 2010, 21–22; Annual Report 2011, 21–22; Annual Report 2011, 27–28; Annual Report 2012, 27–28; Annual Report 2013, 29–30; Annual Report 2014, 20–21; Annual Report 2015, 20–21; Annual Report 2016, 18–19; Annual Report 2017, 17–18. All available at Consumer Affairs Authority, 'Annual Report' <http://caa.gov.lk/web/index.php?option=com_content&view=article&id=94&Itemid=537&lang=en> accessed 29 November 2021.

63 ibid. Between 2010 to 2017 the Council settled, dismissed, or recommended a number of complaints for further action (Annual Report 2010, 28; Annual Report 2011, 27; Annual Report 2012, 34; Annual Report 2013, 36; Annual Report 2014, 26; Annual Report 2015, 27; Annual Report 2016, 24; Annual Report 2017, 23); however, the details of the Council's orders in this regard are not known. Also, the Authority has only issued orders in pursuance of sections 18 <http://caa.gov.lk/web/index.php?option=com_content&view=article&id=113&Itemid=562&lang=en> accessed 6 November 2020, and directions under section 20 of the Act <http://caa.gov.lk/web/index.php?option=com_content&view=article&id=162&Itemid=672&lang=en> accessed 6 November 2020, neither of which relate to competition.

64 UNCTAD *Investment Policy Review: Sri Lanka*, 46 UNCTAD/ITE/PC/2003/8 <https://unctad.org/system/files/official-document/iteipc20038_en.pdf> accessed 7 November 2020.

65 ibid.

'dense web of business regulations' and the high transaction costs of regulatory compliance posed a barrier to the entry of new firms and limited the growth of exiting firms which in turn resulted in the expansion of the informal sector. The report further highlighted the high costs of monitoring incurred by the government in its attempts to 'police market actors' which led to 'irregularities in the written law and its application' as it enhanced the discretionary powers of 'government officials and politicians' and paved 'the way for waste and corruption'.[66] The opinion of multi-lateral agencies regarding the Sri Lankan competition regime is shared by local commentators who highlight the lack of autonomy of the Authority and the Council and[67] the omission from the Sri Lankan Act of a definition of 'unfair trade practices'[68] and of merger regulation[69] and call for extensive reforms of the Sri Lankan Act for the meaningful competition enforcement in the country.

8.3.2.2 Nepal: To Enforce or Not Remains the Question

Although the Nepalese Act was enacted while the country was still ruled by a monarch, almost immediately after its enactment Nepal abolished the monarchy, adopted a new constitution, and transitioned fully to a democratic government.[70] The political confusion that ensued is likely to have created a shift in governmental priorities which is further likely to have contributed to Nepal's neglect of competition enforcement in the years that followed.

A 2012 report of the South Asia Watch on Trade, Economics, and Environment (SAWTEE) prepared in collaboration with the United States Agency for International Development (USAID) assessed the issues relating to competition in Nepal and recommended that the Nepalese Ministry of Commerce and Supplies adopt appropriate enforcement guidelines for the implementation of the Act. In preparing the report, SAWTEE engaged extensively with stakeholders, including representatives of the Nepalese business community, consumer groups, lawyers, judges, academics, and others in the public and private sector, to discuss the parameters of the Nepalese Act and to develop strategies for its implementation.[71]

66 World Bank Group 'Enhancing Competitiveness in Sri Lanka' ©2016 World Bank, section 1. <https://openknowledge.worldbank.org/handle/10986/24927> accessed 9 November 2020.

67 Gamunu Chandrasekera, 'Anti-Competitive Practices & Competition Law of Sri Lanka: A Call for Reform', 5. <www.juniorbarbasl.lk/assets/files/Article%20by%20Gamunu%20Chandrasekera%20-%20Anti-Competative%20Practices%20and%20Competition%20Law%20of%20Sri%20Lanka.pdf> accessed 7 November 2020.

68 ibid 6.

69 ibid 8.

70 n.34.

71 SAWTEE, 'Report on Operational Guidelines to Implement the Competition Promotion and Market Protection Act' <www.sawtee.org/programme/completed-programmes/report-on-operational-guidelines-to-implement-the-competition-promotion-and-market-protection-act.html> accessed 31 October 2020.

Despite these efforts, however, even in 2013 there was no evidence of any competition matters having been decided under the Act,[72] while a 2018 news item not only confirmed that the Board established in pursuance of the Act had remained inactive and was to be re-structured to be made more effective for market regulation, but also called for a meaningful enforcement of the competition legislation.[73] Despite these calls, at the time of writing there was no information regarding any steps that the Nepalese government may have taken to re-vamp the Nepalese competition regime.

8.3.2.3 Bangladesh: Is Competition Forgotten?

Although the Bangladeshi government established the Bangladesh Competition Commission shortly after the Bangladeshi Act had been enacted,[74] it did not appoint the Commission's first secretary until 2013 and then too only tasked him with 'setting up the Commission office'.[75] More than four years later in 2017, the Commission was still experiencing 'operational delays' and was not being consulted by the government even in issues raising competition concerns.[76] Despite these handicaps however, the Commission has organised activities to raise awareness about competition issues[77] and

72 Apurva Kathiwada, 'Nepal' 2 (CUTS 2013) <https://cuts-ccier.org/pdf/23-Nepal.pdf> accessed 30 October 2020.

73 *The Kathmandu Post*, 'Competition Promotion Fails to Curb Cartels' <https://kathmandupost.com/money/2018/04/09/competition-promotion-board-fails-to-curb-cartels> accessed 31 October 2020.

74 According to a US State Department Report (2017), the Bangladesh government had formed an independent agency, the Bangladesh Competition Commission in 2011 under the Ministry of Commerce, '2017 Investment Climate Statements: Bangladesh' <www.state.gov/reports/2017-investment-climate-statements/bangladesh> accessed 24 October 2020; however, other unconfirmed sources suggest that the BCC was actually established in December 2012 nearly six months after the enactment of the Bangladeshi Act.

75 *The Dhaka Tribune*, 'Bangladesh Competition Commission gets Secretary after a Year' <www.dhakatribune.com/uncategorized/2013/09/16/bangladesh-competition-commission-gets-secretary-after-a-year> accessed 31 October 2021.

76 According to the US State Department Report (n.74), in January 2016, the Malaysia-based Robi and India-based Airtel agreed to merge their operations in Bangladesh. The deal, valued at $12.5 million is Bangladesh's largest corporate and first telecommunications merger. Although the merger raised competition concerns, it was completed in November 2016 with approvals from the Bangladesh Telecommunication Regulatory Commission and the prime minister and without any consultation with the Competition Commission.

77 See, for instance the news report on the February 2018 workshop on 'Competition Commission for Economic Growth and Fair Price' jointly organised by the Bangladesh Competition Commission, the South Asian Network on Economic Modeling (SANEM), and the British Council. *The Daily Star*, 'Make Competition Commission Functional: analysists' <www.thedailystar.net/business/make-competition-commission-functional-analysts-1530595> accessed 26 October 2020; the keynote address for a seminar organised by the Commission in March 2019 on 'The Role of Competition Commission in Sustainable and Inclusive Development'; Abdur Razzaque, 'The Role of Competition Commission in Sustainable and Inclusive Development' <www-ccb-gov-bd.translate.goog/site/page/87d2154b-5d3c-4509-a4f4–896016f199f9/সেমিনার-পেপার?_x_tr_sl=bn&_x_tr_tl=en&_x_tr_hl=en&_x_tr_pto=sc&_x_tr_sch=http> accessed 26 October 2020, and a news report of a October 2020 workshop on digital economy, The Business Standard 'E-commerce Sale Grows 24 Times Over Three Years'

to train its officers.[78] Further, in the wake of the Covid-19 pandemic, when competition authorities all over the world were re-evaluating their roles, the Bangladeshi Commission also asserted itself by suggesting that steps be taken to ensure the competitive allocation and spending of the government-announced stimulus funds for stabilising economic activities during the pandemic.[79] The Commission followed up on its proposal by lobbying various government ministries to investigate a suspected onion cartel.[80] Laudable as these efforts may be, at the time of writing there was still no indication of when the Commission may be fully operationalised.[81]

8.3.2.4 Maldives: too early for implementation

In August 2020 when the Maldives president ratified the Maldives Competition Act he also announced that the that the Act would be made effective from 1 March 2021.[82] A visit to the website of the Maldives Ministry of Economic Development shows that it has established an 'anti-trust unit' as part of its Trade and Investment Department; however, at the time of writing there is no information regarding any enforcement or advocacy initiatives undertaken by this unit.[83]

8.3.2.5 Bhutan even policies matter

The Bhutanese Competition Policy does not propose an independent authority for its implementation and designates the Office of Consumer Protection as the

<https://tbsnews.net/economy/e-commerce-sale-grows-24-times-over-three-years-143923> accessed 26 October 2020.

78 See for instance, the April 2018 foundation course organised by the Bangladesh Foreign Trade Institute (Bangladesh Foreign Trade Institute Annual Report 2017–18) and the report of an OECD Conference attended by senior officials of the Commission (Bangladesh Competition Commission 'Report on OECD–GFC Annual International Conference presented by Mr. Md. Abul Hossain Mian, Member Bangladesh Competition Commission, Mr. Md. Monowar Hossain Director Bangladesh Competition Commission, Ms. Dilara Begum Commercial Councellor Bangladesh Embassy, Paris, France 29–30 November 2018 Paris, France' <https://ccb.portal.gov.bd/sites/default/files/files/ccb.portal.gov.bd/page/17510ba7_bdbe_4d2a_99d5_a3da1518b4b4/OECD%20Report%202018%20Final.pdf> accessed 26 October 2020).

79 *The Financial Express*, 'BCC Suggests Steps Against Anti-competitive Activities' <https://thefinancialexpress.com.bd/economy/bangladesh/bcc-suggests-steps-against-anti-competitive-activities-1596771437> accessed 26 October 2020.

80 *The Business Standard*, 'Competition Commission to Break up Onion Syndicate' <https://tbsnews.net/bangladesh/competition-commission-break-onion-syndicate> accessed 26 October 2020.

81 *The Business Standard* n.73.

82 Chapter 3, Section 3.2.1.4.

83 Ministry of Economic Development, Republic of Maldives <https://trade.gov.mv/organizational-structure> accessed 31 October 2021.

Competition Council and entrusts it with the task of reviewing, monitoring, and implementing the policy.[84] However, a visit to the official website of the office at the time of writing suggested that it has yet to take any steps in this regard.[85]

8.3.2.6 Afghanistan ensuring competition without a law

Although Afghanistan has yet to enact its competition legislation, the Afghani government recognises 'Competition Promotion and Consumer Protection' as a pillar of its economic policy and seeks to create and develop 'a competitive marketplace which in that [*sic*] competition is based on supply and demand, and both traders and consumers use from those beneficiaries [*sic*]', and aims to 'standardize and improve business transaction in market'.[86] In the years since the Afghan governmen tcommissioned the drafting of the Afghani Act, the relevant Afghani ministry has also participated in a series of consultations led by the United States Department of Commerce to learn about the political and public awareness challenges faced by Pakistan in developing a competition and consumer protection regime, and to thereby to build 'internal capacity to develop a sustainable competition and consumer protection regime'.[87]

8.3.3 *Links between Adoption and Implementation in these Countries*

Although each of the South Asian Six are likely to offer different explanations for why they have not yet fully operationalised their competition regimes, their inertia in this regard may, in significant part, be attributed to their inability to generate a high level of compatibility and legitimacy for their respective competition legislations due to their particular pre-conditions of transfer and the mechanisms and institutions employed by them in their adoption processes.

Like Pakistan, these countries had acquired their competition legislations through *coercion*, however, unlike Pakistan at least three of these countries (Sri Lanka, Bangladesh, and Maldives) had enacted these legislations through their parliaments, while Nepal like Pakistan had adopted it through an executive order. Although the parliamentary form of enactment in Sri Lanka, Bangladesh, and Maldives resembles the process through which India adopted the Indian Act, the similarity between the enactment in India and in these countries is superficial. For instance, there is no

84 Chapter 3, Section 3.2.2.2.

85 Ministry of Economic Affairs, Office of Consumer Protection, Bhutan <www.moea.gov.bt/?page_id=594> accessed 31 October 2021.

86 Ministry of Industry and Commerce, Competition Promotion and Consumer Protection, Afghanistan <https://moci.gov.af/en/competition-promotion-and-consumer-protection> accessed 31 October 2021.

87 'Commercial Law Development Program, Office of General Counsel, United States Department of Commerce: Improving the Legal Environment for Business Worldwide' <https://cldp.doc.gov/programs/cldp-in-action/details/1183> accessed 31 October 2021.

record of any of these countries having formed any committees, such as the Raghavan Committee in India, to deliberate and draft the proposed legislation, and there is no evidence of parliamentary standing committees engaging with stakeholders to give final form to these legislations or of their judiciaries engaging with the scheme and substance of these legislations to ensure they are in alignment with the constitutions and legal norms prevalent in their contexts. Further, given the turbulent political histories of these countries which have interfered in the smooth functioning of their parliaments (even if not actually suspending these) it is unlikely that their parliaments had the depth of legislative experience of the Indian parliament and therefore were not equipped for *socialising* the proposed legislations for their respective contexts.

Even in the few instances when the competition laws of the South Asian Six were enacted through parliaments the process of enactment could not offset the negative impact of the absence of broad-based consultations. Consequently, whether enacted through parliament or through executive orders the compatibility of these laws remained weak and superficial. This in turn means that those responsible for establishing the competition authorities or enforcing the competition legislations, whether it is the government as in Maldives and Nepal, or the authorities established in pursuance of the competition legislations (as in the case of Sri Lanka and Bangladesh), or the stakeholders who were expected to utilise these legislations, really understood their aims and objectives. In the case of Sri Lanka, this is likely to have been a factor in the Consumer Affairs Authority failing to enforce the competition-related provisions of the Sri Lankan Act as well as for the absence of competition complaints filed before it, while in the case of Bangladesh it is a likely explanation for the government's failure to fully operationalise the Bangladeshi Competition Commission, and in Nepal and Maldives for the lack of application and utilisation of the legislations by the officials appointed for this purpose.

However, the enactment of the competition legislations in Sri Lanka, Bangladesh, and Maldives through parliaments, or in the case of Nepal, by the then all-powerful monarch, does confer on them a reasonable degree of formal legitimacy which is likely to protect them from the kind of constitutional challenges witnessed in Pakistan. However, this formal legitimacy does not automatically translate into productive interactions between the competition enforcement systems set up in pursuance of the adopted competition legislations and the pre-existing legal systems of these countries. As in India and Pakistan, the quality of these interactions is likely to be determined in part by the extent to which the judiciary has engaged with the adoption process, and in part by the extent to which the other organs of state assume ownership and responsibility for these legislations. Given that there is no information or even suggestion that the judiciary in any of these countries has engaged in the adoption process and further given that the extent of ownership of state organs appears weak at best due to their indifference to the enforcement of these laws, it is very likely that the general courts at the adoption stage in these countries would not respond to competition matters as supportively as general courts in India. In fact, the repercussions of the absence of judicial engagement in these countries are likely to be even greater than in Pakistan because some of these legislations give a more central competition enforcement role to the general courts: for instance, appeals from offences under the Bangladeshi Act lie to the lower judiciary; Maldives makes the general courts responsible for reviewing all competition orders; and Nepal entrusts the entire enforcement function to the general courts. In these circumstances the judiciary's lack of understanding of core competition principles and of the rationale for which the countries have adopted competition legislations is likely to have a far greater direct adverse impact on competition enforcement in these countries than even in Pakistan where an adverse direct impact can be offset by reducing the negative indirect impact on enforcement (see Chapter 6).

The considerable pressures on the performance of the adopted competition legislations in Sri Lanka, Nepal, Bangladesh, and Maldives and on their interactions with pre-existing legal systems stem from the quality of the legitimacy and compatibility generated for these legislations the adoption stage, and are likely to present an obstacle to the smooth or early integration of these legislations with the pre-existing legal systems of these countries. While the parliamentary enactment of competition legislations in at least three of the South Asian Six confers a degree of legitimacy on these legislations, the need to satisfy different interest groups represented in their parliaments has remained an obstacle to a decisive start to competition enforcement as witnessed in Pakistan, which had successfully promulgated the 2007 Ordinance and established the CCP entirely through executive action and without any interference from the interest groups represented in the legislature.[88] Further, even the competition legislations (such as those of Sri Lanka, Bangladesh, and Maldives) that have been enacted through elected legislatures have not been made compatible for their contexts for at least two reasons: first, that that their parliaments, like the Pakistani parliament when it enacted the Pakistani Act, were constrained by the advice and direction of multi-lateral agencies supporting them in the adoption and did not have the benefit of broad-based consultations with domestic stakeholders at the deliberation phase; and second, because the turbulent politics of these countries had not equipped their parliaments with the institutional capacity necessry for meaningful legislation. The absence of broad-based understanding of the adopted competition legislations also weakened their domestic legitimacy which in turn manifested in a lack of institutional ownership as witnessed in Pakistan, and the lack of stakeholder

[88] Although a Pakistan-style implementation may theoretically be possible in Nepal, the Nepalese Act lacked the clarity of concepts and a clearly delinated enforcement system as provided in the Pakistani competition legislation.

interest in bringing complaints under these legislations. These factors suggest that the competition experience of these countries is likely to fall somewhere between the two extremes represented by the Indian and Pakistani experiences: the legislations are unlikely to face the kind of fundamental constitutional challenges witnessed in Pakistan that almost choked competition enforcement in the country but they are also equally likely to lack the institutional support and public awareness evident in India and therefore the competition enforcement systems envisaged in these legislations are likely to lack the internal impetus to commence meaningful operations.

Although Bhutan has adopted a competition policy rather than a legislation, its failure to implement this policy may also be attributed to the policy having been introduced through multi-lateral agencies without generating understanding of its rationale and objectives in the country. Similarly, Afghanistan's failure to enact its competition legislation despite receiving a draft in 2011 and despite making efforts to create a competitive culture even without formally enacting the legislation, is at least in part due to the absence of a broad-based understanding of the rationale for the legislation, especially given the other more pressing challenges that the country faces before political events in the country took over and entirely overshadowed any thought of competition enforcement that may have still be lingering in the Afghani context.

8.4 THE HIATUS STAGE: OPPORTUNITY TO LEARN FROM THE INDIAN AND PAKISTANI EXPERIENCE

The mix of mechanisms and institutions through which the South Asian Six engaged with competition legislations or policies have left them at a curious impasse at which despite years of efforts and some important progress, the legislations or policies adopted or contemplated by them remain unable to progress beyond, and at times even through the adoption stage. Although it may be tempting to write off this impasse either as a natural, and, therefore, inconsequential step in the progression of the adopted legislation or policy or, worse still, as the failure of competition reform in these countries, it is too hasty to do so. In fact, the Indian and Pakistani competition experience suggests that this impasse is the hiatus stage in the adoption–implementation continuum, also witnessed in the Indian and Pakistani contexts which despite the enforcement backtracking that came in its wake, provided both those countries with an important opportunity to enhance the compatibility and legitimacy of their adopted competition legislations through advocacy initiatives and in doing so, improved the chances of the subsequent 'success' of the adopted competition legislations.[89]

[89] For a discussion of success, see Chapter 1, Section 1.3.2.3 and for the Indian and Pakistani hiatus stage see Section 8.2.3.

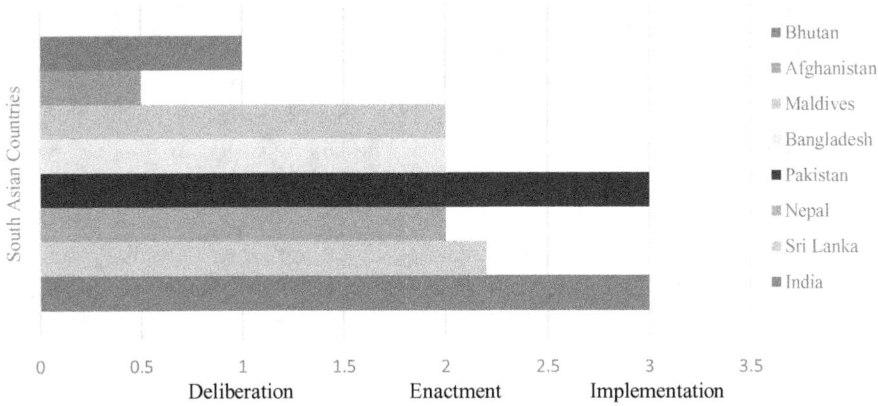

FIGURE 8.1. Progress of South Asian countries along the adoption–implementation continuum

To understand how the South Asian Six may benefit from the Indian and Pakistani experience at the hiatus stage it is first important to identify the point in the adoption–implementation continuum at which each of these countries have entered the hiatus stage. The Indian and Pakistani experience suggests that the probability of a country utilising its hiatus stage for generating compatibility and legitimacy for its adopted competition legislation is greater if the country enters the stage after it has already enacted the competition legislation. This is understandable given that once a competition legislation has been enacted, it already has a degree of compatibility and legitimacy in the country and is, therefore, in a better position to build upon it than if the legislation was still only at the deliberation phase and therefore more vulnerable to the possibility of abandonment altogether. The completion of the enactment phase also means that core competition principles as well as the competition enforcement system for the country have already been clarified, and the country is primed, to popularise these among stakeholders. Sri Lanka, Nepal, and Bangladesh, and Maldives having already adopted competition legislations and Bhutan already having a policy in place, meet this benchmark and may, therefore, be deemed to be well positioned to utilise their hiatus stages meaningfully to enhance the compatiblity and legitimacy of their competition legislations. (Figure 8.1).

The Indian and Pakistani competition experience further suggests that at least three factors other than enactment of the competition legislations helped them utilise their hiatus stage more effectively: first, that the first-tier competition authorities envisaged in the Indian and Pakistani competition legislations – the CCI and the CCP – had already been established, even though, as in the case of India, the CCI was not fully constituted and operationalised when it entered the hiatus stage;

second that these competition authorities were envisaged as independent of the executive, even though in Pakistan this independence was not perfect as the discretion to appoint and remove members from the CCP vested exclusively in the government (acting on the advise of the CCP chairperson); and finally that the competition authorities in both countries are designed as specialist bodies exclusively focused on regulating competition. Among these characteristics 'independence' is a composite of express statutory independence,[90] the degree of the executive control in appointing and removing members to the authority,[91] and the extent to which the authority is dependent on the executive for its budget.[92] Arguably, a country that has already established its national competition authority that is both independent and specialist has the highest probability of effectively utilising the hiatus stage to enhance the compatibility and legitimacy of its competition legislation in anticipation of its effective enforcement at the implementation stage.

Among the enacted competition legislations of the South Asian Six, the Sri Lankan and Bangladeshi Acts provide for independent competition authorities albeit vesting in their governments the power to appoint and remove their members. The budget of the Sri Lankan Consumer Affairs Authority is voted upon by the parliament[93] while that of the Bangladesh Competition Commission is to be determined by the government.[94] In Maldives, competition enforcement is fully embedded in the relevant ministry while in Nepal the enforcement is entrusted entirely to the courts. Further, the Sri Lankan authority is non-exclusive and is interested in consumer protection and trade in addition to competition. Although Bhutan only has a competition policy and Afghanistan has not enacted its competition legislation, the draft Afghan Act's proposes an authority which is both 'independent' and embedded in the relevant ministry[95] and whose members are to be

[90] Indian Act, section 7 and Pakistani Act, section 12 envisage the CCI and CCP as autonomous bodies independent of the governments of the countries.

[91] The greater the involvement of the executive in the appointment and removal of members, the lower the independence of the authority. For instance, under the Indian Act, sections 9 and 11, CCI members are to be appointed on the recommendation of a selection committee and may be removed by the Indian government after an independent Supreme Court inquiry, while under the Pakistani Act, section 14 the power to appoint and remove members of the CCP vests entirely in the government, albeit in case of appointment the government acts in consultation with the chairman and in case of removal, proceeds only after an independent enquiry. On this benchmark the CCI may be deemed to be more independent than the CCP. Also see Chapter 2, Section 2.5.2.

[92] In terms of the Indian Act, section 51 and Pakistani Act, section 20, the budget of the CCI and CCP is paid from the Commission Fund the size of which is largely determined by Indian and Pakistani governments.

[93] Sri Lankan Act, section 49.

[94] Bangladeshi Act, section 31.

[95] ibid section 10(4).

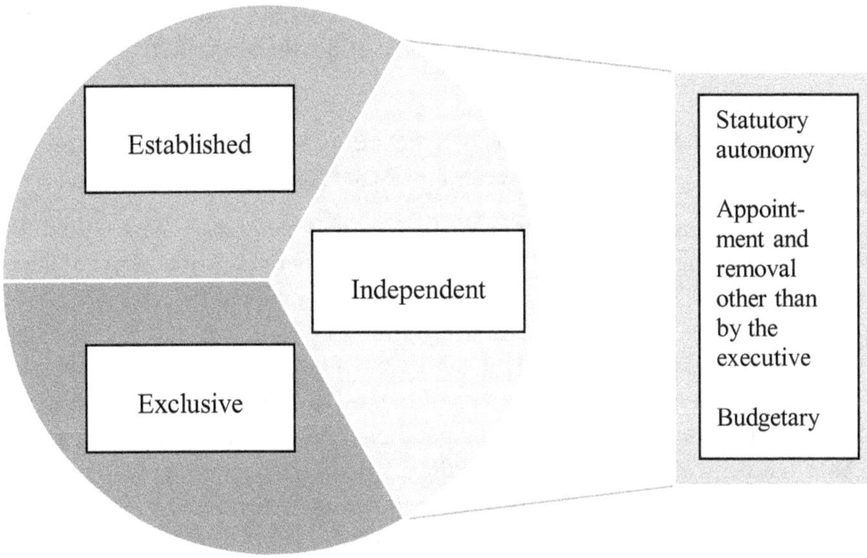

FIGURE 8.2. Anatomy of the potential for utilising the Hiatus Stage

appointed on the advice of the government[96] and may only be removed after an appropriate inquiry,[97] This suggests that Afghanistan's potential for utilising the hiatus stage may be greater than that of Bhutan where the implementation of the policy is vested entirely in a non-specialist government department (Figure 8.2).

Given that none of the competition authorities, whether established or proposed, independent or embedded in the government, fully meet the criteria for effectively utilising the hiatus stage, it may be argued the authority that displays more of these characteristics is more likely to utilise the hiatus stage for creating greater awareness of the competition legislation and thereby enhancing its compatibility and domestic legitimacy and facilitating its future enforcement. Therefore, while the Sri Lankan Consumer Affairs Authority and the Nepalese Competition Promotion Board raise awareness of the competition legislation simply by existing and providing a focal point for competition discourse in their countries,[98] it is the Bangladesh Competition Commission that has utilised the hiatus stage most effectively by organising awareness-enhancing initiatives including trainings, seminars, and workshops and most recently, by issuing a press release highlighting the possibility of it

96 Draft Afghan Act, section 10.

97 ibid section 11.

98 The Sri Lankan Consumer Affairs Authority has also appointed a 'Director' to look after competition matters. Consumer Affairs Authority, Contact Details <http://caa.gov.lk/web/index.php?option=com_content&view=article&id=141&Itemid=591&lang=en> accessed 3 November 2021.

playing a role in checking price hikes in the pandemic, and in doing so has created at least some space for the future enforcement of the Bangladeshi Act.

8.5 PATTERNS OF COMPETITION DIFFUSION AND TRANSFER AND ENFORCEMENT IN SOUTH ASIA

A theme that emerges from this analysis is that countries characterised by relatively more inexperienced or shallower legal and political institutions are more likely to be *coerced* or persuaded by international forces and multi-lateral agencies to adopt competition legislation. It further appears that the forces and agencies that influence the adoption play an important role in defining the competition principles for these countries, albeit mostly leaving it to the countries themselves to stipulate the competition enforcement systems for their respective contexts. However, it seems that while *coercion* succeeds at the adoption stage by bringing the legislations to these countries it is less successful in enforcing these at the implementation stage: despite enacting their competition legislations through their elected legislatures Sri Lanka, Bangladesh, and Maldives remain stranded in the hiatus stage between adoption and implementation. The only outlier is Pakistan, that despite having adopted its competition legislation on the advice and with the support of multi-lateral agencies has also experienced some success in operationalising its competition enforcement system and implementing its adopted legislation. This confirms that countries that adopt competition legislations through the vertical transfer mechanism of *coercion* only generate weak, superficial compatibility and formal legitimacy for their adopted legislations. The combination of these factors not only prevents the adopted legislations from being understood, applied, and utilised in the countries but also hinders them from productively interacting with the pre-existing legal systems in their countries, thereby limiting their ability to be successfully implemented in their respective contexts and over time becoming valid and important components of their pre-existing legal systems.[99]

This analysis also offers interesting, albeit counterintuitive insight into the role of institutions engaged in the adoption process: it appears that a country that combines *coercion* and a limited number of top-down, exclusive institutions in adopting its competition legislation (such as Pakistan) is more likely to be able to operationalise and enforce its adopted legislation than a country that combines *coercion* with bottom-up, participatory, and inclusive institutions. This is a surprising (and somewhat undesirable) discovery given that in theory bottom-up, participatory, and inclusive institutions are expected to enhance the compatibility and legitimacy of the adopted legislation and thereby to facilitate the enforcement of adopted

[99] Chapter 1, Section 1.4.

legislation. However, it is possible to explain this anomaly by recognising that despite their institutional design the bottom-up, participatory, and inclusive institutions through which Sri Lanka, Bangladesh, and Maldives adopted their competition legislations, lacked the capacity to meaningfully aggregate local information or to adapt the law in light of this information and to make the adopted law more compatible with its context. Also while these institutions confer formal legitimacy they lack the historic depth necessary for generating substantive legitimacy. The Pakistani experience suggests that where the bottom-up, participatory, and inclusive institutions are weak, the mechanism of *coercion* delivered through limited, top-down, exclusive institutions which can function without engaging with or requiring consensus from a range of diverse stakeholders is more effective, at least in ithe short run, in meaningfully operationalising the adopted legislation.

This analysis also raises an interesting question about the possibility of convergence among competition legislations across the South Asian countries. The likelihood of convergence arises from all these countries having engaged with their respective legislations primarily at the behest of Western multi-lateral agencies and from the fact that a subset among them – Nepal, Bangladesh, Bhutan, and Afghanistan – also having engaged with India in the adoption process. In Afghanistan, the engagement with India was managed by foreign thinktanks; in Nepal and Bangladesh it was generated by domestic thinktanks and commentators either working in collaboration with their Indian counterparts or studying the adoption of competition legislation in India; and in Bhutan, it stemmed from Bhutan's close economic relationship with India as well as its competition policy being drafted by Indian consultants.

However, this dual common influence does not necessarily lead to substantive convergence among the adopted legislations. There is certainly some convergence among the competition principles embodied in these legislations, evident particularly in the strong resemblance between the Bangladeshi and the Indian Act, which may equally be traced to the *coercive* influence of Western multi-lateral agencies advising Bangladesh to adopt a legislation like that of India, or of India engaging directly with Bangladesh in the adoption process. However, this *coercive* influence whether of multi-lateral agencies or India directly does not extend to the competition enforcement systems prescribed in the different legislations which seem to be based on patterns or institutions already operating in the countries' pre-existing legal systems. Given the significance of enforcement systems to the implementation of the adopted competition legislations, the divergence among them is likely to present an obstacle to convergence not only in the future implementation of these legislations but also in the extent to which they are successful in utilising their present hiatus stage (Table 8.1).

TABLE 8.1. *Review of the adoption–implementation continuum of South Asian countries*

Countries (in order of adoption)	Review of the adoption–implementation continuum				
	Pre-conditions of transfer		Motivation	Deliberation	
	Domestic	International		Status	Strategy
India	Democracy since independence	Member of WTO	▪ WTO ▪ domestic re-evaluation of anti-monopoly regime	Complete	▪ *Socialisation* ▪ through bottom up, participatory, & inclusive institutions
Sri Lanka	▪ British Dominion ▪ Democracy. ▪ Internal strife	Member of WTO	▪ WTO ▪ Evidence of US persuasion also	Complete	▪ *Coercion* ▪ No information regarding domestic institutions of deliberation
Nepal	▪ Traditional monarchy ▪ Constitutional monarchy ▪ Republic ▪ Internal strife	▪ Member of WTO ▪ Extensive engagement with multi-lateral agencies	▪ WTO ▪ Possibly other multi-lateral agencies	Complete	▪ *Coercion* ▪ No information regarding domestic institutions of deliberation
Pakistan	▪ Constitutional democracy ▪ History of martial law and suspension of constitution and parliament	▪ Member of WTO ▪ Extensive engagement with multi-lateral agencies	▪ WTO ▪ World Bank	Complete	▪ *Coercion* ▪ Some information regarding domestic deliberation although led by the World Bank
Bangladesh	▪ Constitutional democracy ▪ Some history of martial law	▪ Member of WTO ▪ Extensive engagement with multi-lateral agencies	▪ WTO ▪ Possibly other multi-lateral agencies	Complete	▪ *Coercion* ▪ No information regarding domestic deliberation
Maldives	▪ Traditional monarchy ▪ Constitutional monarchy ▪ Republic	▪ Member of WTO ▪ Extensive engagement with multi-lateral agencies	▪ WTO ▪ Also other multi-lateral agencies	Complete	▪ *Coercion* ▪ Some information regarding domestic deliberation with support from multi-lateral agencies
Bhutan	▪ Traditional monarchy ▪ Constitutional monarchy	▪ Not a member of WTO ▪ Extensive engagement with multi-lateral agencies	▪ multi-lateral agencies ▪ India	Complete	▪ *Coercion* ▪ No information regarding domestic deliberation.
Afghanistan	▪ Traditional monarchy ▪ Republic ▪ Internal strife and civil war ▪ Republic ▪ More internal strife and civil war	▪ Member of WTO ▪ Extensive engagement with multi-lateral agencies	▪ WTO ▪ Other multi-lateral agencies	Complete	▪ *Coercion* ▪ No information regarding domestic deliberation.

Enactment		First-tier Authority		Implementation	
Status	Strategy	Status	Type	Status	Enforcement
Complete	▪ Through bottom up, participatory, & inclusive institutions ▪ More *socialisation* ▪ Amendment through judiciary	Established	▪ Independent of executive except for budget ▪ Exclusively focused on competition	Delay in commencement but continuous since starting	Orders in respect of anti-competitive agreements, abuse of dominance and mergers
Complete	▪ Through bottom up, participatory, & inclusive institutions ▪ Some *socialisation*	Established	▪ Independent except for appointments ▪ Non-exclusive ▪ Limited mandate; shares power with Council ▪ Lack of clarity regarding appeals from orders of Council	Ongoing	No competition enforcement orders to date.
Complete	▪ Through presidential order. ▪ *Coercion*	No	▪ Embedded in the relevant ministry ▪ Limited mandate-does not include enforcement.	No evidence	Enforcement not in the mandate of the authority
Complete	▪ First three iterations of the competition legislation enacted through presidential order. ▪ *Coercion* ▪ Some evidence of *socialisation* when final version of the legislation enacted through parliament	Established.	▪ Statutorily independent of executive except for appointments, removals and budget ▪ Exclusively focused on competition.	Ongoing with some gaps in enforcement.	Orders in respect of anti-competitive agreements, abuse of dominance and mergers
Complete	▪ Through bottom up, participatory, & inclusive institutions ▪ Limited *socialisation*	Established	▪ Statutorily independent of executive except for appointments and budget. ▪ Exclusively focused on competition.	Only to the extent of advocacy	None
Complete	▪ Through bottom up, participatory, & inclusive institutions ▪ Limited *socialisation*	No	Enforcement entrusted to the relevant ministry	None	None.
Not enacted	▪ Policy adopted through top-down institutions. ▪ Limited *socialisation*	No	Implementation of policy entrusted to Consumer Protection authority	None	None
Not enacted	N/A	N/A	▪ Independent however dependent on government for appointments and budget. ▪ Also part of relevant ministry	N/A	N/A

9

Bridging the Implementation Gap

9.1 INTRODUCTION

In the last two decades, six out of eight South Asian countries have adopted some version of a modern competition law: India was the first to do so in 2002, followed by Sri Lanka in 2003, Pakistan and Nepal in 2007, Bangladesh in 2012, and most recently Maldives in 2020. Although the remaining two countries, Bhutan and Afghanistan have not yet adopted modern competition laws, they have not remained untouched by the growing momentum of what may be called the competition law movement across the region: Bhutan adopted a national competition policy in 2014 which it revised and updated in 2020, and Afghanistan finalised a draft competition legislation in 2011 it is yet to enact. However, with the exception of India and Pakistan, South Asian countries are yet to meaningfully implement their competition laws and policies: among them, Bangladesh has established the first-tier competition authority as envisaged in the Bangladeshi Act, but at the time of writing had still not operationalised it; and Nepal and Sri Lanka though not obliged by their respective competition legislations to establish specialist or fully independent competition authorities, have the requisite competition enforcement infrastructure in place but have not taken up any competition matters. Maldives, despite enacting its competition legislation in 2020, had allowed itself a reprieve until 2021 to implement the law, however, at the time of writing there was still no information as to whether it had commenced competition enforcement beyond the 2021 deadline. Consequently, the region's overall competition enforcement experience remains weak and uneven at best, and the anti-competitive practices that the competition legislations are designed to address, continue unchecked and unabated.

As discussed particularly in Chapter 8, the extent and quality of competition enforcement in the South Asian countries that have already adopted competition legislations is in large part attributable to the strategies and institutions through which they adopted these legislations: while the Indian Act, adopted through *socialisation* and the interplay of a relatively wide range of experienced bottom-up, participatory, and inclusive institutions and the Pakistani Act, adopted by *coercion* through a narrow category of top-down, exclusive institutions have both proceeded to the implementation stage, the Bangladeshi, Sri Lankan, and Maldives competition legislations adopted through a combination of *coercion* and relatively less experienced bottom-up, participatory, and inclusive institutions, and the Nepalese Act, adopted by an executive order, are yet to be enforced. This suggests that competition legislation is more likely to be enforced in one of two situations: if it is *socialised* through extensive, domestic consultations with a wide range of stakeholders, or if it is introduced through *coercion* and delivered through an all-powerful executive.[1] While the former situation generates the compatibility and legitimacy necessary for meaningful implementation, the latter displaces the need for such compatibility and legitimacy, at least temporarily, by keeping the adoption and implementation firmly within the executive. In contrast, legislations introduced through *coercion* and then enacted through parliaments that do not have the history, experience, or even the requisite inclination to aggregate or apply local knowledge, are only superficially compatible with context and have, at best, only a degree of formal legitimacy that does not translate into the ownership and understanding necessary for meaningfully operationalising the adopted legislation.

While the failure of countries to generate sufficient compatibility and legitimacy in the adoption process is not fatal to their ability to implement their competition legislations, the 'success' they are likely to enjoy in this regard depends in large part on their governments' commitment to competition enforcement which in turn is linked to the extent of compatibility and legitimacy that the adopted legislations enjoy in their domestic contexts. In countries where competition legislations mandate independent competition authorities such as in India, Pakistan, and Bangladesh, the governments' support may be discerned by the efforts they make for operationalising these authorities, including appointing their members, and allocating funds for their activities. On the other hand, in countries where legislations do not envisage fully independent competition enforcement authorities (such as Sri Lanka, Nepal, Maldives) or that are yet to adopt competition legislation (such as Bhutan and Afghanistan) the government's support makes the difference by generating greater awareness of and acceptability for the legislation in their contexts.

This chapter argues that regardless of the scenario in which these countries adopted their competition legislations, it is argued that their, governments are more likely to support competition enforcement if they are themselves convinced of competition's potential to help deliver their broader and more pressing economic and social goals. The chapter further argues that not only is it possible for multilateral agencies that have influenced and shaped the diffusion and transfer of

[1] Nepal like Pakistan had introduced its competition legislation through an all powerful executive, however, Nepal still not able to implement the legislation may be explained by the fact that the all-powerful executive that enacted the Nepalese Act was removed from power the very day after the enactment.

competition legislation in nearly all South Asian countries to play a role in generating this understanding, but also it is open to countries to learn from each other in this regard. To this end this chapter is organised as follows: Section 9.2 makes the case for the connection between competition enforcement and economic development across South Asia; Section 9.3 examines the growth in digital economy in these countries and explores how competition enforcement may help South Asian countries address the competition concerns arising from the digital economy; Section 9.4 explores the possibility of South Asian countries benefitting from each other's experiences in competition law enforcement in the traditional as well as the digital economy; and Section 9.5 discusses possible implementation strategies for South Asian countries that can harness competition regulation to realise the potential for traditional as well as digital economic growth in their contexts.

9.2 THE DEVELOPMENT IMPERATIVE

Economic growth and development feature very prominently in the economic and political agenda of South Asian countries. It is likely, therefore, that the governments of these countries may be more inclined to publicise, operationalise and enforce their adopted (or proposed) competition legislations if they understand that doing so would help deliver the development and growth dividends they very much desire. This section identifies the key economic challenges faced by South Asian countries and explores how competition law may help in addressing these.

9.2.1 *Economic Profiles and Challenges of South Asian Countries*

In varying degrees all South Asian countries are characterised by low levels of per capita income, low Gross Domestic Products (GDP) and high economic vulnerability. Among them Bangladesh, Bhutan, India, Nepal, Pakistan, and Sri Lanka are classified by the World Bank as lower-middle-income countries;[2] Maldives is classified as an upper-middle-income country,[3] and Afghanistan as a low-income country.

Afghanistan, Bangladesh, Bhutan, and Nepal are also categorised by the United Nations as 'least developed countries' due to their low GDP and considerable economic vulnerability.[4] All South Asian countries are characterised by

[2] Nepal has recently been re-classified upwards from the low-income category and Sri Lanka re-classified downwards, from the upper-middle-income category. The World Bank, 'Data, Countries and Economies' <https://data.worldbank.org/country> accessed 25 November 2020; Umer Serajuddin, Nada Hamadeh, 'New World Bank Country Classifications by Income Level: 2020–2021' <https://blogs.worldbank.org/opendata/new-world-bank-country-classifications-income-level-2020-2021> (World Bank Blogs, 2020) accessed 25 November 2020.

[3] For the relevant income thresholds 2021 see The World Bank, 'World Bank Country and Lending Groups' <https://datahelpdesk.worldbank.org/knowledgebase/articles/906519-world-bank-country-and-lending-groups> accessed 1 December 2020.

[4] United Nations, 'Country Classifications: Data Sources, Country Classifications and Aggregation Methodology' <www.un.org/en/development/desa/policy/wesp/wesp_current/

considerable income inequality[5] with Gini indices ranging from 39.8 (Sri Lanka) and 31.3 (Maldives):[6] the Gini index in Bhutan and India is 37.4[7] and 37.8[8] respectively; Bangladesh and Nepal have a Gini index of 32.8 and 32.4 respectively;[9] and Pakistan of 33.5.[10] The considerable income equality in all these countries is further exacerbated by a sizeable proportion of their populations living below the poverty line: 54.5 per cent in Afghanistan, 25.2 per cent in Nepal, 24.3 per cent in Bangladesh and Pakistan respectively, and 21.9 per cent in India.[11]

South Asian countries also have an extensive history of state control and central planning which despite efforts at liberalisation persists in the form of state-owned or controlled enterprises (SOEs) operating throughout these countries.[12] Historically, these countries had established a range of SOEs in the belief and hope that these would deliver industrialisation while also safeguarding the public interest. Given the public nature of their mandates these SOEs were not particularly interested in instituting measures for the greater efficiency, accountability, and transparency of their operations, and remained largely unconcerned about the significant losses they incurred in the absence of such measures. In time, several South Asian countries launched privatisation drives in an attempt to address these issues and in response to changing global priorities in this regard: Sri Lanka was the first to do so in 1977,[13] with India, Pakistan, and Bangladesh following suit in 1991, Nepal in 1993,[14] and Maldives in 2006 with technical assistance from the World Bank.[15] Despite these efforts however, these countries were not able to

2> accessed 25 November 2020. Maldives graduated from being an LDC (Least Developed Country) in 2011 while Bhutan is set to graduate in 2023. The classifications of both Bangladesh and Nepal were up for review in 2021, however remained unchanged.

5 Index Mundi 'GINI Index (World Bank estimate)-Country Ranking' <www.indexmundi.com/facts/indicators/SI.POV.GINI/rankings> (updated 2019) accessed 2 February 2021.

6 ibid. The data for Sri Lanka and Maldives relates to 2016.

7 ibid. This is per 2017 data.

8 ibid. There is some discrepancy in the Gini Index for India. According to the World Bank, the Gini Index is 35.7 as per 2011 data while according to the UN, it stands at 37.8 also as per 2011 data. UNDP Human Development Reports 'India' <http://hdr.undp.org/en/countries/profiles/IND> accessed 2 February 2021.

9 ibid. The data for Nepal relates to 2010 and for Bangladesh to 2016.

10 ibid. This is on the basis of 2015 data. There is no data available for Nepal.

11 Bhutan and Maldives with only 8.2 per cent and Sri Lanka with only 4.1 per cent of its population living below the poverty line do not appear to have a significant poverty problem. These figures are obtained from the World Bank data for 2018 with the exception of India and Nepal whose figures are from 2010. See n.1.

12 These are sometimes referred to in the literature as public enterprises and abbreviated as SOEs or PEs.

13 Despite the early start, Sri Lanka's privatisation drive remained slow and was punctuated with long periods of inactivity. Asoka F Balasooriya, Quamrul Alam and Ken Coghill 'Market-based Reforms and Privatization in Sri Lanka' (2008) 21(1) International Journal of Public Sector Management 58–73.

14 Nirmal Kumar Raut, 'Causes and Impact of Privatisation in Nepal: A Theoretical Review' (2012) 2(2) Banking Journal 3.

15 Asian Development Bank, Technical Assessment Completion Report <www.adb.org/sites/default/files/project-document/73639/39664-012-mld-tcr.pdf> accessed 8 December 2020.

reorganise the operations of several remaining or even privatised SOEs along competitive lines and therefore, failed to achieve the desirable levels of economic efficiency.

9.2.2 *Do Multi-lateral Packages of Economic and Institutional Reform Address Development?*

The considerable economic challenges that South Asian countries face have led the majority of them to rely extensively on Western multi-lateral agencies for financial aid. guidance and technical assistance in carrying out their legal reforms. In most cases these countries have have also fully accepted the conditionalities on which multi-lateral agencies have provided this aid and assistance.

The majority of these countries have obtained support from the International Monetary Fund (IMF). From the 1980 onwards, the IMF launched its first-generation reforms, which aimed to alleviate global poverty and inequities[16] by revitalising markets through economic liberalisation and reducing, if not altogether eliminating, state ownership of commercial enterprise and state intervention in market entry, market exit, and product pricing.[17] Within two decades, however, the IMF had realised that market liberalisation and deregulation alone were not sufficient either for establishing sustainable market-led growth or for maximising social welfare. This led to the launch of the IMF's second-generation reforms whose purpose was to sustain, consolidate, and boost market-led growth by 're-regulation' and 'institution building' through positive state action and in co-operation with civil society.[18]

Given the market focus of IMF reforms, it was only natural that the reform packages introduced by it throughout South Asia would also include the market regulating competition laws.[19] However, even as South Asian countries adopted

Bhutan and Afghanistan did not engage in this exercise most likely because their economies were either too underdeveloped, or too small, or both. For Afghanistan see Richard Ghiasy, Jiayi Zhou, Henrik Halgreen, 'Afghanistan's Private Sector: Status and Way Forward' (Stockholm International Peace Research Institute 2015) <www.sipri.org/sites/default/files/2016-04/SIPRI_Afghanistans-Private-Sector_Report-2015.pdf> accessed 8 December 2021, and for Bhutan, Asian Development Bank, Country Partnership Strategy: Bhutan 2014–18 'Private Sector Assessment (Summary)' <www.adb.org/sites/default/files/linked-documents/cps-bhu-2014-2018-psa.pdf> accessed 8 December 2021.

16 James M Boughton 'The IMF and the Silent Revolution: Global Finance and Development in the 1980s' (IMF 2000) <www.imf.org/external/pubs/ft/silent/index.htm> accessed 3 January 2021.

17 Scott H Jacobs, 'The Second Generation of Regulatory Reforms' delivered at the IMF Conference on Second Generation Reforms, November 1999 (IMF 1999) <www.imf.org/external/pubs/ft/seminar/1999/reforms/jacobs.htm#I> accessed 28 December 2020.

18 ibid.

19 South Asian countries had long-standing relationships with the IMF. India had become a member of the IMF in 1945, Pakistan and Sri Lanka in 1950, Afghanistan in 1955, Nepal in 1961, Bangladesh in 1972, Maldives in 1978, and Bhutan in 1981. All these countries have and participated in both first- and second-generation reforms at different points in their histories. International Monetary Fund 'List of Members' <www.imf.org/external/np/sec/memdir/memdate.htm> accessed 28 December 2020.

these laws as part of the reform packages prescribed for them, they often failed to grasp the potential of these laws to contribute to their economic development.[20] This was partly due to the fact that the majority of these countries were adopting competition laws in response to external stimulus rather than indigenous demand, and partly because despite encouraging and urging South Asian countries to adopt competition legislation, the IMF perhaps did not sufficiently clarify or emphasise that these laws were appropriate for their stage of economic development and would support them in realising their economic potential and goals.

The extent to which the different South Asian countries understand the possibility of a connection between competition regulation and economic growth and development may to some extent be deduced from the preambles of their respective competition legislations. A review of these preambles suggests that India and Bangladesh had some awareness of possible links between competition legislation and economic development: the Indian Act adopted through *socialisation* and a range of bottom-up, participatory, and inclusive institutions keeps 'in view the economic development of the country',[21] and the Bangladeshi Act, acquired through *coercion* but enacted through democratic institutions recognises that adopting such legislation is necessary in the 'context of gradual economic development of the country'.[22] However, both the Indian and the Bangladeshi Acts relegate economic growth and development to the background by making it part of the context in which competition takes place rather than acknowledging its potential as a tool for realising economic growth and development. In contrast, the preambles of the Sri Lankan Act[23] and the Pakistani Act (and the Ordinances preceding it),[24] both of which were adopted through *coercion* by multi-lateral agencies albeit with a

[20] India was perhaps the only country among this group of South Asian countries that had some understanding of the reasons for which it needed a modern competition law even if its impetus to develop this understanding came from the WTO's plans of including competition within its framework.

[21] Indian Act, Preamble: 'An Act to provide, keeping in view of the economic development of the country, for the establishment of a Commission to prevent practices having adverse effect on competition, to promote and sustain competition in markets, to protect the interests of consumers and to ensure freedom of trade carried on by other participants in markets, in India, and for matters connected therewith or incidental thereto.'

[22] Bangladeshi Act, Preamble: 'Whereas in the context of gradual economic development of the country, it is expedient and necessary to make provisions to promote, ensure and sustain congenial atmosphere for the competition in trade, and to prevent, control and eradicate collusion, monopoly and oligopoly, combination or abuse of dominant position or activities adverse to the competition.'

[23] Sri Lankan Act, Preamble: 'Whereas it is the policy of the Government of Sri Lanka to provide for the better protection of consumers through the regulation of trade and the prices of goods and services and to protect traders and manufacturers against unfair trade practices and restrictive trade practices; And whereas the Government of Sri Lanka is also desirous of promoting competitive pricing wherever possible and ensure healthy competition among traders and manufacturers of goods and services.'

[24] Pakistani Act, Preamble: 'Whereas it is expedient to make provisions to ensure free competition in all spheres of commercial and economic activity to enhance economic efficiency and to protect consumers from anti-competitive behaviour and to provide for the establishment of the

different combination of institutions, do not appear to recognise the connection between competition and economic growth and development. However, while the Pakistani Act recognises achieving 'economic efficiency' as a goal of competition, the Sri Lankan Act does not even do that. The Nepalese Act is the only South Asian legislation which recognises competition law's potential to enhance 'national productivity'.[25] However, in the Nepalese Act as in all other South Asian competition legislations, the focus on protecting consumer interests and facilitating internal trade overshadows any awareness of the link between competition and economic growth and development. Throughout these countries therefore competition legislation is cast as an essentially consumer protection role and is thereby rendered peripheral if not altogether irrelevant to the economic growth and development priorities of these countries.[26]

9.2.3 *Adapting Competition Legislation for Economic Development*

Scholars argue that for developing countries (including South Asian countries) to be persuaded to enforce, rather than merely adopt their competition legislations, they must be convinced that competition enforcement would spur domestic productivity and economic growth, and while it cannot directly alleviate poverty, may help avoid harm to the poor, create an enabling environment for achieving other social objectives,[27] and generate positive distributional effects.[28] In the South Asian context, it may also be important to make governments appreciate that rigorous competition enforcement would help break up old, politically supported market power, attract fresh capital investment and entrepreneurship, and encourage both investors and entrepreneurs to adopt innovative production and process strategies.[29] Unfortunately, the historically strong nexus between economic and political power in most of these countries, means that their governments may be reluctant to

Competition Commission of Pakistan to maintain and enhance competition; and for matters connected therewith or incidental thereto.'

[25] Nepalese Act, Preamble: 'Whereas, it is expedient to make legal provisions in order to further make national economy more open, liberal, market-oriented and competitive by maintaining fair competition between or among the persons or enterprises producing or distributing goods or services, to enhance national productivity by developing the business capacity of producers or distributors by way of competition, to protect markets against undesirable interference, to encourage to make the produced goods and services available to the consumers at a competitive price by enhancing the quality of goods or services by way of controlling monopoly and restrictive trade practices, and to maintain the economic interests and decency of the general public by doing away with possible unfair competition in trade practices.'

[26] Although Afghanistan has not adopted a competition legislation, its preamble is more in line with that of Sri Lanka and Pakistan. Bhutan, which only has a competition policy is perhaps the only country that articulates the rationale for the policy most clearly, however, it still does not expressly refer to economic growth and development.

[27] Thomas K Cheng, *Competition Law in Developing Countries* (OUP 2020), 5.

[28] ibid 29.

[29] ibid 310–11.

enforce competition in areas where such power is concentrated[30] even if those are the very areas where enforcement is most needed and where doing so is likely to lead to more equitable distribution of both economic and political power.[31]

Matters are likely to become even more complicated when it comes to the question of employing competition law to achieve social objectives such as reduction of inequality, promoting sustainability, and poverty alleviation. Some scholars argue that such social objectives are beyond the remit of competition law and if included in competition analysis are likely to comprise its efficacy. They therefore recommend that competition authorities may at best be mindful of the impact of their enforcement decisions on social welfare rather than actively working towards it.[32] Other scholars, however, are of the view that even though competition law cannot alone be burdened with the 'delicate task of changing the current socio-economic fabric' of developing countries,[33] it has the potential to reduce inequality of opportunity as well as of wealth,[34] and given the often dysfunctional distribution systems in these developing countries, may also be called upon to address distributive concerns without compromising its traditional focus on economic efficiency.[35]

Despite these complications, barring state capture by vested interests, it is entirely plausible that if the governments of South Asian countries and their competition authorities (where they have been established and have the autonomy and capacity to take decisions), appreciate the development dividends that even traditional competition enforcement may deliver for their economies, they may be more amenable to meaningfully implementing their competition legislations. This means that South Asian governments and competition authorities must understand that sanctioning cartels, checking abuses of dominant power, or monitoring mergers and acquisitions that significantly lessen competition will not only generate competitive prices, choice, and transparency for the benefit of consumers (whether natural or legal) and end-users in the short run, but will also spur entrepreneurship in their economies and provide livelihood to more people in the medium run, and thereby

30 A case in point is the reluctance of and delay on the part of the CCP to take up Pakistani sugar cartels. See Amber Darr 'Cartels & the Politics of Competition Law Enforcement in Pakistan' (Competition Policy International 2020) <www.competitionpolicyinternational.com/cartels-the-politics-of-competition-law-enforcement-in-pakistan> accessed 5 August 2021.

31 Lina M Khan, Sandeep Vaheesan, 'Market Power and Inequality: The Antitrust Counterrevolution and Its Discontents' (2017) 11 Harvard Law and Policy Review 235, 237.

32 ibid.

33 Michal S Gal, 'The Social Contract at the Basis of Competition Law: Should we Recalibrate Competition Law to Limit Inequality?' in Damien Gerard, Ioannis Lianos (ed) *Reconciling Efficiency and Equity: A Global Challenge for Competition Policy* (CUP 2019) 108; Ioannis Lianos, 'Competition Law as a Form of Social Regulation' (2020) 65(1) The Antitrust Bulletin 3–86.

34 Gal, ibid 95.

35 Ioannis Lianos, Amber Darr, 'Hunger Games: Connecting Competition Law and the Right to Food' CLES Research Paper Series 2/2019, 9 <www.ucl.ac.uk/cles/sites/cles/files/cles_2-2019 .pdfpapers> accessed 9 February 2021.

help alleviate poverty and re-distribute wealth throughout the economy in the long run. It is also important that multi-lateral agencies working with these countries engaging with these countries in the process of adopting their competition legislations, cast its benefits in development and growth language and thereby help draw competition in from these countries' peripheral consumer protection concerns to their core agenda of economic growth and development.

9.3 COMPETITION IN THE DIGITAL AGE

South Asian countries are increasingly engaging with foreign e-commerce platforms and developing their own e-commerce initiatives primarily for the economic growth and development that such it promises. This section examines the state of e-commerce in South Asia and the regulatory infrastructure individual countries have put into place to faciliate the digital economy and discusses how they may employ their competition legislations to address the challenges presented by e-commerce platforms.

9.3.1 *The State of E-commerce in South Asia*

Among South Asian countries India is a frontrunner in e-commerce and ranks among the top ten countries for e-commerce sales throughout the world:[36] in 2017 India's total e-commerce sales, 91 per cent of which were B2B (Business to Business) sales, were worth US $400 billion and comprised 15 per cent of India's total GDP.[37]

The remaining South Asian countries are only gradually waking up to the potential of e-commerce.[38] However, with the exception of Daraz,[39] which commenced operations as a Pakistani e-commerce platform and swiftly grew to become

[36] UNCTAD, 'Digital Economy Report 2019: Value Creation and Capture: Implications for Developing Countries' (United Nations 2019) ('the Digital Economy Report'), 15.

[37] ibid. India's top ten e-commerce platforms for 2020 were Amazon India, Flipkart, Alibaba, Snapdeal, Myntra, IndiaMart, Book My Show, Nykaa, First Cry, 1mg (e-Commerce Guide, 'Top 10 Ecommerce Sites in India 2020' <https://ecommerceguide.com/top/top-10-ecommerce-sites-in-india> accessed 24 February 2021).

[38] The Digital Report (n.35), 67. The region's exports of digitally deliverable services grew from US $39,260 million in 2005 to US $140,310 million in 2018. Viviana Perego, Sanjay Kathuria, Arti Grover, Aaditya Mattoo, Pritam Banerjee, 'Can E-commerce Drive Trade in South Asia?' (The World Bank Blogs 2019) <https://blogs.worldbank.org/endpovertyinsouthasia/can-e-commerce-drive-trade-south-asia> accessed 24 February 2021.

[39] Daraz was launched in Pakistan in 2012 as 'Daraz.pk' with investment from Rocket Internet SE. In 2018, Alibaba having previously invested in Paytm in India <https://techcrunch.com/2017/03/06/alibaba-paytm-amazon-india> accessed 8 March 2021, acquired Daraz in a move to consolidate its access to South Asian markets <https://techcrunch.com/2018/05/08/alibaba-buys-rocket-internets-daraz/?guccounter=1> accessed 8 March 2021.

a subsidiary of the Chinese giant Alibaba,[40] and has a presence in Pakistan, Bangladesh, Sri Lanka, Nepal, and Myanmar, e-commerce throughout these countries remains largely localised.[41] Pakistan has several specialist and non-specialist local platforms[42] such as Shopify, Tibolli.net, and Dukanlay which connect buyers and sellers, while consumers in Bangladesh rely more on social media websites, particularly Facebook,[43] and platforms such as Daraz Bangladesh, bikroy.com, clickbd.com, and bagdoom.com for their online shopping needs. Global e-commerce players are also largely absent from Sri Lanka where e-commerce is dominated by domestic companies like Kapruka.com, Daraz.lk, WOW.lk, Takas.lk, and MyDeal.lk and from Nepal which hosts emerging online shopping portals such as Sastodeal and Daraz[44] as well as a few platforms such as Foodmandu which allow traditional retailers the opportunity to offer their products online.[45] Maldives, though more digitised than India, Pakistan, and Sri Lanka,[46] appears not to have explored its e-commerce potential: there are only two major e-commerce platforms in Maldives, Ibay.com.mv and koo.mv that connect small businesses and consumers, however, several businesses employ e-commerce components,[47] and as in Bangladesh, Facebook e-commerce pages play an important role in connecting businesses and consumers.[48] Interestingly, Bhutan despite being the smallest South Asian country, has been active in developing its e-commerce: businesses

40 Ming Zeng 'Alibaba and the Future of Business' <https://hbr.org/2018/09/alibaba-and-the-future-of-business> accessed 8 March 2021.

41 Daraz. 'About' <www.daraz.com> accessed 8 March 2021.

42 Freebie Freak 'Best E-commerce Platform in Pakistan to Start an Online Business' <https://medium.com/@tibollinet.2019/which-is-the-best-ecommerce-platform-in-pakistan-189996295067> accessed 8 March 2021. Also see Claritypk, 'List of Online Marketplaces and Ecommerce Stores in Pakistan' <https://clarity.pk/ecommerce/list-online-marketplaces-ecommerce-stores-pakistan> accessed 8 March 2021.

43 The e-commerce Association of Bangladesh (e-Cab) which is the trade body for e-commerce in Bangladesh, estimates that in 2017 there were 700 e-commerce sites and around 8,000 e-commerce pages on Facebook <https://e-cab.net> accessed 8 March 2021.

44 International Trade Association, 'Nepal-Country Commercial Guide' <www.trade.gov/country-commercial-guides/nepal-ecommerce> accessed 12 March 2021.

45 ibid. At present, however, the Nepalese are not allowed to import goods online and, therefore, do not participate in cross-border e-commerce.

46 Raul Katz, 'The Transformative Economic Impact of Digital Technology' contribution to the United Nations Commission on Science and Technology for Development (UNCTAD 2015). <https://unctad.org/system/files/non-official-document/ecn162015p09_Katz_en.pdf> accessed 12 March 2021.

47 See for instance e-Tukuri Local, developed by Maldives Post <www.maldivespost.com/e-commerce> accessed 12 March 2021, and DHL e-commerce <www.dhl.com/mv-en/home/our-divisions/ecommerce/customer-service/contact-ecommerce-consumer.html> accessed 12 March 2021.

48 A simple internet search brings up a large number of Facebook shopping pages, including pages for 'Shop Maldives' <www.facebook.com/shoppersmaldives> 'Maldives online Shop'; <www.facebook.com/MaldivesOnlineShop> 'Asters'; <www.facebook.com/Asters.Maldives> 'Trending Home Maldives'; <www.facebook.com/trendinghome.mv> 'Fashnova'; <www.facebook.com/Fashnova-366264203551737> to name a few; accessed 12 March 2021.

and government organisations have been using social media for sales for some time,[49] and between 2019 and 2020 the Bhutanese Department of Trade issued thirty-one e-commerce licences primarily to cottage and small-scale industries in a bid to facilitate sales in the international market.[50]

Except for India and Bangladesh, South Asian countries primarily engage in homegrown and domestic B2C e-commerce.[51] Although there is some indication that Pakistan is working towards B2B e-commerce, there is no evidence of ny such momentum in Maldives, Nepal, Sri Lanka, and Bhutan. Interestingly, however, the operations of the e-commerce platform Daraz, which is a subsidiary of the Chinese e-commerce platform Alibaba, and operates in four out of the eight South Asian countries – Pakistan, Bangladesh, Sri Lanka, and Nepal – creates the possibility for cross-border e-commerce among these countries.[52] In 2020 Daraz launched a 'Daraz index' in Pakistan and Sri Lanka in which it utilised data it had aggregated from these countries to provide insights into consumer behaviour and to map the growth of the e-commerce.[53]

9.3.2 *Digital and E-commerce Policies in South Asian Countries*

Their varying engagement with e-commerce notwithstanding, South Asian countries are increasingly adopting digitalisation and other policies for facilitating e-commerce. India is the furthest along in this regard: it launched the 'Digital India Programme' in 2015 to create a 'faceless, paperless, and cashless' India,[54] and

[49] See for instance, Bhutan Online Shop <www.facebook.com/pages/biz/topic_shopping_retail/Bhutan-online-shop-1923845024530344> Bhutan e-mart; www.facebook.com/EMartBhutan; and Bhutan Duty Free Limited <www.facebook.com/BhutanDutyFreeLimited> accessed 12 March 2021.

[50] Druksell, '31 E-Commerce Licenses Issued till 2019. More E-commerce Business to Start-up post 2020' <https://druksell.com/blogs/business/e-commerce-in-bhutan> accessed 12 March 2021.

[51] Examples of B2B platforms in Bangladesh include: bfmea.com.bd, bizbangladesh.com The Financial Express Bangladesh 'e-Commerce in Bangladesh: where we are headed' <https://thefinancialexpress.com.bd/views/views/e-commerce-in-bangladesh-where-are-we-headed-1578666791> accessed 22 May 2021.

[52] See n.40 and text thereto.

[53] For Pakistan, see Inisde Daraz, 'Pakistan's First E-commerce Index Powered by Daraz Shows an Increase in Digital Payments and Growing Demand for Online Shopping' <http://insidedaraz.com/pakistans-first-e-commerce-index-powered-by-daraz-shows-an-increase-in-digital-payments-and-growing-demand-for-online-shopping>; and for Sri Lanka, see Daily FT 'Trends and Growth of Sri Lanka's E-commerce Industry: An Overview of Daraz E-commerce Index' <www.ft.lk/business/Trends-and-growth-of-Sri-Lanka-s-e-commerce-industry-An-overview-of-Daraz-e-commerce-Index/34-703498> accessed 22 May 2021.

[54] The programme was launched through a specially constituted Digital Economy & Digital Payment Division in the Ministry of Electronics and Information Technology. Economic Times 'PM Narendra Modi to launch Digital India Programme on July 1' <https://economictimes.indiatimes.com/news/politics-and-nation/pm-narendra-modi-to-launch-digital-india-programme-on-july-1/articleshow/47819644.cms> accessed 20 March 2021.

engaged ministries, governmental departments, and Indian states to develop 'an eco-system to enable digital payments across the country',[55] and to promote a range of measures necessary for building a digital infrastructure.[56] The Indian government also issued Foreign Direct Investment Rules 2016 to facilitate cross-border investment in e-commerce[57] and drafted an e-commerce policy in 2019 to balance data protection and the growth of the e-commerce sector.[58] The government also circulated a 'Model Framework for Guidelines on e-Commerce for Consumer Protection' for consultation with state governments responsible for regulating trade and commerce in their territorial jurisdictions[59] and in June 2019 established a 'Standing Group of Secretaries Constituted for Promotion of Industry and Internal Trade' to streamline and co-ordinate these initiatives.[60] However, despite or perhaps because of these efforts regulation of e-commerce in India remains fragmented giving rise to increasing calls for its rationalisation.[61]

55 Ministry of Electronics and Information Technology, Digital Economy and Digital Payments Division <www.meity.gov.in/digidhan> accessed 20 March 2021. In 2019 the ministry released a vision statement for 'Digital India' which provided a roadmap for India's digital future and projected that by 2025 e-commerce would add USD 15 to 20 billion to the Indian economy, and e-trade would account for 10–15 per cent of the country's total trade. Also see the ministry's 'India's Trillion Dollar Digital Opportunity,' 245 <www.digitalindia.gov.in/ebook/MeitY_TrillionDollarDigitalEconomy.pdf> accessed 22 March 2021.

56 Government of India, Ministry of Electronics and Information Technology, Annual Report 2019–20, 15, 20–24. <www.meity.gov.in/writereaddata/files/Annual_Report_2019–20.pdf> accessed 22 March 2021. The infrastructure proposals include establishing a National Knowledge Network to provide a secure and 'high-speed digital connectivity backbone' for research and education and launching the 'Aadhar system', under which each Indian is issued a unique digital identification number.

57 See for instance, see Ministry of Commerce & Industry, Department of Industrial Policy and Promotion, Press Note no 3 (2016 series), 'Guidelines for Foreign Direct Investment in e-commerce' <https://dipp.gov.in/sites/default/files/pn3_2016_0.pdf>; the Consolidated FDI Policy 2017 <https://dipp.gov.in/sites/default/files/CFPC_2017_FINAL_RELEASED_28.8.17.pdf> as clarified in 'Review of the Policy of Foreign Direct Investment (FDI) in e-commerce'; <https://dipp.gov.in/sites/default/files/pn2_2018.pdf> accessed 24 March 2021.

58 Ministry of Commerce and Industry 'Draft National E-Commerce Policy' <https://dipp.gov.in/sites/default/files/DraftNational_e-commerce_Policy_23February2019.pdf> accessed 22 March 2021, 5.

59 Multiple ministries are at work on their own e-commerce rules <https://economictimes.indiatimes.com/news/economy/policy/multiple-ministries-at-work-on-their-own-ecommerce-rules/articleshow/71191487.cms?from=mdr> accessed 24 March 2021. The Ministry of Consumer Affairs has issued the draft guidelines and invited comments from the public. <https://consumeraffairs.nic.in/sites/default/files/file-uploads/latestnews/Guidelines%20on%20e-Commerce.pdf> accessed 24 March 2021. The Consumer Protection (E-Commerce) Rules were finally issued in July 2020. <https://consumeraffairs.nic.in/sites/default/files/E%20commerce%20rules.pdf> accessed 24 March 2021.

60 *Business Standard*, 'Standing Group of Secretaries Constituted for Promotion of Industry and Internal Trade' <www.business-standard.com/article/news-cm/standing-group-of-secretaries-constituted-for-promotion-of-industry-and-internal-trade-119062100616_1.html> accessed 24 March 2021.

61 *Economic Times*, 'Imminent Need for Uniform Laws for E-commerce in India' <https://economictimes.indiatimes.com/industry/services/retail/imminent-need-for-uniform-laws-for-ecommerce-in_india/articleshow/73692139.cms?utm_source=contentofinter

Sri Lanka, despite being a somewhat late entrant to the world of e-commerce, has already adopted legislation to develop a National Policy on Information and Communication Technology – and has devised an action plan for its implementation. The act establishes a Task Force for Information and Communication Technology as well as the Information and Communication Technology Agency of Sri Lanka.[62] Since it has been operational, the agency has assisted in formulating 'Digital Sri Lanka', a national policy which outlines timebound strategies for utilising information communication technology for citizen empowerment and for establishing an infrastructure for digital government and economy.[63] In 2006, Sri Lanka also enacted the Electronic Transactions Act based on the United Nations Commission on International Trade Law (UNCITRAL), Model Law on Electronic Commerce (1996), and Model Law on Electronic Signatures (2001),[64] which institutes, among other things, a Digital Signature and Authentication regime.[65] More recently, after consulting comparable laws in the United Kingdom, Singapore, Australia, Mauritius, and California, and the draft Indian Bill, Sri Lanka has drafted a Data Protection Bill[66] based on OECD Privacy Guidelines, the APEC Privacy Framework, the Council of Europe Data Protection Convention, and the EU General Data Protection Regulation.[67] At the time of writing this bill awaited certification by the speaker of the Sri Lankan parliament.[68]

Despite making important inroads into e-commerce particularly with Darazpk, Pakistan launched its first comprehensive Digital Policy only in 2018,[69] which was intended to be a precursor to appropriate legislation in this area.[70] Like the Indian policy, Pakistan's Digital Policy is 'based on a multi-stakeholder model'[71] which aims to lay the 'foundation for the construction of a holistic digital ecosystem with infrastructure and institutional frameworks for the rapid delivery of innovative digital services, applications and content';[72] and to capitalise on the rapidly growing connectivity in the country to encourage 'Payment Service Providers (PSP) and

est&utm_medium=text&utm_campaign=cppst> accessed 24 March 2021; Cyril Amarchand Blogs, 'India's Foreign Investment Policy on E-commerce Retail: Is the Time Ripe for a Reworking?' <https://corporate.cyrilamarchandblogs.com/2020/02/indias-foreign-investment-policy-on-e-commerce-retail> accessed 24 March 2021.

62 ibid Preamble.

63 ICTA (official website) <www.icta.lk/digital-srilanka> accessed 14 April 2021.

64 Electronic Transactions Act 2006 as amended in 2017 <www.srilankalaw.lk/Volume-III/electronic-transactions-act.html> accessed 14 April 2021.

65 n.63. 'Enabling Legal Environment' <www.icta.lk/legal-framework> accessed 14 April 2021.

66 Draft Personal Data Protection Act 2019 <www.icta.lk/icta-assets/uploads/2020/06/Data-Protection-Bill-3-10-2019-Amended-Draft-FINAL-LD-Release.pdf> accessed 14 April 2021.

67 n.65.

68 ibid.

69 Ministry of IT and Telecom, Digital Pakistan Policy <https://moitt.gov.pk/SiteImage/Misc/files/DIGITAL%20PAKISTAN%20POLICY.pdf> accessed 25 March 2021.

70 ibid 8, 15.

71 ibid Preface.

72 ibid 5.

Payment Service Operators (PSO)'.[73] In October 2019, Pakistan also launched an e-commerce policy,[74] which identifies a range of 'key players'[75] in e-commerce and proposes 'a National e-Commerce Council' to provide a 'single window for policy oversight to facilitate e-Commerce players'.[76] It highlights the need for global connectivity;[77] establishing an e-payment infrastructure;[78] ensuring consumer protection;[79] and introducing a simplified taxation structure[80] and a data protection regime.[81] In April 2020, the government circulated a Personal Data Protection Bill which aims to provide a framework for data protection and for a data protection authority. However, at the time of writing, this bill was still to be passed into law.[82]

Nepal and Bangladesh, despite their limited engagement with e-commerce, have also developed digital policies: Nepal adopting one in 2019,[83] and Bangladesh in 2021.[84] The Nepalese policy aims to foster holistic economic development by harnessing digital technologies to transform the government, society, and economy;[85] recognises the need for an e-commerce eco-system[86] beyond the Electronics Trading Act (2063) 2008,[87] the Privacy Act (2075)

73 ibid.

74 Commerce Division, 'e-Commerce Policy of Pakistan' <www.commerce.gov.pk/wp-content/uploads/2019/11/e-Commerce_Policy_of_Pakistan_Print.pdf> accessed 25 March 2021.

75 ibid 14.

76 ibid 15.

77 ibid 44.

78 ibid 31.

79 ibid 35.

80 ibid, 37.

81 ibid 42–43.

82 Pakistan Personal Data Protection Bill 2020 <https://moitt.gov.pk/SiteImage/Misc/files/Personal%20Data%20Protection%20Bill%202020(3).pdf> accessed 26 March 2021.

83 Ministry of Communication & Information Technology, 2019 Digital Nepal Framework, <www.mocit.gov.np/application/resources/admin/uploads/source/EConsultation/EN%20Digital%20Nepal%20Framework%20V8.4%2015%20July%20%202019.pdf> accessed 24 May 2021. Also see ICT Frame, 'Digital Samvad: Policy Environment for Digital Agenda in Nepal' <https://ictframe.com/digital-samvad-policy-environment-for-digital-agenda-in-nepal> accessed 24 May 2021.

84 ICT Division, 'Digital Bangladesh and Vision 2021' <https://investindigitalbd.gov.bd/page/digital-bangladesh-vision-2021> accessed 26 March 2021. Bangladesh had first floated a concept note outlining its digital vision in 2009, however, it is only now that this has been formalised as a policy. Access to Information Programme, Prime Minister's Office 'Digital Bangladesh: Concept Note 2009' <http://btri.portal.gov.bd/sites/default/files/files/btri.portal.gov.bd/page/a556434c_e9c9_4269_9f4e_df75d712604d/Digital%20Bangladesh%20Concept%20Note_Final.pdf> accessed 26 March 2021.

85 n.83, 26–27. The policy proposes to utilise digital technologies to transform the government, society, and economy by undertaking eighty timebound initiatives in the eight sectors of digital foundation, agriculture, health, education, energy, tourism, finance, and urban infrastructure.

86 ibid 16, 24.

87 The Electronics Trading Act (2063) 2008 provides, among other things, for the authentication of electronic records (section 3); the recognition of electronic records and signatures (sections 4–6); the security of electronic records (section 6); and the certification

2018,[88] and the Consumer Protection Act, 2075 (2018);[89] and proposes a 'thorough assessment of existing policy provisions on data protection, security and privacy'.[90] The Bangladesh policy, rather than developing e-commerce, is more inclined towards digital government, human resource development, the promotion of the IT industry, and connecting citizens with each other to create a more democratic society and a more balanced and sustainable economy.[91] In 2016, the e-Commerce Association of Bangladesh (e-CAB) had produced an e-commerce policy at the instruction of the Ministry of Commerce, however, at the time of writing it had still not been approved by the Bangladeshi cabinet.[92] Bangladesh also enacted a Digital Security Act in 2018, however, this act addresses data crime rather than data privacy.[93]

Bhutan appears to be as invested in developing the regulatory infrastructure for its digital transformation as it is with developing its e-commerce. Since outlining an 'Information and Communications Technology Policy' in 2003,[94] Bhutan has adopted, among others, the 2014 Telecommunications and Broadband Policy[95] and e-Gov Masterplan[96] and has enacted the Information, Communications, and Media Act in 2018 to provide for e-commerce and digital signatures,[97] consumer protection,[98] and data protection and privacy.[99] Interestingly, the more digitised Maldives lags behind in adopting a holistic regime for regulating electronic

of such records (section 5). <www.tepc.gov.np/uSectionploads/files/12the-electronic-transaction-act55.pdf> accessed 24 May 2021.

88 The Privacy Act (2075) 2018 addresses several forms of privacy including privacy to data (chapter 6); electronics and privacy (chapter 9); and collection and privacy of personal information (chapter 10). <www.lawcommission.gov.np/en/wp-content/uploads/2019/07/The-Privacy-Act-2075-2018.pdf> accessed 24 May 2021.

89 The Consumer Protection Act (2075) 2018 <www.lawcommission.gov.np/en/wp-content/uploads/2019/09/The-Consumer-Protection-Act-2075-2018.pdf> accessed 24 May 2021.

90 n.83, 152.

91 n.84.

92 Tareque Moretaza, 'Revised Digital Commerce Policy Yet to Get Cabinet Approval' (*The Independent* 2019) www.theindependentbd.com/post/222994> accessed 26 March 2021.

93 Nasir Doulah, 'Bangladesh Data Protection Overview' (One Trust Data Guidance 2021), accessed 26 March 2021, and Md Moniruzzaman, 'Personal Data Protection in Bangladesh and GDPR' Bangladesh Journal of Legal Studies (2019) <https://bdjls.org/personal-data-protection-in-bangladesh> accessed 26 March 2021.

94 Ministry of Information and Communications, 'Information and Communications Technology (ICT) Policy for Bhutan: A White Paper 2003' <https://dit.gov.bt/sites/default/files/whitepaper.pdf> accessed 26 May 2021.

95 Bhutan Telecommunications and Broadband Policy 2014 <https://dit.gov.bt/sites/default/files/bhutan_telecommunications_and_broadband_policy_pdf_16764.pdf> accessed 26 May 2021.

96 Bhutan e-Government Masterplan <https://dit.gov.bt/sites/default/files/bhutan_e_gov_master_plan_14953.pdf> accessed 26 May 2021.

97 Information, Communications, and Media Act of Bhutan 2018 <www.moic.gov.bt/wp-content/uploads/2018/02/ICM-Act-2018.pdf> chapter 14 and 15, accessed 26 May 2021.

98 ibid chapter 16.

99 ibid chapters 17 and 21.

transactions and privacy and data protection.[100] However, it is expected that as it rebuilds its economy post-Covid, Maldives will prioritise digitalisation,[101] and will establish a legal and regulatory framework to facilitate it.[102]

9.3.3 *Competition Regulation, the Digital Economy, and E-commerce*

Digital e-commerce platforms present significant competition challenges developing country competition authorities are particularly likely to find it difficult to identify situations in which multi-sided analysis may be properly utilised and to recognise variations between different types of multi-sided platforms.[103] These authorities are also likely to find it difficult to define the relevant market in which the platforms operate, particularly given the zero-pricing policy adopted by the majority of e-commerce platforms, or to understand the complexity of network effects, and the ability of platforms to leverage their power in one market to other markets in which they operate.[104] In time, these competition authorities are also likely to be confronted with privacy concerns which result from the data collection and aggregation function of digital platforms,[105] that in any event changes the dynamics of collusion and abuse of dominance making it harder for the collusion or abuse to be detected.[106] Although privacy concerns are experienced equally in more advanced competition regimes, the adverse impact of breach of privacy in developing countries is likely to be aggravated due to the generally limited understanding of privacy issues, the absence of strong privacy laws or policies, and where these laws or policies do exist, the absence of an infrastructure for implementing them,[107] making it even more important to consider a competition response to these issues.

[100] Maldives enacted a Consumer Protection Act in 2020, however, the legislative framework for electronic transactions, data protection, and privacy is still only in draft stage. UNCTAD, 'Summary of Adoption of E-Commerce Legislation Worldwide' <https://unctad.org/topic/ecommerce-and-digital-economy/ecommerce-law-reform/summary-adoption-e-commerce-legislation-worldwide> accessed 25 May 2021.

[101] World Bank, 'A Digital Dawn' Maldives Development Update (World Bank 2021), 29–31. <https://thedocs.worldbank.org/en/doc/93bdbd79b45eeb504743f4514f1095e1–0310062021/original/April-2021-Maldives-Development-Update.pdf> accessed 25 May 2021.

[102] ibid 35–37, 41.

[103] OECD, 'Rethinking Antitrust Tools for Multi-Sided Platforms (2018)' <www.oecd.org/competition/rethinking-antitrust-tools-for-multi-sided-platforms.htm> accessed 26 February 2021, 10, 16.

[104] ibid.

[105] Digital Economy Report (n.35), 28.

[106] Ioannis Lianos, 'Global Governance of Antitrust and the Need for a BRICS Joint Research Platform in Competition Law and Policy' in Bonakale, Fox and Mncube (eds) *Competition Policy for the New Era: Insights from the BRICS Countries* (OUP 2017), 98.

[107] Michael Kwet, 'Digital Colonialism: US Empire and the New Imperialism in the Global South' (2019) 60(4) Institute of Race Relations 3–26; Renata Ávila Pinto, 'Digital Sovereignty or Digital Colonialism?' (2018) 15 n.27 SUR 27-15–27.

Although all South Asian competition regimes contain provisions which would allow for investigating and sanctioning anti-competitive practices of digital platforms, presently the CCI is the only South Asian competition authority to have initiated proceedings against digital platforms. In its early decisions in respect of platforms the CCI treated online distribution channels as interchangeable with brick-and-mortar distribution outlets,[108] and held that these were simply two different channels of distribution in the same relevant market.[109] In later decisions, however, as the CCI considered platforms in a wider range of sectors including online search engines, cab aggregators, and online travel agencies it refined its understanding of platforms.[110] Between 2015 and 2017 the CCI took up several complaints of abuse of dominance against cab aggregators, but did not find a violation.[111] In 2018 however, the CCI found Google guilty of abuse of dominance for self-preferencing in its search function.[112] In 2019 it ordered an investigation against Amazon and its Indian counterpart, Flipkart for engaging in anti-competitive exclusive vertical agreements with their 'preferred' sellers,[113] and against Google for abusing its dominant position in the licensable Operating System market by forcing smart-phone manufacturers to pre-install Google Mobile Suite and for bundling various Google services.[114] In 2020, the CCI directed an investigation of the online Travel Agents MakeMyTrip (MMT) for abusing its dominant position in the online intermediation services market for booking hotels in India and for entering into an anti-competitive vertical agreement with OYO (providers of franchising services for budget hotels).[115] Also in 2020, the CCI ordered a further investigation against

[108] See for instance, *Jasper Infotech Private Limited (Snapdeal) v Kaff Appliances (India) Pvt Ltd (Kaff)* Case 61/2014 decided 29.12.2014; *Ashish Ahuja v Snapdeal.com & Another* Case 17/2014 decided 19.05.2014.

[109] *Deepak Verma v Clues Network* Case 34/2016 decided 26.07.2016; *KC Marketing, Maharashtra v OPPO Mobiles MU Private Limited* Case 34/2018 decided 08.11.2018.

[110] For instance, *All India Online Vendors Association and Flipkart India Private Limited* Case 20/2018 decided 06.11.2018, para 25, in which it defined the relevant market as the market for 'services provided by online marketplace platforms'.

[111] *Meru Travel Solutions Private Limited (MTSPL) v Uber India Systems (Pvt) Ltd* Case 81/2015 decided 22.12.2015; *Mega Cabs (Pvt) Ltd v ANI Technologies (Pvt) Ltd* Case 82/2015 decided 09.02.2016; *Meru Travel Solutions (Pvt) Ltd v Uber India Systems (Pvt) Ltd* Case 96/2015 decided 10.02.2016; *Fast Track Call Cab (Pvt) Ltd and Meru Travel Solutions (Pvt) Ltd v ANI Technologies (Pvt) Ltd* Cases 6/2015 and 74/2015, decided 19.07.2017.

[112] *Matrimony.com Limited v Google* Cases 07/2012 and 30/2012 decided 08.02.2018.

[113] *Delhi Vyapar Mahasangh v Flipkart and Amazon* Case 40/2019 decided 13.01.2020. Also see Vikas Kathuria 'Digital & Competition: The Indian Scenario' Concurrences N°2-2021, On-Topic: Competition Policy in the Digital Economy, 47. This investigation marks an evolution in the CCI's thinking, as the CCI had not found similar allegations of exclusivity to be anti-competitive in the past. See *Mr Mohit Manglani v Flipkart India Private Limited and others* order Case 80/2014 decided 23.04.2015.

[114] *Mr Umar Javeed and others v Google LLC and others* Case 39/2018 decided 16.04.2019.

[115] *Rubtub Solutions Pvt Ltd v MakeMyTrip India Pvt Ltd (MMT) and others* Case 01/2020 decided 24.02.2020. For a discussion, see Kathuria (n.113), 47.

Google for abusing its dominant position by favouring GooglePay over other competing apps in the Play Store and Android Operating System.[116]

In April 2019 the CCI launched a study of the e-commerce sector to 'better understand the functioning of e-commerce in India and its implications for markets and competition'. The January 2020 report of this study identified a wide range of competition challenges presented by digital platforms and recommended that platforms address these by self-regulating search ranking; collection, use, and sharing of data; user review and rating mechanisms; revision in contract terms; and by adopting a discount policy.[117] Earlier in 2019, the Indian government had constituted a Competition Law Review Committee to assess among other things whether the Indian Act was equipped to respond to the challenges of the digital age. In its July 2019 report, the committee had recommended amendments to the Act to include 'hub and spoke' cartels; to provide for agreements between platforms that do not fit into the traditional categories of horizontal or vertical agreements, and to consider digital mergers.[118] In February 2020 the government incorporated some of these recommendations in a draft Competition Bill 2020, however, at the time of writing this bill had still not been enacted. Encouragingly, in a 2021 report on the study of the telecommunication industry,[119] the CCI expressly acknowledged the relationship between data privacy and competition, albeit without clarifying its position on the treatment of privacy issues in competition enforcement.[120]

In contrast, at the time of writing the CCP had still not decided any anti-trust proceedings against digital e-commerce platforms; however, it had approved a merger between the cab aggregators Uber and Careem on the basis that 'application based Ridesharing Services [are distinct] from all other modes of transport in Pakistan, by reason of [their] characteristics, price and intended usage'.[121] In arriving at this conclusion, the CCP had considered the two-sided structure of ridesharing apps, network effects, and multi-homing[122] and applied the traditional Small but

[116] *XYZ v Alphabet Inc* Case 07/2020 decided 09.11.2020. For details see Kathuria (n.113), 47.

[117] Competition Commission of India, 'Market Study on E-Commerce in India: Key Findings and Observations' (CCI 2020) <www.cci.gov.in/sites/default/files/whats_newdocument/Market-study-on-e-Commerce-in-India.pdf> accessed 4 June 2021. For a summary see Kathuria (n.113), 49–50.

[118] Ministry of Corporate Affairs, 'Report of the Competition Law Review Committee 2019' <www.mca.gov.in/Ministry/pdf/ReportCLRC_14082019.pdf> accessed 4 June 2021.

[119] Competition Commission of India, 'Market Study on the Telecom Sector in India: Key Findings and Observations' 29 para 70. <https://cci.gov.in/sites/default/files/whats_newdocument/Market-Study-on-the-Telecom-Sector-In-India.pdf> accessed 4 June 2021.

[120] India Business Law Journal 'Competition Watchdog Breaks Data Privacy Silence' 9 March 2021 <https://law.asia/competition-watchdog-breaks-data-privacy-silence/#:~:text=Competition%20watchdog%20breaks%20data%20privacy%20silence.%20India's%20antitrust,its%20position%20on%20enforcement%20in%20data%20privacy-related%20matters> accessed 4 June 2021.

[121] *In the Matter Phase II Review of Acquisition of M/S Careem Inc by Uber Technologies, Inc Through Augusta Acquisition BV* File No 1032/Merger-CCP/19 decided 31.012020 para 94.

[122] ibid paras 39–43.

Significant Non-transitory Increase in Price (SSNIP) test to establish the limits of the relevant market.[123] Interestingly, even though after considering the market shares of the merging companies, the CCP noted that the acquisition would substantially lessen competition in the market,[124] it invoked 'mitigating factors'[125] and 'efficiencies'[126] unrelated to the direct economic impact of the proposed merger and approved the merger subject to certain commitments and conditions.[127] In doing so the CCP not only revealed the limits of its understanding of platforms but also its focus on safeguarding and encouraging foreign investment rather than mitigating the adverse impact of increased market power. Although this order has been heavily criticised in the media for causing harm to consumers,[128] it has not prompted the CCP to undertake a holistic study of the e-commerce sector.

These orders of the CCI and the CCP reveal not only the steep learning curve that these authorities have faced and continue to face when it comes to digital e-commerce platforms but also their respective attitude towards foreign investment. While India has made a strong effort towards understanding competition issues that may arise in relation to e-commerce and has initiated the process of amending the Indian Act to address these, Pakistan has adopted a more passive stance, which suggests that at least at present it prefers to address the challenges as they arise.

The remaining South Asian countries are also likely to encounter similar competition and privacy concerns as e-commerce becomes a greater reality for them. However, the response of their competition enforcement authorities to these issues is likely to depend in large part on the mechanisms and institutions through which the countries originally adopted their competition legislations and the degree of independence these competition authorities enjoy in their operations. The Indian and Pakistani examples are instructive in this regard: India had adopted its competition legislation through *socialisation* and a wide range of bottom-up, participatory, and inclusive institutions. It, therefore, has the capacity and the experience to adapt its competition legislation to respond to the challenges emerging in the wake of the ever-growing digital economy. India has also established a largely independent competition authority which has reasonable autonomy to form its own view regarding digital platforms free from other governmental priorities. Pakistan, on the other hand, having acquired its competition legislation through *coercion* and a limited, top-down, and exclusive institutions had established an enforcement authority which, despite having statutory independence, remained subject to governmental discretion in the appointment and removal of its members. Consequently, neither the Pakistani government nor the CCP have taken the

[123] ibid paras 128–35.
[124] ibid para 141.
[125] ibid paras 153–54.
[126] ibid paras 157–59.
[127] ibid paras 242–44.
[128] Business Recorder, 'Consumers Taken for a Ride?' <www.brecorder.com/news/596181> accessed 6 June 2021.

initiative to adapt the Pakistani competition legislation to respond to developments in the economy. The CCP particularly remains susceptible to being persuaded by the broader priorities of the Pakistani government and appears to lack the autonomy to initiate any critical evaluation of the digital economy or the laws proposed to regulate it. Given that the remaining South Asian countries have adopted their laws through *coercion* and that the majority of them have done so through democratic institutions, albeit ones that lack strong legislative experience, their ability to adapt their competition legislations to address the evolving challenges of e-commerce is likely to be limited. However, there is an important option available to these South Asian countries, which is to learn from the Indian and Pakistani examples already available in the region, and to adapt these for their contexts.

9.4 REGIONAL DEVELOPMENTS AND COMPETITION LAW ENFORCEMENT

Notwithstanding competition's potential to support economic growth and development in both the traditional and the digital economy, the limited compatibility and legitimacy of competition legislations in the majority of South Asian countries, due in large part to these countries having adopted these legislations through *coercion* and without the meaningful engagement of bottom-up, participatory, and inclusive institutions, is likely to continue to pose a barrier to effective competition enforcement in these countries.

However, some comfort may be derived from the fact that it is entirely possible for South Asian countries to overcome this barrier by consciously committing to competition enforcement and engaging in activities that enhance the compatibility and legitimacy of their adopted competition legislations. This, in turn, would enhance the extent to which these laws are applied and utilised by stakeholders in these countries and over time will allow them to integrate into and become important features of their pre-exisitng legal systems.[129] Interestingly, regional developments in competition enforcement are likely to offer an important impetus in this regard. As South Asian countries observe their regional counterparts implementing their competition legislations and note the impact this has on their ability to generate investment and entrepreneurial activities in their domestic contexts while also attracting foreign investment to their economies they are more likely to consider competition enforcement as an important tool for growth and development. The possibility and potential of competition enforcement in one South Asian country affecting other countries in the region is reinforced by the fact that notwithstanding

[129] This is likely to be easier in countries whose competition legislations envisage independent competition authorities, which once established have a vested interest in demonstrating their utility by enforcing the legislation (see Chapter 8, Section 8.4). For instance, the CCP's increasing *socialisation* in interpreting the provisions of the Pakistani Act, enhances the CCP's credibility in the eyes of stakeholders and is likely to translate into an increase in the number of orders issued by the CCP and its overall effectiveness.

the very important role of multi-lateral agencies in introducing competition legislations to these countries, a number them have also been influenced by each other in adopting these laws, and for better or worse this though somewhat subtle early influence is as likely to continue through to the implementation stage as the more well-documented influence of the multi-lateral agencies.

South Asian countries had a direct as well indirect impact on each other at the adoption stage: the direct influence is evident in India providing consultation, guidance, and drafting services (whether through its government, the CCI, or thinktanks) to Bangladesh, Nepal, Bhutan, and Afghanistan, and in Pakistan engaging in training and capacity building programmes in Afghanistan, while the indirect influence may be attributed to the *regulatory competition* between these countries[130] which is likely to have been a factor in the South Asian countries adopting their competition legislation in quick succession.[131]

In most instances, the considerable direct and indirect influence of these countries on each other has not diminished even as the competition legislations have entered the implementation stage. For instance, India continues to directly influence several countries in the region through continued consultations and trainings on competition enforcement.[132] It also continues to have an indirect influence simply through publishing its enforcement actions which is likely to encourage its counterparts to remain regulatorily competitive with India. Even though there is no express of official acknowledgement to this effect it is very likely that both the CCI and the CCP without any direct consultative links with each other, are aware of each other's enforcement actions and note the sectors to which these relate. It is further likely that the two countries influence the remaining South Asian countries to match such of their the enforcement initiatives as they find most relevant to their contexts.

There is a danger however, that in the particular context of South Asian countries, regulatory competition may generate 'a race to the bottom' rather than encouraging a race to the top.[133] For instance, there may be a race to the bottom in competition enforcement if the smaller South Asian countries take the view that weaker competition enforcement in their contexts will help them attract more investment. Several factors are likely to play a role in this regard: if a particular country is competing for international investment with another country that has stronger competition enforcement, then it may position itself as a weaker enforcer and, therefore, capable

[130] This means that countries are more likely to adopt a new policy or law in a 'race to the top' if countries similarly situated to it (in terms of economic development or in relation to trade) adopt such law or policy.

[131] Between 2002 when India first adopted the Indian Act and 2020 when Maldives enacted its legislation and Bhutan updated its competition policy Sri Lanka, Nepal, Pakistan, and Bangladesh had adopted modern competition legislations while Afghanistan had a draft legislation by 2011.

[132] India's influence in any of these countries appears to be commensurate with its trading relationship with them.

[133] See n.130.

of offering a more investment-friendly environment, where investors may capture markets reasonably free of competitive constraints. Whether potential investors seek such an environment is likely to depend on the composition of the sector that the investor seeks to enter: if the desired sector comprises of businesses that are operating at a level and a scale that can exert competitive pressure on the investor, then it is likely to prefer strong competition enforcement to keep existing market power in check. If, however, the sector is populated by small businesses, the foreign investor is likely to prefer weaker competition enforcement so that it may achieve economies of scale and leverage its market power with impunity.[134]

Whether South Asian countries engage in a race to the top or to the bottom may also depend in part on the presence of businesses that operate regionally across these countries Regional cross border business may encourage countries in which they operate to adopt comparable competition rules so that they face a broadly similar competition regime across national markets. An important example in this regard is Darazpk, the e-commerce platform that operates in most South Asian countries and forms a significant proportion of all e-commerce activity in these countries. However, with little or no competition enforcement in the greater part of the area in which Daraz operates, it does not appear to have faced the need to call for the rationalisation of competition enforcement. With more platforms operating across South Asian countries either on their own or as subsidiaries of foreign multinationals, regional harmonisation of their competition regimes remains a real possibility.

A 2016 Report issued by the Groupe Spécial Mobile Association (GSMA),[135] on the operations of mobile service providers in certain Asian countries (including India and Pakistan from among South Asian countries) serves as an example of business-led convergence in competition enforcement. The report highlights the importance of effective competition enforcement for countries seeking to move up the digital value chain,[136] and urges co-operation and co-ordination between competition authorities of countries in which GSMA members operate, on the basis, that 'cooperation spreads knowledge and best practice and minimises the risks of diverging decisions and practices among agencies, between countries, making it easier for the market players to operate with legal certainty across borders'.[137] In fact GSMA goes as far as to call for a supra-national body, particularly to regulate

[134] For instance, digital platforms such as Alibaba and Amazon that had first entered India are now exploring the Pakistani market. Pakistan's treatment of the merger in ridesharing apps (see n.121) suggests that it is possible that Pakistan may seek to distinguish itself from India by adopting a different competition stance towards foreign investments.

[135] Groupe Spécial Mobile Association, 'Competition Policy in the Digital Age: Case Studies from Asia and Sub-Saharan Africa' (GSMA 2016) <www.gsma.com/publicpolicy/wp-content/uploads/2016/12/3.CPITDA_Case_Studies_Asia__Sub-SaharanAfrica_Sub-SaharanAfrica-1.pdf> accessed 28 June 2021.

[136] ibid 9.

[137] ibid Foreword.

mergers among telecom service providers in these countries.[138] However, given the complicated political relationships across South Asia, this proposal is unlikely to be realised anytime in the near future.

9.5 POSSIBLE IMPLEMENTATION STRATEGIES FOR SOUTH ASIAN COUNTRIES

The importance of appreciating the growth and development promise of competition law and keeping abreast of regional developments notwithstanding, it is essential that South Asian governments and such competition authorities as have been established, develop competition enforcement strategies that are aligned not only with their core economic objectives but also, and more importantly, take into consideration their resource and capacity limitations.

Given the positive correlation between competition enforcement and investment and productivity growth, South Asian governments and competition authorities need only to meaningfully enforce their competition legislations to attract investment and encourage growth. However, achieving sustainable and inclusive economic growth and alleviating poverty through competition enforcement may require a re-interpretation or even an expansion of the scope of most South Asian competition legislations. Given the compatibility and legitimacy deficit of competition legislations in most of these countries and the considerable resource limitations of their governments and by extension of their competition authorities, it may be more appropriate that in the early stages of enforcement, these governments and authorities prioritise competition advocacy and mainstream competition enforcement. Focusing on these two core areas would not only generate of their operations visibility and thereby enhance the legitimacy of their competition legislations but also start levelling the economic playing field which, in turn, would set the stage for economic growth and development in their contexts. The combination of these factors is likely to generate understanding and experience of enforcing competition principles which is further likely to pave the way for more complex enforcement actions going forward.

In focusing on mainstream competition enforcement, South Asian governments and authorities may also consider the areas of enforcement and sectors that need to be prioritised. In terms of areas of enforcement, these governments and authorities may be advised to focus on detecting and sanctioning cartels not only because of the preponderance of cartels across the region (particularly cartels for rigging bids made to public authorities) but also the harm the cartels cause to consumers particularly given the levels of poverty in South Asian countries.[139] Focusing on the by object or per se anti-competitive cartels is also likely to be within the somewhat limited

[138] ibid.

[139] ibid 323.

resources and capacities of South Asian governments and competition authorities. In nearly all South Asian competition legislations cartels are included in the category of horizontal anti-competitive or prohibited agreements and may be established by demonstrating the existence of an 'agreement' or concerted practice and without requiring complex economic analysis.[140] The governmental bodies and competition authorities responsible for enforcing competition laws may further enhance the impact of their enforcement actions by focusing on cartels in the food and pharmaceuticals sectors that have the most direct and immediate impact on a wide range of consumers.[141]

South Asian governments and competition authorities may also consider recognising the harm that their enforcement orders might cause to the 'poor' employees of the entities that may be the subject of these orders, without going so far as to make poverty alleviation an objective of their enforcement actions. To this end, these governments or authorities may obtain a no-harm commitment from the entity subject to a competition enforcement order. They may also consider the possibility of penalty reduction in exchange for such commitment along the lines traditionally offered in leniency regulations, thereby simultanously preserving the soundness of the legal analysis of the competition violation and addressing the social welfare concerns arising from the matter.

In time, South Asian governments and competition authorities may also consider proceeding against buyer-side cartels and dominant buyers that abuse their position against their smaller suppliers.[142] Buyer power, whether exercised unilaterally by a

[140] For a detailed discussion see Aditya Bhattacharjea, 'Who Needs Antitrust? Or, Is Developing-Country Antitrust Different? A Historical-Comparative Analysis' in D Daniel Sokol, Thomas K Cheng, Ioannis Lianos (eds) *Competition Law and Development* (Stanford University Press 2013), 61.

[141] Cheng (n.26) 315. For instance, the CCP and its operations became topics of public discourse when its first chairman took action against an alleged sugar cartel: <https://tribune.com.pk/story/25343/ccp-to-take-sugar-mills-to-court> accessed 15 February 2021. Similarly, in Nepal there appeared to be widespread demand for action against a transport cartel even though this demand was made of the Supreme Court of Nepal rather than to the board or market protection officer appointed under the Nepalese Act. Although the Nepalese Supreme Court issued an order directing the government to ensure that the transport cartel was duly sanctioned (*Jyoti Baniya v The Federation of Nepali National Transport Entrepreneurs and Others*, Nepal Law Report 2068 (2011/12), Volume 4, Decision No 8598, Decision Date 10-19-2067 (12-5-2010 AD)), there is no information whether the board or the market protection officer played any role in this regard.

[142] There is considerable debate among competition scholars as to whether buyer cartels are appropriately a subject of competition enforcement. However, the CCI has considered these in certain judgments and the concept has been included in the draft Competition Bill 2020 (Priyanka Barik, Bariq P, 'India: Buyer's Cartels Have Now Taken the Driver's Seat in India' (Mondaq 2020) <www.mondaq.com/india/cartels-monopolies/919282/buyer39s-cartels-have-now-taken-the-driver39s-seat-in-india#:~:text=The%20CCI%20observed%20that%20the%20aspect%20of%20the,US%20recognizes%20buyer%27s%20cartel%20as%20anti-competitive%20in%20nature> accessed 13 November 2021. Given India's considerable direct and indirect influence in the region, other competition regimes, may consider moving in a similar direction.

single entity or in conjunction with other buyers, has the potential to cause considerable harm in the labour intensive, relatively unsophisticated South Asian economies that are dependent on their income on large multi-nationals purchasing factors, raw materials, and other inputs from them. In addressing buyer power these countries will also be able to safeguard the interests of the small entrepreneur or the small individual supplier – as, for instance, in the small farmers supplying agricultural produce to the large food processing companies. However, proceeding against buyer power poses considerable challenges, the most significant being the questions of the appropriate welfare standard that may be applied to assess the anti-competitive harm caused by buyer cartels and of extraterritoriality. This is likely to be particularly complicated in situations in which buyer cartels do not lead to increased prices in consumer markets of the country enforcing the competition legislation. At present, due to having adopted their competition regimes on the persuasion of multi-lateral agencies, the majority of South Asian competition regimes also espouse the consumer welfare standard which judges harm primarily on the basis of the price offered to intermediate or end-consumers. However, there is increasing realisation among competition scholars that price does not always capture the harm caused by anti-competitive activities, which creates the possibility for South Asian countries to consider welfare standards more appropriate for their enforcement priorities. A broader conception of consumer welfare is likely to help these authorities establishing anti-competitive effects in their economies rather than seeking extra-territorial application of their laws.

As South Asian competition regimes gain more experience, confidence, and legitimacy in their contexts, they may graduate to addressing the more complex objectives of poverty alleviation, equitable distribution, and enhancing the social, non-economic welfare in their countries. To ensure that in pursuing these complex social objectives the competition regimes do not sacrifice economic efficiency at the altar of populism, it is important that the multi-lateral agencies engaging with them in ongoing trainings provide support on issues ranging from the design of competition authorities, to developing performance and enforcement plans tailored to context, and sanctioning strategies that will punish the offender but not eliminate competition. It is also important that these multi-lateral agencies work with the governments and competition authorities to design trainings in such a way that South Asian countries are able to benefit from each other's enforcement experiences rather than only looking to developed jurisdictions that are distant not only geographically but also institutionally and do not share their economic concerns. Doing so will help develop a pool of tacit competition knowledge in these countries that will not only gradually plug the compatibility and legitimacy deficit left over from the adoption stage, but in time will form the foundation of South Asian competition regimes that not only have competition expertise but also the conviction and the flexibility necessary for realising the all facets of the goals of economic progress for which these countries had adopted these laws in the first place.

Bibliography

BOOKS AND ARTICLES

Acemoglu,D, Robinson JA, *Why Nations Fail: The Origins of Power, Prosperity, and Poverty* (Crown Publishers 2012).

Anand CL, *Constitutional Law and History of Government of India* (8th ed, Universal Law Pub Co 2008).

Areeda PE, Hovenkamp H, *Antitrust Law: An Analysis of Antitrust Principles and Their Application* (Wolters Kluwer 2nd ed 2003), 1507(C).

Balasooriya A, Alam Q, Coghill K., 'Market-Based Reforms: An Empirical Analysis of Privatization in Sri Lanka' (Australian and New Zealand Academy of Management).

Bennett CJ, 'What Is Policy Convergence and What Causes It?' (1991) 1991 *British Journal of Political Science* 215.

Berkowitz D, Pistor K, Richard JF, 'Economic Development, Legality, and the Transplant Effect' (2003) 47(1) *European Economic Review* 165.

Bhattacharjea A, 'Who Needs Antitrust? Or, Is Developing-Country Antitrust Different? A Historical-Comparative Analysis' in D. Daniel Sokol, Thomas K. Cheng, Ioannis Lianos (eds), *Competition Law and Development* (Stanford University Press 2013).

Braun D, Gilardi F, Füglister K, Luyet S, 'Ex Pluribus Unum: Integrating the Different Strands of Policy Diffusion Theory' (2007) 38 *Politische Vierteljahresschrift*.

Carrier MA, 'The Four-Step Rule of Reason' (Spring 2019) 33(2) *Antitrust* 51.

Chen-Wishart M, 'Legal Transplant and Undue Influence: Lost in Translation or a Working Misunderstanding?' (2013) 62 *The International and Comparative Law Quarterly* 1.

Cheng TK, *Competition Law in Developing Countries* (OUP 2020).

Daley D, Garand J, 'Horizontal Diffusion, Vertical Diffusion, and Internal Pressure in State Environmental Policymaking, 1989–1998' (2005) 33 *American Politics Research* 615.

Darr A, Haidermota, K, Akhtar M, 'The Competition Commission Ordinance 2007: A Critical Analysis' *CLD* 2008 *Journal* 37.

Dolowitz D, Marsh D, 'Who Learns What from Whom: A Review of the Policy Transfer Literature' (1996) 44 *Political Studies* 343.

'Learning from Abroad: The Role of Policy Transfer in Contemporary Policy-Making' (2000) 13 *GOVE Governance* 5–23.

'The Future of Policy Transfer Research' (2012) 10 *Political Studies Review* 339.

Evans M, 'Policy Transfer in Critical Perspective' (2009) 30 *Policy Studies* 243.

Ewald W, 'Comparative Jurisprudence (II): The Logic of Legal Transplants' (1995) 43 *The American Journal of Comparative Law* 489.

Gal MS, 'The "Cut and Paste" of Article 82 of the EC Treaty in Israel: Conditions for a Successful Transplant' (2007) 9 *European Journal of Law Reform* 467.

'The Social Contract at the Basis of Competition Law: Should We Recalibrate Competition Law to Limit Inequality?' in Damien Gerard, Ioannis Lianos (eds), *Reconciling Efficiency and Equity: A Global Challenge for Competition Policy* (CUP 2019).

Giraldi F, 'Transnational Diffusion: Norms, Ideas and Policies' in Walter Carlsnaes, Thomas Risse-Kappen, Beth A. Simmons (eds), *Handbook of International Relations* (SAGE 2012), 454.

Grossfeld B, *The Strength and Weakness of Comparative Law* (Clarendon; OUP 1990) 43.

Heinze T, 'Mechanism-Based Thinking on Policy Diffusion: A Review of Current Approaches in Political Science' (Freie Univ. Berlin, FB Politik- und Sozialwiss, Kolleg Forschergruppe, 'The Transformative Power of Europe', 2011) 3.

Hovenkamp HJ, 'The Rule of Reason' (2018) 70 *Florida Law Review* 81 98.

Kahn-Freund O, 'On Uses and Misuses of Comparative Law*' (1974) 37 *The Modern Law Review* 1.

Khan LM, Vaheesan S, 'Market Power and Inequality: The Antitrust Counterrevolution and Its Discontents' (2017) 11 *Harvard Law & Policy Review* 235, 237.

Kumar A, 'The Evolution of Competition Law in India' in Vinod Dhall (ed), *Competition Law Today: Concepts, Issues, and the Law in Practice* (OUP 2007).

Kwet M, 'Digital Colonialism: US Empire and the New Imperialism in the Global South' (2019) 60(4) Institute of Race Relations 3–26.

Legrand P, 'The Impossibility of Legal Transplants' (1997) 4 *Maastricht Journal of European and Comparative Law* 111, 114

Lianos I, 'Global Governance of Antitrust and the Need for a BRICS Joint Research Platform in Competition Law and Policy' in Tembinkosi Bonakele, Eleanor Fox, Liberty Mncube (eds), *Competition Policy for the New Era* (OUP 2017).

'Competition Law as a Form of Social Regulation' 65(1) *The Antitrust Bulletin* 2020.

Lianos I, Darr A, 'Hunger Games: Connecting Competition Law and the Right to Food' (2019) *CLES Research Paper Series* 2.

Linos K, *The Democratic Foundations of Policy Diffusion: How Health, Family and Employment Laws Spread Across Countries* (OUP 2013).

Maggetti M, Gilardi F, 'Problems (and Solutions) in the Measurement of Policy Diffusion Mechanisms' (2016) 36 *Journal of Public Policy* 87.

Marsh D, Sharman JC, 'Policy Diffusion and Policy Transfer' (2009) 30 *Policy Studies* 269.

Mattei U, 'Efficiency in Legal Transplants: An Essay in Comparative Law and Economics' (1994) 14 *IRL International Review of Law & Economics* 3.

Mokal RJ, 'On Fairness and Efficiency' (2003) 66 *The Modern Law Review* 452.

Montesquieu C, et al *The Spirit of the Laws* (CUP 1989).

Morin JF, Gold RE, 'An Integrated Model of Legal Transplantation: The Diffusion of Intellectual Property Law in Developing Countries' (2015) *International Studies Quarterly* 782.

Newmark AJ, 'An Integrated Approach to Policy Transfer and Diffusion' (2002) 19 *Policy Studies Review* 151.

North DC, *Institutions, Institutional Change, and Economic Performance* (CUP 1990).

Örücü E, 'Law as Transposition' (2002) 51(2) *The International and Comparative Law Quarterly* 205.

Pinto RA, 'Digital Sovereignty or Digital Colonialism?' (2018) 15(27) *SUR* 15–27 <https://sur.conectas.org/en/digital-sovereignty-or-digital-colonialism> accessed 5 July 2022.

Raut NK, 'Causes and Impact of Privatisation in Nepal: A Theoretical Review' (2012) 2(2) *Banking Journal* 3.

Reimann M, 'The Progress and Failure of Comparative Law in the Second Half of the Twentieth Century' (2002) 504 *American Journal of Comparative Law* 671.

Rodrik D, *One Economics, Many Recipes: Globalization, Institutions and Economic Growth* (Princeton University Press 2007).

Rose R, 'What Is Lesson-Drawing?' (1991) II *Journal of Public Policy* 3.

Sacco R, 'Legal Formants: A Dynamic Approach to Comparative Law (Installment II of II)' (1991) 39 *The American Journal of Comparative Law* 343.

Shahein H, 'Designing Competition Laws in New Jurisdictions: Three Models to Follow' in Richard Whish, Christopher Townley (eds) *New Competition Jurisdictions: Shaping Policies and Building Institutions* (Edward Elgar 2012).

Shipan CR, Volden C, 'Policy Diffusion: Seven Lessons for Scholars and Practitioners' (Nov/Dec 2012) 72(6)*Public Administration Review* 788–96.

Teubner G, 'Legal Irritants: Good Faith in British Law or How Unifying Law Ends Up in New Divergences' (1998) 61(1) *The Modern Law Review* 11.

Trebilcock MJ, Iacobucci EM, 'Designing Competition Law Institutions' (2002) 25 *World Competition* 361.

Trubek DM, 'The "Rule of Law" in Development Assistance: Past, Present, and Future' in David Trubek, Alvaro Santos (eds) *The New Law and Economic Development: A Critical Appraisal* (CUP 2006).

Twining W, 'Social Science and Diffusion of Law' (2005) 32 *Journal of Law and Society* 203, 205.

Tyler TR and others, 'Procedural Fairness and Compliance with the Law' (1997) 133(I) *Swiss Journal of Economics and Statistics (SJES)* 219 (1997) 225.

Watson A, *The Evolution of Law* (Johns Hopkins University Press 1985).

Legal Transplants: An Approach to Comparative Law (2nd edn. University of Georgia Press 1993).

Weyland KG, *Bounded Rationality and Policy Diffusion: Social Sector Reform in Latin America* (Princeton University Press 2006).

Wilson J, 'At the Crossroads: Making Competition Law Effective in Pakistan Symposium on Competition Law and Policy in Developing Countries' (2006) 26 *Northwestern Journal of International Law & Business* 565.

'Crossing the Crossroads: Making Competition Law Effective in Pakistan' (2011) 8 *Loyola University Chicago International Law Review* 105, 111.

REPORTS, POLICY PAPERS, AND WORKING PAPERS

India

Competition Commission of India

'Market Study on E-Commerce in India: Key Findings and Observations' 2020

'Market Study on the Telecom Sector in India: Key Findings and Observations' 2021

Annual Report 2010–11

Annual Report 2011–12

Annual Report 2012–13
Annual Report 2013–14
Annual Report 2014–15
Annual Report 2015–16
Annual Report 2016–17
Annual Report 2017–18
Annual Report 2018–19
Chakravarthy S, 'Why India Adopted a New Competition Law' (CUTS 2006)
CUTS International, 'Competition Regime in Pakistan: Waiting for a Shake-up' (CUTS 2002)
Government of India, 'Report of the High-Level Committee on Competition Policy & Law 2000'
Ministry of Commerce and Industry India, Department of Industrial Policy and Promotion 'Consolidated FDI Policy 2017'
Ministry of Commerce and Industry, India, Department of Industrial Promotion and Policy, 'Draft National E-Commerce Policy'
Ministry of Consumer Affairs, Food & Public Distribution (Department of Consumer Affairs) 'Advisory to State Governments / Union Territories: Model Framework for Guidelines on e-Commerce for Consumer Protection'
Ministry of Electronics and Information Technology, 'India's Trillion Dollar Digital Opportunity'
Ministry of Electronics and Information Technology, Annual Report 2019–20
Ministry of Electronics and Information Technology, Digital Economy and Digital Payments Division India
Ministry of Corporate Affairs 'Report of the Competition Law Review Committee' (2019)
Mehta P, 'Competition Regimes in the World: A Civil Society Report' (CUTS 2006)

Pakistan

Aurat Foundation Pakistan 'A Five-Year Report on: Performance of Women Parliamentarians in the 12th National Assembly (2002–07) (Aurat Foundation 2009)
Competition Commission of Pakistan
Annual Report 2008
Annual Report 2009
Annual Report 2010
Annual Report 2011
Annual Report 2012
Annual Report 2013
Annual Report 2014
Annual Report 2015
Annual Report 2016
Annual Report 2017
Government of Pakistan, Commerce Division, 'e-Commerce Policy of Pakistan'
Ministry of IT and Telecom, 'Digital Pakistan Policy'
Manes ED, 'A Framework for a New Competition Policy and Law: Pakistan' (The International Bank for Reconstruction and Development 2007).
National Judicial (Policy Making) Committee 'Administrative Tribunals and Special Courts Annual Report 2015' (Law and Justice Commission of Pakistan 2015).

OTHER

Adhikari R, 'Discussion Paper on Competition Policy in Small Economies' (South Asia Watch on Trade, Economics and Environment (SAWTEE) and CUTS Centre for International Trade, Economics and Environment (CUTS-CITEE) 2002

Adhikari R, 'Competition, Competitiveness and Development: Lessons from Developing Countries' UNCTAD/DITC/CLP/2004/1 (UNCTAD 2004)

Bangladesh Competition Commission 'Report on OECD-GFC Annual International Conference presented by Mr. Md. Abul Hossain Mian, Member Bangladesh Competition Commission, Mr. Md. Monowar Hossain Director Bangladesh Competition Commission, Ms.Dilara BegumCommercial Councellor Bangladesh Embassy, Paris, France 29–30 November 2018 Paris, France' (Bangladesh Competition Commission 2018)

Bangladesh Foreign Trade Institute, Annual Report 2017–18

Consumer Affairs Authority (Sri Lanka)

Annual Report 2010

Annual Report 2011

Annual Report 2012

Annual Report 2013

Annual Report 2014

Annual Report 2015

Annual Report 2016

Annual Report 2017

Dutz M, Khemani RS, 'Competition Law and Policy: Challenges in South Asia' (The World Bank 2007)

Freshfields, Brauhaus, Deringer 'Antitrust in Asia: The Business Impact of Fast Evolving Competition Laws' (Freshfields, Brauhaus and Deringer 2017)

Ghiasy R, Zhou J, Halgreen H, 'Afghanistan's Private Sector: Status and Way Forward' (Stockholm International Peace Research Institute 2015)

Government of Bangladesh, Access to Information Programme Prime Minister's Office 'Digital Bangladesh: Concept Note 2009'

ICT Division, 'Digital Bangladesh and Vision 2021'

Government of Bhutan, Ministry of Information and Communications, 'Information and Communications Technology (ICT) Policy for Bhutan: A White Paper 2003'

Ministry of Information & Communications Department of Information Technology & Telecom, 'Bhutan e-Government Masterplan'

Ministry of Information & Communications Department of Information Technology & Telecom, Bhutan Telecommunications and Broadband Policy 2014

Government of Maldives, Ministry of Planning and National Development Maldives 'Strategic Economic Plan, Republic of Maldives'

The President's Office, Republic of Maldives 'Strategic Action Plan 2019–23'

Government of Nepal, Ministry of Communications and Information Technology '2019 Digital Nepal Framework: Unlocking Nepal's Growth Potential'

Groupe Spécial Mobile Association 'Competition Policy in the Digital Age: Case Studies from Asia and Sub-Saharan Africa' (GSMA 2016)

IMF Country Report No. 05/410 'Bangladesh: Poverty Reduction Strategy Paper' (International Monetary Fund 2005)

Country Report No. 19/102 'Maldives: Technical Assistance Report – Public Investment Management Assessment' (International Monetary Fund 2019)

OECD 'Rethinking Antitrust Tools for Multi-Sided Platforms 2018'

Tonmoy NH, Comparative Law Working Papers: Volume 2. No. 3. 2018, 7.
UNCTAD 'Capacity-building on Competition Law and Policy for Development: A Consolidated Report,' UN 2008.
'Investment Policy Review: Sri Lanka' UNCTAD/ITE/PC/2003/8, UN 2003.
'Voluntary Peer Review of Competition Law and Policy: Pakistan' UN 2013
'Digital Economy Report 2019: Value Creation and Capture: Implications for Developing Countries' (UN 2019)
World Bank, 'A Digital Dawn' Maldives Development Update 2021' (World Bank 2021)
'Enhancing Competitiveness in Sri Lanka' (World Bank 2016)

WEB SOURCES

Dictionaries and Encyclopaedias

Cambridge English Dictionary 'Compatibility'
Encyclopaedia Britannica, 'Afghan War 1978–1992' <www.britannica.com/event/Afghan-War>
'Economy of Bangladesh' <www.britannica.com/place/Bangladesh/Economy>

Newspaper Articles and Press Releases

India

Bariq P, 'India: Buyer's Cartels Have Now Taken the Driver's Seat in India' (Mondaq 2020) <www.mondaq.com/india/cartels-monopolies/919282/buyer39s-cartels-have-now-taken-the-driver39s-seat-in-india#:~:text=The%20CCI%20observed%20that%20the%20aspect%20of%20the,US%20recognizes%20buyer%27s%20cartel%20as%20anti-competitive%20in%20nature>
Business Standard 'Standing Group of Secretaries Constituted for Promotion of Industry and Internal Trade' (2019) <www.business-standard.com/article/news-cm/standing-group-of-secretaries-constituted-for-promotion-of-industry-and-internal-trade-119062100616_1.html>
The Economic Times 'PM Narendra Modi to Launch Digital India Programme on July 1' (2015) <https://economictimes.indiatimes.com/news/politics-and-nation/pm-narendra-modi-to-launch-digital-india-programme-on-july-1/articleshow/47819644.cms>
The Financial Express 'Acting CCI Chairman Vinod Dhall Quits' (2008) <www.financialexpress.com/archive/acting-cci-chairman-vinod-dhall-quits/325038>
Government of India, Ministry of Commerce & Industry, Press Information Bureau 'Review of the Policy of Foreign Direct Investment (FDI) in e-commerce' (2018) <www.pib.gov.in/newsite/PrintRelease.aspx?relid=186804>
Ministry of Commerce & Industry, Department of Industrial Policy and Promotion, Press Note no. 3 (2016 series), 'Guidelines for Foreign Direct Investment in e-commerce' <https://dipp.gov.in/sites/default/files/pn3_2016_0.pdf>
The Hindu 'Competition Law for the New Millennium' <www.thehindu.com/2000/06/22/stories/0622000d.htm>
Jain A, Gokhale G, 'Imminent Need for Uniform Laws for E-commerce in India' (The Economic Times 2020) <https://economictimes.indiatimes.com/industry/services/retail/imminent-need-for-uniform-laws-for-ecommerce-in_india/articleshow/73692139.cms?utm_source=contentofinterest&utm_medium=text&utm_campaign=cppst>
Kian Ganz 'Indian Law Firm ELP Drafts Afghanistan's Competition Act' (Legally India 2010) <www.legallyindia.com/content/indian-law-firm-elp-drafts-afghanistans-competition-act-20101210-1604>

Peermohamed A, 'Multiple Ministries at Work on Their Own E-commerce Rules' (The Economic Times 2019) <https://economictimes.indiatimes.com/news/economy/policy/multiple-ministries-at-work-on-their-own-ecommerce-rules/articleshow/71191487.cms>

Pakistan

Ansari I, 'CCP to Take Sugar Mills to Court' (The Express Tribune 2010)

Business Recorder 'Consumers Taken for a Ride?' <recorder.com/news/596181>

'Monopoly Trade Practices Law Being Revamped' (2004) <https://fp.brecorder.com/2004/04/20040428133601>

Other

Al-Jazeera 'Taliban Announces New Government in Afghanistan' (2021) <www.aljazeera.com/news/2021/9/7/taliban-announce-acting-ministers-of-new-government>

Asif Showkat Kallol 'Bangladesh Competition Commission Gets Secretary After a Year' (The Dhaka Tribune 2013) <www.dhakatribune.com/uncategorized/2013/09/16/bangladesh-competition-commission-gets-secretary-after-a-year>

British Broadcasting Corporation 'Nepal Parliament Dissolved' (2002) <http://news.bbc.co.uk/1/hi/world/south_asia/2003085.stm>
<https://ifcext.ifc.org/ifcext/pressroom/IFCPressRoom.nsf/0/27D09BF91AB7305E85257A97001879A2>

The Business Standard 'Competition Commission to Break up Onion Syndicate' (2019) <https://tbsnews.net/bangladesh/competition-commission-break-onion-syndicate>

'E-commerce Sales Grow 24 Times Over Three Years' (2020) <https://tbsnews.net/economy/e-commerce-sale-grows-24-times-over-three-years-143923>

The Daily Star 'Make Competition Commission Functional: Analysts' (2018) <www.thedailystar.net/business/make-competition-commission-functional-analysts-1530595>

The Financial Express 'BCC Suggests Steps Against Anti-competitive Activities' (2020) <https://thefinancialexpress.com.bd/economy/bangladesh/bcc-suggests-steps-against-anti-competitive-activities-1596771437>

'Competition Commission: The Task Ahead' (2016) <https://thefinancialexpress.com.bd/views/columns/competition-commission-the-task-ahead>

Government of Maldives, Presidency, Press Release 'President Ratifies Consumer Protection Act, Competition Act and Fourth Amendment to Land Transportation Act' (2020) <https://presidency.gov.mv/Press/Article/23615>

International Finance Corporation Pressroom 'IFC Helps Bangladesh Implement Mechanism to Make Regulations Efficient, Improving Governance' (2012) <https://pressroom.ifc.org/all/pages/PressDetail.aspx?ID=21398>

The Kathamndu Post 'Competition Promotion Fails to Curb Cartels' (2018) <https://kathmandupost.com/money/2018/04/09/competition-promotion-board-fails-to-curb-cartels>

Khan SS, 'E-commerce in Bangladesh: Where Are We Headed?' <https://thefinancialexpress.com.bd/views/views/e-commerce-in-bangladesh-where-are-we-headed-1578666791> (The Financial Express 2020)

Moretaza T, 'Revised Digital Commerce Policy Yet to Get Cabinet Approval' (The Independent 2019) <www.theindependentbd.com/post/222994>

Other Web Publications and Pages

Aryal M, 'Digital Samvad: Policy Environment for Digital Agenda in Nepal' <https://ictframe.com/digital-samvad-policy-environment-for-digital-agenda-in-nepal> (ICT Frame 2020)

Asian Development Bank, Country Partnership Strategy: Bhutan 2014–18 'Private Sector Assessment (Summary)' <www.adb.org/sites/default/files/linked-documents/cps-bhu-2014-2018-psa.pdf>

'Maldives: Inclusive Micro, Small, and Medium-Sized Enterprise Development Project' <www.adb.org/projects/43566-013/main#project-pds>

'Technical Assessment Completion Report (Maldives) (2009) <www.adb.org/sites/default/files/project-document/73639/39664-012-mld-tcr.pdf>

Bhutan Proceedings and Resolutions of the 75th Session of the National Assembly <www.nab.gov.bt/assets/uploads/docs/resolution/2014/75th_Session.pdf>

Bilaterals.org 'US Ready to Pursue FTA with Sri Lanka' <www.bilaterals.org/?us-ready-to-pursue-fta-with-sri>

Boughton JM, 'The IMF and the Silent Revolution: Global Finance and Development in the 1980s' (IMF 2000) <www.imf.org/external/pubs/ft/silent/index.htm> accessed 3 January 2021.

The British Empire, 'Maldives' <www.britishempire.co.uk/maproom/maldives.htm> 'Nepal' <www.britishempire.co.uk/maproom/nepal.htm>

Chandrasekera G, 'Anti-Competitive Practices & Competition Law of Sri Lanka: A Call for Reform' <www.juniorbarbasl.lk/assets/files/Article%20by%20Gamunu%20Chandrasekera%20-%20Anti-Competative%20Practices%20and%20Competition%20Law%20of%20Sri%20Lanka.pdf>

Choudhury R, 'E-commerce and Developing Countries: The South Asian Experience' No. 173, 2019 <https://us5.campaign-archive.com/?u=fa9cf38799136b5660f367ba6&id=3fb4cb574b>

Clarity.pk 'List of Online Marketplaces and E-commerce Stores in Pakistan, <https://clarity.pk/ecommerce/list-online-marketplaces-ecommerce-stores-pakistan>

Commercial Law Development Program, South Asia <https://cldp.doc.gov/countries-regions/asia-south-asia>

Constitute Project 'Bangladesh' <www.constituteproject.org/countries/Asia/Bangladesh?lang=en>

'Maldives' <www.constituteproject.org/countries/Asia/Maldives?lang=en>

'Nepal' <www.constituteproject.org/countries/Asia/Nepal?lang=en>

'Sri Lanka' <https://www.constituteproject.org/countries/Asia/Sri_Lanka?lang=en>

Constitutionnet 'Constitutional History of Nepal' <https://constitutionnet.org/country/nepal-country-constitutional-profile>

Consumer Affairs Authority Sri Lanka, 'Orders Issued Under Sections 18 and 20' <http://caa.gov.lk/web/index.php?option=com_content&view=article&id=113&Itemid=562&lang=en>

'Contact Details' <http://caa.gov.lk/web/index.php?option=com_content&view=article&id=141&Itemid=591&lang=en>

'Directions Issued Under Section 10' <http://caa.gov.lk/web/index.php?option=com_content&view=article&id=162&Itemid=672&lang=en>

CTL Strategies 'Competition Act' <www.ctlstrategies.com/latest/competition-act>

CUTS Briefing Paper No.4/2003 'Competition Policy in South Asian Countries' <https://cuts-ccier.org/pdf/Competition_Policy_in_South_Asian_Countries.pdf>

CUTS International 'Promoting Competition Policy and Law in Bangladesh: A Civil Society Perspective' (CUTS International 2006) <https://cuts-ccier.org/pdf/BangladeshCAD.pdf>

'Consumer Protection in Bhutan' <https://cuts-ccier.org/consumer-protection-in-bhutan>

Daily FT 'Trends and Growth of Sri Lanka's E-commerce Industry: An Overview of Daraz E-commerce Index' (2020) <www.ft.lk/business/Trends-and-growth-of-Sri-Lanka-s-e-commerce-industry-An-overview-of-Daraz-e-commerce-Index/34-703498>

Daraz 'About' <www.daraz.com>

Darr, Amber 'Cartels & the Politics of Competition Law Enforcement in Pakistan' (Competition Policy International 2020) <www.competitionpolicyinternational.com/cartels-the-politics-of-competition-law-enforcement-in-pakistan>

DHL Maldives, 'DHL E-commerce' <www.dhl.com/mv-en/home/our-divisions/ecommerce-solutions.html>

Doulah N, 'Bangladesh Data Protection Overview' (One Trust Data Guidance 2021) <www.dataguidance.com/notes/bangladesh-data-protection-overview>

E-Commerce Association of Bangladesh <https://e-cab.net>

E-Commerce Guide 'Top 10 Ecommerce Sites in India 2020' <https://ecommerceguide.com/top/top-10-ecommerce-sites-in-india>

Ellis K, Singh R, Eskander S, Huq I, 'Assessing the Economic Impact of Competition: Findings from Bangladesh' (Overseas Development Institute 2010) <https://cdn.odi.org/media/documents/6058.pdf>

Fabienne P, 'Political Legitimacy', The Stanford Encyclopaedia of Philosophy (Summer 2017 edn), Edward N Zalta (ed), <https://plato.stanford.edu/archives/sum2017/entries/legitimacy>

Facebook 'Bhutan Duty Free Limited' <www.facebook.com/BhutanDutyFreeLimited>

'Bhutan Online Shop' <www.facebook.com/pages/biz/topic_shopping_retail/Bhutan-online-shop-1923845024530344>

'Bhutan E-mart' <www.facebook.com/EMartBhutan>

'Shop Maldives' <www.facebook.com/shoppersmaldives>

'Maldives Online Shop' <www.facebook.com/MaldivesOnlineShop>

'Asters' <www.facebook.com/Asters.Maldives>

'Fashnova' <www.facebook.com/Fashnova-366264203551737>

'Trending Home Maldives' <www.facebook.com/trendinghome.mv>

'Best E-commerce Platform in Pakistan to Start an Online Business' <https://medium.com/@tibollinet.2019/which-is-the-best-ecommerce-platform-in-pakistan-1899962950 67> (2019)

Government of Afghanistan, Ministry of Industry and Commerce, Competition Promotion and Consumer Protection <https://moci.gov.af/en/competition-promotion-and-consumer-protection>

Government of Bhutan, Ministry of Economic Affairs, Office of Consumer Protection <www.moea.gov.bt/?page_id=594>

Government of Maldives, Ministry of Economic Development <https://trade.gov.mv/organizational-structure>

Government of Nepal, Ministry of Foreign Affairs, 'History of Nepal' <https://mofa.gov.np/about-nepal/history-of-nepal>

Government of Sri Lanka Parliament of Sri Lanka <www.parliament.lk/en/prime-ministers>

Hurd I, 'Legitimacy' <http://pesd.princeton.edu/?q=node/255>

Index Mundi 'GINI Index (World Bank Estimate): Country Ranking' <www.indexmundi.com/facts/indicators/SI.POV.GINI/rankings> (updated 2019)

'Bhutan Economy Profile' <www.indexmundi.com/bhutan/economy_profile.html>

Information and Communication Technology Agency of Sri Lanka, 'About' <www.icta.lk/digital-srilanka>

'Enabling Legal Environment' <www.icta.lk/legal-framework>

International Monetary Fund 'List of Members' <www.imf.org/external/np/sec/memdir/memdate.htm>

'Maldives' <www.imf.org/en/Countries/MDV>

India Business Law Journal 'Competition Watchdog Breaks Data Privacy Silence' 2021 <https://law.asia/competition-watchdog-breaks-data-privacy-silence/#:~:text=Competition%20watchdog%20breaks%20data%20privacy%20silence.%20India's%20antitrust,its%20position%20on%20enforcement%20in%20data%20privacy-related%20matters>

International Trade Association 'Nepal-Country Commercial Guide: E-commerce' <www.trade.gov/country-commercial-guides/nepal-ecommerce>

IPRsOnline 'Statement of the Hon'ble Minister for Commerce, Mr. Amir K. Mahmud Chowdhury, MP, at the Regional Seminar on Competition Policy and Multilateral Negotiations, Hong Kong: April 2002' <www.iprsonline.org/resources/competition.html>

Jacobs S H, 'The Second Generation of Regulatory Reforms' (International Monetary Fund 1999) <www.imf.org/external/pubs/ft/seminar/1999/reforms/jacobs.htm>

Kathiwada A, 'Nepal' <https://cuts-ccier.org/pdf/23-Nepal.pdf> (CUTS 2013)

Kathuria V, 'Digital & Competition: The Indian Scenario' Concurrences N°2-2021, On-Topic: Competition Policy in the Digital Economy <www.concurrences.com/en/review/issues/no-2-2021/dossier/xxx-digital-xxx>

Katz R, 'The Transformative Economic Impact of Digital Technology' (UNCTAD 2015) <https://unctad.org/system/files/non-official-document/ecn162015p09_Katz_en.pdf>

Maldives Post, 'E-commerce: eTukuri.mv' <www.maldivespost.com/e-commerce>

Minivan News Archive 'A Short Constitutional History of Maldives' <https://minivannewsarchive.com/politics/a-short-constitutional-history-of-the-maldives-73902>

Moniruzzaman, Md. 'Personal Data Protection in Bangladesh and GDPR' Bangladesh Journal of Legal Studies 2019 <https://bdjls.org/personal-data-protection-in-bangladesh>

Nathan 'End of Program Evaluation of Bangladesh Investment Climate Fund (BICF)' <www.nathaninc.com/end-of-program-evaluation-of-bangladesh-investment-climate-fund-bicf>

National Company Law Appellate Tribunal India <www.mca.gov.in/content/mca/global/en/about-us/affiliated-offices/nclat.html>

New Internationalist 'A Brief History of Afghanistan' <https://newint.org/features/2008/11/01/afghanistan-history>

Overseas Development Institute, ODI Briefing Paper November 1990, 'Bangladesh Economic Performance and Prospects' <https://cdn.odi.org/media/documents/6760.pdf>

ODI Briefing Paper November 1990 'Bangladesh: Economic Performance and Prospects' <www.odi.org/sites/odi.org.uk/files/odi-assets/publications-opinion-files/6760.pdf>

Patel P, Anand S, 'India's Foreign Investment Policy on E-commerce Retail: Is the Time Ripe for a Reworking?' (India Corporate Law 2020) <https://corporate.cyrilamarchandblogs.com/2020/02/indias-foreign-investment-policy-on-e-commerce-retail>

Perego V, Kathuria S, Grover A, Mattoo A, Banerjee P, 'Can E-commerce Drive Trade in South Asia?' December 2019 <https://blogs.worldbank.org/endpovertyinsouthasia/can-e-commerce-drive-trade-south-asia> (World Bank Blogs 2021)).

Phuntsho S, '31 E-Commerce Licenses Issued till 2019: More E-commerce Business to Start-up Post 2020' <https://druksell.com/blogs/business/e-commerce-in-bhutan> (Druksell 2020).

Razzaque A, 'The Role of Competition Commission in Sustainable and Inclusive Development' <https://www-ccb-gov-bd.translate.goog/site/page/87d2154b-5d3c-4509-a4f4–896016f199f9/সেমিনার-পেপার_x_tr_sl=bn&_x_tr_tl=en&_x_tr_hl=en&_x_tr_pto=sc&_x_tr_sch=http> (Competition Commission of Bangladesh)

Routledge, 'Authority v. Legitimacy' <http://cw.routledge.com/textbooks/alevelphilosophy/data/AS/WhyShouldIBeGoverned/Authorityandlegitimacy.pdf>

Russell J, 'Alibaba Buys Rocket Internet's Daraz to Expand its E-commerce Empire into South Asia' <https://techcrunch.com/2018/05/08/alibaba-buys-rocket-internets-daraz/?guccounter=1> (Tech Crunch 2018)

SAARC 'About SAARC' <www.saarc-sec.org/index.php/about-saarc/about-saarc>

SAWTEE 'Completed Programmes: Competition Advocacy and Education Programme (CAEP)' <www.sawtee.org/programme/completed-programmes/competition-advocacy-and-education-programme-(caep).html>

'Completed Programmes: Report on Operational Guidelines to Implement the Competition Promotion and Market Protection Act' <www.sawtee.org/programme/completed-programmes/report-on-operational-guidelines-to-implement-the-competition-promotion-and-market-protection-act.html>

Serajuddin U, Hamadeh N, 'New World Bank Country Classifications by Income Level: 2020–2021' <https://blogs.worldbank.org/opendata/new-world-bank-country-classifications-income-level-2020-2021> (World Bank Blogs, 2020).

Shafiq P, 'Pakistan's First E-commerce Index Powered by Daraz Shows an Increase in Digital Payments and Growing Demand for Online Shopping' (Inside Daraz 2020) <http://insidedaraz.com/pakistans-first-e-commerce-index-powered-by-daraz-shows-an-increase-in-digital-payments-and-growing-demand-for-online-shopping>

South Asian Free Trade Area <www.un.org/ldcportal/south-asian-free-trade-area>

Suthakar D, 'Beyond "More Economics-Based Approach": A Legal Perspective on Competition in Sri Lanka' 11th International Research Conference 2018, General Sir John Kotelawala Defence University, Sri Lanka.

Their AJ, 'The Making of a Constitution in Afghanistan' Originally presented at State reconstruction and international engagement in Afghanistan, 30 May–1 June 2003, London School of Economics and Political Science and University of Bonn <http://eprints.lse.ac.uk/28380/1/Thier_LSERO_version.pdf>

Thurairetnam A, 'Competition Regimes: Sri Lanka' <https://competitionregimes.com/pdf/AsiaPacific/30-Sri%20Lanka.pdf>

UKAid 'Bangladesh Investment Climate Fund, Phase 2' <https://devtracker.fcdo.gov.uk/projects/GB-1-204951/documents>

United Nations 'Country Classifications: Data Sources, Country Classifications and Aggregation Methodology' <www.un.org/en/development/desa/policy/wesp/wesp_current/2014wesp_country_classification.pdf>

UNCTAD 'Competition Policy for Development: A Report on UNCTAD's Capacity Building and Technical Assistance Programme' <https://unctad.org/system/files/official-document/ditcclp20042_en.pdf>

Summary of Adoption of E-Commerce Legislation Worldwide <https://unctad.org/topic/ecommerce-and-digital-economy/ecommerce-law-reform/summary-adoption-e-commerce-legislation-worldwide>

UNDP Human Development Reports 'India'. <http://hdr.undp.org/en/countries/profiles/IND>

Maldives 'About UNDP in Maldives' <www.mv.undp.org/content/maldives/en/home/about-us.html>

US Department of State '2017 Investment Climate Statements: Bangladesh' <www.state.gov/reports/2017-investment-climate-statements/bangladesh>

'2019 Investment Climate Statements: Maldives' <www.state.gov/reports/2019-investment-climate-statements/maldives>

The World Bank, 'Data, Countries and Economies' <https://data.worldbank.org/country>

'World Bank Country and Lending Groups' <https://datahelpdesk.worldbank.org/knowledgebase/articles/906519-world-bank-country-and-lending-groups>

The World Bank in Bhutan 'Overview' <www.worldbank.org/en/country/bhutan/overview>

The World Bank in Maldives 'Overview' <www.worldbank.org/en/country/maldives/overview>

The World Bank in Pakistan 'World Bank Discusses Roadmap for Assistance to Pakistan: Approves $500 Million to Support Ongoing Reform Program' <https://documents1.worldbank.org/curated/en/857811627555757196/pdf/Announcement-of-World-Bank-Discusses-Roadmap-for-Assistance-to-Pakistan-Approves-Five-Hundred-Million-Dollars-to-Support-Ongoing-Reform-Program-on-June-11-2002.pdf>

World Trade Organisation, 'Members and Observers' <www.wto.org/english/thewto_e/whatis_e/tif_e/org6_e.htm>

'Trade Policy Review, Sri Lanka November 1995' <www.wto.org/english/tratop_e/tpr_e/tp017_e.htm>

'Working Group on the Interaction between Trade and Competition Policy (WGTCP): History, Mandates and Decisions' <www.wto.org/english/tratop_e/comp_e/history_e.htm>

Zeng M, 'Alibaba and the Future of Business' <https://hbr.org/2018/09/alibaba-and-the-future-of-business> (Harvard Business Review 2018).

Index

www.ingramcontent.com/pod-product-compliance
Lightning Source LLC
LaVergne TN
LVHW011807200926
848484LV00005B/1096
* 9 7 8 1 0 0 9 2 4 7 1 7 7 *